M000105454

ISBN: 1-59777-532-0

Library of Congress Cataloging-In-Publication Data Available

Book Design by: Sonia Fiore

Printed in the United States of America

Phoenix Books
9465 Wilshire Boulevard, Suite 315
Beverly Hills, CA 90212

10 9 8 7 6 5 4 3 2 1

This book is dedicated to the memory of my parents:
[illegible] and [illegible]. And to my family,
(in order of appearance, so no one gets pissed off):
[illegible]
[illegible], Isabella, [illegible], and [illegible]

According to a now-deceased uncle, the first word I spoke as a baby wasn't "mama" or "dada," but Ajax—not the Trojan war hero, but the popular household cleanser. Like most baby boomers, I was weaned on the box. We watched Kennedy get shot, Oswald get silenced, and the Beatles break through on *Ed Sullivan*; gawked at the *Wonderful World of Disney* (in color finally) and sat slack-jawed during the moon landing. If the TV is on, I can't not look at it. I've been hard-wired. Perhaps it was no accident that I ended up as a TV writer. (Though, just to be clear, I'm not a TV savant. I read newspapers, magazines and, if time allows, even the occasional book. I have a B.A. in Philosophy and most of a Masters in Buddhist studies from Colgate University. Despite the opinions of some critics, possessing more than half a brain and writing for television are not mutually exclusive categories.)

In my career, which is how I euphemistically refer to a long-running series of jobs, random assignments, and blown opportunities, I've been on staff for 11 years on two long-running shows—*Wings* and *Becker*—had three studio development deals[1], (including my most recent one at Paramount) written episodes for various shows, including *Frasier*, *The Wonder Years*, and *Get a Life* and, in the course of it all, created and produced three pilots that made it on network schedules. All were cancelled within the first 13 episodes. In fact, after 9/11 I was afraid I wouldn't be allowed on the Paramount lot, as I'd already set off three bombs in Hollywood studios.

---

[1] Development (overall deal). A term contract with a studio, usually for one, two or three years, in which a writer/producer gets an office, assistant, an obscene salary, and a modest expense account, and in return has to pitch shows that will get picked up by the network. And the beauty is, you never have to set foot in your office. You can play golf five days a week. You can go to Hawaii for months, write on a laptop and occasionally fly in for pitch meetings. If, by the end of your deal, you've delivered one show that got on a network schedule, you've earned your keep.

Yeah, I know. Poor, poor pitiful me. Here's the thing. I've made a great living for almost 20 years as a TV writer, or writer/producer, if you want to get technical about the hyphenate. In fact, people who work in this business are paid criminal amounts of money. My friend and colleague David Isaacs jokes that when the revolution comes, we'll be the first to go. Second, actually—after the actors. In my weak defense, I'll offer that I didn't get a break in the business until I was 35, and that was after years in New York of doing shit jobs. (On my first resume I put a heading that read: "My goal is to be a freelance writer," at which point my mother pointed out that I'd misspelled "freelance." My first lesson in proofreading.)

Among the jobs I've held in my life: factory worker, gardener, waiter, English teacher in Japan, bartender, cheese shop clerk, magazine editor for a publishing company where the owner foamed at the mouth and carried a loaded .38 on his belt, associate editor for a porn magazine (the only job I ever had where you had to wear a tie), travel trade magazine editor, advertising copywriter, and freelance joke writer, all punctuated by seemingly interminable stretches on unemployment. But even then, I adhered to a strict, disciplined work ethic. Get up, take the train out to Long Island City[2] to sign up for my check, take the train back, buy a cup of pre-Starbucks watery Greek diner coffee, some lottery tickets, a *New York Times*, *Daily News*, and a pack of cigarettes, then hole up in my studio apartment fighting back winter depression, while circling the Help Wanted ads in the *Times*, calling a few places, chain-smoking, writing spec scripts[3] and praying for four o'clock when *The Odd Couple* came on, and I could bullshit myself into thinking that the day was over and I'd exhausted every opportunity to find employment.

---

[2] Long Island City. A shithole.

[3] Spec scripts. Scripts written "on speculation"; i.e. for free, either for the love of writing it, or as a sample of your ability with the goal of getting an agent and breaking into TV. Basically you keep writing on spec until you either get a break or wisely begin considering another line of work.

OK, it wasn't a West Virginia coal mine, but I'm also not one of those smartass dilettante fucks who went straight from the *Harvard Lampoon* to *Letterman* to instant sitcom success in L.A. And why didn't I take that easier route? Because my high school grades and SAT scores weren't good enough to get me into Harvard because I didn't apply myself and work up to my potential. Shit, my parents were right.

At present, I live in L.A. in a four-bedroom house with 8 TVs and 3 TiVos. (Not a mansion by Hollywood standards, but a modest home behind gates where, at the moment, gophers are eating all my bamboo and I can't get in touch with the guy who was supposed to be here three weeks ago to fix my Jacuzzi. Oh, the humanity!) But I don't have all the TVs because I need to see everything that's on for research purposes. OK, that's part of it. But the reality is I love TV. And I love working in it. So, why write a book?

WHY WRITE A BOOK?

It seems odd that, as prevalent as TV is in our lives, most people have no concept of what goes into creating a show, getting it on the air, and keeping it on. Perhaps they assume that the people in charge simply decide what amuses them at the moment, make those shows, stick them on, and wait to see if the public responds. Or just throw darts at a board. The truth, as with most things in life, is more complicated. Each year hundreds, maybe thousands, of writers, either on their own or in partnership with studios, producers, actors, directors, or managers, pitch the networks their visions for shows. Half-hours ("sitcoms" to the world) both single-camera[4] and multi-camera[5]; hour dramas; animated

---

[4] Single camera. A film-style show shot without an audience.

[5] Multi-camera. Four-camera shows shot on stage in front of a live audience.

shows; reality; variety.... It's referred to as being "in development," and is an annual game of musical chairs in which the goal is to get a show on the air in one of the few coveted timeslots on a network schedule, turn that show into a hit, and have it, at least, reach that 100-episode syndication[6] mark, which allows the writer some measure of creative satisfaction while attaining the gold ring of working in TV—"Fuck you money."

"Fuck you money"[7] is defined as an amount of money that can range from tens to hundreds of millions of dollars and can, depending on one's lifestyle, marital status, and spending habits, allow you the freedom to pursue projects on your own terms, or buy a villa in the south of France, drink a lot of wine and work on a novel. Or take your family and relocate to a spread in Wyoming and live like the actors on *Entertainment Tonight*, who plug their latest movie live from their ranch, where they live year-round and tell the visiting sycophantic reporter how they escaped Hollywood to raise their kids in a normal place amongst regular folk. This is a situation that allows actors to achieve that most rarified actor status: that of being known worldwide as a humble recluse. (It is an interesting Hollywood phenomenon that most people spend half their lives figuring out how to get into the business, and the other half figuring how to get the fuck out. Sorry for the digression, this shit just leaks out.)

Anyway, it occurred to me that keeping a journal while in development might illuminate a side of the business few people get to see, and give them a "behind the scenes" (God, I hate that insipid tabloid TV phrase) look at the day-to-day experience of being a

---

[6] Syndication. Re-runs. Successful shows are sold to independent station groups and the studio and producers cash in.

[7] Fuck you money is, of course, based on whether the studio in fact pays you. In some cases, shows are sold into syndication but the studio insists that there are no profits to be shared as they haven't yet recouped the money they loaned you to make the show in the first place—their "deficit." Eventually, those who own a piece of the show hire lawyers and accountants and sue the studios for a fair accounting of what monies have come in. Another form of "fuck you money" is the studios saying: "Fuck you, just try to collect your money."

writer in Hollywood. OK, that's partly bullshit. I'm not that altruistic. The truth is, after all these years, I found myself bitching about aspects of the business and needed an outlet, which left either writing a book, doing standup, seeing my shrink more often or suffering in silence, but since I don't have the balls to try stand-up, there's no reason to waste a shrink visit bitching about the business when I've got more seriously fucked-up issues to deal with, and there's no money in suffering in silence—that left book.

Actually, the first time I thought of keeping a journal on the development experience was in 1997, as I was driving from Paramount to Sony to meet with the people running Tony Danza's production company to discuss writing a pilot for him. The show I'd been working on—*Wings*—was coming to the end of its 8-year run; Tony had a pilot deal at NBC; and I was about to begin a two-year deal with NBC Productions, their in-house company. It occurred to me, as I was stuck in traffic, that it might be interesting to keep a record detailing the day-to-day experience of creating a television show that might answer some of the legitimate, along with the occasionally inane, questions civilians pose about TV. (See "The Four Predictably Annoying Responses I Get When I Tell People I Write For TV.")

But I told myself that it was way too much work, a waste of time, one of those fleeting notions you get while stuck in traffic and unless you're in therapy, prison, on death row, marooned on a desert island, or happen to be Gandhi, an ex-President, or some other historical figure, who really gives a shit about your experiences? Does the world really need another personal journal? Another "I'm Going to Beat This" cancer diary with a picture of some plucky, 50-something celebrity on the cover with a life-affirming smile and a schmatta[8] on her head? (What is it with

[8] Schmatta. A Hebrew do-rag.

cancer and celebrities? A normal human gets cancer, they call an oncologist. A celebrity gets cancer, they call a publicist.) It's not like I was going to come up with some new insight into the human condition that hasn't been hit on in thousands of years of recorded history. Check out the library, does the world really need another book and, if so, is that a book about working in television? Who gives a shit? Anyway, that's what I told myself, so I bagged it and turned on the radio.

Little did I know at the time that I would meet with those people, go back and pitch an idea they liked, and get hired to write a script. I also didn't know that while they were developing my script, they were simultaneously developing another script for Tony with another writer, a fact conveniently left out of our early discussions. One of those lies by omission you grow to expect and eventually learn to sniff out. ("Hello," lied the agent.) In the end my idea was picked, and after an excruciating and seemingly endless series of notes and revisions, we produced a pilot, which was tested, reviewed, promoted and finally premiered. In all, we shot 13 shows, and got cancelled after the fourth airing—which, as often happens, was during late December. "Merry Christmas, you're cancelled." At which point everyone hugged, cried, got drunk, railed at the unfairness of the business, and promised to stay in touch, while simultaneously reaching for their cell phones to call their agents to find them a job on an existing show.

Looking back, that experience might have made an interesting story about how a TV show comes into and goes out of existence, along with all the shit the writer goes through in between. Like one of those junior high filmstrips about the sperm's journey to the egg. So, this time, as the show I was working on (*Becker*) was winding down, and I faced the prospect of starting a new development deal at Paramount, I decided to keep the journal. My reasons were two-fold: cultural (I need to [illegible] this part of my cultural heritage (or perhaps just my own psychological makeup).) And frustration. Both [illegible].

As I headed back into the development world, an experience I once described to colleagues as sticking your head out of a gopher hole so it can get whacked with a [illegible], I looked out at the landscape of shows and [illegible] that over the past few years network television had gotten [illegible] by the minute, slowly [illegible] for children, adults with children, and adults with the minds of children. Looking at [illegible] of the awful shows that [illegible] the [illegible], I got a pain in my heart like a father [illegible] and wasted potential.

[illegible]

[illegible] and could only [illegible] to lower depths [illegible] they took [illegible] from either door [illegible] the first door, a [illegible] backs, and [illegible]. Behind the second, a [illegible] just as her [illegible] reaching out to hug him. And as the studio audience shouts out "One!" and "Two!" the home audience votes by calling 1-900-DADDY1 or DADDY2 (at 99¢ per call) [illegible]. Really.

Chayefsky's worst nightmare about TV, *Network*, didn't even come close to this. Yet we're living it.

Of course, these shows have their fans. They're all based around the things we worship in America: sex, money, and contests. And, OK, I confess, sometimes I watch them and get suckered in. I also gorge out on the occasional fast food burger. Tastes great going down but as *Super Size Me* proved, a steady diet will make you sick. Or in the case of TV—stupid. But the reason these shows are on is not because some network exec shot up in bed at 3 am in a eureka moment, shouting, "People want to see real people!" It's because one network put one of these shows on the air (MTV's *The Real World* and CBS' *Survivor* being among the first) and they were well received; i.e. they got ratings. So they made more. And the other networks copied them. Why not? If there's gold on the low road, might as well go get it. Or, more to the point, you can't be the only one not getting it. What's unfortunate is while, at one time, those who ran the networks seemed to have a taste/intelligence line they wouldn't cross, the obsession with ratings and being "number one" have squashed that line like a bug on a windshield that gets eaten by a *Fear Factor* contestant. If a show gets numbers, it stays on.

Frankly, if a show about a masturbating monkey got a 20 share, the masturbating monkey would be on *ET*, the cover of *People*, McDonald's would have Masturbating Monkey Meals (some might argue that they already do, but in this case, they would actually call them that) and at Christmastime, parents would flock to the stores to get their kids a "Tickle me, Masturbating Monkey" doll. (Actually, with a few modifications, you could take that wind-up cymbal-clapping monkey and make the prototype. He's already got the smile on his face.)

Meanwhile, the dumber network TV gets, the smarter and more interesting cable gets. Thank God for HBO, Showtime, FX

Comedy Central, A&E, Discovery Channel, The History Channel, or any of the other niche cable channels which collectively have become the room in the house where the adults talk, while network TV is fast becoming the children's playroom. Oh yeah, and then there's PBS, which seems more like the sewing room in the house. Very often a place for reflection, though sometimes it seems like it's gotten a little musty. (Oh, and by the way, stop calling me for money. I gave 100 bucks one time to get the CDs of Bill Moyers' conversations with Joseph Campbell, and now I'm on the permanent suckers list and they're calling me every night at dinnertime to cough up more money. Cough up another interesting giveaway, and I'll think about it. Meanwhile, lose my fucking number. And while we're on the subject, stop the telethons with the silky-voiced intellectuals laying on the guilt and harping on how the world would melt without public TV. OK, I know, I'll write the damn check. Just put the Monty Python retrospective back on and cut your twenty [illegible] off camera.)

Anyway, the aforementioned studio deal—and the subject for most of this memoir—was at Paramount. My job: create shows—either alone or with other writers—and, in partnership with the studio, pitch and sell them to one of the networks, write the script, get it made and hopefully picked up on the fall schedule or for midseason. In the course of that deal, I sold and wrote two pilots. (Later on I sold and wrote two more.) What those experiences were like and how they eventually worked out will be detailed herein in all their gory detail.

Am I worried about offending people? "You'll never pitch in this town again?" Maybe. In writing this, I'm not only biting the hand that feeds me, I'm biting the hand that's fed me steaks. Well, steaks I could eat if my cholesterol weren't so high. Still, if this doesn't get published, no one will know. And if it does, then I've published a book, so what the heck do I care who's upset? (OK, so maybe I care a little: after this comes out, I may not be able to walk down certain network corridors without a brick being lobbed at my head. But what I wrote was exactly what I was feeling at the time and accurately reflected the experience—OK, my experience—of working in television, so I'm leaving the record intact. All I can say to those who may get a little bent out of shape: It wasn't personal; it was strictly business.)

PROLOGUE

There is no method [illegible] anecdotes, or pieces of conversation [illegible] to illustrate a point or explain some aspect of the business, [illegible] information, or just because I found it relevant. As I said, this is mostly subjective, fueled by ambition, money, envy, pride, [illegible] fears, ego, arrogance, and all the other emotions you need to work in TV. Oh, yes, and frustration. [illegible] thanks to the [illegible] network television that is systematically dumbed down. I'm still working on it.

Part of that is financial: I make a lot of money when I work. Part of it's emotional in that I enjoy it. I'm not only addicted to watching TV, I'm addicted to working in it. But although this account is mostly subjective, the occasional conclusions are not simply "my opinions." Somehow, in this country, intellectual relativism has taken hold, thanks to the First Amendment guarantee to freedom of speech, which simply guarantees us equal right to express our ideas; they don't give each idea equal intellectual weight. Some are just dumber or less informed than others, yet it doesn't seem to deflate those who, when they're all out of thoughts, put their hands on their hips and end the argument with a lame "Well, that's my opinion." Frankly (in my opinion), opinions are what stupid people end up with because they either don't know or can't understand all the facts.

The conclusions I arrive at are based on experience, observation, and reflection, and represent an accurate—OK, so maybe a slightly cynical—depiction of this reality. Of course, and someone's going to say it so I might as well, that's just my opinion. Though I'm not alone, as most of this also reflects years of conversations with other writers sitting around bitching about TV, though frankly, anyone out here making the kind of money you can make has absolutely no right to complain. Pissing and moaning about the lack of creative freedom and constant network meddling into a creative product should be a crime, particularly considering how most people have to suffer and sweat to earn a living. Writing for TV is special. It's privileged. If you're lucky enough to create a show that gets on, or get staffed on someone else's show, your job entails getting paid a fortune to sit in a writers' room with funny people, make up stories, and laugh your ass off while people bring you food. It's been described as being very well-paid veal. Despite the erratic hours, and not knowing if you're going to get home to put your kid to sleep, no one in the position of being paid to write for TV has anything to bitch about. That said, I'm now going to bitch.

PART I

THE FOUR PREDICTABLY ANNOYING RESPONSES I GET WHEN I TELL PEOPLE I WRITE FOR TV

As I said: I love TV. Or, to be more precise, I'm addicted to it, as are most people, if they're honest enough to admit it. Which most people aren't. In fact, when I tell civilians what I do, I get one of four predictably annoying responses (which was also one of the catalysts for writing this book. I can now set some of this shit straight, while putting in print what I wish I'd been clever enough to say in the moment).

1. The first response comes from people who must immediately inform you that what you do is foreign to them; i.e. beneath them, and always comes out with the same rising intonation carrying an air of intellectual superiority as they say: "Oh…well, I (or "we" if it's a couple) don't really watch TV," as if this disclaimer carried with it proof of one's intelligence, breeding, and superior cultural taste. Then they feign ignorance of what shows might be on, almost to the point where you have to remind them what the TV is—you know, the box in the living room, with the lights and sounds coming out of it. Once in a while one of them will confess to some occasional viewing—the news, a PBS or Animal Planet documentary, or perhaps C-SPAN, when there's an important Congressional debate. And, of course, no one ever admits to letting their kids watch. Especially during the week. To do otherwise is looked on as an only slightly less despicable form of child abuse, or at least bad parenting, which most parents aren't above telling you. You get the disapproving stare, along with the head shake, and the tongue clack, as preface to "Do you now or have you ever let your

are setting programming standards, based on the premise that there is an adult audience out there that wants a funnier, more intelligent product than the networks are offering. Even one-hour network drama shows mostly about doctors, cops, or lawyers play to a brighter audience. *House* and *24* are just two current examples of hour TV at its best. When people criticize TV for being dumb they're usually referring to half-hour comedy (sitcoms), or the more lame reality shows. And in this respect, they're mostly right.

But the question is why? Are the people in charge of which shows get on pre-dumbing it, or are they simply responding to the nation's taste by offering more of the dumb shit they've already expressed a desire for? Ratings determine what's on the box, so, like water seeking its own level, the audience is going to get more of what it's said it wants. There's no taste police, no intelligence minimum. No standards and practices for what should be on TV, just one as a watchdog for what *can't* be on—tits and profanity. There is no longer any pretense of content driving network TV. It's ratings and nothing but ratings, to the point that even the word "good" has been corrupted. Once upon a time "good" denoted quality. Now it denotes success. A good movie is one that does well at the box office. A good show is one that gets numbers but still may be crap. It's a simple syllogism: what's good is what sells; sometimes shit sells; therefore, sometimes shit is good. Good ratings=life. Bad ratings=cancellation and death. Bottom line: it's McTelevision. It's unfortunate, because over time, this process limits the audience's choices and they become almost like convicts in the mess hall being served a diet of shit sandwiches and cold ketchup soup. Eventually you're going to start thinking: "You know, the soup's not that bad." H.L. Mencken said it best: "No one ever went broke underestimating the taste of the American public."

3. The third response when I tell people I work in television comes from someone who absolutely must tell you, since you're in

the "comedy field," that they've got a "great idea" for a show usually based on either their personal lives or the madcap antics in their office, which is "just the funniest place. In fact there's a guy down in shipping, he does these impressions of the boss, I swear we're all in stitches in the lunchroom, so you should write a show about that." The assumption in this one is that TV writers couldn't possibly have ideas of their own and just sit around waiting for a friend or relative to call with an amusing true-life anecdote, for someone to lob a spec script over the transom, or for some innocent rube to get off the bus with a million-dollar idea they can steal.

[illegible]

Let's put this one to rest right now: Hollywood doesn't steal. There have been an infinite number of lawsuits brought by people who pitched ideas or sent scripts to a studio and have had them rejected, only to see that same studio produce a similar project. Most have probably been frivolous; others may have had some merit. But ultimately, unless someone rips the title page off your script and puts their name on it (which has happened), it's not really theft. Hollywood copies, imitates, parodies and plagiarizes, rips off and robs, but Hollywood does not steal ideas for one reason and one reason only: It's not ethical. (Just kidding. Sorry, I couldn't resist that.) No, it's because in Hollywood, IDEAS ARE SHIT. That's right. They're almost worthless. EVERYTHING IS EXECUTION—how a show or movie is written, cast, directed, edited, even marketed. And while there are an infinite number of examples from TV that illustrate this point, the one that always occurs to me is from the movie side. Between 1987 and 1988 four movies were released with virtually an identical premise: through

Along with the fear that if you don't get a project set up somewhere, a few years down the road, you'll be the fat fuck in shipping who does hilarious impression of the boss.

4. The fourth and most dreaded response of all is: "What's it like working in TV? I hear there's a lot of money in it, and most of those shows are so lame it couldn't be all that difficult to write so do you think I could get one of those jobs and cash in?" Answer: "No, you can't. Or maybe you can, it's just not easy." Want to hear the war stories? Visit any deli in town and look for a table of 30-to-50-year-old guys (and women) in jeans, sneakers, and baseball hats. Or check out Nate 'n' Al's in Beverly Hills and look for a bunch of 70-year-old Jews in jogging suits, or Members Only jackets and Greek fisherman's caps. This is where show business goes to relax, bitch and/or die by gorging itself on corned beef. (Note to American men over 60: Lose the Members Only jackets already. It's a fucking windbreaker with epaulettes that looked idiotic 20 years ago. Wearing it now simply leaves others with the impression that you're either too poor, too old or too fashion-retarded to have purchased a new coat in the last two decades. And, oh yeah, what's with the jaunty cap? Do you first get old and then decide you look good in it? Or do you put the cap on first, and it turns you old? I'm not just trying to be an asshole. I really need to know.)

Working in TV is great. What's a bitch is not working, either when you're trying to break in and get your first job, or when the show you've been on gets cancelled and you're trying to get your next one. And the money in TV is criminal. Salaries range from the hundreds of thousands a year to the millions. And beyond.

"Sounds great, but do I have to actually write something or can I just tell you my idea so you can write it and we'll split the money?" Answer: Fuck off. This is not how shows or careers in TV come about. Just ask any producer who's staffing a show about the hundreds of spec scripts lying in piles on the floor, each representing a writer or team looking for a job. And those are just the writers with agents who could get their material through.

"Yeah, but I don't know what a script looks like." Go online and search for copies of scripts from existing shows. Someone will be selling them somewhere. Or write the studio or production company requesting one. They might be nice enough to send you a copy or two, as someone did for me, years ago when I was in New York. Then watch those shows and try to come up with an idea for an episode.

"OK, I've written some scripts but I can't get them read by an agent. What do I do?" Everyone who ever broke into TV faced this same dilemma and somehow managed to get in, so figure it out for yourself; shit, I'm not your mother. For starters, move to L.A. and either meet or sleep with the right people. And don't bother with sitcom writing classes or the "how to" section of the bookstore. The shelves are filled with "How to Sell Your Idea to TV" books. By and large, they're worthless. They might as well be titled: "How to Get a Sense of Humor." "Developing a Dyspeptic Personality." "A Dystopian World View for Idiots." "You, Too, Can be Cynical." "Insecurity, Self-doubt, and Self-loathing—Your Ticket To Success." "The Art of Rejection." Or "The Complete Idiot's Guide to Dealing With Complete Idiots." You're either funny or you're not. You can either write or you can't. No book or class will ever give you talent. At best, some may give you the correct format in which to channel your ideas and maybe a rough idea of how the business works. (You think Larry David got that way by reading a book on sitcom writing?)

In terms of what it's really like to work in TV, read on, or buy one of the only books that got it right, both written by writers: *Artistic Differences* by Charlie Hauck and *Conversations With My*

Agent by Rob Long. By the time you're done reading, you may not want to go near TV. It's a cold fucking business.

DEVELOPMENT IN THEORY "The Agony and the Entropy"

The reality of how television shows are created and developed involves an annual feeding frenzy that begins in early fall and lasts through mid-May, although at some networks development goes on all year long. In either case, it's a creative merry-go-round where everyone's grabbing for the precious few brass rings. You succeed, you're rich, and are greeted by agents and executives with a hug usually reserved for a reunion with a long-lost birth mother. You fail, you're shunned like an Amish whore. OK, you're not really shunned, but your phone will immediately stop ringing, and you will be harassing your agent to get you on staff on some show some other bastard was lucky enough to get picked up.

THE ODDS

Each year hundreds, maybe even thousands, of ideas are pitched. Maybe 500 are picked up "for script" (the network pays the writer to write it) and turned in either right before the Christmas/New Year break, or soon after. By the end of January or early February, most are winnowed out and a relatively select few, 120 or so, are picked up to be shot, which begins a casting, rewriting, and rehearsal process that goes through the next few months. Most pilots are shot and delivered by April, when the networks screen and test them. Let's say maybe 35 make it to series, either on the fall schedule or midseason. Maybe 12 get cancelled quickly, 7 more get pulled for November sweeps[9] and eventually cancelled, leaving 16 that stay on for all 13 shows. Of those, maybe 10 get a back nine order[10], allowing them to stay in production, while 3 more get cancelled, and 3 get a somewhat less enthusiastic script order and eventually fade away. Of the remaining 10, maybe 6 get pulled for February sweeps, and end up getting cancelled. The final 4 shows stay on the air and are on the schedule the following fall, though there's always a chance that a couple of those won't make it through a second season. So, in the end, of those 500 pilot scripts written, let's say two shows end up going the distance. That's about 250-to-1 odds of ultimate success. Then it begins all over again.

Television is a business based on the presumption of failure. In fact, not long after the fall shows premiere, the networks open their doors for new pitches. And many of the cable channels are open year-round. But it's also a business maintained by people, many of whom, from a creative standpoint, and with some notable exceptions, have no business running it; namely, the network comedy development executive.

THE NETWORK COMEDY DEVELOPMENT EXECUTIVE

In 1876, German-American archaeologist Heinrich Schliemann excavating at Mycenae uncovered a set of funeral masks and communicated his awe in a telegraph to the king of Greece, stating: "I have gazed upon the face of Agamemnon." I would feel equally awestruck if I ever found myself gazing upon the

[9] Sweeps. November, February and May periods when ad rates are set and networks pull any stunt they can concoct to artificially goose their ratings.

[10] Back nine. Traditionally, the TV season is built around 22 episodes, broken up into the pilot, and an additional 12 episodes that are part of the initial order. If the show does well, it's given an extra nine episode order — "the back nine"— as opposed to the back nine holes of a golf course, which is where you will traditionally finds writers whose shows didn't get a back nine.

fact of a network development executive who had ever created, written, or produced an episode of television. Not that there aren't intelligent people. They are. Most are extremely bright. You have to be to get these jobs. Some are even funny or know funny when they see it and try to nurture it. Others seem to attack it like white blood cells going after a lung infection. And a few I've encountered over the years wouldn't recognize an original idea if it got shot up their asses on the tip of a flaming arrow.

In the past, there have been network presidents who came from the producing ranks. Grant Tinker, who ran MTM and went on to run NBC, is one who comes to mind. As far as an executive writers respected, the person most often mentioned is the late Brandon Tartikoff. Both of them ran NBC during the eighties, when the relationship between writer and network seemed more collaborative. These days, it seems most development executives are business people and corporate climbers who have worked their way up the ladder to land these coveted jobs: MBAs, lawyers, publicity execs. Again, with some exceptions, few have actually worked as a writer or producer—broken a story, run a writers' room, [illegible] an outline, written a script, done a rewrite, supervised the production work, sat in on an edit [illegible] or any of the various jobs associated with producing television. Honestly, I'm not even sure some of them have ever told a joke, let alone written one. Yet their jobs entail passing judgment on what's funny or not and altering it along the way with veto power over the person who actually had the idea in the first place along with the vision to guide it creatively. Somehow the ascension of the ranks of development executives carries with it the assumption of actual creative ability.

Though most development executives can't be held ultimately responsible for the content on TV, as they are part of a corporate hierarchy that often dictates creative policy, influencing what they buy, how they alter what they buy, and how hands-on they are during the process. Their jobs have one requirement: deliver hit shows—meaning successful shows—no matter what form they come in. Bottom line: it's not about pushing a show to its creative limits. It's just about putting something on the air that gets ratings. A friend and colleague Dave Hackel cynically describes TV shows as "the train cars that bring us the commercials." Could be *The West Wing*. Could be *The Biggest Loser*. The people who make Cheerios ultimately don't give a shit. Nor do their ad agency media buyers, who look at a show in terms of its ratings, particularly the 18-49 demo and CPM (cost per thousand—how much it costs to reach 1000 people).

When you're pitching your show, these are the thoughts rattling around the mind of the network comedy development executive. Their job is to sift through all the pitches they hear, or spec scripts they read, and determine which ones to buy. In their defense, the pressure is on them to find a hit by using their own judgement while simultaneously operating under mandates from above, ranging from:

More half hour, because one hour is dead or we need a comedy to launch behind an established hit.

More one hour, because half hour is dead, or because we're getting killed in the 10 o'clock slot by some other network's one-hour drama.

No shows starring anyone over 20.

No shows starring anyone over 30.

No shows starring anyone over 40.

No kid shows, this isn't the fucking Disney Channel. (Unless it's the fucking Disney Channel.)

No workplace comedies. Family shows are succeeding on our network.

No family shows. Workplace comedies are succeeding on our network.

More edgy, non-traditional shows.

No edgy shows. Give us a nice, traditional, meat-and-potatoes sitcom.

No single camera. Too expensive.

More single camera. We just had one of them succeed.

And no shows about show business. They never work.

Whatever the edict of the day, or the moment, network executives know where the holes are in their schedule and how their bosses wanted them filled, so any pitch they hear goes through that filter. They also know how many producers have projects with on-air commitments[11] that often involve huge penalties if they're not put on. Given these parameters, more often than not they know two minutes into a pitch whether your project is something they're interested in, or something their bosses would allow them to buy.

If their interest starts to wane, you immediately see it in their body language, the patronizing smiles, the way their eyes drop, and their pencils slowly fall to their laps, while you have to continue tap dancing, sensing inside that your idea just isn't going to fly. So while you're rambling on about your amusing little show, they really just wish you'd shut up, stop wasting their time and leave, so that the next person can come in, hopefully with something they can use. (If I were a network exec, I'd have a gong to ring to signal I'd heard enough, or a button to push that opens the floor under the writer so I could drop his ass out of the room and into the parking lot the moment I knew I was done with him.) With

[11] Commitments by a network to a writer, actor, or producer guaranteeing that either their show will be put on the schedule or they'll be paid a huge penalty. Having network commitments strengthens one's leverage when it comes to attracting talent.

those pressures, it's easy to see why some give you the feeling they're in the serious business of comedy.

Then there are studio development executives. Similar types of people, different situations. Studios are in the position of teaming up with writers to sell shows to the networks. In short, they are salespeople. "Sell 'em, don't smell 'em" is something you hear occasionally. It's about finding writers and setting up as many projects as you can. (And while for some it's more about quality than quantity, the "how many shows did you sell" mentality is still part of the game.)

Studio people tend to be more flexible. They naturally don't know what the networks will buy, so they'll usually take a shot with any idea, however bizarre, although they will occasionally tell you not to waste your time with something, either because networks aren't buying it, or they've bought too many already. Their notes tend to be sharper. More strategic. With the eventual goal of shaping the show so that it will sell. Studio people tend to laugh more. Though the pressure is on them to sell and you can often feel it, even while they're making jokes in the network waiting room before a pitch.

And then there are the "current programming" executives, who are basically the liaisons between a production and the studio or network. They tend to be the funniest, most easygoing, and light-hearted. Almost like they're part of the show. Writers tend to like them. Except the one or two who get so puffed up with self-importance that they try to put their own stamp or impose their own tastes on whatever you're doing. Those you want to strangle with their own entrails.

In TV, especially on a pilot, you are deluged with executives. One of the strangest sights you'll see is an executive walking on stage for a shoot, carrying a script, sidling up to the quad[12] and staring at it quizzically—much like when my car stalls and I pop open the hood and stare at the engine because I know it's what I'm supposed to look at but I honestly have no clue what I'm looking for, what's broken, or how to fix it. The difference is, with my car, I take it to a mechanic, say: "It's broken," and give him the freedom to fix it and screw me. There is no scarier sight than a group of them huddling after a table read or run-through, while you stand aside and wait for the judgment from on high. Experientially, as a writer, it's like waiting to get directions from a blind seeing-eye dog. Even though they have the power, few will accept that writers are more qualified to come up with ideas and produce better, funnier, more unique shows, rendering their role more advisory. These days, executives don't advise. They dictate. They are the gatekeepers. The ones who filter the ideas that come in, guide them along the note process and ultimately decide which projects go through and in what way. Again, it's not that they're clueless. Or humorless. It's just that most often they don't have the insight or experience to know why something works or doesn't. Why it's funny or not. Some do. Others know it when they see it. And a few, well, perhaps as a result of being humor-adjacent for so many years, they get the notion that they might actually be funny, much like a cow pushed out of airplane might momentarily think it can fly.

THE PITCH

If a camel is a horse built by a committee, a network pilot is a horse that's been gang-raped by a committee, then put back in the

[12] Quad. The quad split. On a four-camera show, a single monitor is split into four quadrants (quads) showing the shots from each of the four cameras. This is how the director checks coverage, makes sure the respective camera operators get their shots and where the writers and producers gather during a shoot to laugh at their own brilliance.

stable with the warning to shut its fucking mouth. And other than in cases where a network buys a spec pilot, it all begins innocently enough with the pitch. Sometime in early fall, writers who can get in to pitch will visit a studio development VP, or production company development exec. (Some go directly in to the network, which means you could end up doing the show with their in-house production company, but for the sake of this example, let's go through the entire food chain.)

Question: "So you mean if I have an idea, all I have to do is call up a studio?" Answer: "No. If you haven't worked on a show, you won't even get on the lot, let alone in the door." Not even a few produced scripts and a WGA[13] card gets you in. It's based on experience, relationships, and a track record. The less experienced you are, the more you need to have proven yourself in production on an existing show while developing a relationship with someone at the studio who would be open to hearing your idea. If you've never written a pilot or "run a show"[14], you'll have to team up with an established writer who can godfather[15] your script, making the studio and network feel that at least someone who knows how to do the job will be involved.

As to the usual lament of "That's why TV sucks, they keep relying on the same people," the answer is, in part: fuck off. A half-hour show costs over a million dollars to produce, an hour show over 2 million. Each involves hundreds of decisions that have to be made on a daily basis, from dealing with scenes that don't work, actors who are upset or confused because those scenes don't work, directors who are caught in the middle, wardrobe mismatches, ruined takes due to boom shadows or a hundred other personal,

---

[13] WGA. Writers' Guild of America

[14] Run a show. A showrunner. Most often the creator and Executive Producer who is the ultimate creative judge on all aspects of the show.

[15] Godfather. To back up a less experienced writer who's being entrusted to write his or her first pilot.

professional, or technical glitches. Only someone with years of experience in the trenches of TV production will be able to make those calls as quickly as they need to be made.

But if you've got the credentials to pitch your idea, you or your agent will make the call to a studio development VP, saying "So-and-so has an idea they want to pitch." A meeting is set, and you prepare your little notion into an entertaining 20- or 30-minute presentation during which you tell them the arena, the characters, maybe an idea for a pilot story, a few potential future episodes, and maybe cite an example of similar shows that hit or actors from those shows who might work in yours. If you're lucky, you'll find it's right for someone a network has on a deal. If you've done your homework, you'll know that in advance. Just to fast-track this scenario, let's assume they like it, maybe have a few adjustments or suggestions you incorporate, and they begin scheduling network meetings for you to go pitch.

Finally, the day comes. The meeting is on. Or it's been cancelled at the last minute because, frankly, network people often have more important things to do than hear about your little skit. But let's say it's not cancelled. The meeting day arrives. You go to the guard gate, praying they haven't screwed up your drive-on[16], you seek out visitor parking, passing rows of reserved spaces—the network's way of saying "Don't get too comfortable, you're only visiting." You find your way to the proper office, sit in the waiting room while they conduct more important business, go over last-minute stuff with your studio partners, then a door opens and you're ushered inside and greeted with a warm smile, handshake and/or hug, with cheek kiss or without, depending on whether you're already acquainted. Then you meet a few more junior execs and assistants with notepads.

---

[16] Drive-on. A list at the gate with your name on it, allowing you to pass through. There's no smaller feeling than looking into the eyes of a guard looking back at you and saying, "You're not on the list."

You find a comfortable spot and after the obligatory beverage offering (water—it's free, so take it), followed by 5 minutes of general chit-chat in the guise of "Let's make believe we're actual human beings having an actual conversation." After the "Where do you live?" "Who do we know in common?" and "Do you have kids?" there will be the eventual dramatic pause, followed by the exec's: "So, what have you got?"

Now you're on. The floor is yours. You remember the goal is to be funny and entertaining, then get the hell out. You get out your notes and take a dramatic pause to collect your thoughts, the emotions running through you a schizophrenic mix of arrogance and insecurity. Arrogance, because you need to pitch with the certainty that they're assholes if they don't buy this. And insecurity, because you know the odds are against them buying it and, deep down, you're just jerking off. Still, you pitch your heart out, hopefully getting some laughs along the way, until finally there's another pause and they say "Thanks, let us talk," which means "We're done with you. Take your shit and go."

So you gather your notes and leave, passing the next group waiting to get in. During pilot season, writers are queued up like guys at Dodger stadium waiting to pee. You see them on your way in, and on your way out. Occasionally it's someone you know. You stop, smile, make small talk and, as you leave, you secretly hope they fall miserably on their asses, just as they hope you've just fallen miserably on yours. Especially if they're good friends. It's been said that in Hollywood, friends don't want friends to fail; friends want friends to die. After all, their success is your failure. They're the ones keeping you from your goal of making millions, buying a Porsche, a house in the hills, and fucking a movie star. Oh, and creative satisfaction.

Now you're in "waiting to hear" mode, which is where show business spends most of its time. Bernie Brillstein once commented that "There are only ten people in show business," meaning only the heads of studios and networks have any real greenlight[17] power. Everyone else waits by the phone. You pace your apartment or house. You play with your kids or work on your show if you're in production at the time. Or play golf if you don't. You try desperately not to read the trades[18] for fear of seeing that a project just like yours got picked up somewhere else. Or worse, someone you hate just had some good fortune. A writer I once worked with, Jim Vallely, remarked, "*Variety* takes fifteen minutes to read and four hours to get over." You try to put the project out of your mind, which is impossible. Every phone ring gives you an adrenaline rush.

Eventually, the call will, most likely, go to your agent, who relays the news to you. Again, given the odds, most often it's "They passed." If you're experienced, you take it as fact of life, and move on to pitch it elsewhere, or to another project. If you're new, you take a moment to whine to your agent "But *why????*" sounding somewhat like a petulant child who's been told he can't have more ice cream. Even then, the explanation is sketchy, coming in the form of "It was too soft," "Too edgy," "They have ten like it in development," or "They hate you." It doesn't matter. You didn't sell it, so your agent will tell you any bit of encouraging bullshit to get you off the line so they can talk to their writer clients who did sell their shows.

For future reference, if you intend on working as a writer, you need to be aware that there are only two responses to any pitch, script, or show that you will ever hear in your entire professional life. The first is: "I loved it! I laughed! I cried! The characters are fresh! The dialogue sharp! The jokes hilarious! The touching,

---

[17] Greenlight. The okay to start spending money on a project.
[18] Trades. Show business trade papers – *Variety* and *The Hollywood Reporter*.

profound moments...profoundly touching! This is a work of genius, and the genius is you!" The other response...is everything else. It begins with a pause. Followed by "Uh, well, I only read it once in the can or in bed and it was late," backed up by a weak "I really liked that joke on page 3," or "Do you think it's a little dark?" and "Let's have breakfast and talk about it," all delivered with that rising intonation people use when they're trying to hide their true feelings or soften the blow. In other words, most of what you will hear in your show business career will be some form of bullshit.

BULLSHIT

Lies fuel show business. Along with the lie's country cousin—bullshit. Bullshit is Hollywood oxygen. It's necessary for survival. In fact, most everything you will be told in the course of your career will contain some degree of bullshit, either from people who care about you enough to spare your feelings, people who need you so they're blowing so much smoke up your ass that your eyes begin to cloud up, or people who don't give a shit about you but are looking for the most efficient way to reject you. Rarely will anyone tell you the absolute truth, unless you ask. Then they'll adopt a sincere voice and tell you a version of the absolute truth, only with a bit less bullshit. In time, you'll come to realize that people say more by what they don't say than by what they do and you learn to read the silences. (Along with the hesitations, the lilting quality in people's voices when they're offering faint praise, or a left-handed compliment. "I like this one so much more than your last script.") People lie to protect their own interests, occasionally to spare your feelings, or to keep you working until such time as you fail and they don't need you, or you succeed, in which case, the lie becomes irrelevant.

But it really doesn't matter. Anything less than "I loved it" means "I hated it. You suck. You'll never make a living as a writer. Go bag groceries." Also FYI, in the world of meals, agent dinners are reserved for true friends or clients who have had or are about to have a major success. Lunch is for clients who have had some success and have a solid chance of continued employment, or for poaching other agents' clients. (Note that there is a time limit on lunch, giving the agent a built-in excuse to cut off the conversation.) Breakfast is basically for clients who haven't worked in a while, and is set up with the agenda "Let's strategize," though the true meaning of it is "If you don't get work soon I'll have to drop you."

OK, back to the present. The phone rings. You check the caller ID. It's your agent. Your heart is pounding as you pick up the phone and say hi, ready to hear the words that could change your life. Then your agent's assistant asks you to hold on while the agent wraps up another call. Shit. You hold for what seems like an eternity, and then he or she jumps off their previous call. (In Hollywood, people either "jump" on or off calls. If they like you, they "take" your calls. If not, they silently shake their heads to their assistants and mouth the words "call back," and the assistant then gets back on and tells you that person is in a meeting and will call you back. This is either the truth or bullshit. You'll know by whether your phone rings again.)

OK, so your agent gets on the phone. The tension is high as he starts the conversation with "I talked to the executive…" You say "And…" Then he or she says: "They passed." Then your heart sinks and you consider suicide, which is usually preferable to having to tell friends and acquaintances that your show didn't go. But the mood usually passes when you remember that you had several other ideas and maybe one of them will sell. Or you're in denial or heavily sedated.

But for the sake of this example, let's say it's good news, which you'll know by their tone of voice and how quickly it arrives. Agents deliver so much bad news to their clients that it's exciting to them when they don't have to. "Congratulations," he says. Your heart soars. "They bought it." Your heart soars even more. Then there's a pause. If you're new, the pause confuses you. You think "Shouldn't there be more praise coming?" If you've done this before, you understand the pause. It's quickly followed by a "But." "BUT" means you're fucked but comes in the form of "They had a few concerns."

"Concerns" is studio- or network-speak for shit they want changed, which might range from a few caveats either in story or tone, to dislike for the main character, to the complete evisceration of everything you pitched. "Oh, and there's a funny, young black kid from some candy commercial they just made a holding deal with so they want him in there as the son of the sexy neighbor, who could also be a love interest for the main character." Then you say "There is no sexy neighbor, it's a show about firemen, set in a fire-house, and the main character's got a girlfriend and I based the entire pilot story around their relationship." And your agent says "I'm getting to that."

And he does. Then, for a brief second, you consider whether you can make the changes they want, or if your creative integrity is such that you just can't stomach your pet project being turned into pet food. 99% bend over and make the changes, as they can somehow make all your ambitions suddenly feel like pre-tensions. Sure, occasionally you'll hear the story of the writer who absolutely refused to compromise his or her creative vision and made the pilot the way they saw it, and it went on to become a hit. Of course, the only reason you're hearing that story is, like *Seinfeld*, the show went on to become a hit. You don't hear the stories of writers who told the studio or network to piss off because, most often, the network said "OK" and those shows never came into existence. It's like Robert Townsend and *Hollywood Shuffle*. The story of how he maxed out his credit cards to make the movie is legendary. What you never hear about is how many people maxed out their cards with the same dream but without the same talent or luck and ended up with nothing but debt, obscurity, and a commemorative DVD.

But at this stage it doesn't matter. You say, "Sure, whatever, anything," due to the sheer relief of not having been rejected and the fact that you are now officially being paid to write and can hold your head up at any social gathering where other writers are present and say with confidence: "I have a project in development! I am somebody!" Then there's a moment of panic as you begin to wonder if you can even write this the way they now seem to want it. Yet you put those fears aside, as dollar amounts and deal points are discussed. Actors' names are dropped in the "You think we can get DeNiro?" moments of casting self-delusion. A subsequent meeting or notes conference call is set to discuss the changes and how you plan to deal with them. Still, it doesn't matter how much more you have to go through. You've reached the level where you're being paid to write a pilot, which means you can pay your rent, mortgage, alimony, and car insurance and feed your kids…well, for a while.

So, off you go to write the brilliant script that's going to become a huge hit, redefine the face of television, and get you on the Emmy red carpet, on your way to hanging out with celebrities and scamming one of those swag bags with all the free shit in them, right? Wrong.

THE OUTLINE

The next step in the process is the outline in which you'll incorporate all the studio and network changes, flesh out the pilot story while making good on the rough version you pitched—even on the parts where you knew you were blowing smoke up their asses and praying you weren't called on it. Then you'll turn it back in and go through the notes process again, (and again, and again, and again) each time addressing more of their "concerns," but eventually you'll get your story approved. Now, you've been cleared to write something that, more or less, resembles what you originally pitched.

WRITING THE SCRIPT

It's now somewhere in October or November. This is the writing honeymoon period. The script is yours. You're still a virgin. You procrastinate for a few days, mulling things over, making some notes, basically letting it take shape in your head, while getting ready to sit down and begin to spew out a vomit draft[19]. Then you read it, get depressed and begin to rewrite, rewrite, and rewrite more. ("Writing is rewriting.") You come up with more jokes. Better moments. New insights. You stay in touch with agents and executives who are all waiting eagerly for the script that might become the fall's big hit and will change everyone's fortunes. Maybe you show it to a writer friend and get some helpful suggestions or a few extra jokes.

---

[19] Vomit draft. A quick first draft of a script in which you just move forward through the outline, trying not to get stuck on minutiae or bad jokes. The goal is to get to the end and have a document to begin to revise.

OK, let's fast-track this. You finally turn in your 45-50 page script (for a multi-camera show; 30-35 pages for single camera). Now they have a document in their hands and a new development phase has begun. The communal euphoria over your clever pitch and amusing story turns is about to replaced by a dispassionate, businesslike analysis of every word, moment, joke, and punctuation mark. This part of the process could be titled: Joy Takes A Holiday. Now it's time to get serious. It's time to get your notes.

NOTES

Check out any writer who's just come from getting notes on a script. They look tired, frustrated and beaten up. (I've rarely been through a note session in which I wasn't privately regurgitating or rolling my eyes.) Even those times when the notes were dead on and I was caught with a sloppy outline or lazy first draft. Or sometimes, just a bad one. It's not that those note sessions are less annoying. It's just that ultimately they're easier to digest because, if you're at all honest with yourself, you have to admit they were right. But most often, the phrase "I just got my network notes" is uttered in the same tone people use to say: "I've just come from a colonoscopy." But if you're in development, there's no avoiding them.

It's like that old joke about three explorers who get captured by some native tribe. The chief strides up to the captives and announces they have two choices: death…or chi-chi. The first guy doesn't want to die and says he'll take chi-chi, at which point he's stripped down and sexually defiled in every way known to man by every member of the tribe. The second guy gulps, nervously, but figures there's no way out and opts for chi-chi. He is similarly defiled. The third guy goes, Fuck this, I've got my dignity, I'm not going through that shit—and says "Give me death." And the chief goes "OK, death!... But first—chi-chi!"

Sad, but true. You can't escape notes. Or the fact that they tend to arrive in the same predictable form, couched in the same familiar phrases. A character's "too mean" and "not likeable enough." "The story starts too late." "We need more heart." "Shine a light on this." "I need to root for her more." "The ending's not satisfying." "There's not enough fun." Not that every draft of every script is perfect. Far from it—every writer knows you need notes at some point to get you out of your own head and give you some perspective or objective viewpoint. The difference is you trust your own kind because they know how to make suggestions that help you achieve what you're after. Notes among writers usually take a more Socratic approach, i.e., the search for the best idea. Studio or network notes traditionally take the form of smoothing every edge, removing every subtlety, softening every extreme and are part of a two-step development process: Step one: Give us something different; Step two: Now make it more the same.

I've experienced it personally a dozen times and heard hundreds of similar stories. It's what drives writers insane. If you put a dozen writers in a room, you'd get horror stories for hours, but none relates the experience better than an article from *Written By* magazine, from the Writers' Guild. In terms of the emotional response to getting notes, this says it all.

On Receiving "Notes"

Why Arthur Miller never wrote *Free and Clear*.

Written by Nicholas Kazan

(From the January 2005 issue of "Written By")

Death of a Salesman

This harrowing story is the most instructive one I've ever heard about script notes. I repeat it to every producer and studio executive I meet.

The story reflects poorly on my parents. As a matter of privacy, I don't normally reference my family. In this case, it's unavoidable.

My father was director Elia Kazan. He died in September 2003, a few weeks after his 94th birthday. When I flew to New York for his funeral, I heard that critic Martin Gottfried had just published a book about Arthur Miller and was giving a reading. Out of curiosity and perversity, I went, hoping to see Miller there and invite him to my father's service.

Miller was not in attendance, but this story was waiting for me.

In 1947, Miller's play *All My Sons* won the New York Drama Critics prize for Best Play, besting Eugene O'Neill's *The Iceman Cometh*. (No comment.) Everyone eagerly awaited Miller's next play. In anticipation, a Broadway theater was booked and a production company formed. The most eminent producer in town, Kermit Bloomgarden, wanted to produce the play. Many prominent investors, including the famous producer and director Joshua Logan, lined up to put money into the production.

Miller finished his new play, *Death of a Salesman,* and gave it to Elia, who loved it and agreed to direct it. Bloomgarden was equally enthusiastic. (Another prominent producer, Cheryl Crawfold, had right of first refusal but read the play and turned it down, paving the way for Bloomgarden. Crawford was the first of many experienced readers to misjudge the text. She wept at opening night, both in response to the play and to her own poor judgment.)

Having pleased his director and producer, Miller gave the play to the investors. To everyone's shock, Josh Logan and others were horrified. They said they were withdrawing their investment because the play was "unproducable." Not flawed. Unproducable.

Their reason? They said the audience would be unable to follow the story, unable to distinguish what was in the past from what was in the present.

Miller was plunged into despair. He consulted Elia, who now agreed with Logan's assessment. Elia suggested Miller consolidate the impressionistic "flashbacks" into one section. Bloomgarden agreed. Miller then consulted my mother, who was a mentor to him and other playwrights; she suggested he eliminate the flashbacks altogether.

Fortified with this abominable advice, Miller rewrote his play. No one quite knows what Miller did, but when he finished, everyone agreed the result was God-awful.

Investors conducted an informal poll.

Miller decided to stand by his original text: "If it's going to fail, let it fail the way I wrote it, rather than the way I rewrote it." Elia changed his mind again and decided to direct the play in its original form. Bloomgarten produced it. I don't know whether Josh Logan remained an investor. I do know some investors dropped out and the financing became shaky. Miller's former agent Leland Hayward (another extremely experienced theater person) had, sight unseen, signed on to put up $4,000; after reading the play, he cut his investment to $1,000.

According to Arthur Miller, 98 percent of those asked said they would not go see a play called *Death of a Salesman*. Fortified with abominable advice, Miller rewrote his play.

Before the play went into rehearsal, there was another bump in the road. Bloomgarden decided audiences wouldn't go see a play with *death* in the title. He suggested something sunnier: *Free and Clear* (a phrase from the play's final scene). Those involved conducted an informal poll. According to Miller, 98 percent of those asked said they would not go see a play called *Death of a Salesman*.

Miller refused to budge, and this time Elia supported him. We can ask ourselves now: *What would this play be if we -didn't know from the outset that Willie Loman was going to die? Would it still feel tragic? Would it work at all?*

The play opened with the original structure and title, and the rest is history. The audience on opening night sat in silent shock and then exploded, rising to their feet and applauding, hooting, screaming. Many continued to clap long after the actors had finished their curtain calls. Others sat in their seats, stunned or sobbing, unable or unwilling to leave the theater.

Since then, *Salesman* has been done thousands of times, in virtually every country in the world. By almost any standard, it is one of the five best American dramas of the 20th century. Many critics consider it the best.

And no one has ever been confused about what was in the past and what was in the present.

Principled and Passionate

I am sure you can see my questions:

--If the most successful producer of that era wanted to change the title, *and* if he and two of the leading directors of the time considered the play "unproducable" and further agreed on what the problem was, *and* if all these "experts" were wrong in every respect about a play regarded as a masterpiece, how does anyone ever dare to give notes?

--Why is it that, in Hollywood, every producer, studio executive, and development person just out of college feels entitled to make suggestions on every script they receive? How can they be so confident of their opinions? Are they truly unaware of the damage they can do?

--Why is every draft from every writer considered just a "work in progress," a rough approximation waiting to be improved by the wise counsel of a dozen or more readers?

--Why do we writers accept notes which will destroy what we have so painstakingly created?

--And if we refuse to make destructive changes, why are we considered "difficult" rather than "principled and passionate"? Why are we not considered experts, both in general and, most especially, on the distinct universe of the script which we have written?

I told the preceding story to, and asked these questions of, a friend who runs a major studio. She said, "So what does this mean? Are we supposed to give no notes at all?!"

I said, "No. Give notes, but as suggestions, not mandates. Feed the writer. If the writer is inspired by your idea, great; if not, drop the subject because the note is probably wrong. The writer may not be able to tell you why it's wrong, but trust him or her, it is."

The fact is: We know. We live with a script for months, often years, and we know what a script wants to be--and what it doesn't. We also know that if, with the best of intentions, the DNA of a script is altered, the animal that results will not be pretty to look at.

I made another suggestion to my friend at the studio: "If a writer you respect believes in the script, hold a reading. Hear the text. Before you say with confidence that something -doesn't work, find out what the movie is. It's drama, it's alive: Give it a chance to breathe."

Of course, a reading won't always validate the writer's view . . . and that's its beauty: It simply exposes the text, usually revealing problems of some sort--either the same problems the studio sees, ones the writer fears, or problems neither anticipates. Regardless of the "result," a reading is always a valuable and revelatory tool. It should be standard practice.

Let me be clear. I don't mean to suggest here--to do so would be absurd--that every screenplay is a cinematic equivalent of *Death of a Salesman*. But accomplished and experienced writers work for months or years on a screenplay and then are given notes by executives who have to read three or six or nine screenplays over a weekend and are expected (or expect themselves) to give detailed, helpful, and well-considered notes. A lot of good work and careful thought can be overlooked by tired or overwhelmed executives.

I think there's one more lesson to be gleaned from this story. *Salesman* broke new ground, and that was part of the problem: Being unfamiliar with what the play was doing and how it worked, readers thought it wouldn't work at all.

Similarly, it often seems that the better a script is (the more novel and daring its approach), the less likely it is to be properly read and understood. Again: I don't mean that every "daring" script is good or unappreciated. I do mean that the best scripts may have the most difficult time being recognized.

So the next time someone reads your script and either really hates something that you know works or makes cavalier and foolish suggestions--"just spitballing"--perhaps you should ask them: Did you ever hear a song for the first time and hate it and then two weeks later find yourself singing it?

Anyway, you digest the first set of notes, scribbling them all over your beautiful first draft. Emotionally, it's like that scene in *The Accused*, only you're Jodie Foster...*and* the pinball machine. Then you bitch aloud in your car on the way home, or call your agent and bitch, all the while knowing you have no choice but to sit down and begin the rewrite that will satisfy the studio in preparation for turning it into the network. It's not fun. It's never fun. Although sometimes the notes are dead on, and even open up opportunities and provide insights you hadn't previously seen. Again, depending on the specifics, your next draft is either an unholy perversion of your original idea, or a greatly enhanced version of it. In either case, it eventually goes back to the studio, usually leading to more last-minute revisions before it's passed in to the network. Then you wait for them to respond for what seems like an eternity. Then they respond, with little more than a phone call to arrange a meeting or notes call to address those notes. Rarely are you given any indication of their initial reaction, so either you beg your producing partners or studio exec to scope it out or you suffer in silence.

Reaction day finally arrives. The conference call is set up. It's you and all the other entities involved. Your phone rings. Everyone's on. First some initial pleasantries. Then, after a beat, they move the big guns into position, because the more real this gets, the more the network needs to shape your project into something similar to what they already have on or something they're comfortable with or need. The notes begin with "We like some/much/most/a bit of what you've done"—the emotional equivalent of "Your kid doesn't look all that retarded."

Then there's a dramatic pause as your smile remains frozen like one of those Beverly Hills face jobs that make actresses over 50 look like some weird amalgam of Prune Face and the Joker from *Batman*. Or the eye jobs that make them look like Catwoman. (Makes you wonder what Adam West is doing these days and if he went into plastic surgery.) And, while we're on the subject, would somebody please explain the collagen, killer-bee-stung lips? Exactly who decreed that this was a sign of beauty? In all the conversations I've had with other guys over the years, I can't recall one where someone said "If only I could find a woman who looked like she just got smashed in the mouth by a brick."

The other day, I was leaving a building in Beverly Hills and passed a relatively famous actress on her way in. She had about $10,000 worth of clothing on her back, but her face looked like she was just French-kissed by the grill of a speeding Humvee. Now, obviously, many actresses (and actors) get face work, and you don't know it because it's well done. Which is great. When I was growing up on Long Island, the $1000 Jewish nose job was the thing. A girl finished sixth grade with, as David Steinberg once described it, "a nose like a Macaw," and came back in the fall for seventh grade with a svelte, oddly contoured little button. Wasn't bad. It was just no longer a beak. No one can fault the impulse to look better. Ugly's a bitch. So's aging. No one in his or her right mind looks forward to the day when their face, balls or tits hit the floor. And if you need your looks to make your living, or if it just helps you face the mirror and get out of the house in the morning or to sleep at night, then you do what you've got to do. But if the Joker look is the state of the art, then please, somebody bring back the Audrey Hepburn/Grace Kelly school of aging gracefully. We all want to appear as attractive as possible, for as long as possible, but the idea is to look like Grace Kelly *before* she got in the car wreck. Not after.

Sorry, sidetracked... Right, network notes. Usually along party lines. More backstory on the characters. Clarify their relationships. Take out some jokes that seem too mean, usually your favorite ones, but which is often the intro to the big, overall note: "Yes, the jokes are funny, but we have to know these people like each other." This is a note you hear so often you want to puke.

If Shakespeare were writing for TV, Romeo and Juliet would never have died (too depressing), Romeo would have to be butched up (he's too whiny, too weak—in network-speak, a loser). Women won't be attracted to him. Guys won't want to hang out with him. Mercutio would be Romeo's great-looking best friend who gets laid constantly, but deep down is still looking for someone special (Charlie Sheen). Tybalt would be the neurotic gay neighbor (Nathan Lane), and Friar Lawrence, the grumpy, wise-cracking bar owner of the place where they all hang out (John Goodman, Ed Asner, Brian Dennehy), 'cause you need somewhere they can all go and sit six abreast on the couch facing camera—you know, like most people do when having a group conversation. By the time they're done, Romeo and Juliet would be Dharma and Greg. A pair of newlyweds with bickering families who "just drive them so-o-o crazy" 'cause they can't get along. They might even be from different ethnic backgrounds, which would add hairy moles, silly wigs, and amusing accents to the arguments between the new in-laws. "Julio and Juliet." You could sell that to CBS tomorrow.

So, while the few specific notes involve just laying in more pipe[20] on the characters, the broad note is the most daunting, because it changes your entire emotional approach to the script and affects the overall tone and every single line and moment you put in there. Which leaves you, frankly, barren and clueless on how to proceed. For a moment, you think about fighting, but that can lead to you getting a reputation for being "difficult" and your project will die. The dilemma is, if you cave, you're easy to work with but your project may have begun its Bataan death march to mediocrity. So you agree to the notes you think you can handle. Maybe fight a few battles. But in the end, the experience is like having them dismantle your child, telling you to lose the ears, double the number of toes, stick the eye on the elbow, and have the left arm protrude from the asshole. "Now, go play catch with the mutant little bastard. Oh, and…"—in network parlance —"have fun with it." (OK, this is a gross generalization and an unfair stereotype. There are projects that glide through the process due to strong producers and intelligent executives who trust the writer and actually have some good insights. It does happen. Unfortunately, it's not the norm.)

---

[20] Pipe. Background information. The character's personal history.

So, you go back and rewrite. Again. And again. And again. (Most every script I've worked on resulted in a pile of notes, outlines, and drafts about a foot high. When it results in a pick-up, it's all been worth it. When it's a pass, you take that pile and drop it in a file box. Or in the garbage. And move on.)

But for now, you're still alive. You turn the revised draft back in to the producers, or studio, or whoever is next in the development chain. This results in a few more notes. Last-minute stuff. Let's just make it perfect. More notes. More rewrites. Finally, it goes back again to the network and you wait for that phone call, which eventually arrives bearing more notes. You rewrite again. And again. And again. Then, sometime, usually before Christmas or in early January, it's time to let it go and turn it in, which you do thinking it may be OK, but deep down you've got this disturbing sensation that you've just given birth to the son of the devil.

A while ago I saw a comic at The Laugh Factory on Sunset. He was the original writer of *Malibu's Most Wanted*, that Jamie Kennedy movie about a spoiled rich white kid who acts black. The comic joked about it, saying (I'm paraphrasing): "People asked me if my script got changed a lot. All I know is, when I wrote the first draft, it was about the Holocaust." Funny line. Experientially, very true.

So... after all the drafts, conversations, note sessions, and emails, your script is now on the pile with hundreds of other pilots. You begin to hear buzz about some hot spec that got an order, or someone who hooked up with a star and is on the fast track to production. You hate these people because with their success they narrow your chances. Essentially, at this point, you have one chip on a roulette table. Only this table has a few hundred numbers. Those are your odds. Now you sweat it out, along with everyone else, with a combination of hope that you'll succeed, backed up by the nagging fear of failure.

January. Now it kicks into high gear.. The network execs, assistants, their assistants, and their assistants have all taken pilot scripts home or to Hawaii over the holidays, read them, and now reconvene to determine what they think, individually and as a group. According to legend, a writer once called someone at the network to ask what that person thought of his script. The response: "I don't know. I'm the only one who's read it." May be apocryphal; doesn't matter. In terms of what goes on, it's often true. So, once again, you wait by a phone that doesn't ring. Then it rings.

Given the odds, it's mostly bad news. "They liked it, but didn't love it." "The rewrite didn't address enough of their concerns," or a flat-out "They passed." But let's say it's not. Let's say the news is good. You're picked up to shoot your pilot. Joy, elation, sighs of relief. Now your phone begins to ring like fucking crazy as the news spreads all over town. Agents offer congratulations disguised as a request to get their actor clients in to read, or their writer clients in to consult on the pilot so that they might get hired on staff if it goes to series. Friends call to offer congratulations and consulting help while silently gritting their teeth over your good fortune and/or lack of theirs.

PILOT PRODUCTION

If you've made it this far you've beaten most of the odds, and, if you're at all human, you've got a giant ego pump stuck up your ass, blowing in a steady stream of arrogance and self-importance, with a sidebar of fear over all the work there is to do. You set up offices, hire a line producer[21], casting director, and set designer and begin digesting the inevitable notes that accompanied the

[21] Line Producer. The producer who oversees the money you're spending and flips out over how much it's costing and how to justify that to the studio.

pick-up. (Optimistic asshole that you are, you actually thought you were done hearing notes.) You break out sides[22] for the casting director and begin the process of putting out offers to established stars, who are offer-only[23], while setting up casting sessions for when those stars tell you to fuck off or when their agents ask for obscene amounts of money and/or an Executive Producer credit.

The casting director will generate a list of actors who are available and/or potentially interested. This is called the "jerk off list." Most of the time, the actors you want, you can't get. The actors you can get, you don't want. Or worse, you find out that an established star is interested in your show. The network is excited. The studio is excited. Getting this person would put a ton of heat on your project. The problem is, that person is totally wrong for the part. You know it in your bones and could recite a hundred reasons why they're wrong. Doesn't matter. If the network wants them, you change the part since, at this point, who's in it becomes more important than what it is or was. Doesn't matter anymore, you're in development, a hazy netherworld in which emotionally you feel like Jack Nicholson when the guy turns to him at the end of the movie and says, "Forget it, Jake. It's Chinatown."

CASTING

While all this is going on, the casting people are busy pre-reading hundreds of actors. Eventually, a percentage will leak through, getting callbacks to read for the producers. You will hear your material read so many times, often so badly, that by the time

[22] Sides. Scenes from the script that are used in casting. You pick out the best material to showcase each part, giving actors the best chance to shine while ensuring that after you hear your favorite jokes read a hundred times you'll be completely sick of them by the time you're ready to shoot. That is, assuming anything resembling what you initially wrote is still left in the script.

[23] Offer-only. Actors who, by virtue of their stature in the business, won't audition for a part. You want them, you give them the part.

it's over you will despise every word you've written and will have convinced yourself it's not only not funny, but needs to be buried wherever they stick uranium and other nuclear byproduct so it won't create generations of genetic mutants.

Years ago on a pilot, I made the rookie mistake of handing the casting director a 7-page audition scene for the main character that began with a long monologue. I liked the speech. It provided insight into the guy's state of mind as he sat on the ledge of his dreary office building, eating his lunch, saying something like "How the hell did I get here?" By the time the 50th actor walked in, sat on the arm of the chair pretending it was a ledge and launched into "How the hell did I get here?" I wanted to blow my brains out. After about 100 readings, Tim Matheson got the part without auditioning. The speech stayed in the script and the finished pilot and he did a great job. The show lasted 7 episodes and died.

Now, if anyone wonders why some stars seem to be out of their fucking minds—why they throw tantrums if their trailers are a few square feet shorter than their co-star's, or if the milk in the latte is low-fat instead of non-fat, or if their morning call is too early, rehearsals last too long, they're not being lit right, the director's being disrespectful or the studio sent a town car instead of a stretch limo—there's a simple answer: Some stars are out of their fucking minds. Children in adult clothes, who are coddled by an entourage of agents, managers, publicists, lawyers, and personal assistants while getting paid obscene amounts of money to play "make-pretend." OK, they're not all like that, and even the ones who are don't all start like that. They start as ordinary actors, who are driven to insanity via the casting process.

Casting, both for pilots or movies, will at some point involve an actor getting called in by a casting director to audition, whereupon entering the outer office they will bump into every other actor in town who's the exact same age and type. Or, in the case of actresses, women who are their type but 5-10 years younger, all part of the five stages of an actor's life: 1) Who's X? 2) Get me X! 3) Get me an X-type! 4) Get me a young X! 5) Who was X? After awhile the actors all know each other and know what to expect. They shake hands, but inside every one is thinking *I hope you all tank 'cause I want this part.* Most don't make it through, but those who do are called back to read for the producers, where they come in one by one, do the scene or scenes, the producers say "Thank you," and then they leave with no indication of how they did, short of the one person who got the part getting a call.

Everyone else is left wondering: "Did I suck?" "Did I at least come in second?" "Did they say anything?" "Did they like me at all or is this a sign to give it up already?" But they're given nothing. Not a word. Just silence, until the next audition. This would drive anyone crazy. Eventually, the response from the business arrives in the form of whether they ever get cast in anything. You nail a few guest-star parts; you can start to have hope that you're building a career. You get nothing over a period of years; you can start thinking about getting married and having kids if you're a woman, or becoming a waiter or hanging yourself if you're a guy. Or you can go into real estate. At least actresses have the built-in excuse of: "Well, I quit the business when I had my kids." And if they happen to marry a guy with some clout, they can harangue him to death to cast them in whatever they're doing. Note how many wives end up with parts in their husband's films. (Or conversely, how many husbands end up managing their wives' careers or directing their films.) It's not because they were necessarily best suited for the job. It's because they communicated to their husbands that they've seen their last blowjob unless they get to act.

In all, making it as an actor is hell on earth. Worse than trying to break in as a writer. When writers are rejected, it's just their material. They can always go home and write another script and live off the hope (or delusion) that one day it will sell and they'll be vindicated. Actors not only get rejected personally, but short of plastic surgery (see above), they can't reinvent themselves. Nor can they go home and act. (My sister was once in a restaurant in New York and was getting ignored by the waiter/actor. She finally yelled out, "Hey, this isn't a play about a restaurant, it *is* a restaurant!") It's no accident actors occasionally lose it when they become famous. They go through a ton of humiliation to get there.

If you're a producer in casting sessions, you try to be gracious and compassionate for one reason and one reason only: it's basic human decency. (Just kidding. Couldn't resist that either.) The reality is, one day, someone who read for you will go on to become a star and, if you're a prick, they'll never forget it and, given the opportunity, will stick it back up your ass. Hey, who wouldn't? (One of the biggest stars in Hollywood right now once got fired off a network pilot by a producer, who screamed at him over the P.A. that he'd see to it that the actor would never work in this town again. That actor recently won an Oscar.)

In any case, if you're an actor in casting sessions, your goal is to get the part. Coming in second is meaningless. Toward that end, here are some audition tips.

10 AUDITION TIPS

OK, there aren't just 10. There aren't just 10 of anything. Nature doesn't work in decimals. When I worked for a magazine publisher years ago, the one who foamed at the mouth and carried a loaded .38, we were in a meeting discussing cover lines (the attention-getting headlines on magazine covers) and someone had written something about beauty tips, to which he said: "Make it '10' beauty tips." The editor said: "But there aren't just 10." To which he said: "I don't care. People like numbers." At the time, I thought "What a fucking, low-rent clod." But just look at the cover of most any magazine. I think he was right. Still, while there are probably thousands of tips you could get from working actors, from a producer's standpoint, there is only one:

1. BE GREAT. It's that simple. That's all you have to do. Go in and do the part letter perfect. You're even allowed to have the script in hand, which you should do. You don't have to be off-book[24]. Actors who do this often look like they're trying to show off and appear overeager. ("Look how good I am, I already memorized my lines! Wasn't that good, daddy?") Then, invariably, they drop a line during the read, and need to ask for a script. Now they're embarrassed and worried that they've fucked themselves. And, most often, they have. Either way, it's usually a tip-off that someone could be annoying during the week. Don't be super actor. Just be great. You're walking into a room full of people who desperately want to find the perfect person for the part. And quickly. The producers want you to be great. Just go in, do it one time, smile, say thank you and leave. The other nine tips really fall under the heading of shit *not* to do. No matter what any acting coach or cold reading seminar expert tells you.

2. DON'T BRING IN PROPS. Mime it. Once on *Becker* we had a two- or three-line part for a corporate CEO. The scene was simple. He's sitting at home, gets a phone call that upsets him, and reacts. That's it. One actor walked in carrying a smoking jacket, TV remote, large bowl of popcorn and pair of slippers to show that he

[24] Off-book. Having one's lines memorized.

was a rich guy having a night in. Then he took ten minutes to set up all the props while we waited. When the time came for him to get upset, he let out a howl that sounded like an elephant being fisted. By that time, it didn't matter. He lost the part the second he walked in the room with those stupid props. And while we're on the subject of props, we need to discuss cleavage, or, as an actress I worked with referred to them, her "show tits." Whether natural or store bought, have the good sense to keep them holstered. Not that they won't be appreciated—I promise you, they will be. But if you enter the room and it's just tits for miles, several things will happen: privately, every guy in the room will stand up and cheer but, as this is a professional situation, they will keep their poker faces plastered on and applaud the moment you leave the room. Secondly, if there are women producers in the room, you will immediately lose their vote. Now, while the guys will be secretly hoping you do well, everyone will also be thinking that you've brought these props as misdirection from your acting abilities. So, unless the part is "Slut #1," just bring your talent to the read. Get the part based on that. How much you cleavage you choose to flash during the week is your choice.

3. DON'T COME IN AND LOVE-BOMB THE PLACE. Don't light up the room with your presence and magnetic personality, like some cheesy Vegas comic. You will be hated instantly. And don't go overboard complimenting the producers. On one of the first shows I did, an actress came in and went on and on about how much she admired my work and had always wanted to work with me. I was relatively new in the business, so it actually gave me an ego rush for a moment, until I remembered that I was new in the business and hadn't done anything of note, so she couldn't possibly have known who I was, what I'd done, or had any burning desire to work with me. She couldn't have loved my work. I had no "work." In that one

moment I decided she was full of shit. Didn't matter what she did in the audition, she wasn't getting the part.

4. DON'T GO OVERBOARD COMPLIMENTING THE WRITING. One "I really loved this script" is usually the right amount of smoke to blow up a writer's ass, and will instantly endear you to him. Anything more and you'll be seen as a suck-up and it will work against you. Compliment the writing by doing the part well. Even if it sucks. Even if it's profoundly unfunny and the most hackneyed sitcom crap you've ever read. You agreed to be here, so leave your dignity at the door, treat it like it's Shakespeare, do it as well as you can, and pick up your dignity again on the way out.

5. DON'T TRADE OFF ON ANY PERSONAL RELATIONSHIPS you may have with any one of the producers. No big hugs. No chatty conversation about your kids going to the same school. Keep it professional. Respond to any overtures, but don't make them.

6. DON'T CHANGE A SINGLE WORD IN THE SCRIPT. Not an "and," not a "but," not a beat. Nothing. Most likely the writer is sitting there and wants to hear their words exactly as they were written. By that time, with all the rewrites on their script before it even got to this stage, those might be the only words they wrote that have been left intact. Even if it's "hello," they're going to want to hear "hello." If you ad lib "hi," "'s up?" or "howdy," they'll hate you and you won't get the part.

7. DON'T ASK UP FRONT HOW THEY WANT IT. Don't inquire if they want to see it with or without an accent, standing up or sitting down, or hopping on one leg. Just make a choice and go with it. And when you're done, don't ask if they want to see it

another way. If they do, they'll let you know. That's one of those acting school bits of bullshit advice they tell you to do in a room, and it backfires because it makes your initial choice feel arbitrary. If they want to see it slower, faster, louder, lower, with a French accent, or with you wearing a bandito moustache, they'll ask in the moment or send the casting director outside to give you an adjustment and give you time to prepare.

8. FOR KIDS: DON'T BE A TINY LITTLE PROFESSIONAL. Don't walk up to the producers, look them in the eyes, and offer a smile and firm handshake. This shit reeks of parent coaching and will be a warning flag that you've got a baby actor on your hands. And quite possibly, a pain-in-the-ass stage parent.

9. IF YOU GET THE PART, DO THE PART. Don't change a thing. Don't go bigger or broader. Some actors think: "If I got this many laughs in the reading doing it this way, I'll get twice as many going twice as big." Wrong. Dead wrong. In fact, most often the opposite is true: Less is more. Just throw the words away. Don't spin. Don't show off. Don't angle for attention. If you see a producer writing SPF on a script, it stands for "Small Part Fever," signifying an actor who's trying to make the producers, studio, network, and the world stand up and take notice through their three little lines. It's a disease that can get you fired.

10. DON'T BE TOO CHUMMY. Don't hustle producers for more lines or a recurring role. "You know, my character could come back," is the kiss of death. And don't think you've suddenly got an audience that wants to hear about your pet projects. Don't pitch your pilots. Don't give out your music CDs or flyers to your one-person show. Don't do anything other than what you did per-

fectly in the audition. And at the end of the week, say thank you and split. And don't visit next week like you've suddenly become one of this merry band of players. If anyone wants you to come back, they'll call your agent and ask. Which has happened. One actor on *Becker* came in for one episode and stayed for five years. Just be great. The opportunities will take care of themselves.

I know it's seductive. After all the struggling, you finally get a break and it's natural to want to shine as much as possible. But if breaking any of these rules occurs to you, imagine the phone call that will come from another producer to the producers of this show. It will go something like: "We heard you just worked with X actor on your show. We're thinking of casting them. What was the week like?" Think about it.

OK, back to the pilot. So, after endless casting sessions, you finally choose your three or four people per role and take them into the network to audition, where they are traditionally hated. You're sent back to scour the universe for fresh faces, while you entertain the thought of casting the star you thought was totally wrong for the part and reconsider actors you've previously rejected. Then, unless your pilot is cast-contingent[25], you finally scrape a cast together, usually jamming in someone at the last minute who you'd rejected earlier as totally wrong but you hire them just to get you to the table. This happened on the Tony Danza pilot. We had a role we just couldn't cast, so we just gave it to someone, though the thought was that the role would be cut in series. It was.

[25] Cast-contingent. A pilot that is given the go-ahead pending network-approved casting of a key role or roles.

THE TABLE READ

A maternity ward with hundreds of parents and a deli spread. The producers are nervous, despite having writer friends around as consultants who, being that writers are a venal, selfish group, simultaneously hope it goes well and sucks. The cast is nervous, but temporarily preening, as they've been cast in a pilot, which puts them ahead of most of their contemporaries. The network and studio people drift in, usually on cell phones, putting on a face that says they are focused on the birth of this particular child, but the fact is they're thinking of every other pilot that's going on simultaneously all over town. Agents also show up, assigned to "cover" the table reading for their actor or writer clients. Somehow everyone manages to look excited and jaded at the same time.

After some nervous chatter, these hundred people take their seats, either in a large conference room or on stage, a few clever introductory remarks are made, the director takes over, introduces the cast (polite applause for each, or loud, sycophantic applause for the star), then the director take a beat and starts reading the opening stage directions. "Interior kitchen—morning. Julio comes down for breakfast..." As the writer, you feel a sudden blockage in your colon as you approach that first joke. It gets a big laugh—good start. Medium laugh—you lean forward, concerned. It dies—you crap your pants. You're in for a long ride.

The reading ends. Applause all around. Either it went "through the roof"—a success, or "in the toilet"—not a success. Most Hollywood events—table readings, rehearsals, test screenings, pilot testing, weekend grosses—are described in one of those two ways; for some reason the metaphors seem to center around blasting through the ceiling or going down in a whirl of shit. People incapable of original thought often need stock expressions to communicate. It's why many notes tend to arrive wrapped up in the same stock phrases. "Hang a lantern on this."[26] "Make this character more likeable." "Redeem that character."[27] "We need the ending to be more satisfying."[28] But whether it went through the roof or in the toilet, the respective groups break off into mini-cells to put their heads together. Meanwhile, you shake hands with people if it went well or try not to notice that they're avoiding looking you in the eyes if it didn't.

You dismiss the cast and other irrelevant people, and wait for the inevitable notes, trading glances with the writers you brought in as consultants because, having heard the reading, you all know what worked and what didn't. What jokes need to be replaced. What story beats didn't play and how they might be fixed. And you're all aware of the fact that the reading was seven minutes too long because of all the pipe you had to cram in there during the notes sessions, so the script needs to be cut. You could leave right now and start fixing. But you can't. Because the other folks need to ring in. And they do, often in predictable fashion. "Change this joke." "That character's too mean." "Start the story sooner." "Change the act break."[29] "Hate this actor, let's recast." "The set's too dark, lighten it up." Or the ever-popular "It's a train wreck, we need to page-one[30] the script, or even shut down production and re-think this." Either way, they'll eventually leave and, assuming it's not a train wreck, you retire to the writers' room with the other writers to have Chinese food, bitch about the dumbass notes and jokes the actors killed. Then you begin your rewrite.

---

[26] Hang a lantern. Make something clearer, hence the light image.

[27] Redeem this character. Make them feel sorry for the bad thing they've done. Atonement. No one gets away with anything in American fiction. At least not without punishment.

[28] More satisfying—a happy ending.

[29] Act break. The halfway point in a show that traditionally involves some sort of dramatic cliffhanger.

[30] Page one. Totally rewrite from page one.

THE PRODUCTION WEEK

Rehearsals and rewrites. First for the producers, just among family. Then for the studio and network. More notes, more rewrites. Eventually, you'll get to the point where you barely recognize a comma from your original script. What was once 45 pure script pages with jokes and dramatic moments that almost made you come, thinking of your own brilliance, is now this ugly beast—this Frankenstein monster that, while born from the idealistic notion of unraveling the secret of life, has now crawled off the table, punched you in the throat, kicked down the castle door, and is marauding the countryside, strangling villagers, throwing children down wells and ripping the arm off the local constable. And every asshole in town has an opinion on how to fix it.

When I did the *Tony Danza* pilot, at one point during a notes session there were five couches worth of opinions—the producers, Tony's two development people and Tony, three development execs from NBC Productions, three from Sony (co-partners), three from NBC, and the director. A virtual cluster fuck of opinions. At one point, an executive gave Tony what amounted to an acting note and he nearly took her head off. Inside, I smiled.

But you keep going 'cause you're on the train. Finally you get to shoot night. High energy. Usually goes "through the roof" based on all the effort that's been focused on it and the warm-up guy[31] whipping the audience into a frenzy with some time-tested material. I once consulted on a friend's pilot, and the warm-up guy was a well-known performer whose act included a bit where he hypnotized several audience members. Unfortunately, that night

[31] Warm-up guy. A comedian who entertains the live audience before and during the shoot. The job is to get them laughing, while refocusing them back on the story when it's time. They're usually very energetic and enthusiastic. One of the most successful warm-up guys in town for years was Ray Coombs, who also hosted *Family Feud*. He eventually committed suicide.

the pilot didn't go through the roof. It was headed into the toilet, as evidenced by the fact that everyone working on the show, almost including the actors on stage, was more focused on a group of ballet-dancing Marines than they were on the pilot. It never went any further.

But let's say that doesn't happen. Let's say it goes through the roof. You survive the night. Go through editing, cutting it to time which invariably involves losing one or two of your favorite jokes, mixing[32], adding temp music[33], titles[34], then finally deliver your completed show to the network. Now....

TESTING

OK, I swear I'm not making this up. Before shows are picked up, they are tested by the network. Either to back up their gut feeling, or determine it, executives seem to need quantifiable facts. "I laughed 'til I peed myself" doesn't cut it. "96% of the focus group between 18 and 49 evenly split between men and women found the main character likeable and sympathetic, and 88% indicated they were more-than-likely to make a point of watching this show as appointment television" does.

The writer, along with representatives of all the various production entities, convene in a small facility in Burbank. Basically, it's two large rooms: one with a console with video monitors, speakers, warm Coke, and dry, crusty roast beef sandwiches. (Nothing breaks a Jew's heart more than bad deli, but this is no accident. It is a precursor of the heartache to come.) The other room is behind a pane of one-way glass, where there are about 25

[32] Mixing. Combining all the elements of sound, sound effects, and balancing the laughs.
[33] Temp music. A theme song you like that evokes the mood of the show, since no one's paying for that music until you go to series, at which point it becomes prohibitively expensive and you get original music written.
[34] Titles. The credits.

"Timmies"[35] who've been paid a few bucks to watch the pilot and offer their opinions—something that, I imagine, doesn't happen often.

First, the dial test. Each audience member sits at a desk and is given a small box with levers. The job: push it up when you like something, down when you don't. Then they run the pilot and you watch a TV monitor over which a bar graph is superimposed, broken up into men and women, showing their reactions, line by line, moment by moment, joke by joke. You sit there in disbelief, watching the show you slaved over being given a creative EKG. A joke gets laughs. The bar goes up. A woman with big tits enters. The guy meter goes up, the women's goes down. You get the picture. Then it ends.

Then they take the boxes away and a moderator begins a discussion group. "What did you like?" "What didn't you like?" "Would you watch this show again?" At which point people try to show off their knowledge by saying I like this or that. Sort of on the level of I like chocolate ice cream or I like vanilla. There's usually one smart-ass who trots out terms like "character motivation" just to impress the others with his intimate knowledge of show business or to get the attention of the blond chick next to him, 'cause you know this guy doesn't get out much and he's only doing the focus group for the forty bucks, the free sandwiches and the chance to get out and meet someone instead of staying home, jerking off, and crying himself to sleep.

At the end, they dismiss the panel and you think "That wasn't so bad. They seemed to laugh. They seemed to like it." Then a cocky little martinet in a bad suit walks in with a couple of flunkies holding clipboards and tells you, in short, why your show's going to fail. And the sad thing is, about 85% of the time, the tiny little prick

[35] Timmies. The general audience. People not in the business. See Charlie Hauck's book–*Artistic Differences*.

is right. (Most new shows fail, so how wrong could he be?) In an article dated 3/29/04 from *Television Week*, Jordan Levin, then head of the WB, talked about eschewing formal testing and instead trusting his management team to make the tough decisions by trusting their guts. (Cut to 6/15/04, when *The Hollywood Reporter* runs the story that Levin is resigning from the WB. This seems like one of those Hollywood-style resignations, much in the same way a guy with his head clamped under a falling guillotine blade decides he's going to opt for death. Cut to the present: the WB, as such, no longer exists.)

THE FALL SCHEDULE

You've delivered your pilot. Once again, you wait by the phone as the networks screen all their shows, analyze the testing, consult with the sales and promotion departments and figure out their schedule, which they will announce to the media in May in New York at the upfronts[36]. Now the rumors are flying. Who's on? Who's not. Who's on for midseason? Everyone waits by phones. False schedules are leaked all over town as the networks try to out-fox one another. It's the emotional equivalent of having put all your money on the pass line and the dice are tumbling but haven't landed yet. But let's say the phone rings, and you're on the schedule. This is a moment of pure joy. One simple idea from your imagination has now taken shape as a network television show. You swell with pride at the prospect of upcoming success. Then, being the neurotic you are, you can't let the moment live for more than a millisecond before you're compelled to ask: what's the time slot?

[36] Upfronts. Annual event in New York where the network execs trot out their fall lineup for advertisers, media buyers and critics. The hope is to pre-sell as much advertising time as possible and generate some good buzz for your shows, while getting as drunk as possible.

TIME SLOT

In retail, the adage is: the three most important things are location, location, location. The TV equivalent of location is "time slot"—what night and what time your show will air. A network schedule is little more than a block of stores—virtual real estate. They put in a sushi place and people eat there, it stays open. The food sucks. Someone gets a tapeworm (as happened to a friend), they shut it down and stick in a shoe store. But at this point, your time slot is an indication of how much the network likes your show and how much faith they have in it. If they're excited, you premiere in some coveted 8:30 or 9:30 Monday through Thursday slot behind an established hit. Less excited, you're exiled to Friday, Saturday, or Sunday night, or thrown up like cannon fodder against some other network's ratings juggernaut, left to hold your own or die a quick death.

While many established hits spent several years bouncing around the network schedule looking for a home, that was a time when networks actually stuck with shows because they believed in them. These days, they have a hair trigger. You drop considerably from your lead-in, do worse than what used to be in that slot last year, don't pull in the coveted "18-49 demo," you're staring down the barrel of cancellation. With that in mind, you get on a plane and go to New York for the upfronts.

THE UPFRONTS

The Athens flea market of television. You're flown to New York first class. Limos. Nice hotel. Big dog and pony show. The head of the network gets up in front of several hundred ad agency media buyers and reporters and tells them why he (or she) is just so damn excited about the network's fall schedule, which is exactly the same level of excitement he had in this same room a year ago talking about last year's fall schedule, before canceling most of those shows.

The stars trot out on stage, often doing some lame-ass skit. Then they run a clip from your show. For thirty seconds, you're the most popular girl at the party. Agents circle, setting you up to hire their clients. You drink and run around the city for a few days, then go back to L.A., ready to make television history.

PRODUCTION

Let's say you're on the air with a 13-show order—the pilot plus 12. You set up offices. Hire a writing staff, interviewing maybe fifty people for ten jobs, thus guaranteeing that forty people you just met now hate you and hope you die. Then you start pre-production: breaking stories (once you've gotten them through the studio/network approval mill) while setting directors, having endless production meetings about sets, wardrobe, hair, and schedules, followed by the traditional "writers meet the cast" luncheon, during which everyone sizes each other up.

The cute blond actress playing the sleazy best friend across the hall thinks "Which one of these pasty Jews should I suck up to so they'll write more for my character?" The writers think "Whoa, the blond chick's really into me." This goes on from June through early August. Then you start shooting with almost the same level of scrutiny and micromanagement as the pilot. During this time you also screen other pilots that have been picked up, usually during lunch in the writers' room. This is "writer's Christmas" because you get to be all smug and superior and crap all over everything. There is no greater joy than dumping on a bad pilot. "Can you believe they picked up this shit?" is often the refrain. Plus, you want to feel secure that there won't be much competition this year.

Occasionally, you see a pilot and go "Damn, that's good." One I still remember was *Malcolm in the Middle*. You knew it would last. More recently, among the over 60 pilots I watched last fall, the ones that stood out were *Desperate Housewives*, *Lost*, *Complete Savages*, and a John Stamos show. All for ABC. Two are already huge hits. One got pulled off the air, and the Stamos show has come back on the schedule, but with sagging ratings, making its future uncertain. (Fast forward: it died.)

THE PREMIERE

So, you've shot a few shows, things are going well. The writers and actors are getting along. The stories are working. The cast is starting to jell, finding nuances in their individual characters as well as learning to play off each other. Now it's time to premiere. There's been promotion, your actors do talk show appearances, there are radio spots, billboard and bus ads, all heralding your show as the funniest show that's ever been and a cure for cancer. NBC traditionally does this very well. They call everything "that breakout hit comedy everyone's talking about!" Frankly, the only people talking about it are the NBC promo people, but they know if they keep saying it over and over, Americans are so gullible and insecure they'll believe that if someone else likes it, they should, too, especially since those other people must be smarter than they are.

Finally, you all gather at a restaurant for the premiere party. Everyone's in dress-up clothes. Fingers crossed on one hand, straight Scotch clutched in the other. The feed gets pumped in over several monitors, in real time, and everyone creams over it, applauding the credits, and laughing at jokes they've heard a million times. It's fun. It's uplifting. The end result of a lot of hard work, and hope for the future. In short, a giant circle jerk. You're sure you're going to have a hit. Except for...

THE REVIEWS

By the time of the premiere, the show has been sent out for review all over the country to entertainment critics who traditionally hate everything. Chances are they've already pre-hated your show because it's a TV show, so they despise it on principle. Now, I know they're part of the system, but TV reviewers, with some notable exceptions, are useless individuals with little reason to exist.

Shows could be produced, go on the air, get ratings and either succeed or fail based on the audience's desire to watch them. Yet somehow, a tradition of legitimate literary, theater, and film criticism has descended to the level of the "TV review," often a snippy little diatribe kitty-littered with sarcasm, asinine alliteration, and lame attempts at word play. This is because many reviewers seem like arrogant scumbags with B.A.s in literature and unfinished novels or screenplays in their drawers, which they pull out late at night after everyone's gone home and pound away at the computer, secure in the knowledge that, once their masterpiece is published, the world and their mommies will finally know their true genius and they can take their rightful place at clever cocktail parties or be photographed at some hot club finger-banging a supermodel but, meanwhile, they're stuck in some cubicle at *Entertainment Weakly* pounding out sitcom reviews. (That's my review of TV critics. OK, so maybe it's a little one-sided, opinionated, and more indicative of my personal prejudices than grounded in fact, leaving critics no chance for rebuttal. How's it feel, asshole?)

Anyway, this is why most pilot reviews are negative. Dumping on a TV pilot is easy. The literary equivalent of clubbing a baby seal. I have been reading reviews all my life, and I have never read one that praised a writer or script while pointing out how the incompetent director and talentless actors conspired to trash this great piece of material. (Unless it's some version of a Shakespeare play, in which case the reviewer usually beats up the creative force behind this feeble and arrogant attempt to fuck with the master.) More often, it's some form of "The script is lame, and the noble actors and director did what they could to rise above it, considering the shit they had to work with." Or why did this respected actor agree to do this crappy show? Note: if an actor with clout signs on to a project, know for sure that very often, for better or worse, their creative paw prints were all over that script, as well as every other aspect of the production—from casting and wardrobe to hand-picking the director. But because stars are so beloved by many ass-kissing reviewers, they just can't bring themselves to believe that they had anything to do with creating this turd.

Now, there are insightful TV reviewers who care about the medium and are motivated by a desire to see it reach a level of excellence, while rightfully chastising its lesser offerings. Paul Brownstein of the *L.A. Times* and Tom Shales of *The Washington Post* are just two of many around the country who come to mind. Shales, especially, can be pretty funny. Unless you're on the business end of a bad review, as some friends once were. Then he's not so damn funny. Still, I recently read a piece of his on the *Happy Days Reunion* show that was brilliant, meaning I agreed with it.

"HELLO," LIED THE AGENT

'Happy Days': Little More Than Fonz Memories

By Tom Shales

" 'Happy Days' trivia" is a redundant term, because the show was trivia itself, or at least trivial. It was one of the dopiest hits in prime-time history, almost amateurish in execution, but people who watched it in their youth may feel great affection for it just the same. We always love the TV we grew up with.

Garry Marshall, the obnoxious huckster who put the show together and produced it, still has a lot of energy -- and the zest for life common to multimillionaires. He's all over ABC's "Happy Days 30th Anniversary Reunion" (8 p.m. on Channel 7), a very long two hours that brings together most of the show's core cast for a feast of clips and a round of reminiscence. And a bevy of bloopers -- but a small bevy, alas, and you have to wait forever for them.

The special really could have been called "When We Return," not because the cast is returning but because Marshall and others must say "When We Return" a dozen times within the two hours. The program seems even more perforated with commercial breaks than other ABC fare, and that's unconscionable.

People who liked "Happy Days" will, nevertheless, probably like the special, and those who found "Happy Days" a farce in the bad sense of that word are likely to be bored to death, though they may want to watch in a kind of anthropological way: Here is how America of the 1970s imagined America of the 1950s -- through rose-colored camera lenses that made the decade a celebration of teenage years and a blatant rip-off of "American Graffiti."

Marshall says bluntly that he liked the idea of doing a series about the '50s because he realized that it could play forever in reruns; it wouldn't age because it was supposed to look old. "Happy Days" evolved not into a show about the '50s, but a show about growing up and about whatever days people look back on as having been happy for them.

Among those gathered together for the reunion, taped in Hollywood, are Henry Winkler, whose friendly tough guy, Fonzie, became the most popular figure on the show and probably the key factor in its success. Winkler discusses very seriously how he wanted to play a "hood" who did not stand in front of the mirror combing his hair, unlike all other TV and movie hoods, but the writers thought this absolutely had to be seen in the show, following the dictates of the stereotype.

So Winkler came up with a cute compromise: Fonzie takes out his comb and looks into the mirror, then, realizing his looks are perfect and cannot be improved upon, shrugs and puts the comb away. "I was being true to myself and respectful to what was written," he says, as if he'd been doing Shakespeare.

Other appearances include Ron Howard, who was Richie Cunningham not long after playing the adorable little tot on "The Andy Griffith Show" (and is now a filmmaker worth zillions); Penny Marshall, Garry's sister, and Cindy Williams, who played Laverne and Shirley and who later, of course, got a show of their own; and Marion Ross, somehow one of the sexiest "moms" ever in a sitcom.

Ross's outlook may or may not have broadened over the years; the rest of her certainly has. But she's still a good sport, a charmer, much too good to be married to Tom Bosley, who'd become a star on Broadway and always looked cranky about starring in a mere TV show, even one that made him rich.

Happily, Garry Marshall takes time on the special to acknowledge that "Happy Days" inspired the phrase "jumping the shark," which in showbiz lingo and in everyday language has come to mean going too far, exploiting something beyond even the usual American excess. It emanates from a week in which the writers, having run out of sane ideas, decided to build a story line around Fonzie jumping over a shark while on water skis.

Certain mysteries about "Happy Days" are not solved. Two actors who played the part of Richie's older brother are brought out to take bows, but no one ever explains how the character later came to be written out of the show, even after having been around long enough to be played by two different actors. Another curious fact is that all the clips from "Happy Days" look terrible, as did the series -- photographically grubby, washed-out and cheap. It's as if the film were sent to the corner drugstore for developing.

Probably this was a case of Paramount Television or Marshall or both being penny-pinching tightwads. Reruns of sitcoms like "Bewitched" and even 50-year-old "I Love Lucys" can look gorgeous restored for DVD, but "Happy Days" will probably never look anything but cruddy. Maybe that is somehow part of the show's charm.

Also unhappily absent from the reunion special is the ingenious video that a group called Weezer made a few years ago for their song "Buddy Holly." Spike Jonze, the brilliant director, managed to shoot new footage of the band and mix it almost seamlessly with clips from the original show, even going so far as to make the color look putrid. The video was a '90s look at a '70s look at the '50s -- sort of déjà-déjà-déjà vu -- and wittier than anything ever seen on "Happy Days" itself.

Happy Days 30th Anniversary Reunion (two hours) will be shown at 8 p.m. on Channel 7.

Zap2it - TV news - 'Happy Days,' Indeed: ABC Starts Sweeps Hot

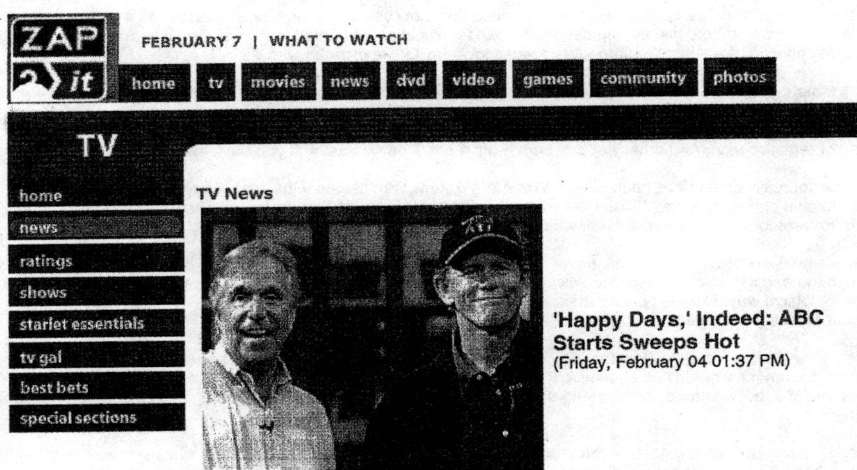

'Happy Days,' Indeed: ABC Starts Sweeps Hot
(Friday, February 04 01:37 PM)

LOS ANGELES (Zap2it.com) It doesn't matter whether or not Joanie still loves Chachi, because America, it seems, still loves "Happy Days." ABC's "Happy Days 30th Anniversary Reunion" proved to be an across-the-board ratings smash on Thursday (Feb. 3) night, getting ABC off to a strong start for the all-important February sweeps period.

Thursday's "Happy Days" special averaged 19.9 million viewers during its two-hour run, a particularly impressive total given the tough competition it faced, as the other networks trotted out new episodes for the launch of the sweep. Averaging 16.2 million viewers overall, Thursday marked ABC's best opening night for a sweeps period since 2000. ABC's 5.2 rating among adults 18-49 was the network's best demographic start for a sweep since 2002.

ABC's reunion special was particularly strong for the 8 p.m. hour, where it averaged just under 20.5 million viewers, spanking around new episodes of "Joey" and "Will & Grace." ABC doubled up NBC's struggling comedies for the hour in total viewers as both "Joey" and "Will & Grace" approached record lows for new episodes.

In its second hour, "Happy Days" dipped slightly to 19.3 million and the reunion fell below CBS' "CSI: Crime Scene Investigation" and NBC's "The Apprentice 3" in the young adult demographic and behind "CSI" in total

viewers. Still, the special held "CSI" to under 25 million total viewers, one of the drama's smallest audiences for a new episode this season and the show's 18-49 rating of 8.9 was its lowest of the year. CBS still won the night in viewers with 18.54 million.

Although CBS' "Without a Trace" (19.3 million viewers) topped NBC's "ER" (18.1 million) in total viewers, "ER" crushed the CBS procedural in the 18-49 demographic, helping NBC to a nightly 18-49 win with a 6.9 rating.

The review was vicious. The *Happy Days Reunion* got huge ratings. If you liked *Happy Days*, it proves that reviews mean nothing. If you didn't, it means that America likes safe, silly, simple-minded TV.

I guess it boils down to the fact that there are intelligent, insightful media critics who evaluate new shows on their own merits, while keeping an eye on how they affect the TV landscape and the culture in general. And then there are just some snide, superior, hyper-educated little dickheads who got jobs as TV reviewers to whom I would just say, OK, if it's shit, call it shit, but it's just a TV show. It's not like the writer was selling crack to minors or peddling phony cancer cures. So, lighten up on the vitriol. (He said vitriolically.)

So...given the odds, let's say the reviews haven't been stellar. Well, why sugarcoat it; let's say they blew. Not only in the national papers but, more importantly, in the *Hollywood Reporter* and *Variety*, which you know everyone in town is reading that morning and shaking their heads because they know your show is D.O.A. If that wasn't enough to trash your spirits, there are the advertising pundits who've already placed your show on the endangered species list in the advertising tip sheets that start floating around at the upfronts. But you press on, assuring one another that "reviews are meaningless." They're gone in a day. Only ratings matter.

A day or two before the premiere of the *Tony Danza Show* I had the unique experience of being called at work early one afternoon by the babysitter, telling me that my house was flooded. I drove home and sloshed through the flood, only to have it slowly dawn on me that this was not ordinary floodwater. This was sewage. A conclusion I arrived at after staring dumbfounded at a toilet spewing out geyser-force shit. It flooded the second floor and shit-rained down onto the first. We relocated the cats to the vet, ourselves to the Bel Age hotel, called some environmental clean-up company, and I waited nine hours for the city to arrive and stop the shitstorm. I stood in the street with the DWP guys at 11 o'clock and smoked the first cigarette I'd had in three years.

The next day I returned to the house to survey the damage caused by the "effluence," as the LA city attorney later referred to it, standing on my balcony overlooking the city and talking on my cell phone to Tony's development person, who read me the excoriating reviews of the pilot from both the *New York Times* and *Variety*. So there it was. In one day I was crapped on both literally and figuratively. To this day, I'm not sure which felt worse. But still, even though most of the reviews were negative, there were still the ratings.

THE RATINGS

Rating—the percentage of households (homes with TV sets) watching your show. Share—the percentage of households that happened to be watching TV at that time that watched your show. For a quick education on the world of TV ratings, check out this piece from thefutoncritic.com.

frequently asked questions about nielsen ratings
(last updated: wednesday, march 1, 2006)

Every so often we like to revisit our frequently asked questions about Nielsen Ratings. Here's the latest update:

1. In your daily ratings breakdown, I always see the following information: "7th Heaven" (households: 4.4/8, #9; adults 18-49: 2.7, #T4). What does it mean?

Let's break it down piece by piece. In the example given for "7th Heaven," here's what each number signifies:

household rating = 4.4
household share = 8
household rank (for the night) = #9
adults 18-49 rating = 2.7
adults 18-49 rank (for the night) = tied for #4

2. So what does a 4.4 household rating mean?

A 4.4 household rating means that 4.4% of all households (that is to say homes with a TV set) watched this episode of "7th Heaven."

For the 2005-06 season, Nielsen Media Research has determined there are an estimated 110,213,910 television households in the U.S. This means that a single national household ratings point represents 1%, or 1,102,139 households.

With the above in mind, a 4.4 household rating equals 4.4% of 110,213,910 million television households or 4,849,412 households.

3. So that's great and all. How do I find out exactly how many people (not just households) watched the show?

Unfortunately, we do not have access to the total viewers numbers on a daily basis.

Also keep in mind, the number of actual total viewers CANNOT be determined from the household rating or household share. Obviously since there is at least one person in a household, the total viewers will be "at least" 4,849,412 people in the above case.

3. So what does an 8 household share mean?

An 8 household share means that 8% of all households that happened to be watching TV watched this episode of "7th Heaven."

So in keeping with the above example, the 4,849,412 households that watched "7th Heaven" accounted for 8% of the television audience that was watching television at the time the show was on.

Also note that the share will always be larger than the rating. This is because the number of households watching television at any give time will always be less than those who own a television period.

4. So what does a 2.7 adults 18-49 rating mean?

A 2.7 adults 18-49 rating means that 2.7% of all adults 18-49 watched this episode of "7th Heaven."

For the 2005-06 season, Nielsen Media Research has determined there are an estimated 130.0 million adults between the ages of 18 and 49 in the U.S. This means that a single national adults 18-49 ratings point represents 1%, or 1.30 million people.

With the above in mind, a 2.7 adults 18-49 rating equals 2.7% of 130.0 million adults between the ages of 18 and 49 or 3,510,000 people.

5. Okay, I've got all that. But how come the information I see here is different from the information I see elsewhere (i.e. Mediaweek, Zap2It.com, etc.)?

This is where a lot of confusion about ratings comes from. To better understand the answer, we must quickly go through what Nielsen Media Research does.

Nielsen collects data from two different samples: a "National Measurement" and a "Local Measurement." Households in each sample are given a device that tracks their viewing habits.

The 5,100 participating households in the "National Measurement" are outfitted with what's called a "Nielsen People Meter." This device measures two things - what program or channel is being watched and who in the household is watching. It accomplishes this by instructing each member in the household to press a button indicating that they have begun watching television on that particular set. This process allows Nielsen to electronically gather demographic information.

Every night this data is transmitted to Nielsen Media Research's Operations Center in Dunedin, Florida. Around 8:00 a.m. EST the next day Nielsen releases the preliminary "fast national" ratings from this data. **This is the information you see reported every morning on The Futon Critic and Zap2It.**

That afternoon, around 3:00 p.m. EST, Nielsen releases the "final national" ratings. These are the revised numbers which take into account various scheduling changes from across the country, most notably those due to live events (such as ABC's "Monday Night Football"). Unfortunately, we do not have access to the "final national" ratings on a daily basis.

Nevertheless, the "final national" ratings are what you see reported in places like The New York Times, L.A. Times and USA Today as well as the various "weekly roundup" press releases we post to the site.

6. So far so good. Now what about that "Local Measurement" sample you mentioned?

The "Local Measurement" sample is used to track, as you might guess, information in a specific market, as opposed to the entire country in the "National Measurement."

Approximately 22,400-28,000 total households participate in the "Local Measurement" sample or about 400-500 households in each of 56 of the largest markets in the U.S. These are what are commonly referred to as the "metered markets" (**click here for the complete list**).

In total, the 56 metered markets account for 69.66% of all households in the U.S. This means that 30.34% of U.S. households are not included in the "Local Measurement" sample.

Homes recruited for the "Local Measurement" sample are NOT equipped with People Meters. Instead they're given more generic electronic meters, which can only measure what is being watched in the household NOT who in the household is watching what (i.e. demographic information). Because of this, only household ratings and shares can be reported.

In any case, every night this data is also transmitted to Nielsen and the following morning the "metered market" ratings are released. These numbers obviously will be different (but not obnoxiously different) from the "fast national" ratings also released by Nielsen. Generally speaking, since "metered market" ratings come from the largest urban areas, the numbers will skew in favor of more "urban" shows.

These are the household ratings and shares you see reported every morning at Mediaweek. But, as we mentioned previously, since demographic information (total viewers, adults 18-49, etc.) isn't obtained in the "Local Measurement" sample - Mediaweek also reports the "fast national" information for total viewers and adults 18-49 (even though they're from a different sample than the "metered market" ratings).

This hopefully clears up the differences between the numbers reported by The Futon Critic, Zap2It and Mediaweek.

7. One other thing - while I understand that The Futon Critic and Zap2It both report "fast national" ratings, how come sometimes the numbers are different by 1 or 2 digits?

The short answer is human error. Nielsen reports the "fast nationals" in half-hour form, meaning we have to average them to get the numbers for programs longer than a half-hour. Sometimes this leads to small variances.

8. So what about those paper diaries I hear about? Don't they count to?

Yes, but they're aren't a factor in the numbers that are electronically reported each day. Basically, paper diaries exist as a supplement to the "Local Measurement" sample.

Paper diaries are filled out during the months of November, February, May and July - periods generally referred to as "sweeps months." These diaries are used to record viewer habits, allowing each market to get some sort of demographic information.

As any regular TV viewer knows, the "sweep periods" are used by the networks to drum up ratings for their affiliate stations and often feature various stunts and special programming.

9. What about TiVos (or other DVR services)? Does Nielsen track those viewers?

As of January 1, Nielsen has added DVR viewership to its audience sample. In the case of "fast national" ratings, the data includes all DVR playback through 3:00 a.m. eastern time that day.

Overall, keep in mind that there are more than 110 million households in the U.S., only 7.09% of which own DVRs of some kind (about 7.8 million according to the latest estimates). The viewership of those households reflect the habits of those willing to buy a TiVo (or other DVR) and subscribe to its service, not a random sample of everyone in the U.S.

I hope that clears it up.

Along with your show's actual ratings, other considerations include its performance in context. Did it go up from your lead-in[37] or (God forbid) down? Ratings first arrive as Overnights, a measure of the major urban markets, and eventually as Nationals, folding in the ratings from cities across the country. Now the sad truth of this moment is, by this time, most people in town already know

[37] Lead in. The show on before you.

your fate. Tapes of the pilot have been floating all over. They've seen the testing. Read the ad guys' predictions and the reviews. You've either got some buzz going or not. But, still, you try to keep your hopes up, as you awaken around 6am, make coffee, and clutch the piece of paper with the ratings hot-line numbers in one hand as you nervously dial with the other, poised to hear the cold, emotionless recorded voice rattle off the numbers that will determine your fate.

On the *Tony Danza Show*, Tony had huge ratings expectations. He lived through *Who's the Boss*? with 20 shares. Big numbers. Big affirmation. Big love from the public. We premiered to a 12 share. Up three points from our lead-in, another new show called *Built to Last* with Paul Winfield. The next day was solemn. He was disappointed, as were we all. I instantly went into cheerleader mode. "At least we went up. We're in double digits. We'll build. Word of mouth, etc… I mean, if we were *Built to Last* with a 9 share that'd be different. That would be it. Pack your bags, turn out the lights, and go home. It's over."

The next week we got a 9 and I was all out of bullshit. We shot our 13 shows to ever-dwindling numbers. The week of our 13th episode, the network VP came to the set and told us that the network loved the show, loved what we were doing and were behind us 1000% percent. Then she smiled and left. The next day we were cancelled.

CANCELLATION

There is no more pathetic figure than the writer who just found out his show's been cancelled. Especially while you're still in production. It's like having a miscarriage while you're in the baby store picking out cribs. You stand there with this stupefied look on your face, mired in the first stage of Kubler-Ross denial as you're flooded with sadness, rage and embarrassment, followed soon after by the fear of poverty 'cause you're mortgaged up the ass and you've got kids in private school. Basically, you're Brando in the back of the cab in *On the Waterfront*, going "I coulda been a contender, I coulda been somebody. Instead of a bum, which is what I am."

Millions in syndication money have just eluded your grasp. Maybe the studio will take your 13 episodes and sell them abroad so Bolivian cocaine workers can be delighted by your amusing little skits, but basically a year's work has just culminated in nothing but 13 commemorative DVD's for your shelf, a group cast and crew picture, and a quickie wrap party, followed by reassuring calls from your agent saying it'll be OK. If you're fortunate enough to be on a development deal, which I was at the time, you crawl back to the solitude of your office to think of something else. If not, you slink home in shame and start figuring how to sell your shit on Ebay.

IT'S NOT CALLED "SHOW ART" IT'S "SHOW BUSINESS."

OK, so now that you've got a rough idea what it takes to get a show on the air, time for some grad school in the business side. Who are the players? Due to a 1991 change in FCC regulations, in which restrictions against network ownership of shows were relaxed, the "fin-syn" ruling (financial interest in syndication) allowed networks to own their own shows, giving them a taste of future syndication profits and an incentive to put on more of their own product. Networks instantly started in-house production companies followed by mergers or co-production deals with independent studios. At present, this is who owns and controls TV.

The source is a website called "Muslim Access" and it's dated Dhul Hijjah 15, 1425, so I'm sure it's factual and current. (I'm surprised they didn't just say "The Jews own the media," though, as some comic once pointed out: "If the Jews owned the media, do you really think we'd let the story out?")

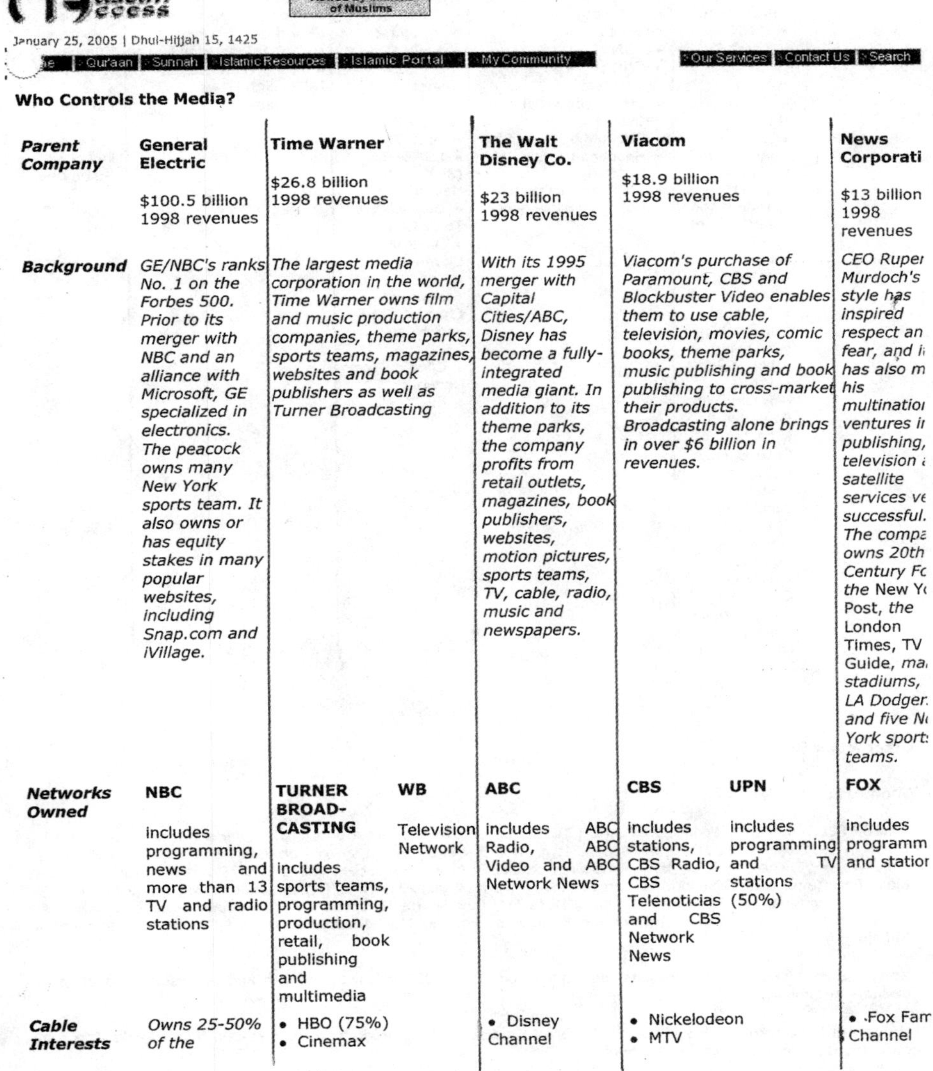

Muslim Access

Place Your Ad Here
Viewed by Millions
of Muslims

January 25, 2005 | Dhul-Hijjah 15, 1425

e | Quraan | Sunnah | Islamic Resources | Islamic Portal | My Community | Our Services | Contact Us | Search

Who Controls the Media?

Parent Company	**General Electric** $100.5 billion 1998 revenues	**Time Warner** $26.8 billion 1998 revenues		**The Walt Disney Co.** $23 billion 1998 revenues	**Viacom** $18.9 billion 1998 revenues		**News Corporati** $13 billion 1998 revenues
Background	*GE/NBC's ranks No. 1 on the Forbes 500. Prior to its merger with NBC and an alliance with Microsoft, GE specialized in electronics. The peacock owns many New York sports team. It also owns or has equity stakes in many popular websites, including Snap.com and iVillage.*	*The largest media corporation in the world, Time Warner owns film and music production companies, theme parks, sports teams, magazines, websites and book publishers as well as Turner Broadcasting*		*With its 1995 merger with Capital Cities/ABC, Disney has become a fully-integrated media giant. In addition to its theme parks, the company profits from retail outlets, magazines, book publishers, websites, motion pictures, sports teams, TV, cable, radio, music and newspapers.*	*Viacom's purchase of Paramount, CBS and Blockbuster Video enables them to use cable, television, movies, comic books, theme parks, music publishing and book publishing to cross-market their products. Broadcasting alone brings in over $6 billion in revenues.*		*CEO Ruper Murdoch's style has inspired respect an fear, and i has also m his multinatio ventures ii publishing, television a satellite services ve successful. The compa owns 20th Century Fo the* New Y Post, *the* London Times, TV Guide, *ma stadiums, LA Dodger and five N York sport teams.*
Networks Owned	**NBC** includes programming, news and more than 13 TV and radio stations	**TURNER BROAD-CASTING** includes sports teams, programming, production, retail, book publishing and multimedia	**WB** Television Network	**ABC** includes ABC Radio, ABC Video and ABC Network News	**CBS** includes stations, CBS Radio, CBS Telenoticias and CBS Network News	**UPN** includes programming and TV stations (50%)	**FOX** includes programm and statio
Cable Interests	*Owns 25-50% of the*	• HBO (75%) • Cinemax		• Disney Channel	• Nickelodeon • MTV		• Fox Fam Channel

following:

- A & E (with Disney and Hearst)
- American Movie Classics (25%)
- Biography Channel (with Disney and Hearst)
- Bravo (50%)
- Bravo International
- CNBC
- Court TV (with Time Warner)
- Fox Sports Net
- History Channel (with Disney and Hearst)
- Independent Film Channel
- MSG Network
- MSNBC (50%)
- National Geographic Worldwide
- News Sport
- Prime
- Prism (with Rainbow, a subsidiary of Cablevision, and Liberty Media, a subsidiary of TCI)
- Romance Classics
- Sports Channel Cincinnati, Chicago, Florida, New England, Pacific, Ohio, Philadelphia

- HBO Direct Broadcast
- Court TV (33% with GE)
- TBS Superstation
- Turner Classic Movies
- TNT
- Cartoon Network
- Comedy Central (37.5% with Viacom)
- Sega Channel
- OVATION (50%)
- Women's Information Television (WIN) (partial)
- TVKO (75%)
- 4 regional all-news channels
- CNN
- CNN/SI (with *Sports Illustrated*)
- CNNfn (financial network)
- CNNRadio
- Headline News
- Sportsouth
- CNN International
- CNN Airport Network

- Disney Television (58 hours/week syndicated programming)
- Toon Disney
- Touchstone Television
- A&E (37.5% with Hearst and GE)
- Lifetime Network (50%)
- ESPN (80% with Hearst)
- ESPN2 (80% with Hearst)
- ESPN Classic (80% with Hearst)
- ESPN West (80% with Hearst)
- ESPNews (80% with Hearst)
- Buena Vista Television
- Biography Channel (with GE and Hearst)
- History Channel (37.5% with Hearst and GE)
- Classic Sports Network
- E! (35%)

- M2: Music Television
- VH1
- Showtime
- Nick at Nite's TVLand
- Paramount Networks Comedy Central (50% with Time Warner)
- TNN: The Nashville Network
- Movie Channel
- FLIX
- All News Channel (50%)
- Sundance Channel (45%)
- Midwest Sports Channel
- CBS Telenoticias (30%)
- Home Team Sports (66% with News Corporation)

(50%)
- Fox New Channel
- fx (50% with TCI's Liberty Me
- fxM (50 with TCI's Liberty Me
- Fox Spo Net (25% with TCI, C and Cablevisio
- The National Geographi Channel (50%)
- FIT TV Partnershi
- Regiona networks, including T Guide Cha and Fox Sports Nev York

Other Major Players:

Who Controls the Media?

Page 3 of 3

AT&T (TCI) - Recently acquired by AT&T, TCI's hold on cable, internet and local phone services contributed to billion in 1997 revenues. TCI is the second-largest US cable television system provider, and it has 10% ownersh Time-Warner/Turner. The company owns all or part of USA Network, Sci-Fi Network, E!, Court TV, Starz! and Star Black Entertainment Television, BET on Jazz, BET Movies/Starz! 3, CNN, TNT, Headline News, Prime Sports Cha Learning Channel, Discovery Channel, QVC, Q2, Fox Sports Net, The Travel Channel, Prevue Channel, An net, The Box, Telemundo, International Channel, Encore, MSG Network, Action Pay-per-view, and the H Shopping Network.

Sony - Sony's main media interests, earning $9 billion in 1997 sales, are in film and television production, m theaters and music.

Universal (Seagram) - In addition to Universal Studios, with its production facilities and theme parks, the com owns the USA and Sci-Fi cable networks.

Source: NOW Foundation

(Fast forward. There have been two big changes in ownership since this writing. Dreamworks has been bought by Paramount. And the WB and UPN have merged into one network, which will be known as The CW. You can check the Muslim website to see if these changes have been incorporated, but The Patriot Act and other moves by the administration to ease restrictions on wiretapping and surveillance being what they are, I'm not going near it. My passport picture already makes me look like a terrorist and I've got enough shit going on right now without the FBI showing up at my door.)

Anyway the studio goal is still to sell to the networks, though at present, each studio entity's primary goal is to feed their own network, and each network's intention is to pick up as much in-house product as possible. If you're on a deal at one of these studios, they don't necessarily want you pitching outside, at least without checking first with the mother ship. By way of illustration, here's a chart from *Variety*, showing the list of drama pilots. Note how many are either in-house productions or co-productions. On a similar note, check out an article from *Variety* about networks muscling their way into co-productions.

IAN GURVITZ

2/4/2004

2004-05 drama pilots

THE REPORTER

TITLE	STUDIO	PRODUCTION TEAM	DESCRIPTION
abc			
43 Minutes	Touchstone TV/FremantleMedia	Graham Yost, Marla Ginsburg	SWAT team handles the final 43 minutes of a major crisis in real time
The Catch ****	Touchstone TV	J.J. Abrams	Drama about two bounty hunters starring Greg Grunberg
Desperate Housewives	Touchstone TV	Marc Cherry, Chuck Pratt, Michael Edelstein	The sexy and secret lives of the inhabitants of a cul-de-sac
Doing It	Touchstone TV	G. Sachs, J. Judah, S. Bloomberg, F. Calfo	Coming-of-age drama about the sexual antics of three teen boys in Seattle
Empire * ‡	Touchstone TV/Storyline Ent.	T. Wheeler, C. Johannessen, C. Zadan, N. Meron	The rise of ancient Rome's Octavius to the emperor's throne
Eyes	WBTV/McNamara Paper Products	John McNamara, John Amiel	Centers on the workings of high-powered risk management corporation
Gramercy Park	Warner Bros. TV/the Tannenbaum Co.	S. Robinson, E. Tannenbaum, K. Tannenbaum	Three nannies and the families they work for in a tony N.Y. building
Harry Green and Eugene	Paramount/Frequency Films/Littlefield Co.	J. Wyman, S. West, W. Littlefield, J. Polhemus	L.A. private eye Harry Green (Mark Valley) and his inept brother, Eugene
Kat Plus One	Warner Bros. TV/Berlanti-Liddell Prods.	G. Berlanti, M. Friedman, M. Liddell	Young N.Y. publicist's life turns upside down when she has to raise her nephew
Untitled Kelley/Katims	20th TV/David E. Kelley Prods.	Jason Katims, David E. Kelley	Romantic comedy about three sisters running the family's wedding-planning business
Lost *****	Touchstone TV	J.J. Abrams, Damon Lindelof	Plane crashes on a desert island, and the survivors have to live together
The Secret Service	Touchstone TV	A. Kurtzman-Counter, R. Orci, F. Calfo	Procedural drama about a married woman who works for the Secret Service
Untitled Shonda Rhimes	Touchstone TV	Shonda Rhimes, Mark Gordon	Female residents in a surgical training program; "Sex and the Surgery"
cbs			
Untitled Bounty Hunters	Spelling TV	T. Hughes, R. Milbauer, A. Spelling, E.D. Vincent, R. Holcolmb	Father and his two sons earn a living as bounty hunters
Cooking Lessons	WBTV/the Tannenbaum Co.	E. Fox, E. Tannenbaum, K. Tannenbaum	Centers on a woman who writes a food column; based on Amanda Hesser's book
CSI: New York *	CBS Prods./Alliance Atlantis/Bruckheimer TV	A. Zuiker, C. Mendelsohn, A. Donahue, J. Bruckheimer, J. Littman, A. Lipsitz	Crime-scene investigators in New York
Clubhouse	Spelling TV/Icon Prods.	M. Gibson, B. Davey, A. Spelling, E.D. Vincent, D. Cerone	Coming-of-age drama about a Yankees batboy; based on M. McGough's book
Dr. Vegas ** †	WBTV/CBS Prods./Bender Brown Prods.	J. Herzfeld, L. Bender, K. Brown, M. Sennet	Centers on a Las Vegas casino in-house physician
Nice Guys**	WBTV/Silver Pics/Shoe Money Prods.	S. Black, A. Bagarozzi, J. Silver, T. Schlamme	Private eyes in Los Angeles; buddy action drama in the vein of "Lethal Weapon"
Numbers	Paramount TV/Scott Free Prods.	R. Scott, T. Scott, C. Heuton, N. Falacci	Mathematician from MIT is recruited by the FBI to help solve crimes
Sudbury ** †	Warner Bros. TV	B. Hartman-Edwards, D. DiNovi, S. Bullock	The trials and tribulations of a family of witches
Wanted **	WBTV/25C Prods./CBS Prods.	C. Cidre, S. Timberman, C. Beverly, T. Carter	Thriller set in the fugitive section of the LAPD
The Webster Report **	WBTV/25C Prods./CBS Prods.	T. Rebeck, S. Timberman, C. Beverly, B. Sonnenfeld	Centers on an offbeat N.Y. private investigator
nbc			
City of Dreams	WBTV/Jerry Bruckheimer TV	D. Mills, J. Bruckheimer, J. Littman	Jimmy Smits as an L.A. private eye fixing problems for the rich and famous
Eden †† ‡	Mark Burnett Prods.	Mark Burnett, Douglas Day Stewart	Members of a summer-study cruise are marooned on a remote island
Hawaii	NBC Studios	Jeff Eastin	Ensemble cop drama set in Hawaii
HUB	NBC Studios	Mark Gordon, Nick Thiel	Offbeat ensemble drama set behind the scenes at a large U.S. airport
Untitled Medical Mystery **	NBC Studios/Paramount/Landscape Ent.	B. Cooper, S. Vila, J. Horwitch, M. Ashford	Medical mystery procedural show
Medium	Paramount/Grammnet/Picturemaker	G. Gordon Caron, K. Grammer, S. Stark	Suburban mom uses her psychic powers to solve crimes
Revelations *** ‡	Pariah	David Seltzer, Gavin Polone	Group tries to forestall the apocalypse; "The X-Files" meets "The Da Vinci Code"
fox			
Untitled Attanasio/Shore	Universal Network TV/Heel & Toe Films	Paul Attanasio, David Shore, Katie Jacobs	Team of doctors diagnose the toughest medical cases
Untitled Bigelow/Kessler bros.	20th Century Fox TV/Imagine TV	K. Bigelow, T. Kessler, G. Kessler, B. Grazer, D. Nevins	Woman goes undercover in a high school to investigate a drug ring
Hollywood Division	Universal Network TV	Barry Schindel, Rob Port	Cop drama about detectives working undercover at a Hollywood high school
Johnny Zero	WBTV/John Wells Prods.	J. Wells, R. Scott Gemmill, L. Wells	Ex-con with a notorious street rep (Franky G) struggles to go legit and becomes a PI
The Jury *	20th Century Fox TV	T. Fontana, J. Yoshimura, B. Levinson, J. Finnerty	Legal drama from the point of view of a New York jury
Oahu	20th Century Fox TV	Kevin Falls, Peter Elkoff	"Upstairs, Downstairs" look at the guests & staffers of a luxury Hawaiian hotel
One Big Happy	20th Century Fox TV	Gretchen Berg, Aaron Harberts, Shawn Levy	Dysfunctional blended family with five kids; loosely based on Levy's life
Point Pleasant	20th TV/Original TV	M. Noxon, J. McLaughlin, N. Moritz, M. Adelstein, D. Parouse	Beachside community turns upside down when a girl washes ashore
Ricochet	Touchstone TV	Rene Echevarria, Jeff Kline	Cop drama in the vein of "Memento"
wb			
Dark Shadows	WBTV/John Wells Prods.	Mark Verheiden, John Wells, Dan Curtis	Remake of the ABC soap about a wealthy Maine family under a vampire curse
Global Frequency	WBTV/Mark Burnett Prods.	Mark Burnett, John Rogers	Based on DC comic about an intelligence agency where agents are ordinary folk
Jack & Bobby	WBTV/Berlanti-Liddell/Shoe Money	G. Berlanti, M. Liddell, T. Schlamme, V. Taylor	Drama about the teen years of a future president and his brother
Prodigy	WBTV/Silver Pictures	J. Friedman, J. Silver, D. Stokdyk, J. Gwartz	Centers on a family raising a child prodigy son
The Robinsons: Lost in Space	20th TV/Fox TV St./Lion Rock/Synthesis	D. Petrie, J. Woo, K. Burns, J. Jashni, T. Chang, S. Zizzi	A remake of Irwin Allen's fantasy-adventure drama set in 2097
Rocky Point	Warner Bros. TV	John Stockwell, Lizzy Weiss	Young woman living on Hawaii's North Shore takes in her estranged father
upn			
Beck and Call †	WBTV, Shephard/Robin Co.	D. Bucatinsky, L. Kudrow, M. Robin, G. Shephard	Revolves around the lives of three twentysomethings in their first jobs
Kevin Hill	Touchstone TV/ Icon Prods.	Jorge Reyes, Mel Gibson, Bruce Davey	Young attorney gives up his playboy lifestyle to raise his niece
Mystery Girl †	20th Century Fox TV	L. Heldens, H. Gordon, R. Dwek	Alex Breckenridge as a magazine writer who solves mysteries
Nikki & Nora	Warner Bros. TV	Nancylee Myatt, Lynne Litt	Centers on two lesbian private investigators
Silver Lake †	Spelling Television	Justin Tanner, Aaron Spelling, E. Duke Vincent	Dramedy about an L.A. record store owner who communicates with the dead
Veronica Mars	Warner Bros. TV/Silver Pictures	Rob Thomas, Joel Silver	Hip teen girl helps her father with his private detective agency

*SERIES COMMITMENT **CAST-CONTINGENT ***TWO-HOUR PILOT ****MIDSEASON 2004-05 *****PILOT PLUS 6 SCRIPTS †PRESENTATION ††TWO SCRIPTS AND BIBLE ‡LIMITED SERIES

Eye mandate ruffles rivals

CBS is eyeing more co-prods

By JOSEF ADALIAN

A new skirmish in the ongoing battle of the congloms has broken out, with Viacom-owned CBS asking for co-productions on many of its fall 2005 pilots – much to the chagrin of Disney-owned Touchstone and News Corp.'s 20th Century Fox TV.

CBS has told Touchstone it won't move forward with drama projects "The Ghost Whisperer" (working title) or "Quantico" unless Touchstone agrees to produce them with Eye sister studio Paramount Network TV. Touchstone has told CBS, "No thanks."

Production on both pilots is moving forward, with the impasse essentially being put off until May. At that point, should CBS want to order the projects to series, either Touchstone or the Eye will have to blink.

Likewise, the formal announcement of at least two 20th-produced comedy pilots is being held up, insiders said, because the studio isn't thrilled with CBS' request that Par come on board to produce. A similar situation played out earlier this month on the drama front, with 20th eventually agreeing to a co-prod on one drama and holding the line on another.

Duo balking

It's believed 20th and Touchstone are balking because CBS wants a co-prod, even though the net isn't bringing a major bit of talent to the table. They wonder if the Viacom net is simply trying to use its clout (and status as the No. 1 net) to artificially inflate Par's roster.

Insiders say CBS, by contrast, believes it's simply protecting its creative investment by ensuring it has a hand in the production of as many pilots as possible. What's more, industry insiders say the net is also probably still gun-shy about doing business with 20th and Touchstone because of prior run-ins with the studios.

Touchstone, quite famously, bailed out of "CSI" after the show was on the schedule, while 20th asked to get out of "Joan of Arcadia" late in the development process.

Notably, both of Warner Bros. TV's drama pilots at CBS are *not* co-prods. And Sony just snagged a comedy order for a pilot it'll produce all by itself.

Co-prods more common

Co-prods had become commonplace in recent years, as studios looked to limit financial risk and networks sought to get a piece of backend profits. Often times, the co-prod requests have come in May, when webs are deciding whether to put new shows on the air.

But this year, with Paramount and CBS both under the control of Viacom co-prexy Moonves and Tellem, the net seems to be flexing its muscles -- perhaps wanting to avoid any messy hold-ups come May.

One industry observer believes studios are balking at the Eye's co-prod requests because of a change in the financial landscape.

Thanks to scripted hits like "Without a Trace," "Desperate Housewives" and "Medium," there's a new sense that the network biz may not be as risky as it seemed just a few years ago. Hit dramas are fetching huge sums in off-net coin, and studios like 20th and Touchstone don't want to have to share, some believe.

What's more, nets like CBS increasingly feel they invest millions in marketing and license fees to launch hits, and don't want to be left out of the backend.

There's also the sense at some networks that a show produced by a non-aligned outlet -- think Paramount producing "Medium" for NBC -- won't get the same love from a studio as a skein produced inhouse.

Not surprisingly, those who rep the creative community are concerned about the latest conglom skirmish. Some worry that good projects might die because of corporate politics.

"It's all very scary," one tenpercenter said.

Reps for Par, Touchstone and 20th all declined comment.

As far as cable goes, until recently it has been considered a loss leader, though that is dramatically changing given the big syndication sales of *Sex and the City* and *The Sopranos*, not to mention ancillary markets like foreign sales and DVDs. But as of now, the main goal for the studios is to get a network hit that will lead to syndication and millions for the creators, and billions for the studios. The next *Frasier*, *Seinfeld*, *Raymond*, or *Friends*.

THE MONEY

Most people are generally aware that this is a high-paying business for writers. If they knew the reality, it would foment revolution. Per the current WGA contract, this is the kind of money involved.

Writing a half-hour script—$20,044
Hour show script—$29,482
Ninety-minute teleplay—$41,480
Pilot script—anywhere from $50,000 to $150,000 and more, depending on the writer's status in the business. Plus:
Residuals—each time an episode you write re-runs, whether in prime time, on cable or in syndication you get a check for a percentage of the script fee. If it airs in another country you get a check. If a clip from a show you wrote is used on one of those network bleeper shows, you get a check. Sweet.

Residuals are financial orgasms you get to relive over and over. Just ask any writer who's gone to the mailbox and seen that green envelope. But that's nothing compared with what we earn working on staff of a show. Depending on one's position, a writer or writer/producer can earn anywhere from $3,477 per week, to upwards of $50,000 per show (22 shows per year)...and more. On a hit, salaries can easily go into the millions per year. And, if the show you create gets sold into syndication, it's worth anywhere from tens to, in some cases, hundreds of millions. (See "fuck you money.") This is the goal. This is the world. This is why you go through the shit you go through. Oh, and for creative satisfaction.

PART II: THE JOURNAL

DEVELOPMENT IN PRACTICE
The Agony, the agony, the agony and (occasionally) the ecstasy of writing for television

You now have a rough idea how the TV business works, and of the stakes involved. Now to try to answer the question: What's it like to work in TV? This record begins in June of 2003. At that time I was working on *Becker*—a Paramount-produced show for CBS—as an Executive Producer, although I hadn't expected to be back there at all. In May, after five years on the air, we were unceremoniously bounced off the schedule in favor of a new show developed by the network called *The Stones*, about a newly divorced couple who decide to still live together with their kids. There had been mention of giving us a midseason order[38] but through May and most of June, there had been no official pickup.

The writers, actors and crew were nervous. We had all been together for five years and now faced uncertainty and the prospect of saying goodbye and having to look for work. No one knew our fate. All we got from the network was silence and, frankly, denial will only take you so far before you reach the point of "Who are we kidding—it's over." So Dave Hackel —the creator of the show—and I had a final sushi lunch, got a little drunk, and figured we'd just bury this thing. And because we finally gave up, that afternoon the call came through picking us up for 13 midseason, which led to a mad scramble to reassemble a writing staff and get to work on what we figured were the last 13 shows, though in the back of our minds was the hope that if we did well there might be an official reprieve and we'd stay on. But even further back was

[38] Midseason order. A network insurance policy. They order 6 or sometimes even 13 shows, preparing to slot them in the second one of the new shows is cancelled.

the certainty that this wouldn't happen, and it was time to start preparing for the future.

Toward that end, I'd been writing a spec pilot during the last year called *The Guys*. In pitching shorthand it's a male *Sex and the City*. Writing on spec is like masturbation. Not in the sense of it being a hairy-palmed sin or pointless exercise, but in the good sense of having no limits on your imagination, and no one around telling you to do it differently. You can do it when you want, where you want, and as often as you want. It's pure. It feels good. It makes you smile. The jokes you like, the chances you take, they all stay in. But now, I felt it was time to lift my skirt and show the development executives at Paramount what I'd been working on.

(Just for perspective, since show business can get somewhat myopic to the point that people assume that *Variety* and the *Hollywood Reporter* are actual newspapers instead of trade papers, I'll include along the way any news events, observations, anecdotes about the business or the world in general, just for perspective, to set this in context, or simply because I feel like it.)

JULY 2003

California votes for a recall of Gray Davis. Personally, I don't exactly know what he did that was so bad, other than being very, very grey. Kobe Bryant is charged with sexual assault. Bob Hope dies in his sleep, officially putting him On The Road To The Afterlife. Scott McClellan replaces Ari Fleischer as White House press secretary. His initial comment on being appointed to the position: "no comment." Oh, and there's a war in Iraq.

July 15

Pitched the idea for my pilot to Garry Hart, President of Paramount television; Rose Catherine Pinckney, VP of Development; and Kevin Plunkett, another VP; all of whom I know and like but we've never worked together in development. (Fast forward: None of those people are still in those jobs. Another fact of executive life: there is no such thing as job security. If your agent makes a good deal going in, sometimes you have next-job security. See "Indy Prod.")

Though I'd already written a draft of the script, I didn't want to reveal that before testing the waters. They sparked to the idea. I told them I didn't want to repeat the mistakes I made last time on *Tony Danza*, most importantly getting into bed with so many production entities that by the time all the notes had been given, the development experience felt like a three-stage process of date, date rape, and gang rape. I did mention that I had lunch with Steve Stark, a former Paramount development exec who was now running Kelsey Grammer's company. Steve said he might be interested in developing the project but, as for now, I want to go it alone.

July 18

Kevin called and said they're meeting with NBC in a week and a half to gauge what they're looking for this year. Being that Kevin Reilly, the new president of NBC, is facing the demise of *Friends* and *Frasier*, he may be looking to put his particular stamp on the crop of new shows. Given that his previous job was at F/X, where *The Shield* and *Nip/Tuck* were developed, he might be willing to entertain a show that is darker than most fluffy NBC comedies. If it turns out to be something NBC is looking for, maybe we can go right in and beat the fall rush. I like the show I wrote, which is a dangerous experience because when you actually care about something you're writing it stings more when the people in charge start to dick with it. But I take it one step at a time, trying not to get pre-angry before the process has even begun.

AUGUST 2003

Largest blackout in U.S. history leaves 50 million people in 8 states without electricity. There's still a war in Iraq. Thousands die in Europe's heat wave. Michael Jackson is charged with child molestation.

August 20

Talked with Kevin, who said they were ready to set up pitch meetings. Based on my experience on *Becker*, where we had absolutely no creative interference from the network, I tell them I'd like to go to CBS first. He says they can set something up in a couple of weeks, but first want a pre-pitch meeting here just as a dry run, which is probably good for me because I've been in production on *Becker* for over five years and haven't been pitching anything new in all that time.

As I think about what I went through the last time, I am already pre-angry in anticipation of every idiotic comment I'm going to get back. Do they all have to be guys? Couldn't it be guys and girls? One gay guy? A gay couple? How about the gay odd couple? Basically, how can we duplicate the success we've had by morphing it back into something that's familiar? As I said, for some reason, studio development people tend to be more open, more lighthearted. They seem to laugh more, probably because their job is to sell and, as such, they're open to trying anything. Network development people, by and large, tend to be more discerning about what they buy, and don't (or maybe they aren't allowed to) think in terms of new and exciting as much as what's road tested and familiar. If somebody takes a chance with something new and it fails their bosses come down on them and say, "What were you thinking?" If they take a chance on something familiar or an actor who's recently been on a hit show, they can never be accused of taking a stupid risk, just a familiar one that didn't pay off. Give us another

Will & Grace, another *Friends*. Funny, pretty people living near each other, looking for love—and if some could be gay and do Cher impressions, so much the better. Then we'll actually get Cher to guest star during sweeps and everyone will talk like Cher and we'll all giggle and it'll be such fun!

But I know the reality I'm walking into. I'm going in to pitch for the first time in years. I'm excited, and I'm furious. And I haven't even started yet.

SEPTEMBER 2003

John Ritter dies after collapsing on the set of "8 Simple Rules." I knew him a bit. I'd worked with his wife, Amy Yasbeck, for years on "Wings" where John did a guest shot and our kids played together once in the park. Feeling sad for her and pathetically helpless, I send a card. Michael Jackson charged with child molestation. Still a war in Iraq.

September 11

Rehearsal pitch meeting with Rose Catherine and Kevin. Made my notes, went in early, and played video poker on my cell phone. I bet heavily and win big. I'm up like 20 grand from a five-hundred-dollar stake. I figure I'm on a run of luck and those don't come often, so I start betting heavier, thinking if I can parlay this into millions I could retire and not have to deal with show business, except on my own terms. Then the people I'm here to see show up and I remember I'm not playing with real money; it's just a game on my cell phone. Shit.

We sit down, and I go into my pitch. It goes well. Then they tell me that the women we'll be pitching to at CBS are notoriously unresponsive, and that I'll kill myself trying to get a laugh out of them, but they will give us a direct answer in a very short time. I'm still confident in my decision to go there first, as opposed to NBC, who may just want to clone more *Will and Graces*. Of course I'm afraid CBS just wants to clone more Monday night shows with fat, dickless husbands and the brown-haired wives who browbeat the shit out of them and dole out sexual favors like a dog owner rewarding a mutt for rolling over. Essentially, it's *The Honeymooners*, which has been pitched for decades in one form or another. A great show in its time but a painfully old-fashioned paradigm in the 21st century. Yet, for some reason America likes its husbands fat, and dopey, and its wives tough, pretty and smart. Or, development executives imagine they do.

Maybe it's not an accident. Half-hour comedies are supposed to be funny. Comics are funny. And in the 70s, the networks discovered that comedy clubs were virtual trout farms for funny people. But comics tend not to be great-looking guys, which was probably part of the reason they went into comedy—to have an outlet for the pain they felt because pretty girls wouldn't fuck them because they were unattractive. The irony is that, once they were funny on stage, pretty girls *would* fuck them because being funny suddenly made them attractive, even if they looked like something that lived under a bridge. Which was fine if you were doing a week headlining some club in the middle of nowhere and staying in some shithole motel. At least you weren't sleeping alone. But that still didn't make the comic better looking in front of the camera, and casts of TV shows are supposed to be attractive, so if the funny male lead isn't, his TV wife damn well better be so that the cast photo doesn't look like some group of mutants. (Maybe the reason the pretty wife is traditionally so bitchy is that she knows she's too pretty to be married to this hideous-looking guy.)

Anyway, I mention my concern during the meeting. We laugh about it and Rose Catherine and Kevin allay my fears, while suggesting I don't mention any of this during the CBS pitch. I agree not to.

Now it's a matter of getting ready for Monday morning and beginning the process. But one hit show and I'll never have to go through this again. I walk down the hall thinking I fully expect them to buy this, because I think it's better than most of the shit I see and they should recognize that. Of course everyone who goes in to pitch has that same attitude. Then I go back into pre-anger mode over all the changes they're going to want, none of which I want to hear, because I've already written it and unless someone has some brilliant insight, I don't want to change it. The question is, at this point, do I have the balls to tell a network, "Sorry, not interested in doing it your way." Answer: Probably not. In reality, I'm a shitty poker player.

On the way out, I pass the Paramount Theater and suddenly remember that it's September 11. Two years since the planes hit the World Trade Center. I think of my one connection to it—other than being a native New Yorker—that of knowing David and Lynn Angell, who were on the first plane. David was one of the creators of *Wings* who hired me 12 years ago. A smart, warm, soft-spoken guy, he also co-created *Frasier* and was ready to take the cash and get out. He and his wife had built a house on the East Coast to which they were going to retire. They were only returning to L.A. for the Emmys.

The Paramount Theater was where they held the memorial service for David and Lynn. As I walk past it, the sad irony hits me. You work your ass off here to get a show on the air. It's a hit. You spend years in production, slogging through endless rewrites in rooms that reek of sweat and goopy Chinese food. Finally you succeed: great ratings, truckloads of Emmys, huge syndication sale—and you cash out, ready to live the rest of your sweet life in comfort, but how the fuck are you supposed to know that the flight you've taken a thousand times is going to get hijacked by suicidal terrorists and flown into a building? So much for plans.

September 14

The morning of the CBS pitch and the beginning of the fall TV season which, ironically, *Becker* is once again part of. We were put back on the schedule after CBS took a critical look at *The Stones* and decided it blew, which it did. How they didn't know that from the script stage is beyond me. So we went from virtual cancellation, to midseason order, to back on the schedule with hope for new life. I'm on my way to pick up my daughter Hana for school, just having read the first of the many articles in magazines by TV critics offering their assessment of the fall TV season. The articles are usually snide, the underlying assumption being "meet the new crap, same as the old crap." Which brings me back to—

CRITICS

I've been to about a dozen TCA (Television Critics Association) fall premiere events. They're mostly held at the Ritz-Carlton in Pasadena. I've talked to a few nice reporters, though as a group they look like the surliest collection of hard-core cynics and borderline alcoholics I've ever seen—though this may just be the result of spending nearly a week sequestered in a hotel room screening one pilot after another. By the time they're done, they're gnarly as hell and either in need of a drink or already lit from the minibar, but either way, they seem ready and eager to shit on everything in sight. And TV is an easy target. It's like going to a trout farm and blasting away at the pond with a .12 gauge. They're already handicapping the new shows, and, with regard to *Becker*, using terms like time slot hit[39] to explain its re-emergence, which must be one of those phrases they learned in entertainment critic

[39] Time slot hit. A bad show that succeeds because it's in a good time slot, usually following a huge hit.

school to explain the success or non-cancellation of the shows they called shit the previous year.

In reality, very few really bad shows succeed no matter what their time slots. In fact, the show that preceded *Becker* on the air five years ago in the coveted post-*Raymond* time slot was *The Brian Benben Show*. Brian Benben was the actor on *Dream On*; an early HBO success that featured cleverly intercut old movie clips, along with topless women. The actor was funny in the show, though occasionally just a spritzer at a wet T-shirt contest. Anyway, *Benben* lasted three and out. Similarly, the post *Seinfeld*, *Cheers*, *Frasier* and *Will and Grace* time slots are littered with the bodies of past critical and/or ratings failures such as *Grand*, *Madman of the People*, *Caroline in the City*, *Suddenly Susan*, *Veronica's Closet*, *Stark Raving Mad*, *Coupling* or *Good Morning, Miami*. Good time slots don't create hits. Like advertising, they merely induce trial, delivering an audience to check out the product. But if there's no way to explain the success of something you went on record saying you didn't like, you pull out the "time slot hit" criticism and that gets you off the hook. Each magazine has their own little handicapper, whether some lone schmuck in a cubicle or an entire editorial staff. There is no greater sport, no easier way to feel superior than dumping on the crap the networks offer up every year even though in many cases, it is, indeed, crap.

Sorry, I digressed. Where was I? Oh, right, the fall season. Lots of on-air promo on NBC for the two shows that got off to a good start: *Whoopi* with Whoopi Goldberg, and *Happy Family* with John Laroquette and Christine Baranski. Still, one magazine I read picks them both as early cancellations. (They were.)

Back to me. As I head to CBS, I've got visions of success combined with a damage control plan for failure, which would be going to NBC, possibly even with Kelsey Grammer's company, because they have commitments there. It may make for a stronger approach, enabling me to circumvent the pitch and just reposition this as a script with strong production partners. That's the nature of this business: work for success; plan for failure.

I pull into CBS early, go over my notes, and play a little video poker on my cell phone as I wait for the meeting, trying to lose this pre-anger I've got coursing through my system. I'm going to be pissed if they don't buy it. I'm gonna be pissed if they're a lousy audience. I'm going to be pissed if they buy it and start to meddle with it. Anything short of "We love it," I'm going to be pissed. It's amazing the level of importance you can put on this shit. Ultimately you know it's just television. Is it really that important? When you're in production, "the show" is the first thought in your mind in the morning and last before you go to sleep. And that's not including jolting up in bed at 3am with some great story idea or the paralyzing fear that you've fucked up an edit on a show that's already been locked and delivered for broadcast. Still, you try to remind yourself that it's just television. On the other hand, a successful show can employ hundreds of people for years and, if it's good, become part of the culture. Someone's going to succeed, might as well be you.

We go in. Obligatory hello's and offers of water. I take out my file and lay it on the table, more as a prop, just to show them there's more than what they're hearing, maybe even a script. Then, after a beat, I go into my pitch, setting up the basic premise and characters, while getting as quickly as possible to the first joke, which will get them laughing, give them an idea of how funny this will be, and put them in a mood to hear more. I deliver the joke that made my studio partners laugh when I pitched it to them. This time—silence. Not a smile, not a movement. Nothing. I instantly go to a place not unlike a comic who's bombing—I pretend it didn't happen and press on, getting quickly to the next joke. Silence. I look over at the heads of CBS Comedy Development, sitting there motionless, expressionless, and think "Someone call 9-1-1; these women are dead. Or catatonic." I mean, maybe I've bored one or two people in my life with a story that went on a few beats too long, but I've never actually turned anyone into stone. This is, like, Biblical.

Still, I keep going. Finally one of their mouths moves and she emits a sound. A laugh? A nervous tic? Maybe just the noise and crooked, involuntary smile a baby lets out when it farts. Either way, I'm grateful for the response, however slight, which gives me the confidence to power through to the end and get the fuck out.

The Paramount executives hang around behind closed doors for a few moments, either for a quick post-mortem or to make fun of me. Then they emerge and we walk to the parking lot. I press Rose Catherine for some feedback, along the lines of "What the fuck was that?" but she insists it went well, saying she knows when they hate something because they make faces after, but she said they liked it. I don't believe her but choose to anyway. Which puts us in "waiting to hear" mode, which is where everyone other than the ten people really in show business spend most of their time. She reiterates that they're known for quick responses. Maybe we'll hear today, maybe tomorrow. Either way, it'll be a quick yes or no. I run out to the parking lot and drive back to Paramount, just to see the faces of people who (I think) like me.

Still September 14

End of day. I finish the day's work on *Becker* and I'm driving home on Gower when my cell phone rings. It's my agent, Jay Sures from UTA, and my brother, Marc Gurvitz, who's also my manager at Brillstein-Grey. They sound excited as they tell me they've heard I sold the pilot. Sure enough, the second I hang up the phone rings again. It's Rose Catherine confirming it. This kind of good news is unusual. And will not help the vein of cynicism I've got permanently running through me. But I'll take a sale as opposed to a pass. I privately applaud the network on their good judgment, and as a satisfied smirk creeps across my face, I drive up toward Sunset, passing Sunset/Gower studios, where we produced the first show I ever created, with Moon and Dweezil Zappa, called *Normal Life*. Don't remember it? No reason you should.

I'd only been writing TV for about a year. Getting a pilot on was a total fluke, and only happened because I did a last-minute rewrite on someone else's script, more as a face-saving device for the production company. There was little hope of actually getting it picked up. Then it got picked up. As I wait for the turning signal, I think back to the creative fights we had over the direction of the show, firing an actress I was very fond of, personally and professionally, the cast storming into the writers' room en masse, throwing that week's script on the table with the pronouncement: "We're not doing this shit, " the horrible reviews, the lousy ratings, getting cancelled, getting nasty drunk on the day of our last shoot and throwing a stapler through a window, then coming in the next day, hung over, and asking who the asshole was who threw the stapler through the window.

With the benefit of hindsight, I now realize the show *was* shit, though it didn't start that way. As originally conceived, it was modeled after the Zappa family—sort of the *Addams Family Ties* as we referred to it then—an atypical family on the surface, a loving one underneath. And that was the pilot we shot. That pilot never aired. It was thrown out and, over time, replaced by a show that was improved to death by the experts brought in to save it by using every hoary sitcom story and dumbass cliché known to man. I turn on to Sunset, heading home, vowing it won't happen that way this time.

September 23

I deliver a five-page pilot outline on *The Guys* to Rose Catherine and am waiting for a response. It was exactly what I pitched, but now that people get a chance to look at in on paper, suddenly problems can arise. Once again, I'm pre-pissed over the comments I might hear. I finally get a call from Rose Catherine. She says everything's fine, good job, just a couple of minor notes. I say I can address them and turn it back in next week so it can go on to CBS, where I am, once again, anticipating disaster at every turn.

OCTOBER 2003

Gray Davis ousted. Arnold Schwarzenegger elected governor in total recall. No sooner is he in office than he starts making noises about changing the Constitution to allow naturalized citizens to run for President. Amazing. The last time the world saw this much ambition combined with that accent, they burned down the Reichstag. Michael Jackson charged with child molestation. Rush Limbaugh admits he's a prescription drug addict and announces plans to compete in the Fattest American Hypocrite Pageant being held in Atlantic City. Liza Minelli's estranged husband sues her for $10 million in damages for spousal abuse. Roy Horn of Sigfried and Roy is attacked by one of his famed white tigers. Weeks later, paparazzi catch the tiger and Liza having lunch at Spago in Beverly Hills. A spokesperson for Liza insists they're just good friends comforting one another during difficult times, though the tiger confides to a close friend that "Liza's the greatest piece of ass I've ever had, and I've had them all over the world."

October 3

The outline has been at CBS for days. Silence. No response. Shit. I start calling Rose Catherine to find out what's going on and hear that CBS had called, but am given no information beyond that.

In the history of turning in material, there's a simple equation: Silence=Death. Nothing I can do but go through my day on *Becker* and wait for the call. We have a good run-thru after a late-night rewrite the night before. We deal with a few changes, as well as the slam we took in *Entertainment Weekly* based on the premiere episode that I wrote. Though the article didn't slam me personally, this publication has had a snarky disdain for the show from day one. For revenge, we stick in a couple gratuitous *Entertainment Weekly* shots in the show. Why not? No one will notice or care, but we'll feel better.

I call Rose Catherine again. Not there. I try to pump her assistant for information. Nothing. She's on her way to a pitch meeting. She'll try you later. I start driving home. My cell rings. It's her assistant, saying she's going into another pitch meeting but will be out at 6:00 and I will be her first call. This is the nature of communication during pilot season—you need to set up appointments to speak to people.

The traffic on Laurel Canyon is backed up. It's 5:30 and I need to get home by 6 because my cell phone cuts out near my house and I don't want to miss this call and sweat out the weekend with no information, followed by Monday, which is Yom Kippur, a show business holiday. I'm already grinding my teeth, because I smell it. No information means they have problems with the story. My guess—it's too dark, it's too mean, and too many people have problems. They want it happier. Could you make it more like *Raymond*? Could you make it more like *King of Queens*? I already know they're backing off what I pitched and what I'm going to hear is that they have concerns. "Concerns" is network-speak for what they intend to throw out. I am now itching for a fight. I curse out every driver in front of me for having the fucking temerity to be on my road when I'm in a hurry. But I try to calm myself down and figure out how to play it.

I do not want to soften this. I don't want to sanitize it. I think of the line by Jerry Belson, a veteran comedy writer who supposedly said the title of his autobiography would be: "I Did It Their Way." I'm now ready to slam my Porsche into a mailbox. (Yes, I have a Porsche. Yes, it's a cliché. But I bought it used and, according to the salesman, who would never lie, the car was "previously owned by a drummer for Guns 'n' Roses, who only drove it when he wasn't touring," that being the L.A. version of the little old lady who only drove it to church on Sundays. Anyway, it was used, and I've had it for 10 years. So fuck off.)

Where was I? Oh yeah, the fight. Or the one I could have if I had the wherewithal to just say no to their changes. Once again, I'm kicking myself for going against my original feeling, which was just to put the script out there. Say here it is, take it or leave it. That's what happened on *Becker*. Dave Hackel wrote the pilot on spec and refused to change it for NBC, who felt they needed to "develop" it, meaning cut its soul out. That was before Les Moonves at CBS bought it and, to his credit, left us alone. That's also what happened on *Oliver Beene* at Fox, with a friend, Howard Gewirtz, who wrote the script on spec, based on his life and stories he used to tell in the *Wings* room about his family growing up in the Bronx. Whether or not it ultimately succeeds (it got cancelled after a season and a half) it did get on the network intact, based on Howard's vision. This is the way good shows happen. From producers who say this is what I want to do, take it leave it.

Cheers was based on the vision of the writers, as was *Seinfeld. Union Square* was *Cheers* built by a network. *The Single Guy* was *Seinfeld* built by a network. If you don't remember those shows, that's because you shouldn't—but they are indicative of network–think: *Seinfeld* worked because it was a show about some New Yorkers who hung out together, so those kind of shows must work. Similarly, *Cheers* was about people who hung out in a bar, so if we just change the bar into a diner and stick some wacky people in there, that'll work, too. Again, ideas are shit. It's all execution.

I finally make it home without slamming my car into anything or anyone. It's a few minutes before 6. I'm pacing, pissed off, because I can already hear it. "They have some concerns." "Can you take the edge off?" "We don't want to do anything about divorce." " We don't want anything about alcoholism. (One character's in AA.) "We don't want anything about gambling." (Another has a gambling problem.) I wait for the phone to ring, almost totally consumed by what their notes are going to be about my show. "My show." You'd think I was in the waiting room of a maternity ward waiting to see if my kid has been born with an extra head. I feel ridiculous. But it is what it is. So I wait. And wait. All night. No call comes in.

October 4

9am. After agonizing all night and all morning, I can't stand the suspense any longer and I call Rose Catherine. Miracles being what they are, I get through to her and figure she'll tell me they only have a few little notes and I've been driving myself insane for no reason. She doesn't. The network response is exactly as I feared: make the lead character more sympathetic, but, most importantly, they think all the characters feel like—and here's the dreaded network term—"losers."

If there is one note that boils a writer's blood more than anything, it's this. You can even hear them whining as they give it. "I don't know. They're all so screwed up. They feel like loo-o-sers..." This is a classic dumbshit network note: "These people are too damaged, nobody's going to want to hang out with them." My response to her was immediate, and expressed with a combination of anger, disdain, and cobra venom. Just look at any successful series. *Cheers*, *Taxi*, *Seinfeld*. These people are all, on paper, "losers." Cheers had a washed-up alcoholic baseball player; a horny, terminally single, pontificating mailman who lived with his mother; a barfly with no career and a crappy marriage; a pretentious snob of a woman who gets dumped by her fiancée; a barmaid with a bunch of kids and no husband; and a failed career woman. And *Taxi*—Jesus. It was all about cab drivers with life ambitions they'll never fulfill. *Seinfeld* was basically four people who hung out and ragged on each other. All losers, if you choose to categorize them this way. Nobody's getting what he or she wants. They're all damaged. That's why they're interesting characters.

This is one of the prime examples of network development people not understanding the nature of what they do. Characters need faults. That's where the humor comes from. But the notes you get back demonstrate that what they truly want is just fluff and silliness and characters who just run around and slam doors and have silly little adventures with no style, wit, intelligence or emotional depth whatsoever. The problem is that sometimes this shit succeeds (meaning it gets ratings) which gives network people the proof to say you should do it like that because, obviously, that's what the audience wants.

But at this point, you can rant and rave all you like. Ultimately you're screaming at the wind. Unless your response is "No, I won't change a thing." In which case, most often, you're done. They just won't put it on. I finally finish bitching and one of my cats looks up at me with this expression that says, "What's your fucking problem, man? We need food, a roof over our heads, furniture to fuck up and rugs to shit on, so take your creative integrity and stick it up your ass!"

Rose Catherine and I talk a little longer, and then agree on a plan, the basic premise of which is I'm going to calm down and think of ways to adjust the main character to make him more sympathetic without eviscerating him, and we'll talk again on Monday. But I tell her if they want to turn all these characters into successful, happy, well-adjusted unfunny people, then let's agree to part company now, and we'll take the project to another network. That's my brave stand. To the studio. I know full well it will never fly at the network, and that I'm on the slippery slope toward homogenization.

I swear, this is the only business I know where the people who know how to do the jobs are governed over by people who don't. Though in all fairness, there are exceptions. There are executives who get it. One that comes to mind has to do with *Frasier*. The story goes that very early on the creators of the show wanted to change Kelsey's character from *Cheers* and do something else, some sort of rich, bedridden industralist with a nurse he bickered with. They wanted to avoid *Frasier* entirely, until one of the then-executives at Paramount said, Are you out of your minds? You've got an entire country with a *Cheers* hangover; you're doing *Frasier*. Turns out he wasn't wrong. Another involves Rick Ludwin, an NBC executive not even in comedy development, who put up money from his budget to produce more *Seinfeld* episodes in the early stages of the series when NBC wasn't sure of what they had. He should be known as the show's patron saint. Every once in a while there's an executive with some intelligence and insight to know funny when they see it, or to stop writers from outsmarting themselves. It does happen. I just haven't seen it happen much.

Now, I don't want to come off as misogynistic, but for some reason it's often women executives who have these reactions. I wonder if it's due to the fact that, for a woman to crash through the glass ceiling and attain a position of power such as Network Development Executive, it usually requires a strong personality. Women executives have to overcompensate for the perception of weakness by being overly tough, as a way of proving that they belong there. And toughness in a woman doesn't often go hand in hand with a sense of humor. Many of them have a Faye-Dunaway-in-*Network* thing going on. They may be tough enough to have risen through the ranks, but I think the very quality that enabled that to occur can be an Achilles heel when it comes to judging what's funny.

I bitch to Rose Catherine. (A female development exec who *is* funny and also knows it when she sees it; i.e., she laughs.) She completely gets it but is also pragmatic and wants this to go forward, as I do, and we both know there's no future in shoving something down network throats because they'll just pass on it. So now they not only need to be reassured that this won't be sad, but we need to make some (hopefully small) adjustments so everyone doesn't end up feeling…down. Screw reality. Give us more fun. I will churn this over in my guts all weekend. It's exasperating that the people in these jobs don't get that funny doesn't mean "fun," and characters need conflict to…ah, fuck it.

Bitched out, I think about my monthly nut, lock my self-righteousness and creative integrity in the bathroom, and start considering adjustments I can make, which is fine because I've already written a draft and know that a) the script's too long and b) I'm kidding myself if I think it's going to remain intact. I am now in development. The days of having it all my way are over. I have left masturbation and have begun dating. I also consider that I'm trying to do a show about guys and the development people are all women. One of the other notes was that the characters don't talk *to* each other, they talk *at* each other, even thought I told them explicitly in the pitch that that's what I was going to do. Because guys don't usually run up and throw their arms around each other and say, "Tell me what's bothering you, sweetheart." They talk around it, they joke their way out of it. Either way, it doesn't matter. I start making notes, planning to talk to Rose Catherine Monday, hoping she can figure out how to communicate "my" concerns to CBS and figure out some way that I won't have to do another outline because, basically, I don't want to.

What angers me is that writers who work in this form are rarely afforded any respect. In fact, the word "sitcom hack" crops up more often than not. But, given the power structure of television, you're only as good as you're allowed to be. You have to thread the eye of the needle to get a decent show on the air. Some writers say: "give them *their* pilot, then do *your* show." Easily said. Not so easily done. No matter how good your ideas are, no matter how smart your characters, you have to get it through this filtration system. Then it gets on. Then you get reviewed for doing a stupid show. Then you get cancelled and walk around with this failure hangover for six months, quoting chapter and verse of how you never got a chance, how your time slot sucked, and how you got rat-fucked by network notes. And no one wants to listen because, frankly, it's boring.

This is happening on a show right now that friends—a writing team—have on one of the networks where there are three or four producing entities—including one set of dilettante non-writing producers (see "Pod Producers")—all in all, just a cluster fuck of notes and opinions. Like hyena tearing apart a dead gazelle. They're so frustrated and exhausted by all the hoops they have to jump through just to get a story approved, it's amazing they get any work done at all. (That show was eventually cancelled. When I saw them afterward, they were smiling. A couple years later, I consulted on a pilot of theirs for another network, and watched it get similarly opinion-fucked to death. It never made it to air. Last I heard, they were on staff on a show at another network, but one that's definitely headed for cancellation. By the way, these people have won multiple Emmy awards for writing and producing.)

I just don't know how to play it this time. First pilot I did, when I gave into everybody's notes, trying to be agreeable, I got accused of having no passion or no vision. Second time I tried to hold firm and got accused of being difficult to work with and threatened with being bounced off my own show. Third time I got lost in the sauce of four production entities and a very strong-willed star who was used to having everything his way. It was his show, not mine. We'll see what happens this time.

THE NON-WRITING "POD" PRODUCER

Up until a few years ago, my only reference for the term "pods" was from *Invasion of the Body Snatchers*. Pods were the pea-like cocoons that aliens placed in peoples' homes, so that as soon as the people fell asleep, the pods stole their essential being, killing the person and leaving in their place some kind of replicant. I'll try not to draw too heavily on that analogy in explaining the show business phenomenon of "pods" and the "non-writing producer."

When an upper-level studio or network executive "ankles" their job, as it's put in *Variety*—in English, that means they got fired—they very often parachute into a 2- or 3-year development deal, complete with office, assistant, golf cart, their own development person, and sometimes even on-air commitments, so that they soon become important players in the development chain. They know the people. They know the system.

On the upside, they are experienced executives who are, frankly, trusted more by studio and network people than the writer. They speak the same language. They've inhabited the same space. Their connections are stronger. They have a better chance of picking up a phone and getting the person they need on the line quickly. Since they know the system, they can be indispensable in guiding a show through the development process, not only strategically but, on occasion, even creatively. They know where the minefields are. They can even be instrumental in lobbying to get a show on the air, or to help it stay on the air. On the downside, the non-writing producer most resembles the non-swimming lifeguard or the non-flying pilot, leaving the writers in the room asking each other behind closed doors: "What the fuck is this idiot doing here?" But for better or worse, they are now a reality of the TV business.

Now, the adage in TV has always been that the writer is king. That is true, usually, once a show is up and running. (While in features, the writer is often the schmuck who can be dispensed with, once they've turned in a draft and set of revisions. No one gives a shit about their vision. Fuck their vision. This is now a movie.) But in TV, the writer's vision is vital not only to launching the show, but to sustaining it. The network buys an idea as well as the writer behind it, hoping that the individual has this show in his or her blood, and can shepherd the creative process through 22 episodes a year.

The problem can arise, though, once a show has been picked up and the non-writing producer no longer has a creative function. But very often they want one. At best, they can be helpful as liaisons with all the various entities involved in the production, helping to get stories approved, extra money for stunt casting[40] during sweeps, or just as someone who can grease the wheels, making the writer/producers' lives easer by handling some of the disagreeable or time-consuming tasks that go with the job. At worst, having been part of the creative process, they often feel justified in staying with it and want to be in the writers' room. This often results in the writers either begrudgingly accepting their presence, bitching about it or, on occasion, banning them from the room.

---

[40] Stunt casting. Shows casting the biggest stars they can get during sweeps so that the network can promote the shit out of it and, hopefully, get bigger ratings, so they can charge more for advertising.

I inherited one of these producers on a show once. Granted, the show was in deep shit, and going down, thanks to the initial vision for it having long since been dispensed with, along with the substance abuse problems of the star, but the presence of a non-writer in the room was not the answer. But it is a phenomenon of the TV business that is here to stay. Some work. Some don't. But, and most writers would agree, the last thing you want is a non-writer constantly in the room. If I'm flying to New York, I want to know that everyone in the cockpit is an experienced pilot. I'd feel less comfortable with the notion that the person sitting in the co-pilot's seat is there because he or she helped the airline negotiate a good deal on the plane.

October 8

Spoke with Rose Catherine, who tried to get through to CBS. No response. She'll try again tomorrow. Tonight is the *Becker* premiere party—the premiere that a few months ago nobody thought would happen. But thanks to their swift development department they don't have a lot in the bank, so the only reason we're still in production is because we became the less ugly girl in the bar at last call. We're up against the last half-hour of *The Bachelor* on ABC, the last half hour of *The West Wing* on NBC and either *The O.C.* on FOX or baseball playoffs. All that's left is to schedule the second coming of Christ on UPN to ensure that no one will watch. Still, all we have to do is hold on to as much of the *King of Queens*' lead-in as we've gotten in the past holding onto *Raymond's*. A two-share fall-off isn't bad. Anything more than three and it's over.

October 9

I call the ratings hotline in the morning. The numbers were OK. Not bad, not great. I do my work on *Becker*. Don't hear anything on the pilot all day, so I call Rose Catherine while I'm on stage, right before the show. She's unavailable. The show starts. I set my phone to vibrate because I don't want to miss her call, but the last thing you want is your cell phone ringing during a scene and blowing a take and having two hundred people look at you simultaneously thinking "Asshole." A few minutes into the show, it vibrates. I have to take the call, which I have time to do, as we're on a break, trying to deal with a broken camera and the Marines in the audience who are hooting and howling like it's a USO review. Otherwise the show's going fine.

I walk to the side of the stage, hoping to hear good news: that she explained my concerns to CBS, smoothed it over, and they've given me the go-ahead to go to script. This is not what I hear. She says they still want to be reassured that these are "people we want to hang out with." In network-speak, they're still afraid the characters aren't likeable enough, which is exactly the problem I feared going in. And this is what I told Rose Catherine. She insists they get it, but they don't get it enough to trust me, so I have to do another outline to address their problems and have to schedule time for us to talk so she can give me everything in detail. She insists there's no rush, but I don't want to get stuck doing outline revisions while having to write half of the next *Becker* script.

I am now mired in seller's remorse. This experience is pushing every fear button I have about development. Pitch them your best ideas, they sanitize it, you shoot it, and it fails based on its newfound mediocrity. Then, and at the end of the day, they walk away and you're stuck holding the failure bag with your name on it. These are the fortunes of this business. It's amazing how fast people will run from a failure. But every executive who was taking a crap in the NBC building when *Cheers* was pitched became "instrumental in its development" in their bio in *Variety* after they ankled their job and went "indy prod."

October 10

Talked to Rose Catherine and got CBS's notes. I try to rework my outline, using some more emotional language, thinking this might get through to them, and adding a beat at the end where the main character gets his ex-wife's engagement ring out of hock as a way of showing he still cares. All this just to get approval on an outline so I can get the OK to change a script I've already written.

October 21

Still waiting for an answer from the network on the revised outline I turned back in. Monday. Nothing. Tuesday I get a call from Rose Catherine from her cell phone. She asks, "How are you?" I say, "You tell me, how am I?" She says "Great!" with a rising intonation, which means oh, shit, what now? She says they're "pretty satisfied" with the changes and it's "heading in the right direction," but now they want to schedule a conference call to discuss the main character and how he can be more prominent. At this point, I'm getting a serious case of writing blue balls. But I'm in the process and have to keep going, so the call gets set up for Friday at 4:00. Of course, it has to be several days away to give me plenty of time to stew over this and imagine the next wave of shit.

October 23

Driving on Gower toward Paramount, I pass the line of people waiting to get into *Dr. Phil*. The expectant looks on their faces makes it seem like they're lepers lining up to get healed by Jesus, not to sit in the audience to watch this Texas spawn of Oprah drawl out homespun platitudes and fob them off as solutions to complex problems. But he's obviously tapped a goldmine, based on the Maserati, Porsche, Mercedes and Escalade parked in his space on alternate days. I mean, shit, the guy doesn't even go by a last name. Dr. Phil. My daughter calls her pediatrician "Dr. Susan." I guess it's appropriate, as this is the way children refer to the people they think are going to magically make them all better.

Bumped into Garry Hart, President of Paramount TV, and told him that I feel like I'm being dicked around by CBS on the story. He said, "Don't do it if it's not what you want," which is exactly what you want to hear from an executive. Though I know what he really means is we've sold it, so find a way to make it work.

October 25

We finally have the conference call with Paramount and CBS. They say they're happy with what I did and just have a few more points to make, which they do. I say I can handle them except for one note that I fight and they agree to reserve judgment, which simply means they'll postpone hating it until later. And then, almost a month after delivering them an outline, they finally say, "Go write." Now I have about a month to turn the script in and go back through the same system I just crawled out of on the outline.

Oddly enough I saw something on-line this morning that said that CBS had beaten NBC on Thursday night in the 18-49 demo for the first time in ten years. A combination of *CSI* and some other show beat *Friends* and maybe *Coupling*. This may mark a turning point in the network domination game, which happens every decade or so as one network loses successful shows and their number-one position is usurped by another. It also means NBC is vulnerable on Thursday night and they're going to be looking for comedies to replace *Friends* and *Frasier*. This is the way it usually goes. Success or failure in doing a pilot always occurs in context of what the network needs at any given moment. Shit. Maybe I should've gone to NBC. Too late.

NOVEMBER 2003

George Bush makes secret visit to troops in Iraq over Thanksgiving. Has dinner. Then gets the fuck out. Police raid Michael Jackson's Neverland Ranch looking for evidence supporting allegations that he molested a 12-year-old boy. Apparently the fact that his house is a kiddie playground and he's accused of molestation every other day and looks like a freak isn't considered "evidence." The Paris Hilton sex tape shows up on the Internet. Is it just me, or did she just seem really bored? I mean, the guy's doing all the work and she's just lying there doing her nails and tossing off the occasional, dispirited "Oh, God, fuck me," seemingly just to be polite. Maybe they should've cast someone else.

PRODUCERS

One thing you hear from people when they look at the credits on shows and see a million producers is "Why do they need all those producers?"—the innuendo being "Does it really take that many chefs to make a shit sandwich?" The truth is that most every one of these people began their careers as writers. And they still are. The producing titles come with experience, and represent the hierarchy on writing staffs. Staff writer, Story Editor, Executive Story Editor, Co-Producer, Producer, Supervising Producer, Co-Executive Producer, and Executive Producer. With each credit comes additional responsibility, along with bumps in salary. As well, there is the non-writing Line Producer, who deals with the budget and cost of doing each episode, as well as an Associate Producer, who handles post-production, including all the technical aspects involved in delivering the finished product for broadcast. On occasion, various other Producer titles are handed out, either to the star of the show, his or her manager, or significant other.

Another assumption people make is that you all work on one show every week, then go on to the next. In truth, in any given week, a writing/producing staff is working on this week's show, going over a story outline for a show a month away, giving first draft notes on a script three weeks away, second draft notes on a script two weeks away, doing a rewrite/joke pass on a script going to the table next week, as well as looking at edits and mixes from past shows, going to casting, trying to line up guest stars for sweeps, and dealing with the problems on stage that week. So, do you really need that many producers? The answer is: yeah, sometimes.

As to what producers do—here's an example. On this week's *Becker*, part of the story has to do with Alex Desert's character buying a $500 bottle of Bordeaux, and sharing it with the others so they can all know the experience of drinking such expensive wine. The story leads up to a moment where the entire cast, along with some homeless people who are part of the plot, simultaneously drink the wine and do a spit take, meaning they're so repulsed by the taste they instantly spit it out, showing that this expensive bottle of wine has turned. It's hardly an unfamiliar bit. In fact, it's pretty clammy[41] going all the way back to vaudeville, but it did fit the moment so we decided to embrace its very clamminess and go for it. Nothing complicated. People drink and spit. Then the discussions started.

---

[41] Clammy. A bit, joke, or story that's so old it's almost got a slimy film over it. David Lee, one of the creators of *Wings* and *Frasier* used to use the more genteel phrase, "It seems a bit dusty." Almost universally acknowledged clammy stories are "The Cabin Show," in which the cast gets stuck in a cabin in the woods or some other confined space; The Pregnancy Scare, where the wife fears she's pregnant, though it's usually a false alarm, unless it leads to another clam—The New Baby, which usually comes in around year 5 or 6 when the story lines are running dry; The Camping Trip, a version of The Cabin Show; and The Ruined or Mistaken Identity Dinner Party, revolving around a disastrous party or, in the latter case, some miscommunication, leading to silly hijinks and crosstalk. (Crosstalk: a device through which characters make unintented jokes based on what another character mistakenly believes; e.g., one of the characters is gay, when he really isn't.) Also involved in clammy episodes is the concept of "Schmuckbait," as in a story only a schmuck would believe, or one for which the audience has to suspend a great deal of disbelief, like when a main character says they're leaving, unless, of course, the actor is quitting or was fired, in which case, they do in fact leave. Still, clams aside, it always comes down to execution, and some shows have done great episodes based on clammy stories, like the "Shoebootie" episode of *All In The Family*, where Archie and Meathead got stuck in a meat locker.

First at the production meeting.[42] Do we need to preshoot[43] this scene because everybody's going to get all wet? That was followed by a long discussion with the wardrobe people, who were worried they wouldn't have enough time to get doubles and triples on all the shirts, pants, or jackets, meaning buying two or three of them so the actors can change for another take and it obviously looks like the same piece of clothing. This was further complicated by the fact that all the homeless people on the show needed special wardrobe because even if the wardrobe people bought regular clothes, they would have to look distressed, faded or oily and once they buy it and treat it they can't return it. And they can't just go to a thrift shop and buy shitty clothes because of the need for more than one identical outfit in the same size. So that's going to double or triple their budget for that week and they wanted to made that clear, along with the fact that they were pressed for time and needed to know as soon as possible if this would stay in the show, which is something you often don't even know until you see it in rehearsals and know if it works. Some ideas are great on paper. Hysterical at a table reading. Then they die on stage.

That conversation was followed by another about whether the actors would spit in each other's direction or spit to the side or would they have to actually spit on one another. I make the point that the "spit take" moment is not funny if people are deliberately angling the direction of the spit. It has to be spontaneous and land on other people. That's part of the joke. It won't have a shot otherwise. A short time later I was called to the line producer's office. He was worried because people are actually expelling bodily fluids mixed with grape juice disguised as wine onto someone else,

[42] Production meeting. The meeting of the department heads and producers before each table reading, going over the specifics of that week's production and flagging any concerns or problems.
[43] Pre-shoot. While multi-camera shows are shot in front of an audience, occasionally a scene will be more intricate and will take up too much time on shoot night, so it's done a day before, edited quickly and then shown to the live audience on the monitors, while sound is recorded to capture their laughs and edit in later.

possibly into someone's eye or mouth which could theoretically transmit diseases so he was concerned and wanted to cover our asses and call the Paramount legal department to see whether we had to have actors sign releases. We said fine, go ahead. Unfortunately at these times, bringing up a potential problem to legal can run the risk of raising a red flag so instead of taking a chance that they might be held liable for something, the danger is they'll say don't do it and you've just screwed yourself by bringing up a problem that may not have existed in the first place. An hour later we find out that legal had no problem with it and we were good to go.

So the irony of this is that something they did in vaudeville years ago and has been in so many movies, TV shows, and stage plays that it's become hackneyed, now involves endless discussions about the time it takes, whether you have to shoot it in advance, can you do it in front of the audience, where will they spit, can they get all the wardrobe in time, will it cost too much, and finally if there's a legal problem because somebody's afraid they could get AIDS by being spat on. A sad state of affairs, but nevertheless, if anybody wonders what producing is, that's one of the things that's involved—long discussions about spit. It's one of those moments where your child says "What did you do at work today, daddy?" and you reply that you navigated your way through a complex maze just to make sure that a group of actors could spit on each other. Howard Gewirtz used to say at these moments, after a long pause, "And they pay you like a CEO." Which they do.

November 7

I'm writing (or actually rewriting) my pilot for *The Guys*, per the network notes, thinking that even if it doesn't get on, maybe *Becker* will get picked up for another year and I'll still have work. It's just one of those little denial games you play to handle the fact that your fortunes are subject to the whims of others. But television shows, like people, are mortal. No matter how long your run is, you'll eventually get the call from the studio or network saying you've been cancelled. Sometimes, as it happened on the three shows I did before, it's during your initial run. You either know it's coming or you don't. You either dread it or pray for it, just to make the pain stop. Sometimes you know based on the ratings. You can do six shows and out, thirteen and out, or as in my last case, shoot thirteen, air four and on the day of shooting your thirteenth show, get that call and have to power through the last episode with a lot of tears and emotion.

So while I was in the middle of a rewrite, Tim Berry, the line producer, came in and I could instantly tell by his serious expression that something was off. He said Garry Hart was calling me, a rare occurrence. I suddenly knew what was going on. I went to Tim's office, picked up the phone to hear Garry tell me that he's just spoken to the network and that they're not going to order any more shows. English translation; we're cancelled. I ask if they gave any reason, knowing it didn't matter. All he said was they promised *The Stones* a chance to air and it was going to be in our time slot, which was once their time slot, and so we were done.

I hang up the phone, speak with Tim for a while, then go back in the room and power through the rest of the rewrite. When it was done I asked the rest of the office staff to come in the room and informed them of what was going on. Sadness all around. It's like waiting for someone who's terminally ill to finally pass away. Even though you know it's coming, your emotions in that moment change. You have crossed a bridge, it's officially over and you know you're going to have to start saying good-bye to the writers, the cast, the office staff, and hundreds of crew members. That ritual will begin on Monday morning as producers, cast and crew walk on stage with long faces and we begin the mourning process, which will occur during the last six shows.

Talked to Dave at the end of the day and commiserated. We both knew this was a possibility; still we were hoping against hope that since the show had been given a reprieve and been put back on the air this fall and the ratings were, even by CBS's accounts, pretty good—we'd only fallen off a couple of shares from *King of Queens*, less than one rating point—that we might have pulled off a second chance. Compounding the strangeness, only a day before the head of current programming at CBS called and said they couldn't have been happier with the ratings. Next day—cancellation.

Selfish bastard that I am, my thoughts immediately turn back to my pilot, and the hope that, by Christmas, I might have some indication of whether I'll be going into production, which will certainly affect whatever holiday mood I happen to be in. Still, I have a development deal to fall back on, so I'm not panicking right now, as opposed to most everyone else in the production who will be out of work come December 23, leading to a mad scramble for jobs on existing shows, which is tough as most shows don't look for new staff at this point. Most likely everyone knows they're out of work until May or June (for writers, when new shows hire staff) or April (for production people doing pilots and eventually August for shows that go into production). The sidebar to this is that, chances are, someone you interviewed for a job and didn't hire now has his own show. It's this annual game of musical chairs. Today you pass judgment on someone else, tomorrow the roles are reversed, and they're doing it to you. So other than just being a nice human being in general, there are pragmatic reasons for not pissing too many people off.

Driving up Laurel Canyon on my way home, I start thinking about saying goodbye to people I've spent 5 1/2 years with. At the same time I'm excited about the prospect of getting a shot again with my own show coupled with the fear that a year from now I could be driving the same road at the same time in the same car, having totally crapped out.

Under the heading of misery loves company, I just heard that *Coupling* was cancelled. It was a high-profile show on NBC, with a solid time slot following *Will and Grace*. So much for "time slot hits." *Coupling* was a remake of a British show about three guys and three girls who had all slept together at one point, yet remained fast friends as they jumped in and out of relationships with one another. The English show was smart and the American producers were supposedly using the British scripts almost verbatim. Almost from the beginning, since writers gossip like fishwives, not only about who's fucking whom, but about who's going through what kind of hell on what show, the word filtered back that NBC was all over the producers, meddling at every turn, trying to get them to sex the show up. Even the billboard for the show featured the actors naked behind a banner. No subtlety as to what we're selling. The critics, by and large, stomped all over it. The ratings were poor. They were doing thirteen shows. They aired a few. Got cancelled. And, at the end of the day, NBC president Jeff Zucker's epitaph on the show to a group of critics: "It sucked."

On a side note, I read an interview with one of the creators of the English series, who said that the American executives just didn't get it. Their show was about gender. The American version was just about sex.

Zap2it Print Ready Page

'Coupling' Creators Slam Zucker Comments
By Kate O'Hare

Beryl Vertue, one of the executive producers of both the British and American versions of "Coupling," is taking NBC's swift cancellation of the U.S. show in stride, but the veteran producer does object to what NBC entertainment chief Jeff Zucker said afterward.

"We were outraged," she tells *Zap2it.com*.

In a Nov. 5 *Hollywood Reporter* article about Zucker's appearance the previous day at an International Television Society breakfast panel at New York's Waldorf-Astoria, the NBC chief is quoted as saying, "Some of our programs just sucked."

"I thought it was a dreadfully vulgar thing to say," Vertue says, "unless I'm being too British by far."

In particular reference to "Coupling," which was yanked off NBC's Thursday-night schedule before November sweeps, Zucker said, "We didn't develop the characters well enough. If we had listened to the research, 'Coupling' would not have been on the air."

These comments led to an angry retort from Steven Moffat, the writer of the British version (and Vertue's son-in-law), in a Nov. 6 posting at the Web site of BBC America, which airs the U.K. "Coupling," now going into its fourth season.

"I have no knowledge of the research," Moffat wrote. "Truth is, I don't have much knowledge of anything. I was barred, by NBC, from attending the taping of the second pilot, as was Sue [his wife, and 'Coupling' producer, Sue Vertue], and we were told, quite firmly, to take a creative 'back seat' thereafter.

"So! Four episodes in and cancelled. Well done at the wheel, guys! See that thing on the horizon over there? That'll be our fourth U.K. season. See ya!

"Been keeping my mouth shut about this for a while, professional decorum and all that. But with NBC's shameful backstabbing of its own creative team -- a creative team who were hobbled throughout by NBC's own continual, flat-footed interference -- clearly professional decorum hasn't made it as far as L.A.

"Sometimes shows have to be cancelled. Of course, they do. You can't argue with the backs of a departing audience. But for the head of a network to announce, in public, that the show 'sucked' -- such educated language! -- and pretend he'd never liked it ... words fail me. But not as badly as they appear to fail him."

In the *Philadelphia Enquirer* on Nov. 4, Zucker was also quoted as saying, "It just wasn't working. It was time to move on. Shows come and go all the time. I can't take any of it personally."

In a posting the next day at *bbcamerica.com*, Moffatt wrote, "U.S. 'Coupling' was commissioned by NBC, promoted as the new 'Friends' by NBC [we asked them not to], promoted as the sexiest show on TV by NBC [we begged them not to], promoted as the 'show you're all talking about' by NBC [no one had seen it, how could they be talking about it?], scheduled by NBC, noted to death by NBC, cancelled by NBC, and publicly blamed and disowned by NBC.

"Tell me -- please, I want to know -- at exactly what level of involvement would they take it personally?"

"What I thought was dreadful," Vertue says, "and what made us so angry was that it completely disowned [the show] and, you might say, laid the blame entirely on the American team. That was very unfair. That's what made us annoyed.

"I'm not sure how any series could succeed with that amount of publicity and then not appear as the Second Coming. The sex angle was sold to a ridiculous and actually erroneous degree. It's a show about gender, it's not a show about sex."

Vertue, who received an Order of the British Empire for her television work, has a theory why "Coupling," despite its success in the U.K. and other countries, didn't translate.

"It's now over 30 years since I pioneered the format deal in America," she says, "before people like Jeff Zucker had left school. And those were two huge successes, 'All in the Family' and 'Sanford and Son.' That was because, not only were they terribly good ideas, also Norman Lear was really creative and talented and understood how to do it.

"And the third, most important thing is, he was allowed to do it. He would not accept any interference. That's what I've noticed over the years, this increasing amount of interference in the creative process, to what is now, I think, quite alarming proportions.

"It's like painting by numbers, everybody's having a go of it. And 'Coupling' is my personal experience of how alarming and detrimental that interference has become, not just in our program, but in all of them."

The British "Coupling" has just lost original cast member Richard Coyle, who played the idiosyncratic Jeff.

"He'll kind of just not be there," Vertue says of Jeff's absence. "We'll see what Steven does, because I haven't seen it. He doesn't fall under a train. It's nothing drastic."

In his place is actor Richard Mylan, as a new character, Oliver.

"He will probably eventually be one of the gang," Vertue says. "He's not sitting on the sofa in the first episode, let's put it that way. He has to build himself into that group."

Vertue is also working on transferring another U.K. show, a "quirky" family comedy called "The Savages" to an American network. Asked if it's for NBC, Vertue says, "No."

Not the first time a network's stepped in, screwed with a show, and then backed off when it tanked. I'm sure the mood over there is exactly the same as the mood will be over here. We did good work. Nobody understands. They didn't give us time. Whatever the excuses, you know in your heart they're just excuses. Facts are facts.

You've been cancelled. We'll lick our wounds over the weekend and come back Monday to start planning the last episodes.

November 15

With a newfound desire to concentrate on my pilot, I finally finish a draft and give a copy to my brother and agent. Both say they like it. A few notes, but general praise. Which is all you want to hear. "It's perfect. Don't change a thing." I make some revisions based on their notes, planning to hand it in after Thanksgiving to the studio. Why ruin my holiday sweating out a response. In the meantime I also have to write half of the last episode of *Becker*, and I've also just put my ass on the line by pushing my way to direct the second-to-last episode of the show. My first time directing but I know if I don't do it now I'll never get a chance. It felt very much like the decision to buy my first motorcycle, which took two and a half hours in the showroom of sitting on it and getting off—the male midlife crisis version of a young girl's decision to lose her virginity.

DECEMBER 2003

A bearded and gaunt Saddam Hussein is caught by American troops hiding in an underground bunker. Jubilant Iraqis topple statues and loot his palaces. Bush speaks to the nation: "Let joy be unconfined. The wicked witch is dead." Michael Jackson raises a "V" for victory as he's led into a courtroom to face child molestation charges. Then, to prove he's straight, sticks his tongue through the "v" and wiggles it, provocatively.

December 1

Went over the pilot for what seems like the millionth time, then slapped on a title page, walked it over to Rose Catherine's office and handed it to her personally. We talk for a few minutes, then I tell her I'm going to be busy the next few weeks with the end of *Becker*—co-writing one episode and directing another—so I need her notes as soon as possible. She promises she'll get them to me. Once again, I'm waiting for a phone to ring.

December 3

Get several messages from Rose Catherine's assistant trying to reach me to talk about the script. No message, just "Call back." Oh, shit. Trouble. When people have something good to say, they lead with it. "Call back," means there are problems. Sure enough, when we talk, it starts with "We're happy with most of what's there, there's just a few things that go to character." Essentially they don't get a few of the characters or they're not fleshed out, and—I was waiting for this one—"We need to root more for the main character."

"Rooting interest" is one of those phrases you hear constantly. Why they feel they always need to root for someone, I don't know. It's a comedy show, not the fucking Super Bowl. *Seinfeld* made billions; I've got the DVDs. I watch it in syndication and laugh my ass off over episodes I've seen a hundred times. And I still have no idea who I was rooting for. But I have to account for their notes because they won't turn it in until their thoughts are reflected in the script; but, more importantly, they know how the network thinks, so I know I'm going to be facing the same comments when I get there.

December 16

Haven't been able to touch the pilot in a week because I've been directing my *Becker* episode. It's gone well. The shoot is tonight. I walk onstage to check out the audience. You don't want them too quiet, or too rowdy. Or, as you get once a year, the group from drug rehab who are just glad to be outdoors but tend to nod out between scenes.

I think back to New York, almost twenty-five years ago, sitting in my studio apartment on 2nd Ave, writing spec scripts and jokes for comedians for $25 a pop, having no idea of how Hollywood worked, knowing I wanted to get out here and be part of it, while nursing the underlying fear that I'd never even get close. And twenty-five years later, I'm on a Paramount sound stage, yelling Action and Cut, feeling like I reached some sort of goal. I try to stop for a moment to appreciate it which, amid all the bitching, is occasionally necessary. I once had lunch with a friend, Sally Robinson, a writer who gave me my first job, and we got on the subject of happiness. I said I thought it was basically a myth. That all we can hope for in life were moments, maybe a half-dozen or so, to play back on our deathbed. First kiss. First love. Getting married. Holding your newborn child. And mingled in there somewhere, some kind of career success, or at least the achievement of some personal milestone. I guess this seemed like one. So, I savor it for a minute...then resume agonizing about this pilot, hoping it gets picked up, shot, and on the air, and knowing that the odds are ultimately against any of that happening. The momentary appreciation of life fades quickly into the more ever-present neurosis and fear of failure.

December 23

We wrap our final *Becker* episode of the season, 129th of the series, two days before Christmas. I also turn in a revised copy of the pilot, reflecting the notes I got from the earlier draft. If by some miracle the pilot goes, I already have most of the essential production people from *Becker* ready to jump on it. We can use the same offices, though I hope not the same stage. It would feel lousy to be walking over the bones of this show. Still, that's not today's problem.

The mood onstage is bittersweet. We had a good run, genuinely liked each other personally and professionally, and wanted it to go on. It didn't. Everybody says the right things, "I'll keep in touch." And at the end of the day everyone moves on because they have to.

Caught a glimpse of an article, an interview with Les Moonves about the CBS schedule. Much of it just the party line, "We're in great shape," though the last line was "I don't see us needing much new product in 2004-2005," which is always encouraging if you have a pilot under consideration. Also ran into a writer I know who ran a hit show for a couple years until he was unceremoniously booted out, but with a huge golden parachute as a way of softening the blow. His comment on the experience: he said he felt like he "had a winning lottery ticket shoved up his ass." Perfect. Describes much of what goes on here.

December 29

Rose Catherine calls. Very happy with the rewrite. They're sending it on to CBS. So this year's work is over. I can now relax over the holidays. Or I could if I was genetically and culturally disposed to relaxation. Which I'm not. Either way, no more work to do until January.

JANUARY, 2004

Happy New Year. War still on. Michael Jackson charged with child molestation. Circle of life.

January 1

Sitting home pondering what misery there is to come in the new year and do what I usually do to relax—turn on the TV. Oh shit, it's the Rose Parade.

I HATE A PARADE

I hate a parade. Pretty much across the board. Although, growing up in New York, I have some affection for the Macy's Thanksgiving Day Parade with its overactive thyroid Snoopys and Underdogs. At least you can stand there and go: "Wow, that's a big Snoopy." Or "Hey, check out that huge Underdog." And they mix it up a bit. But the fucking Rose Parade. Old-money Pasadena's gift to the nation. I guess the Republican idea of a ripping good time is to tart up a Chevy with flowers around some goofball theme, stick a debutante on top doing the Queen's wave, and slowly motor down the street, backed up by the thumping rhythms of the obligatory marching band pounding out white-people funk while two inane commentators narrate the procession.

"Ooh, here's a Chevy with 50,000 American Beauty roses commemorating international brotherhood. And how about that band." And it's the same shit year after year after year. It's not like there's going to be a surprise. It's cars and roses and teenage girls on top, and still people camp out overnight just to get a good spot like they've been told aliens are going to land and start handing out cash. It was with this holiday spirit that I prepared to go into the new year, hoping my show gets picked up so that I can bring a smile to the face of America.

January 2

Real development. No squeezing in a spec pilot while working in production. There's no more production, other than editing and maybe going to a mix of the show I directed. This is pure development deal. I set up my office on the lot, with a computer, an assistant, a modest expense account, and an obscene salary, along with the brand-new pressure to get this pilot picked up. Considering most people I worked with are now unemployed, this is not a bad position to be in.

Development deals are what you make of them. Many writers use the time to play golf twice a week, with side trips to Vegas, or weeks in Hawaii, eventually phoning in an idea for a show. Like an asshole, I plan to show up every day for work, motivated less by an American work ethic than by fear of failure. I fish out a couple pilots I'd been playing with over the years and think about rewriting them. I have lunch with colleagues to discuss any ideas we might want to pursue together. I check my email often and wonder exactly why it is I'm not in Vegas getting lap dances on the company dime.

As I prepare to dive into this, it occurs to me that I have to stop thinking as a writer—getting passionate about one project that may or may not go into production. I have to diversify and get as many things going as possible, whether or not I'm passionate about them, because networks can be passion-killers, chipping away at the soul of an idea, then with almost radar-like precision, zooming in on your half-dozen favorite jokes and killing them as well—sort of like Keyser Soze in *The Usual Suspects* in that flashback scene where he kills someone's entire family before burning their house down. Just to make sure nothing lives in this spot—ever. But their ability to rub out your favorite jokes is no accident. By and large, the ones that make you laugh the hardest will be the riskiest ones. Those die an early death because they are the jokes they'll never let through. The fart jokes stay in. For some reason, the things we laugh at are the things that are most natural to us as human beings while being the very things we're most disconnected with, embarrassed about, and afraid of—namely, sex, bodily functions, bodily fluids and death. In over 300 shows in front of live audiences, I've never seen a fart joke die.

January 12

I've heard nothing on the pilot and am now officially neurotic, sweating out a reaction. Another Hollywood equation: success=love. The way people treat you is contingent on your level of success. If this pilot goes I will be inundated with calls from agents, representing writers, actors and directors all looking for work. They will say they're thrilled for me, reminding me of whatever personal connection we might have, and act as if we're old friends. If it doesn't happen, I will be inundated with silence, apathy and will have to start over again. Years of work for nothing. Money, success, ego gratification, prestige and, most of all, the opportunity to do more work and have your ideas received with greater respect. At the moment, all this hangs on one phone call. This may seem overly dramatic, but anyone who has ever waited out one of these phone calls knows exactly what I'm talking about.

January 13

I get a call from Rose Catherine's assistant saying they want to have a meeting over the phone on Wednesday at 5:00 to discuss the script. No reaction, no comment, no nothing. Just word of a meeting being set. Once again, I smell bad things. I try calling her back for specifics. She's in meetings. She'll call back. So I wait. And wait. I fucking hate this.

January 14

I'm in a post-production house on Sunset Boulevard in Hollywood, looking at a mix of the *Becker* episode I directed and still sweating out the silence, though, at least to divert my attention, in the last two days I lost a credit card and had a car accident. Life's way of reminding you that if you thought you've been fucked over enough, there's always more it can do. Then my cell phone rings. My agent and brother, together. Right away I know this isn't good. And it's made worse by the fact that my cell phone has a bad connection and I can't get a damn signal. So I run around the halls, finally making it outside to the back alley where the reception is better so that I can stand there amid the garbage cans and sun-baked trash and clearly hear my agent say, "The network has problems with the script."

The top line—it's too dark. Too depressing. These guys aren't fun to be around. Where is the fun going to come from? The key word, if you're trying to discern what they're looking for, is "fun." They're also afraid it doesn't fit the other shows on their network. Now, most of the other shows on their network suck ass so, at first, I take this as a compliment. I'm now in full defensive mode, but one lesson I've learned is that things are what they are. All the bitching and complaining about the unfairness of it all amounts to absolutely nothing. And so, along with my worst fears being confirmed, I now have to wait a day until 5:00 to have this phone session and find out exactly what they want changed. Which won't matter because I'm starting with a foot in the hole. But I'll go through the formality of taking their notes, giving them back a rewrite that I'll break my balls on, and try not to lose my soul in the process. Their response will be, and I can predict this right now, "We like it. We appreciate the changes you made. We just think the subject matter is too rough or too dark for us so thank you but we're going to pass."

And while part of the grieving process at this point is thinking you can get the script back and sell it to another network, the only places I think might be interested would be NBC or Fox. This is probably not an ABC show. Compared to the half-hours on ABC right now, the CBS lineup looks like a slasher film.

This experience begins to remind me of a similar incident the day I moved out to LA in 1987. I'd already been here for a summer. I'd optioned a movie to Zanuck/Brown and was doing a rewrite. But in the process I was hooked up at Lorimar because my brother's boss was running the studio and they wanted a rewrite on, of all things, a mummy movie. So I pitched my version and got the assignment, along with a one-year development deal which was my ticket out of New York and into L.A. I worked feverishly on the script, doing draft after draft. Went home to New York to pack up my wife, stepdaughter and cat, and moved into an apartment in Beverly Hills. The second we landed, I called my brother to see what they thought of the script. Silence. Then, "They have problems." Turns out, this was code for "They hated it." No specifics. Just hate.

Cut to three months of trying to get a meeting with the VP of Development to get some feedback. Getting meetings cancelled over and over. Finally, I get in. Ten people in the room. The producers, assistants, assistants' assistants, and I make my plea to the exec. "Give me specifics. Tell me what you want." I'm on my hands and knees. "Just tell me what you want changed," I say. "I don't like failing on assignments." Her reply: "I don't give a fuck about your personal philosophies. I'm here to make movies." Welcome to Hollywood.

Sixteen, seventeen years later I'm having the same experience all over again. In some ways it never stops. The only way to make it stop is to get a hit. Another equation in the quantum physics of show business: one hit equals multiple opportunities and the power to ignore notes you don't agree with. But first you need the hit.

January 15

Went in for my notes meeting. We huddled around the speakerphone like cave dwellers around fire, waiting for the network voices to arise from the box. After a few seconds of fake pleasantries, they launch into their notes, again starting with the obligatory "We liked (not loved) your script." In my mind, I can see them rolling their eyes. Still, I get their "top line." It's too dark." "Too mean." "It's not fun to be around these guys." "We need to see the fun of hanging around them." She singles out a few moments on several pages and, as is their nature, killed two or three of my favorite jokes pronouncing them "too mean" or "too snarky." I sigh, say "fine" and let them go, as it's suicide to try to shove anything down their throats at this point.

In a somewhat odd moment and in an effort toward conciliation, I offer to strip away a character's back-story[44] of being a widower and make him happily married instead. She said, no, she liked that part. It made you pull for the character. In all, it takes about twenty minutes, then fifteen more for the post-mortem after we hang up. Rose Catherine assures me this was not the waste of time I knew it was, saying their going page-by-page showed sincere interest; otherwise it would have simply been sweeping generalizations. I'm given a week to turn around another draft.

I walk out toward the parking lot, mulling over a game plan, but knowing I have none. The only shot I have is to take the script I loved writing and turn it into their version of a network television show. I also had to navigate the political waters. If I don't give them what they want, they bury it. If I do, then maybe they pass it on with some enthusiasm. I have been reading in the trades about the networks picking up their drama pilots and I know of several comedy pilots already beginning production, so this is the eleventh hour. I have to get this draft to the studio by Wednesday so they

---

[44] Backstory. A character's personal history.

can read it that night, give me more notes Thursday so I can rewrite Thursday and Friday and get them yet another new draft on Friday so it can go back to the network for the "weekend read," studio/network parlance for the ton of scripts they take home and have to plow through before Monday. Still, in my heart, I know it's dead. According to my agent, who has always had the ability to tell me what I need to know instead of what I want to hear, I have an uphill battle.

Additionally, I read online this morning that CBS has picked up yet a third installment of *CSI*, this time set in New York. This is fast becoming the franchise for CBS that *Law & Order* is for NBC. (Why not just drop the pretense and change the name of the network from CBS to CSI?) But every hour drama that gets on represents two half-hour comedies that don't. It also occurs to me that this will make three shows on the network that have to do with dead bodies, crime scenes, and autopsies of victims who were brutally murdered and abused in the most vile ways the writers can think of. That's OK to show on one-hour TV. You just can't joke about it in a half-hour comedy. But, what the fuck. That's the way it is so, as an act of faith, I decide to keep rewriting, opening my mind to try to give them what they want.

January 20

I submit my most recent revision to Paramount a day earlier than requested because I have to start jury duty today. It's a case of acquaintance rape. Having worked in television all these years, I'm familiar with the concept. In fact, I'm waiting to be called as an expert witness.

January 22

Paramount likes the rewrite, albeit with some last-minute

notes. I work all night and get it back to them for Friday morning as I rush back to jury duty, asking them to call if any last-minute revisions are needed. No call. No need. I assume it went back to CBS for the weekend. I know it's not going to happen, but in the back of my mind I feel like I've answered all their notes so, curse me, I've got hope again. Asshole, I'll just never learn.

January 30

Silence=Death. Also, Death=Death. No word from CBS. Still hoping against hope, knowing all the while that good news travels immediately and bad news hangs back like a mugger in a dark alley waiting to strike. Finally couldn't stand the suspense any longer so I call my agent to see if he can scope it out. He does and calls back. Bad news. They didn't like the rewrite. Chances are like 95% it's a pass. I take the hit and walk around with it for the afternoon, thinking about other scripts I've been working on, trying not to dwell on the fact that this represents several years' work down the drain. A few hours later I talk to the Paramount VP, who confirms it. "They appreciated the work but still wanted it lighter." Short of putting in kids and a puppy I don't know what to do. At this point, short of a miracle, this project is dead.

FEBRUARY 2004

Creators of NBC's "Will & Grace" file a multi-million dollar lawsuit against the network, claiming they failed to negotiate a fair license fee; in short, screwing them out of money. After much fanfare and pre-game analysis, Mel Gibson's "Passion of the Christ" opens huge. Christians rejoice. Mel Gibson rejoices even more. Variety reports Jesus has hired an attorney and is suing for larger cut of the profits. (I wonder if he'll hire a Jewish lawyer.) Either way, good luck finding the money.

Turning water into wine is one thing. Turning studio gross revenues into participants' profit participation is occasionally quite another. (See "studio accounting," or "ledger-de-main.")

February 1

With no project in play, I am officially a writer alone on a development deal. And what better day to contemplate how the American public might want to be entertained than to watch the Super Bowl—this bloated circus that once upon a time was a football game. It opens with some military type walking Beyonce to midfield to belt out the national anthem while American flags are unfurled and choppers fly over the stadium. Basically a *Wag the Dog*-style promo for war. Watching this spectacle, my first reaction was to put my hand over my heart and regurgitate every meal I've ever eaten, back to and including mother's milk.

Then, just to add insult, I'm in the bathroom when Justin Timberlake exposes Janet Jackson's breast. Fifty near-naked cheerleaders on either sideline, flashing ass and cleavage, and the country goes batshit over one bare tit, leading to millions of angry calls, emails and "imagine my pain" letters to the networks. These are the letters that occasionally show up at production offices over a joke in an episode that—who knew—was construed as offensive by someone. The letter usually begins with the phrase "Imagine my pain as I sat down to watch your show, and..." You get the idea. We got a few on *Wings*, and one on *Becker* for making fun of the name of a disease called "Asperger's Syndrome." I know it's serious, but c'mon, I defy anyone to hear that and not think Ass Burgers.

February 2

Back in my office, checking the trades to see which pilots are being picked up. Mostly family fare. People reuniting with families they haven't seen, lost or estranged relatives showing up on doorsteps (a perennial network favorite), single parents struggling to take care of children. Same shit, different faces. I can play sour grapes for a while, bitching about how mundane and ordinary they all seem, but the truth is that it ultimately doesn't do any good and in reality I have no idea how good any of these shows might be because the one-line descriptions always sound the same. There's no way to tell how good they really are until you either read the pilot or see the final cut. I know it's time to stop bitching and move on.

February 20

A friend, Wayne Rice, who has written and produced features (*Suicide Kings; Dude, Where's My Car?*) pitches me a TV idea. Very simple. About his family growing up. It's safe, familiar, very TV-friendly. After the year I've had of trying to fight the system, I figure it couldn't hurt to pitch something they're familiar with. I call Kevin at Paramount. He thinks it might be right for Fox. We talk about setting up a time to come in and pitch in a couple weeks.

MARCH 2004

Kobe Bryant goes to trial in Colorado, wearing a "How did I fuck up this bad" expression as he strolls into the courtroom with his white, female attorney (what are the odds) by his side. Somehow I don't think you want Johnnie Cochran in on this one. The one-year anniversary of the US invasion of Iraq. Martha Stewart found guilty.

As the world falls apart I focus on what's important and call to set up a meeting to go in with my friend and pitch his family show. We're set for April 15. Hurry up and wait.

APRIL 2005

In a colossal non-event, Bill Rancic gets hired as the first Apprentice, on the show "The Apprentice." He's immediately given a silly hard hat along with marching orders to relocate to Chicago and supervise the construction of a new Trump high-rise. Before he leaves, the Donald takes him aside, kisses him on both cheeks, and whispers in his ear: "It's just a make-pretend TV show. You go anywhere near that building, I'll cut your balls off." (He's since "quit the project" and reappeared on the show as a judge.) In what seems like a similar non-event, John Kerry emerges as Democratic front-runner in the U.S. presidential race. (He lost.) Howard Dean locks himself in a room and kicks himself in the ass repeatedly, causing him to make that shrieking/whooping noise that made him look like a maniac in the first place and cost him the nomination.

April 12

The Hollywood Reporter publishes the list of 125 pilot orders. 71 half-hour comedies, 54 one-hour dramas, along with sidebar interviews with the respective network executives. Out of about 500 scripts, the networks green-lit a quarter, so you can imagine that every single writer went through a version of the same agonizing process of writing, notes, phone calls, and more rewrites. That's a lot of angst, but at least these fuckers got to go into production, with a chance to get on the fall schedule or be picked up for midseason. Over the course of the season, we'll track how they do.

COMEDY

Unt. Rodney Carrington

Studio: Touchstone TV
Prod. Team: Ric Swartzlander, David Himelfarb
Synopsis: Family show based on Carrington's comedy routine; Carrington, Jennifer Aspen star

Earthquake (presentation)
- Touchstone TV, Tollin/Robbins Prods.
- L. Firestein, M. Tollin, B. Robbins, J. Davola, D. Himelfarb, D. Goldman
- Earthquake as unlucky father of four

Unt. Victor Fresco (presentation)
- Paramount Network TV
- Victor Fresco
- Lewis Black in a workplace high-school comedy

The Furst Family
- Touchstone TV/Granada TV
- Alan Zweibel
- Blue-collar family show starring Laurie Metcalf, Marissa Jaret Winokur, French Stewart

Unt. J.L. Hewitt (presentation)
- Touchstone TV/Handprint Entertainment
- Gabe Sachs, Jeff Judah, Jennifer Love Hewitt
- Sports producer (Jennifer Love Hewitt) unwillingly becomes on-camera reporter; Ed O'Neill co-stars

Hot Mom
- Warner Bros. TV
- Suzanne Martin, Andy Ackerman
- Hip wedding planner/single mom (Gina Gershon) and her more conservative teen daughter

I Married Sofia
- Touchstone/DDJ
- Don Reo, Damon Wayans, Jeff Sagansky
- Colombian actress (Sofia Vergara) pays an American (Joe Lawrence) to marry her for a green card

Plan B
- Universal Network TV, Sternin/Ventimilia Prods.
- Joshua Sternin, Jeffrey Ventimilia
- Thirtysomething single woman (Caroline Rhea) juggles romance, career, weight; w/ Willie Garson

Savages
- Universal Network TV/Icon Prods.
- M. Scully, J. Thacker-Scully, M. Gibson, B. Davey
- Fireman father (Keith Carradine) raises five boys

Untitled Jessica Simpson
- Touchstone TV
- Gayle Abrams, Ted Harbert, Joe Simpson
- Pop culture star (Simpson) creates chaos when she joins a TV newsmagazine as a reporter

Untitled Staley/Long
- Touchstone TV
- Timothy Fall, Dan Staley, Rob Long
- Man (T.E. Scott) and his estranged father (W. Devane) reconnect when they become dads

Untitled John Stamos
- 20th Century Fox TV/Brad Grey TV
- A. Winsberg, T. Doyle, B. Grey, J. Stamos
- Couple (Stamos, Madchen Amick) on a daylong date, chronicled over an entire season

Untitled Joel Stein
- Warner Bros. TV/Acme Prods.
- J. Stein, M. McCall, M. Schultheis, M. Hanel
- Young reporter (Colin Hanks) at a top magazine

Thank God It's Monday
- Touchstone TV
- Warren Bell
- Guys talk about their home life at work

DRAMA

Blind Justice
- Paramount Network TV/Steven Bochco Prods.
- M. Olmstead, N. Wootton, S. Bochco
- Police officer (Ron Eldard) blinded on the job

The Catch (midseason)
- Touchstone TV
- J.J. Abrams
- Centers on two bounty hunters (Greg Grunberg, Orlando Jones)

Countdown
- Touchstone TV/FremantleMedia
- Graham Yost, Marla Ginsburg
- SWAT team handles the final 43 minutes of a major crisis in real time; w/ Jason O'Mara

The DeMarco Affairs
- 20th Century Fox TV/David E. Kelley Prods.
- J. Katims, D.E. Kelley, J. Pontell
- Three sisters (S. Blair, L. Sloane, S. Lloyd) run the family's wedding-planning business

Desperate Housewives
- Touchstone TV
- Marc Cherry, Chuck Pratt, Michael Edelstein
- The secret lives of four suburban women (F. Huffman, T. Hatcher, E. Longoria, M. Cross)

Doing It
- Touchstone TV
- G. Sachs, J. Judah, S. Bloomberg, F. Calfo
- The sexual antics of three teen boys in Seattle

Empire (series order)
- Taranus Ltd./Storyline Entertainment
- T. Wheeler, C. Johannessen, C. Zadan, N. M
- Julius Caesar's nephew Gaius Octavius a the disgraced gladiator tapped to protect him

Eyes
- Warner Bros. TV/McNamara Paper Products
- John McNamara
- The workings of high-tech risk management corporation; Tim Daly, AJ Langer star

Gramercy Park
- Warner Bros. TV/the Tannenbaum Co.
- S. Robinson, E. Tannenbaum, K. Tannenbaum
- Three nannies working at a tony N.Y. building

Harry Green and Eugene
- Paramount/ Frequency Films/Littlefield Co.
- J. Wyman, S. West, W. Littlefield, J. Polhemus
- L.A. private eye Harry Green (Mark Valley) and his inept brother, Eugene (Jason Segel)

Kat Plus One
- Warner Bros. TV/ Berlanti-Liddell Prods.
- G. Berlanti, M. Friedman, M. Liddell
- N.Y. publicist's (Marisa Coughlan) life changes when she has to raise her nephew

Untitled David E. Kelley (series order)
- 20th Century Fox TV/David E. Kelley Prods.
- David E. Kelley
- Legal show centered on "The Practice's" Alan Shore (James Spader); w/ William Shatner

Lost (pilot plus 6 scripts)
- Touchstone TV
- J.J. Abrams, Damon Lindelof
- Crash survivors on a mysterious desert island; Dominic Monaghan, Matthew Fox co-star

The Service
- Touchstone TV
- A. Kurtzman-Counter, R. Orci, F. Calfo
- Married woman (S.W. Callies) works for t Secret Service; Shohreh Aghdashloo co-stars

Untitled Shonda Rhimes
- Touchstone TV
- Shonda Rhimes, Mark Gordon
- Female residents in a surgical training program; Ellen Pompeo, Patrick Dempsey star

COMEDY

Untitled Jason Alexander

Studio: Regency TV/CBS Prods.
Prod. Team: Jeff Martin, Lindy De Koven, Jason Alexander
Synopsis: Jason Alexander as a columnist, TV sports co-anchor and father of two; Malcolm-Jamal Warner co-stars

The Amazing Westerbergs

- Sony Pictures TV/CBS Prods.
- Jay Scherick, David Ronn
- Two brothers (Chris O'Donnell, Jay Harrington), raised to think they're special, realize they're not; Monica Potter co-stars

Center of the Universe

- Warner Bros. TV, CBS Prods., Tannenbaum Co., Katlin/Bernstein Prods.
- Mitchel Katlin, Nat Bernstein, Eric Tannenbaum, Kim Tannenbaum
- Family man (John Goodman) tries to keep the peace with his extended Chicago family; Jean Smart, Olympia Dukakis, Diedrich Bader co-star

Untitled Andrew Kennedy

- Sony Pictures TV/CBS Prods.
- Andy Gordon, Eileen Conn
- Centers on a young couple (Kennedy, Christa Miller) whose parents (John Ratzenberger, Julia Duffy) are in their lives

Saint Louie

- Warner Bros. TV/Mohawk Prods.
- Bruce Rasmussen, Bruce Helford, Deborah Oppenheimer
- New York couple (Louis C.K., Cynthia Watros) overcomplicate the raising of their 2-year-old; Evan Handler co-stars

Untitled Staley/Long

- Paramount Network TV
- Dan Staley, Rob Long
- Young cop's widow (Ricki Lake) and her mom (Kirstie Alley) raise the widow's kids and run a bar frequented by cops

Taste

- Regency TV/CBS Prods.
- Kirk Rudell
- Culinary school graduate (Jane Krakowski) gets her first shot at a high-pressure restaurant job; Richard Ruccolo co-stars

Untitled Aisha Tyler

- Warner Bros. TV/Is or Isn't Entertainment
- Bill Martin, Mike Schiff, Lisa Kudrow, Dan Bucatinsky
- Single New York woman (Tyler) leaves an edgy fashion house to get a corporate job; Adam Goldberg, Richard Kind co-star

Vinyl Cafe

(presentation, midseason)

- Paramount Network TV
- Phil Rosenthal, Steve Skrovan, Saul Rubinek, Eleanor Reid
- Animated show based on Stuart McLean's short stories about an idiosyncratic family of four

Washington Street

(cast-contingent, midseason)

- Warner Bros. TV/CBS Prods.
- Julie Ann Larson
- The tenants in a modest apartment building form a family led by a nurturing single mom

DRAMA

Bounty Hunter

- Spelling TV
- Terri Hughes, Ron Milbauer, Aaron Spelling, E. Duke Vincent, Rod Holcolmb, John Wirth
- Father (Robert Forster) and his two sons earn a living as bounty hunters; Lauren Holly co-stars

Clubhouse

- Spelling TV/Icon Prods.
- Daniel Cerone, Mel Gibson, Bruce Davey, Aaron Spelling, E. Duke Vincent
- Coming-of-age drama about a Yankees batboy (Jeremy Sumpter); Mare Winningham, Dean Cain, Christopher Lloyd co-star

Colderon (presentation)

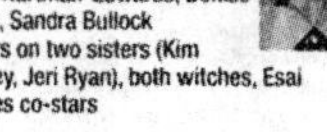

- Warner Bros. TV/CBS Prods./ DiNovi Pictures/Fortis Films
- Becky Hartman-Edwards, Denise DiNovi, Sandra Bullock
- Centers on two sisters (Kim Delaney, Jeri Ryan), both witches, Esai Morales co-stars

Cooking Lessons

- Warner Bros. TV/the Tannenbaum Co.
- Emily Fox, Eric Tannenbaum, Kim Tannenbaum
- Centers on a woman (Lisa Lackey) who writes a food column; Paula Marshall, Constance Zimmer, Gil Bellows co-star

CSI: NY (series order)

- CBS Prods./ Alliance Atlantis/ Bruckheimer TV
- Anthony Zuiker, Carol Mendelsohn, Ann Donahue, Jerry Bruckheimer, Jonathan Littman, Andrew Lipsitz
- Spinoff of "CSI: Miami" about CSIs in New York; Gary Sinise, Melina Kanakaredes star

Dr. Vegas

- Warner Bros. TV/CBS Prods./ Bender Brown Prods.
- John Herzfeld, Lawrence Bender, Kevin Brown
- Centers on an unconventional Las Vegas casino physician (Rob Lowe); Joe Pantoliano co-stars

Nice Guys (midseason)

- Warner Bros. TV/Silver Pictures TV/ Shoe Money Prods.
- Shane Black, Anthony Bagarozzi, Joel Silver, Thomas Schlamme, Shaun Cassidy
- Centers on two Los Angeles private eyes

Numbers

- Paramount Network TV/Scott Free Prods.
- Ridley Scott, Tony Scott, Cheryl Heuton, Nick Falacci
- Mathematician from MIT (David Krumholtz) is recruited by his FBI agent brother (Gabriel Macht) to help solve crimes; Peter MacNicol, Michael Rooker co-star

Wanted

- Warner Bros. TV/25C Prods./CBS Prods.
- Cynthia Cidre, Sarah Timberman, Carl Beverly, Thomas Carter, Gregory Hoblit
- Thriller set in the fugitive section of the LAPD; Scott Glenn, Yancey Arias star

The Webster Report

- Warner Bros. TV/25C Prods./ CBS Prods.
- Theresa Rebeck, Sarah Timberman, Carl Beverly, Barry Sonnenfeld
- Centers on an offbeat private investigator (Stanley Tucci) in New York; w/ Bobby Cannavale, Ben Gazzara

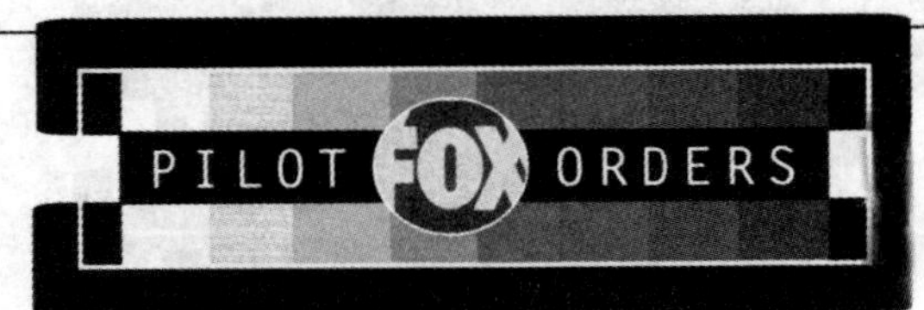

COMEDY

American Dad
(presentation, midseason)

Studio: 20th Century Fox TV
Prod. Team: Seth MacFarlane, Mike Barker, Matt Weitzman
Synopsis: Animated family comedy

Blue Aloha (presentation, midseason)
- Carsey-Werner-Mandabach
- B. Forrester, M. Carsey, T. Werner, C. Mandabach
- Animated family comedy set in Hawaii

The Boondocks
(presentation, midseason)
- Sony Pictures TV
- Aaron McGruder, Reggie Hudlin
- Animated comedy based on the comic strip

The Phil Hendrie Show
(presentation, midseason)
- 20th Century Fox TV
- Phil Lord, Christopher Miller, Steve Levitan
- Animated family comedy about a radio talk show host/family man (Hendrie)

Unt. Katz/Snyder
(presentation, midseason)
- Touchstone TV, Wass/Stein Prods.
- J. Katz, T. Snyder, N. Wass, G. Stein
- Animated family comedy; w/ voices of Jonathan Katz, Lisa Kudrow

The Kelsey Grammer Sketch Show (presentation)
- Grammnet Prods./Avalon TV
- K. Grammer, S. Stark, D. Patterson, J. Thoday
- U.S. version of an ITV sketch comedy series

Lucky Us
- 20th Century Fox TV/Original TV
- H. Hester, N. Moritz, M. Adelstein, D. Parouse
- Pair (Chyler Leigh, Ethan Embry) go on a blind date and end up having a baby

Method & Red (series order)
- Regency TV/20th Century Fox TV
- Kell Cahoon, Will Gluck
- Centers on two rappers (Method Man, Redman) living in an affluent suburb

Mr. Ed
- 20th Century Fox TV/Original TV
- M. Pennette, N. Moritz, M. Adelstein, D. Parouse
- New take on the classic Saturday Evening Post stories w/ Sherman Hemsley as voice of Mr. Ed; David Alan Basche, Sherilyn Fenn star

The Perez Family (cast-contingent)
- Carsey-Werner-Mandabach/Martin-Stein Co.
- M. Perez, M. Carsey, T. Werner, C. Mandabach, S. Martin, J. Stein
- Multigenerational Cuban-American family in Miami through the eyes of a 16-year-old boy

Quintuplets
- 20th Century Fox TV/Imagine TV
- Mark Reisman, Brian Grazer, David Nevins
- Centers on 15-year-old quintuplets; Andy Richter, Rebecca Creskoff star

Related by Family
- Paramount Network TV
- Victor Fresco
- Blended family with two very different teenagers forced to live under the same roof; Amy Yasbeck, Mathew Glave star

The Robinson Brothers
- 20th Century Fox TV/Original TV
- M. O'Keefe, M. Adelstein, N. Moritz, D. Parouse
- Centers on three adult brothers (Dave Annable, Jay Baruchel, Eddie McClintock)

Untitled Chris Rock
- 20th Century Fox TV/3 Arts TV
- Chris Rock, Saladin Patterson, Ali LeRoi, Michael Rotenberg, Dave Becky
- Coming-of-age comedy loosely based on Rock's experience growing up

Sorry Charlie
- Sony Pictures TV/Jersey TV
- Michael Jacobs, Danny DeVito, Michael Shamberg, Stacey Sher, John Landgraf
- Parents struggle with the fact that their kids are growing up; Stephen Root stars

Spellbound (midseason)
- Warner Bros. TV
- R. Greenberg, S. Martin, A. Ackerman
- Modern-day male witch falls in love with a mortal woman

Sweden, OH
- Warner Bros. TV
- Bill Fritz, Kurt Voelker, Greg Malins
- Teen boy's life changes when a sexy swedish exchange student (Helena Mattsson) moves in

DRAMA

The Deerings
- 20th Century Fox TV
- Gretchen Berg, Aaron Harberts, Shawn Levy
- Dysfunctional blended family with five kids; D. W. Moffett, Noelle Beck star

Hollywood Division
- Universal Network TV
- Barry Schindel, Robert Port
- Detectives investigate crimes in Hollywood; w/ D.J. Cotrona, Nathan Fillion

House
- Universal Network TV/Heel & Toe Films
- P. Attanasio, D. Shore, K. Jacobs, B. Singer
- Team of doctors diagnose the toughest medical cases; w/ Hugh Laurie, Omar Epps

The Inside
- 20th Century Fox TV/Imagine TV
- K. Bigelow, T. Kessler, B. Grazer, D. Nevins
- Young FBI agent (Rachel Nichols) goes undercover in a high school; Peter Facinelli co-stars

Johnny Zero
- Warner Bros. TV/John Wells Prods.
- John Wells, R. Scott Gemmill, Llewellyn Wells
- Ex-con (Franky G) struggles to go legit and becomes a PI; GQ co-stars

The Jury (series order)
- 20th Century Fox TV
- Tom Fontana, James Yoshimura, Barry Levinson, James Finnerty
- Legal drama from the point of view of a New York jury; w/ Billy Burke, Shalom Harlow

The North Shore (series order)
- 20th Century Fox TV
- Peter Elkoff, Bert Salke, Chris Brancato
- "Upstairs, Downstairs" look at the guests & staffers at Hawaiian hotel; Kristoffer Polaha, Navi Rawat co-star

Point Pleasant
- 20th Century Fox TV/Original TV
- M. Noxon, J. McLaughlin, N. Moritz, M. Adelstein, D. Parouse
- Beachside community turns upside down w. a girl (Elisabeth Harnois) washes ashore

Ricochet
- Touchstone TV
- Rene Echevarria, Jeff Kline
- Cop drama in the vein of "Memento"; Josh Hopkins, Johnny Messner, Dondre Whitfield co-star

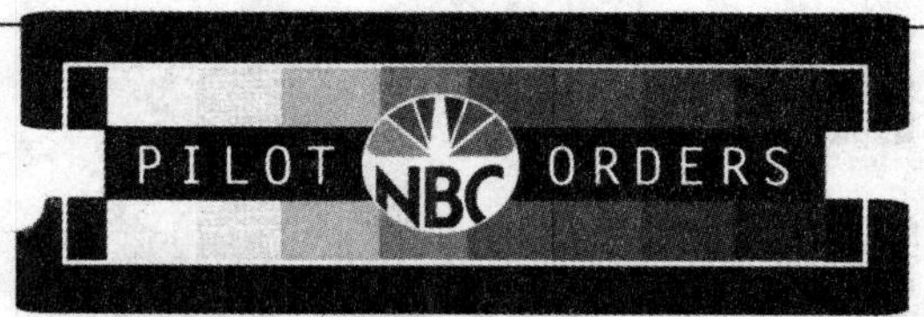

COMEDY

Beverly Hills S.U.V.
Studio: NBC Studios
Prod. Team: Larry Wilmore
Synopsis: Colorful, unlikely ensemble of salespeople at an upscale Beverly Hills car boutique; Jeffrey Nordling, Henry Winkler star

D.O.T.S.
- Pariah
- Todd Greenwald, Rob Cohen, Gavin Polone
- Set in the world of meter maids; Steve Hytner, Stephen Dunham co-star

Everyday Life
- Universal Network TV
- Rob Reiner, Dan Paige, Sue Paige, Alan Greisman
- Part scripted/part improv comedy about a family of shrinks; Reiner, Mercedes Ruehl, Josh Radnor, Mary Gallagher star

Father of the Pride
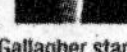
(series order)
- DreamWorks TV
- Jonathan Groff, Peter Mehlman, Jeffrey Katzenberg, Jon Pollack
- Lions performing in Siegfried & Roy's show; w/ voices of John Goodman, Cheryl Hines, Carl Reiner, Orlando Jones

Foster Hall
- NBC Studios/Conaco Prods./E. Gerson Saines Prods.
- Christopher Moynihan, Conan O'Brien, Jeff Ross, A.J. Morewitz, Tom Palmer, Ron West, Emily Gerson Saines
- Brother (Macaulay Culkin) and sister (Busy Philipps) reunite after years of being bumped from foster home to foster home; Greg Germann co-stars

The Friendlys
- NBC Studios
- Robb Cullen, Mark Cullen
- Recently deceased mogul's boozy wife (Ana Gasteyer) and his daughter (Julie Bowen) wrangle over the business; Dave Foley co-stars

Untitled Heline/Heisler
- NBC Studios
- DeAnn Heline, Eileen Heisler
- Love story between two people (Josh Cooke, Jennifer Finnigan) whose biggest obstacle is themselves

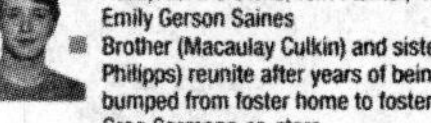

Joey (series order)
- Warner Bros. TV
- Scott Silveri, Shana Goldberg-Meehan, Kevin S. Bright
- Set-in-Los Angeles spinoff of "Friends" centered on Joey Tribbiani (Matt LeBlanc) and his sister (Drea De Matteo)

The MacGregors
- Warner Bros. TV
- Marsh McCall
- Centers on the relationship between an adult son (Mitch Rouse), a successful writer and his newly divorced professor father (Tom Conti); Shelley Long co-stars

The Men's Room
- NBC Studios
- Danny Zuker
- Revolves around three men (Scott Cohen, John Cho, Eric Lively) at different stages of their lives

My 11:30
- NBC Studios/Nuance Prods.
- Steven Sater, Paul Reiser, Keith Addis
- Playboy New York businessman (Jeff Goldblum) and his no-nonsense shrink

Nevermind Nirvana
- NBC Studios, the Untitled Burke/Tarses Project
- Ajay Sahgal, Karey Burke, Jamie Tarses, David Schwimmer
- Indian-American guy (Kal Penn) and his Caucasian fiancee (Judy Greer) deal with his family

The Office
- Reveille/Universal Network TV
- Greg Daniels, Ben Silverman, Ricky Gervais, Stephen Merchant, Howard Klein
- Based on the cult BBC comedy about the employees of a midsized paper company; Steve Carell stars

Untitled Tarses/Wrubel
- NBC Studios, the Untitled Burke/Tarses Project
- Matt Tarses, Bill Wrubel, Karey Burke, Jamie Tarses
- Ex nerd's (Alyson Hannigan) life turns upside down when her slacker brother (Michael Landes) reappears in her life

Weekends
- NBC Studios/Spyglass Entertainment
- Craig Doyle, Roger Birnbaum, Gary Barber, Judd Pillot, John Peaslee
- Centers on a Generation X Orange County couple (Eddie Kaye Thomas, Caitlin Mowrey) with a baby

DRAMA

Hawaii
- NBC Studios
- Jeff Eastin
- Ensemble police drama set on a Hawaiian island; Ivan Sergei, Eric Balfour, Sharif Atkins co-star

HUB
- NBC Studios
- Mark Gordon, Nick Thiel
- Offbeat ensemble drama set behind the scenes at a large U.S. airport starring Heather Locklear and Blair Underwood

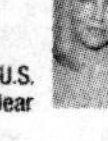

Law & Order 4: Trial by Jury
- Wolf Films/Universal Network TV
- Dick Wolf, Walon Green
- Courtroom drama; fourth installment in the "Law & Order" franchise

Untitled Medical Mystery
- NBC Studios/Paramount Network TV/Landscape Entertainment
- Bob Cooper, Scott Vila, Jason Horwitch
- Medical mystery procedural drama toplined by Neal McDonough; Kelli Williams co-stars

Medium
- Paramount Network TV/Grammnet Prods./Picturemaker Prods.
- Glenn Gordon Caron, Kelsey Grammer, Steve Stark
- Suburban mom (Patrica Arquette) uses her psychic powers to solve crimes; Miguel Sandoval co-stars

Revelations
- Pariah
- David Seltzer, Gavin Polone
- Group tries to forestall the apocalypse; Bill Pullman, Natascha McElhone, John Rhys-Davies star

COMEDY

The Bad Girl's Guide
(presentation)

Studio: Paramount Network TV/Flame Ent.
Prod. Team: Jennifer Heath, Michele Wolff, Cameron Tuttle, Tony Krantz
Synopsis: Based on Cameron Tuttle's book; centers on three women who adhere to the bad girls' attitude and live life to the fullest with no excuses; Jenny McCarthy stars

Humor Me (presentation)
- Sony Pictures TV
- Michael Curtis, Ken Mok, Barry Katz
- Stand-up comedian (Dane Cook) faces a quarter-life crisis when he loses it all and tries to get his life back on track

Me, Me, Me (presentation)
- 20th Century Fox TV
- Tom Straw, Lisa Birnbach
- Centers on two good-looking New York women who shamelessly climb the social ladder

Second Time Around
(presentation)
- Paramount Network TV/C to the B Prods.
- Ralph Farquhar, Michelle Listenbee-Brown, Claude Brooks
- After a quick divorce, a couple (Boris Kodjoe, Nicole Ari Parker) marries again

Untitled Andrew Secunda
(presentation)
- Paramount Network TV/ the Littlefield Co./Nervous Properties
- Andrew Secunda, Adam Chase, Warren Littlefield
- Centers on an uptight, career-minded woman (Charisma Carpenter) and her fun-loving brother (Tyler Labine)

Untitled Soluna (presentation)
- DePasse Entertainment/ Grammnet Prods./Paramount Network TV
- Jacque Edmonds, Suzanne DePasse, Kelsey Grammer, Irene Dreayer
- Comedic look at the lives, passions, and ambitions of the members (Jessica Castellanos, Christina Lopez, America Olivo, Aurora Rodriguez) of Soluna, a hot and rising Latina singing quartet

7.
Splitting Hairs
(backdoor pilot)
- Paramount Network TV/ the Greenblatt Janollari Studio
- Eunetta Boone, Bennie Richburg, Robert Greenblatt, David Janollari
- Spinoff of "One on One" centered on Flex's barber brother (Marques Houston) co-managing a barber-shop with a corporation heiress (Shannon Elizabeth)

DRAMA

2 Kings
- Blueprint Entertainment/ Edmonds Entertainment
- Seth Zvi Rosenfeld, Henry Bromell, Tracey E. Edmonds, Keri Selig, John Morayniss, Noreen Halpern
- Two high school boys from different sides of the tracks discover friendship in 1970s New York

Beck and Call (presentation)
- Warner Bros. TV, Shephard/Robin Co., Is or Isn't Entertainment
- Dan Bucatinsky, Lisa Kudrow, Michael M. Robin, Greer Shephard

- Revolves around the lives of three young assistants and their bosses; Christina Vidal, Vanessa Williams, Adam Kaufman, Jordana Spiro, David Conrad co-star

Kevin Hill
- Touchstone TV/Icon Prods.
- Jorge Reyes, Mel Gibson, Bruce Davey, Alex Taub

- Young attorney (Taye Diggs) gives up his playboy lifestyle to raise his cousin's infant daughter; Jon Seda, Michael Michele co-star

Mystery Girl (presentation)
- 20th Century Fox TV
- Liz Heldens, Howard Gordon, Rob Dwek
- Alex Breckenridge as a magazine writer who solves mysteries; Grant Show, Eric Paladino co-star

Nikki & Nora
- Warner Bros. TV, Green/Epstein/Bacino Prods.
- Nancylee Myatt, Lynne Litt
- Centers on two free-spirited New Orleans lesbian private investigators (Liz Vassey, Christina Cox); Shemar Moore co-stars

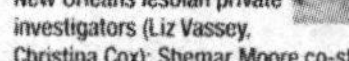

Silver Lake (presentation)
- Spelling Television
- Justin Tanner, Aaron Spelling, E. Duke Vincent, Jorge Zamacona
- Dramedy about a Los Angeles record store owner (Kerr Smith) who communicates with the dead; Sandra Bernhard co-stars

Veronica Mars
- Warner Bros. TV/Silver Pictures/ Stu Segall Prods.
- Rob Thomas, Joel Silver
- Hip teen girl (Kristen Bell) helps her private investigator father (Enrico Colantoni) so' crimes

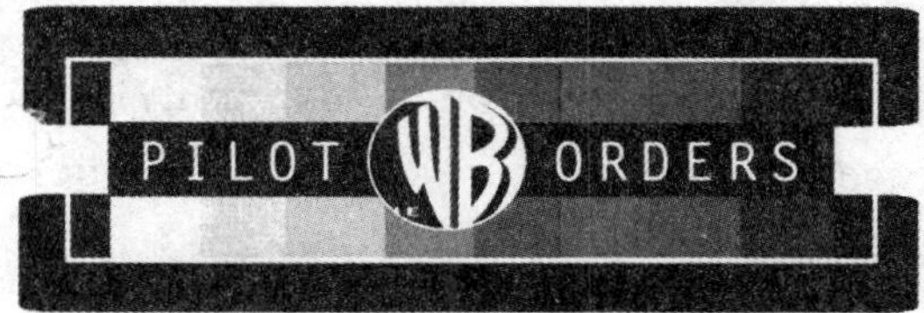

COMEDY

Blue Collar TV
(series commitment)

Studio: Warner Bros. TV
Prod. Team: Fax Bahr, Adam Small, JP Williams
Synopsis: Sketch comedy show based on the Blue Collar Comedy Tour starring Jeff Foxworthy, Bill Engvall & Larry the Cable Guy

Commando Nanny
- Warner Bros. TV/Mark Burnett Prods.
- David Flebotte, Mark Burnett, Conrad Riggs
- Based on Burnett's experience as a British military commando-turned-Beverly Hills nanny; Philip Winchester, Gerald McRaney, Kristin Bauer star

Dana & Julia
- Sony Pictures TV/Happy Madison
- Tom Brady, Doug Robinson, Adam Sandler, Jack Giarraputo
- Modern-day "Laverne & Shirley" starring Dana Goodman and Julia Wolov

Green Screen
- Michigan J Prods./Acme Filmworks
- Drew Carey, Ron Diamond
- The show blends improv comedy and elements from different animation styles added during postproduction using green-screen technique

Joint Custody
- Warner Bros. TV
- Dottie Dartland-Zicklin
- Liberal and permissive divorced mom (Kate Walsh) shares custody of her kids with penny-pinching disciplinarian former husband (Jon Tenney)

Untitled Robert Schimmel
(midseason)
- Michigan J Prods.
- Bob Myer, Robert Schimmel, Howard Stern, Lee Kernis
- Cancer survivor marries a friend of his 25-year-old daughter; based on Schimmel's life

Shacking Up
- Regency TV/Wannabe Producers
- David Garrett, Jason Ward, Jamie Kennedy, Mike Langworthy, Josh Etting
- 24-year-old moves back home with his mom (Fran Drescher) and her 24-year-old boyfriend

hen Comes Marriage
- 20th Century Fox TV/Brad Grey TV
- Boyce Bugliari, Jamie McLaughlin, Brad Grey, Peter Traugott
- Young married couple balances life between their single friends and their own relationship

DRAMA

Dark Shadows
- Warner Bros. TV/John Wells Prods.
- Mark Verheiden, John Wells, Dan Curtis
- Remake of the original 1960s Gothic soap opera about a wealthy Maine family under a vampire curse; Marley Shelton, Martin Donovan, Alexander Gould co-star

Global Frequency (midseason)
- Warner Bros. TV/Mark Burnett Prods.
- Mark Burnett, John Rogers
- Based on DC comic about a top-secret rogue intelligence agency that calls on everyday people to help solve global crimes

Jack & Bobby
- Warner Bros. TV/Berlanti-Liddell/Shoe Money Prods.
- Greg Berlanti, Mickey Liddell, Thomas Schlamme, Vanessa Taylor
- Drama about the teen years of a future president and his brother raised by a single mother (Christine Lahti)

The Mountain
- Warner Bros. TV/ Wonderland Sound and Vision
- Stephanie Savage, McG, David Barrett, Shaun Cassidy
- 25-year-old (Oliver Hudson) inherits his family's mountain resort when his grandfather dies; Barbara Hershey co-stars

Prodigy
- Warner Bros. TV/Silver Pictures
- Josh Friedman, Joel Silver, Danielle Stokdyk, Jennifer Gwartz
- A teenager (Kate Mara) hides her prodigious musical talents from her family, while her 9-year-old brother (Coby Arens) struggles with being a genius; Stacy Edwards, David Newsom co-star

The Robinsons: Lost in Space
- 20th Century Fox TV/Fox TV Studios/ Lion Rock Prods./Synthesis Entertainment
- Doug Petrie, John Woo, Kevin Burns, Jon Jashni, Terence Chang, Suzanne Zizzi
- En route to colonize a new planet, the Robinson family is ambushed by aliens and gets lost in space; a remake of Irwin Allen's fantasy-adventure drama set in 2097

Rocky Point (midseason)
- Warner Bros. TV
- John Stockwell, Lizzy Weiss
- Young woman living on Hawaii's North Shore takes in her estranged father

April 15

Wayne and I are set to pitch his family show idea. Then Paramount cancels the meeting, rescheduling for next week.

April 22

Wayne and I get ready again. Meeting cancelled again. Rescheduled for next week. He's getting tired of driving all the way to Hollywood for meetings that don't happen. I assure him it won't happen again. Meanwhile, I'm getting pissed and embarrassed. My own studio is making me look like a schmuck.

April 27

Zap2it.com reports that a California appeals court has ruled that a harassment lawsuit by a former writers' assistant on *Friends* can go forward. Amaani Lyle, a black, female writers' assistant, had sued several producers, along with Warner Brothers and NBC studios, claiming that the writers made racist jokes and crude comments about women and sex. The defendants argue that their vulgarity was part of the creative process on *Friends* whose characters are all sexually active.

WRITERS' ROOMS

I have no idea if she was sexually harassed in the room. I wasn't there; I can't say. But in almost 20 years of working in these rooms, I've never seen it happen. Most assistants are treated with respect by the writers since assistants make considerably less money, work even longer hours, and they're in the room all day and are part of the family. They also know that writers' rooms are disgusting places. Most of the time, they join in. But it has practically nothing to do with the content of the show. Without getting too lofty, rooms are sanctuaries where the rule is you are free to say any vile thing that pops into your head, as long as it's funny, whether it's "on story," meaning something that is meant for the script, or "off-story," meaning funny shit for its own sake. The underlying joke is to see who can be more disgusting. It's a contest. It's humor calisthenics. It's fun. And it's not just a boys club. All the women writers I've worked with were just as vile as the men. It's not about gender. It's about the type of people who like to make sick jokes and laugh, while working on a comedy show.

It's misguided that the defense in this case is trying to draw a parallel between the content of *Friends* and the "loose sexual talk" in the room. There is no direct parallel. In fact, it's almost inversely proportional. One of the sickest rooms I've ever heard about was on *Full House*. When you're working on something that sanitized, the other shit's going to need to come out even more. Other than the few heated debates and arguments that went on over story, or changes in a script, I've never seen one person get singled out as the "room schmuck." If the *Friends* writers tormented her personally, she may have a case. But if she was simply offended by all this crude talk, then she shouldn't have taken the job in the first place as everyone knows that this is how rooms function. And if she didn't know, then she should have complained earlier, at which point she would have been told politely or not that this is the way rooms function; either get used to it or quit.

There is rarely a direct link from a discussion about a cast member's body to a story in the show. It's room chatter. The bullshit that goes on before, during, and after the actual work. Some sick comment at midnight during a long rewrite can break a painful silence and get people laughing again. Ask any writer who's sat bleary-eyed at 2am if they didn't need the gross shit to get through the night. When a rewrite goes past midnight, you not only start getting punchy, but your standards get progressively lower by the hour. Bob Ellison, a veteran of *The Mary Tyler Moore Show* and *Cheers*, was in a late rewrite when a stale joke was pitched. The reaction was "It's too lame," "it's too stupid," to which Bob responded: "It's 2:30, put it in." At any rate, soldiers in trenches smoke cigarettes, play harmonicas and look at pictures of their sweethearts back home. Writers talk about sex. Because if you're in a room 16 hours a day, and crawl home at 3am reeking of Chinese food and room stank, chances are you're not getting any. Again, this is not a complaint. We are obscenely overpaid people who like to complain and come off like martyrs. It's the equivalent of retirees sitting around bragging about their operations. But, as far as writers' rooms being racist, sexist, vile places—they are. But not really.

The joke is to say shit to be funny and because it's extreme, not because you mean it. Rooms also tend to be more liberal, so that if anyone were truly racist, they wouldn't last long. (Has anyone ever known a truly amusing racist?) As for talk about sex, that's most often the main topic of conversation, along with politics, religion, news, music, movies, TV and what celebrity or world figure died that morning. In the equation: humor=tragedy plus time (from Alan Alda's oily TV producer character in *Crimes and Misdemeanors)*, the "time" factor is usually how long it takes someone to hear about a death on morning TV, get in their car, drive to work, and get into the room to start making jokes. But it's just about the joke. It's about being funny because that is what you do. This case has to be understood in that context. If they simply read the room jokes out loud in open court, without that context, those writers are fucked.

(Cut to April, 2006. An article on AOL News reports that the California Supreme Court threw out the case, saying "sometimes vulgarity is not just acceptable, but necessary in the workplace," meaning that the trash talk was part of the creative process.)

April 30

Wayne and I take every precaution before assuming the meeting's on before he drives over in midday traffic. The second he steps in my office, the meeting's cancelled again. Excuse: it's pilot season. This is becoming a fucking joke.

MAY 2004

"Friends" ends its run on NBC after 10 seasons. "Frasier" ends after 11 seasons. A day of national mourning is declared. European Union expands to 25 nations. No one gives a shit. In a feat of Orwellian Newspeak, an organization calling itself "Swift Boat Veterans for Truth" launches a series of TV commercials branding John Kerry as unfit to serve as commander in chief, smearing his war record, casting doubt on the severity of the wounds he received and later knocking his post-service anti-war activities. So, somehow the guy who went where the bullets were is branded a liar, traitor, and unfit for command, while the guy who used daddy's connections to dodge military service in time of war and even fucked off in the National Guard is a fearless leader of men.

May 6

A friend and colleague, David Isaacs, tells me about an idea he has for a show. Divorced woman with kids falls in love with single guy and tries to balance her career and high-maintenance family life to pursue love for the second time. I like it, and we agree to partner up and develop it. The more we discuss it, the more we agree it's perfect for Julia Louis-Dreyfus, whom neither of us knows nor has any idea if we can get, but her involvement would certainly add some heat to this.

We call agents to check out whether she's looking to do another show after having failed with *Watching Ellie*, the post-*Seinfeld* starring vehicle she did with her husband, based on the interesting notion of doing the show in 22 minutes real time. One of the best *Frasier*s I'd ever seen was done this way, with Niles and Frasier in the coffee shop, asking each other if they were happy. It was written by David Angell and Peter Casey, two of the creators of the show. It was brilliant. But to do an entire series with this device is risky. Then again, *24* makes it work on Fox with a similar time conceit. Also, it's the kind of idea networks usually love during the pilot stage, then panic over and change once it becomes real or if the ratings are lousy. Which they were. And they changed it. Still, it was different and it was well done, it just didn't catch fire. Turns out, she's potentially interested. Not necessarily in us. Just in doing another show in theory. At least it's not a no. We start to work, along with David's partner, Ken Levine and Dave Hackel, getting ready to pitch to Paramount.

May 10

Right before the network upfronts, the rumors start to circulate about which shows are getting on the air. This is a report from thefutoncritic.com. We'll track these through the year and see just how accurate the "pilot buzz" was.

home >> newswire >> monday, may 10, 2004

Monday, May 10, 2004 - 12:04 PM
Pilots Build, Lose Buzz for 2004-05 Schedule
By The Futon Critic Staff

LOS ANGELES (thefutoncritic.com) -- With the upfronts just one week away, pilot "buzz" has kicked into high gear as the vague picture of the broadcast networks' new 2004-05 series is starting to come into focus.

Here's a round-up of how each pilot is faring, according to various reports:

NBC

COMEDIES - Peacock executives apparently are breathing a big sigh of relief as "Joey" tested well internally and more importantly got solid thumbs-up from independent sources. While there was no doubt the show would make the fall schedule, said results will no doubt make Jeff Zucker and co. sleep easier. Brief promos for the series began running during the "Friends" finale. As for its other comedies, both "D.O.T.S." and its untitled Deann Heline/Elieen Heisler project have repeatedly been mentioned as testing well, and the opposite is true for "Foster Hall," "The Friendlys," "Weekends" and "Americana." Straddling the middle are "My 11:30," "Beverly Hills, S.U.V." and "Men's Room." Yet to be mentioned are Rob Reiner's "Everyday Life," Marsh McCall's "The MacGregors," "Nevermind Nirvana," "The Office" and "The Father of the Pride," the latter of which already has a series order.

DRAMAS - With just a handful of drama pilots in the works, at best two new hours will make the schedule. Leading the buzz are "Revelations," "Hawaii" and Jason Horwitch's untitled medical mystery project while "HUB" and "Medium" remain off the radar.

ABC

COMEDIES - Rodney Carrington, John Stamos and Jessica Simpson's half-hours seem to be the strongest contenders, as does the Colin Hanks-led "News to Me" and Jennifer Love Hewitt's untitled comedy. On the flip side, "Earthquake" doesn't seem to be getting any traction, while "The Furst Family," "Hot Homma," "I Married Sofia," "Plan B," "The Savages," "Thank God It's Monday" and Lewis Black's project remain under the radar.

DRAMAS - Gushing in the word that best describes the Alphabet's reaction to "Desperate Housewives," which seems as sure as anything to make the fall schedule. Not surprisingly "Housewives" comes from new ABC topper Steve McPherson's former home, Touchstone Television. Also considered strong or having fans are "Eyes," "Doing It," "Blind Justice" and "Under the Knife" (a.k.a. "Surgeons"). "Lost" is set to be screened this week, while mum is the word on "Countdown," "DeMarco Affairs," "Gramercy Park," "Kat Plus One" and "The Secret Service." Only "Harry Green & Eugene" has been singled out as not likely for a fall 2004 berth.

The WB

COMEDIES - The Fran Drescher-led "Shacking Up" and the Mark Burnett-produced "Miles to Go" both seem to be the biggest favorites while "Blue Collar TV" is expected to launch this summer and continue on through the fall should it perform well. Yet to be mentioned are "The Dana & Julia Show," "The Green Screen," "Joint Custody," "Then Came Marriage" and the untitled Fleiss/Sheridan project.

DRAMAS - With "Jack & Bobby" already getting a go for fall 2004 and "The Mountain" also considered a sure thing, that leaves little room for other projects. "Dark Shadows" is widely considered a long shot to make the schedule after strong initial buzz. The same goes for "The Robinsons: Lost in Space," while "Prodigy" has yet to appear on any reports.

FOX

COMEDIES - Seth MacFarlane's animated pilot "American Dad" is the only comedy looking good for a series order thus far while "Blue Aloha," "The Boondocks," "The Deerings," "Lucky Us," "Mr. Ed," "Related by Family," "The Robinson Brothers," "The Sketch Show," "Sorry Charlie," "Sweden, Ohio" and the animated projects from Jonathan Katz and Phil Hendrie remain invisible for the time being. Keep in mind FOX is already launching "Method & Red" and "Quintuplets" this summer.

DRAMAS - Dark dramas "Point Pleasant" and "House" are said to have their fans for 2004-05 series orders, while "On the Inside" is also generating buzz. Off the radar then are "Hollywood Division," "Johnny Zero" and "Ricochet."

CBS

COMEDIES - As usual, the Eye is fairly mum on its pilot reactions however the Ricki Lake/Kirstie Alley, Chris O'Donnell, Jason Alexander and John Goodman projects are said to be leading candidates. Fellow newcomers "Taste," "Saint Louie" and untitled projects from Aisha Tyler and Andrew Kennedy remain under the radar.

DRAMAS - Both of Sarah Timberman and Carl Beverly's pilot's, "Wanted" and "The Webster Report," are said to have screen well, as have "Colderon" and "The Clubhouse." Still yet to appear on any reports are "Bounty Hunter," "Cooking Lessons," "Dr. Vegas" and "Numbers."

UPN

COMEDIES - Not surprisingly the "One on One" spin-off "Splitting Hairs" and Jenny McCarthy's "The Bad Girl's Guide" lead the netlet's comedy buzz, leaving behind "Humor Me," "Me, Me, Me," "Play Nice" and "Second Time Around" as well as the untitled Soluna project for the time being.

DRAMAS - Again, it's not surprising to learn "Beck & Call" and "Kevin Hill" are considered at the top of the list to make UPN's fall schedule. Nevertheless "Veronica Mars" and "Silver Lake" are said to also be possibilities, while "Nikki & Nora" and "Mystery Girl" bring up the rear.

May 17

Finally Wayne and I get in to pitch Paramount the family show. Jokes all around about the cancelled meetings. Four in a row. Real damn funny. Still, they like the pitch. Nothing to dislike. It's safe, right down main street. Possibly for ABC. Maybe Fox. They're on their way to New York for the Upfronts and we agree to talk when they get back and start setting up meetings.

May 21

They return from the upfronts. And pass. Reason: it's too typical, nothing unique about it. I know there was nothing unique about it. It's just another family show, just like the ones getting picked up this season. Fucked if you do, fucked if you don't.

THE 2004-2005 NETWORK TV SCHEDULE

You saw the list of pilots produced. Here's what made it on the fall schedule or got ordered for midseason. The article is dated August 30, but it reflects the decisions set down in May. Of the 125

A6 TUNE IN: THE NEW SEASON Variety AUGUST 30, 2004

2004-2005 fall primetime schedule

Day	Network	8:00 PM	8:30 PM	9:00 PM	9:30 PM	10:00 PM	10:30 PM
MONDAY	abc	**The Benefactor** (12 Yard/29 29) *Sept. 13*		**Monday Night Football** (ABC Sports) *Sept. 13*			
	CBS	**Still Standing** (20th Century Fox) *Sept. 20*	**Listen Up** (CBSP/Regency) *Sept. 20*	**Everybody Loves Raymond** (Worldwide Pants/HBO) *Sept. 20*	**Two and a Half Men** (Warner Bros.) *Sept. 20*	**CSI: Miami** (CBSP/Bruckheimer/Alliance Atlantis) *Sept. 20*	
	NBC	**Fear Factor** (Endemol) *Aug. 30*		**Las Vegas** (NBCU/DreamWorks) *Sept. 13*		**LAX** (NBCU) *Sept. 13*	
	FOX	**North Shore** (20th Century Fox TV) *Sept. 6*		**The Complex: Malibu/The Swan 2** (Fremantle Media) *Aug. 30/ Oct. 25*			
	UPN	**One on One** (Par) *Sept. 20*	**Half and Half** (CBS Prods.) *Sept. 20*	**Girlfriends** (Par.) *Sept. 20*	**Second Time Around** (Par.) *Sept. 20*		
	WB	**7th Heaven** (Spelling) *Sept. 13*		**Everwood** (Warner Bros.) *Sept. 13*			
TUESDAY	abc	**My Wife and Kids** (Touchstone) *Sept. 21*	**George Lopez** (Warner Bros.) *Sept. 21*	**According to Jim** (Touchstone/ Brad Grey) *Sept. 21*	**Rodney** (Touchstone) *Sept. 21*	**NYPD Blue** (Bochco) *Sept. 21*	
	CBS	**NCIS** (Par.) *Sept. 28*		**Clubhouse** (Spelling/Icon) *Sept. 28*		**Judging Amy** (20th Century Fox TV) *Sept. 28*	
	NBC	**Last Comic Standing/The Contender** (Peter Engel Prods./Mark Burnett/ DreamWorks) *Aug. 31*		**Father of the Pride** (DreamWorks) *Aug. 31*	**Scrubs** (Touchstone) *Aug. 31*	**Law & Order: SVU** (NBCU/Wolf) *Sept. 21*	
	FOX	**The Billionaire: Branson's Quest for the Best** (Bunim-Murray) *Nov. 9*		**The Next Great Champ/House** (Endemol/NBCU) *Sept. 7/Nov. 16*			
	UPN	**All of Us** (Warner Bros.) *Sept. 21*	**Eve** (Warner Bros.) *Sept. 21*	**Veronica Mars** (Warner Bros.) *Sept. 28*			
	WB	**Gilmore Girls** (Warner Bros.) *Sept. 21*		**One Tree Hill** (Warner Bros.) *Sept. 21*			
WEDNESDAY	abc	**Lost** (Touchstone/Bad Robot) *Sept. 22*		**The Bachelor** (Telepictures/Next Entertainment) *Sept. 22*		**Wife Swap** (RDF Media) *Sept. 29*	
	CBS	**60 Minutes** (CBS News) *Sept. 29*		**King of Queens** (Sony/CBS Prods.) *Sept. 29*	**Center of the Universe** (CBSP/ Warner Bros.) *Sept. 29*	**CSI: NY** (CBSP/Bruckheimer/Alliance Atlantis) *Sept. 22*	
	NBC	**Hawaii** (NBCU) *Sept. 1*		**The West Wing** (Warner Bros.) *Oct. 20*		**Law & Order** (NBCU/Wolf) *Sept. 22*	
	FOX	**That 70s Show** (Carsey-Werner) *Sept. 8*	**Quintuplets** (20th Century Fox/ Imagine) *Sept. 8*	**Bernie Mac** (20th Century Fox/ Regency) *Sept. 8*	**Method & Red** (20th Century Fox/ Regency) *Sept. 8*		
	UPN	**America's Next Top Model** (10 x 10 Entertainment) *Sept. 22*		**Kevin Hill** (Touchstone/Icon) *Sept. 29*			
	WB	**Smallville** (Warner Bros./Tollin-Robbins) *Sept. 22*		**The Mountain** (Warner Bros.) *Sept. 22*			
THURSDAY	abc	**Extreme Makeover** (Mindless) *Sept. 23*		**Life as We Know It** (Touchstone) *Oct. 7*		**Primetime Live** (ABC News) *Sept. 23*	
	CBS	**Survivor: Vanuatu** (Mark Burnett Prods.) *Sept. 16*		**CSI** (CBSP/Bruckheimer/Alliance Atlantis) *Sep. 23*		**Without a Trace** (Warner Bros./CBS Prods.) *Sep. 23*	
	NBC	**Joey** (Warner Bros.) *Sept. 9*	**Will & Grace** (NBCU) *Sept. 16*	**The Apprentice** (Mark Burnett Prods.) *Sept. 9*		**ER** (Warner Bros.) *Sep. 23*	
	FOX	**The OC** (Warner Bros.) *Nov. 4*		**Tru Calling** (20th Century Fox TV/Original) *Nov. 4*			
	UPN	**WWE Smackdown** (WWE) *Sept. 23*					
	WB	**Blue Collar TV** (Warner Bros.) *July 29*	**Drew Carey's Green Screen Show** (Michigan J) *Sept. 16*	**One Tree Hill (R)** *Sept. 16*			
FRIDAY	abc	**8 Simple Rules** (Touchstone) *Sept. 24*	**Complete Savages** (NBCU/Icon) *Sept. 24*	**Hope & Faith** (Touchstone) *Sept. 24*	**Less Than Perfect** (Touchstone) *Sept. 24*	**20/20** (ABC News) *Sept. 24*	
	CBS	**Joan of Arcadia** (Sony/CBS Prods.) *Sept. 24*		**JAG** (Par.) *Sept. 24*		**Dr. Vegas** (CBSP/Warner Bros.) *Sept. 24*	
	NBC	**Dateline** (NBC News) *Sept. 3*		**Third Watch** (Warner Bros.) *Sept. 17*		**Medical Investigation** (NBCU/Par.) *Sept. 10*	
	FOX	**Totally Outrageous Behavior** (Bruce Nash) *Sept. 10*	**World's Craziest Videos** (Brad Lachman) *Sept. 10*	**The Next Great Champ** (Endemol/Lock &Key)			
	UPN	**Star Trek: Enterprise** (Par.) *Oct. 8*		**America's Next Top Model (R)** *Oct. 8*			
	WB	**What I Like About You** (Warner Bros./Tollin-Robbins) *Sept. 17*	**Commando Nanny** (Warner Bros./Mark Burnett) *Sept. 17*	**Reba** (20th Century Fox) *Sept. 17*	**Grounded for Life** (Carsey-Warner) *Sept. 17*		
SATURDAY	abc	**Wonderful World of Disney** (Various) *Sept. 25*					
	CBS	**Amazing Race** (CBSP/Bruckheimer/Touchstone) *Sept. 25*		**Crimetime Saturday** (Various) *Sept. 25*		**48 Hours: Mystery** (CBS News) *Sept. 25*	
	NBC	**The Apprentice (R)** (Mark Burnett) *Sept. 11*		**NBC Saturday Night Movie** (Various) *Sept. 11*			
	FOX	**Cops** (Barbour/Langley) *Sept. 11*	**Cops** (Barbour/Langley) *Sept. 11*	**America's Most Wanted** (Fox TV Stations) *Sept. 11*			
	UPN						
	WB						

Day	Network	7:00 PM	7:30 PM	8:00 PM	8:30 PM	9:00 PM	9:30 PM	10:00 PM	10:30 PM
SUNDAY	abc	**America's Funniest Home Videos** (Vin Di Bona) *Sept. 26*		**Extreme Makeover: Home Edition** (Endemol) *Sept. 26*		**Desperate Housewives** (Touchstone) *Oct. 3*		**Boston Legal** (20th Century Fox TV/David E. Kelly) *Oct. 3*	
	CBS	**60 Minutes** (CBS News) *Sept. 26*		**Cold Case** (Warner Bros./CBS Prods.) *Oct. 3*		**CBS Sunday Night Movie** (Various) *Sept. 26*			
	NBC	**Dateline** (NBC News) *Sept. 12*		**American Dreams** (NBCU) *Sept. 26*		**Law & Order: Criminal Intent** (NBCU/Wolf) *Sept. 26*		**Crossing Jordan** (NBCU) *Sept. 26*	
	FOX	**King of the Hill** (20th Century Fox) *Nov. 7*	**Malcolm** (Regency) *Nov. 7*	**The Simpsons** (20th Century Fox) Nov. 14	**Arrested Development** (Fox/Imagine) Nov. 7	**The Partner** (Rocket Science) *Nov. 7*			
	UPN								
	WB	**Steve Harvey's Big Time** (Telepictures) *Nov. 7*		**Charmed** (Spelling) Sept. 12		**Jack & Bobby** (Warner Bros.) *Sept. 12*			

New programs in RED New time slot in BLUE

Gotham slugfest: 'CSI' will fight the 'Law'

By MICHAEL SCHNEIDER

Operating from a position of strength, CBS enters the fall with few major schedule shuffles.

That gives the net a chance to focus on a few key battlegrounds. At the top of that list: The launch of "CSI: NY" opposite NBC's storied "Law & Order."

STRATEGY

The Eye has had trouble filling the Wednesday 10 p.m. slot for years, going bust with entries such as "The Brotherhood of Poland, N.H.," "Presidio Med" and "Wolf Lake." Given the power of the "CSI" franchise, that will likely change.

"We finally have a weapon that can go in there and do some business, which is a time period we haven't done business in for many, many years," says Viacom co-prexy/co-COO Leslie Moonves. "'CSI: NY' is not going to beat 'Law & Order.' However, 'CSI: NY' will do better than we've done in that time period in decades, so it's very exciting to be able to attack that."

Earlier this year at the web's upfront presentation, Moonves even guaranteed advertisers that "CSI: NY" would be "next year's top new drama."

Eye also is bowing the baseball-themed drama "Clubhouse" and Rob Lowe/Joe Pantoliano vehicle "Dr. Vegas," as well as the Jason Alexander laffer "Listen Up" and John Goodman comedy "Center of the Universe."

So far the comedies have been a bust with critics, and they may quickly go the way of Alexander's ("Bob Patterson") and Goodman's ("Normal, Ohio") other recent tries.

CBS

Still, CBS Entertainment prexy Nancy Tellem says she's fine with the caliber of the new series so far. And, she points out, most of them have been scheduled in safe timeslots.

"We believe we're well-positioned to introduce another strong freshman class," Tellem says. "All of our new shows will benefit from an established show as a lead-in, except, of course, 'CSI: NY,' which already has a built-in identity."

Emboldened by CBS' continued strength, Moonves resurrected the "Tiffany network" moniker in May.

"The title of the Tiffany network, because of the quality of our shows and our performance, once again rings true," Moonves says.

NEW SHOWS

Center of the Universe

Clubhouse

Dr. Vegas

Listen Up

CSI: NY

The plot: Spinoff of "CSI: Miami" follows forensic investigators (led by Gary Sinise and Melina Kanakaredes) in the Big Apple.

Exec producers: Anthony Zuiker, Carol Mendelsohn, Ann Donahue, Danny Cannon, Andrew Lipsitz, Jonathan Littman, Jerry Bruckheimer

What works: Don't mess with success. The "CSI" formula fits just fine in Gotham, and Sinise and Kanakaredes are big-time stars to make it work.

What doesn't: How many different variations on the same theme can you do?

Bottom line: Apparently, at least three. "CSI: NY" is a no-brainer, destined to be a hit and perhaps even better than predecessor "CSI: Miami."

CENTER OF THE UNIVERSE

The plot: John Goodman is a family man surrounded by an eccentric family, including a sex-obsessed father, wacky mother, oddball brother and goofy son.

Exec producers: Mitch Katlin and Nat Bernstein, Eric Tannenbaum and Kim Tannenbaum, Alan Kirschenbaum

What works: Excellent cast includes Jean Smart, Ed Asner, Diedrich Bader and Olympia Dukakis.

What doesn't: Too bad they're wasted on this. Show offers few laughs.

Bottom line: Appears to be the latest in a string of busted laffers for Goodman.

CLUBHOUSE

The plot: Teenager defies his mother (Mare Winningham) and becomes a batboy for the Yankees-esque New York Empires, where he works under Christopher Lloyd and meets his idol (Dean Cain).

Exec producers: Daniel Cerone, Ken Topolsky, Mel Gibson, Bruce Davey, Aaron Spelling, E. Duke Vincent

What works: The show elicits a youthful exuberance not found elsewhere on the Eye (outside "Joan of Arcadia").

What doesn't: Baseball theme may turn off some viewers. Show may feel out of place on the CBS lineup.

Bottom line: Ball's in the viewer's court, but it's not quite a home run.

DR. VEGAS

The plot: Rob Lowe is an unconventional physician who becomes the inhouse doctor at the high-end Las Vegas casino run by Joe Pantoliano.

Exec producers: Jack Orman, Steve Pearlman

What works: Solid popcorn fare with two compelling leads, while the Vegas backdrop remains interesting.

What doesn't: Plot seems all over the map.

Bottom line: It's a gamble, but with light Friday night competish, Rob Lowe and Joey Pants may have hit the series jackpot.

LISTEN UP

The plot: Jason Alexander plays a family man and sports talkshow host/newspaper columnist, based on real-life Washington Post scribe Tony Kornheiser.

Exec producers: Jeff Martin, Lindy DeKoven

What works: Sitcom vets Alexander and Malcolm Jamal-Warner are seasoned pros. There's a comfort level in seeing these two familiar faces on the small screen, and the maleled family laffers appear to be working for CBS.

What doesn't: There just aren't enough laughs to go around. Show suffers, rightly or wrongly, from the so-called "Seinfeld curse" — in other words, "Listen Up" pales in comparison.

Bottom line: These kind of inoffensive, middle-of-the-road sitcoms seem to work on Monday nights for the Eye, but Alexander's *thisclose* to hawking KFC again.

—M.S.

RETURNING SHOWS

THE AMAZING RACE

Premiere: Sept. 25 (sixth edition)
Timeslot: 8 p.m. Saturday

COLD CASE

Premiere: Oct. 3 (season 2)
Timeslot: 8 p.m. Sunday
Cast changes: None.
Storyline: Det. Lilly Rush and her investigators track down old murder caes.

CSI

Premiere: Sept. 23 (season 5)
Timeslot: 9 p.m. Thursday
Cast changes: None
Storyline: Producers say "don't blink" during the premiere.

CSI: MIAMI

Premiere: Sept. 20 (season 3)
Timeslot: 10 p.m. Monday
Cast changes: Who's off the show will be revealed in premiere. A new cast member will come aboard.
Storyline: In the season opener, one of the team dies on the job.

EVERYBODY LOVES RAYMOND

Premiere: Sept. 20 (season 9)
Timeslot: 9 p.m. Monday
Cast changes: Monica Horan becomes a regular cast member.
Storyline: Ray tries to shirk responsibility whenever possible. So what else is new?

JAG

Premiere: Sept. 24 (season 9)
Timeslot: 9 p.m. Friday
Cast changes: John M. Jackson and Kari Turner have departed.
Storyline: Harm and Mac resolve some of their personal issues.

JOAN OF ARCADIA

Premiere: Sept. 24 (season 2)
Timeslot: 8 p.m. Friday
Cast changes: Christopher Marqute and Becky Wahlstrom officially become regulars.
Storyline: After being hospitalized, Joan continues to struggle.

JUDGING AMY

Premiere: Sept. 28 (season 6)
Timeslot: 10 p.m. Tuesday
Cast changes: Dan Futterman returns; Kevin Rahm will only be in a few episodes this season.
Storyline: Amy and the Grays focus on changes in their family life.

KING OF QUEENS

Premiere: Sept. 22 (season 7)
Timeslot: 9 p.m. Wednesday
Cast changes: None
Storyline: Doug takes Carrie to a wellness spa to get her in a giving mood before he asks for permission to go to Las Vegas.

NCIS (formerly NAVY NCIS)

Premiere: Sept. 28 (season 2)
Timeslot: 8 p.m. Tuesday
Cast changes: Sean Murray becomes a regular.
Storyline: Gibbs and the NCIS team investigate more unusual cases.

STILL STANDING

Premiere: Sept. 20 (season 3)
Timeslot: 8 p.m. Monday
Cast changes: None
Storyline: An older Brian keeps testing the limits.

SURVIVOR: VANUATU

Premiere: Sept. 16 (9th edition)
Timeslot: 8 p.m. Thursday

TWO AND A HALF MEN

Premiere: Sept. 20 (season 2)
Timeslot: 9:30 p.m. Monday
Cast changes: Conchata Ferrell becomes a series regular.
Storyline: Charlie dates an elusive woman who gets the better of him.

WITHOUT A TRACE

Premiere: Sept. 23 (season 3)
Timeslot: 10 p.m. Thursday
Cast changes: None
Storyline: Martin and Samantha start a relationship outside of work.

YES, DEAR

Premiere: Midseason (season 5)
Timeslot: 8:30 Monday
Cast changes: None
Storyline: To be determined

Baseball pitches programmers a curve

JOSEF ADALIAN

For execs at Fox these days, the concept of a new fall season has become a relic of yesterday, right up there with rotary dial phones and cassette tapes.

STRATEGY

During September and October, while other webheads are busy playing with their new fall toys, Fox will defy decades of tradition and premiere not a single new scripted series.

Zero. Zilch. Nada.

That doesn't mean Fox will be in repeats, however. It's just that for Fox, the fall season started three months ago.

Ignoring skeptics, the Murdoch web went ahead and launched a slew of new shows in June, just days after its veteran hits aired their season finales. It's part of a year-round programming strategy meant to help Fox solve its October dilemma. Because of post-season baseball coverage, if Fox premieres a show when everyone else does, in September, it then has to take it off the air for nearly a month, just weeks after its bow.

"We have a unique set of circumstances that prevents us from launching any scripted programming in or around October," says Fox Entertainment prexy Gail Berman. "We have to program in a calendar type of way rather than a seasonal type of way."

Some of the skeins Fox launched this summer ("The Jury," "The Casino") didn't survive. But the strategy worked well enough that Fox will head into the September onslaught with two newish shows already familiar to viewers — "North Shore" and "Method & Red" — as well as comedy hit "Quintuplets" and unscripted smash "Trading Spouses."

Add in several high-profile reality shows, and Fox execs think they'll be competitive enough to survive until tentpoles such as "The Simpsons" and "The OC" return in November — and "American Idol" roars back in January.

FOX

"We go into September and baseball with a tremendous wind at our backs," Berman says. "We're playing our own game here."

The lack of new scripted skeins in early fall doesn't mean Fox won't have some fizz in the fourth quarter.

Net's one new scripted show of the fourth quarter, medical mystery "House," is drawing critical buzz in advance of its November premiere. It also has the benefit of being the only new comedy or drama Fox has to promote during baseball.

Boxing reality skein "The Next Great Champ" could help Fox boost its weak Friday night average. And the web will take a big step toward Thursday night respectability by shifting hit sudser "The OC" to the night — easily this season's bravest scheduling gamble.

Berman says she doesn't mind sitting out the annual September onslaught of new skeins. Her only goal is closing the one-tenth of a ratings point gap that separated Fox and first-place NBC when the season ended last spring.

"I hope to have one time of the year when I can celebrate," she says, "and that's next May."

NEW SHOWS

HOUSE

The plot: Emotionally and physically challenged doctor (Hugh Laurie), with zero bedside manner, tackles medicine's toughest mysteries with help from a sort of medical "A-Team."

Exec producers: Paul Attanasio, Katie Jacobs, David Shore, Bryan Singer

What works: Smart writing, fascinating stories and a powerhouse perf by Laurie make this one of the few must-see shows of the fall.

What doesn't: Fox has never had a successful medical show — and this one may be too smart for the room.

Bottom line: It'll take a miracle for this ›w to survive, but if there's any justice, it will.

THE NEXT GREAT CHAMP

The plot: A dozen would-be boxing stars fight for a shot at a title and a contract with host Oscar De La Hoya's company.

Exec producers: Paul Buccieri, Joe Livecchi, Oscar De La Hoya, Richard Schaefer

What works: Could be a good alternative for young males on Friday nights.

What doesn't: Boxing hasn't been a regular part of network primetime in decades, and viewers might want to wait for the more star-studded NBC boxing skein from Mark Burnett.

Bottom line: It won't take much to improve on Fox's dismal Friday track record of recent years.

RENOVATE MY FAMILY

The plot: Put every home-, self- and car-improvement makeover skein in a blender, and this is what you get.

Exec producers: Jean-Michel Michenaud, Chris Cowan, Ray Giuliani

What works: Makeover and wish-fulfillment shows are red-hot, and this one's got something for everyone. Making Jay McGraw host ensures at least one plug on "Dr. Phil."

What doesn't: It's the 400th makeover show on the scene.

Bottom line: A good way to keep the Tuesday 9 p.m. slot warm before "House" moves in come November.

THE COMPLEX: MALIBU

The plot: Eight couples perform extreme makeovers on rundown apartments, then auction off units to the highest bidder. The couple whose unit snags the highest coin gets to keep the profit from all the sales.

Exec producer: Ted Haimes

What works: Original Australian version of this show was a monster hit.

What doesn't: It all seems a little confusing to us.

Bottom line: After the Olympics, viewers could be looking for a new reality fix.

THE BILLIONAIRE: BRANSON'S QUEST FOR THE BEST

The plot: A little "Amazing Race," a little "Apprentice," as Richard Branson orders around a bunch of would-be moguls out to win an undisclosed prize.

Exec producer: Jon Murray, Richard Branson, Lori Levin-Hyams, Kevin Lee, Laura Fuest, Tod Dahlke

What works: Branson doesn't say, "You're *fired*." We think.

What doesn't: The Donald and Mark Cuban may have filled America's billionaire jones.

Bottom line: Whatever.

—J.A.

House

The Next Great Champ

The Complex: Malibu

The Billionaire

RETURNING SHOWS

24

Premiere: Mideason (season 4)
Timeslot: 9 p.m. Monday
Cast changes: Oscar nominee Shoreh Aghdashloo joins the cast.
Storyline: Jack, now working for the Secretary of Defense, heads back to CTU after an explosion on a commuter train.

AMERICA'S MOST WANTED

Premiere: Sept. 11 (season 17)
Timeslot: 9 p.m. Saturday

ARRESTED DEVELOPMENT

Premiere: Nov. 7 (season 2)
Timeslot: 8:30 p.m. Sunday
Cast changes: None
Storyline: George Sr. has escaped from prison and Michael must figure out how to keep the family business operational.

THE BERNIE MAC SHOW

Premiere: Sept. 8 (season 4)
Timeslot: 9 p.m. Wednesday (new)
Cast changes: None
Storyline: Bernie and Wanda decide to have a baby of their own, but find it more difficult than they thought.

COPS

Premiere: Sept. 11 (season 16)
Timeslot: 8 and 8:30 p.m. Saturday

KING OF THE HILL

Premiere: Nov. 7 (season 9)
Timeslot: 7 p.m. Sunday
Cast changes: None
Storyline: An upcoming story has Hank turned into the Office of Homeland Security as a traitor.

MAD TV

Premiere: Sept. 18 (season 10)
Timeslot: 11 p.m. Saturday
Cast changes: Josh Meyers departs.

MALCOLM IN THE MIDDLE

Premiere: Nov. 7 (season 6)
Timeslot: 7:30 p.m. Sunday (new)
Cast changes: None
Storyline: Reese, still in the army, winds up in Afghanistan. Malcolm volunteers at a veteran's hospital.

THE OC

Premiere: Nov. 4 (season 2)
Timeslot: 8 p.m. Thursday
Cast changes: Alan Dale is now a series regular.
Storyline: Summer's over and the gang returns for more relationship turmoil.

THE SIMPSONS

Premiere: Nov. 14 (season 16)
Timeslot: 8 p.m. Sunday
Cast changes: None
Storyline: Homer gets a new best friend and Marge's former high school pal returns.

THE SWAN 2

Premiere: Oct. 25 (second edition)
Timeslot: 8 p.m. Monday

THAT '70s SHOW

Premiere: Sept. 8 (season 7)
Timeslot: 8 p.m. Wednesday
Cast changes: None
Storyline: As Eric and Donna deal with their broken engagement, Hyde discovers his father is a successful businessman and Fez finds his true calling.

TRU CALLING

Premiere: Nov. 4 (season 2)
Timeslot: 9 p.m. Thursday (new)
Cast changes: Jason Preistly becomes series regular.
Storyline: Tru's father moves to town, and continues his alliance with Jack, unbeknownst to Tru, who enrolls in med school.

'Desperate' Alphabet not looking for quick fix

By MICHAEL SCHNEIDER

STRATEGY

Another year, another comeback attempt.

This time, the faces at ABC are different, but the problems the same. For the past two seasons, the net has shown signs of life in the fall, only to lose that momentum come midseason (when Fox's "American Idol" smacks everything in its path).

Incoming entertainment prexy Steve McPherson is realistic: ABC's not going to find an instant fix.

"We certainly think that it's a building-block process," he says. "We're not of the belief that it is one show that saves the network. If that walks in the door, fantastic, and we'll hopefully use it effectively.

"But we're looking to get on some solid performers, improved time periods, improved nights and start to get a momentum back," he says.

Part of the problem remains ABC's inability to find a signature scripted megahit in the vein of "CSI" or "Law & Order."

The web's signature comedies perform decently but none recall the power of classic staples such as "Roseanne" and "Home Improvement." And the net's drama woes have been well documented.

"It's no secret to anyone that we haven't had a drama that has really broken out in the last few years," McPherson says. "We think we have some good shots with some of the new development. We just want to make sure that we give each of them the appropriate launching pad."

Stuck in fourth place, ABC execs believe they have no place to go but up. And so far, the critics like the Alphabet web's odds.

Buzz is high on new ABC entries "Wife Swap," "Desperate Housewives," "Lost" and "Life as We Know It." "Boston Legal" trades on its "The Practice" familiarity, while "Rodney" and "Complete Savages" attempt to re-create the classic ABC formula of family comedy with a male center.

Given ABC's position, McPherson believes the net has more leeway to stick with the shows it believes in, despite low ratings.

"When you're in this position, you absolutely approach things differently than if you were on top and trying to hold on to that," he says.

"We really want to look at time periods, we want to look at nights, and we want to hopefully improve in those specific places and then slowly build out from there.

"I do think it allows you to be a little more patient, but you also have to be better. You absolutely have to be more competitive, more strategic than the people who are right now beating you."

NEW SHOWS

Complete Savages

Life as We Know It

Lost

Wife Swap

THE BENEFACTOR

The plot: Mark Cuban does his best Donald Trump impersonation, putting 16 contestants through a series of tests and eventually awarding $1 million to one lucky winner.

Executive producers: David Young, Clay Newbill, Todd Wagner

What works: Like Trump, Cuban is an eccentric figure and could be interesting to watch as he makes players jump through hoops.

What doesn't: Even the show admits "some of the rules are made up along the way," which could make for some sloppy TV.

Bottom line: Show is paired with "Monday Night Football," and those male sports fans definitely know who Cuban is. But will they watch him?

BOSTON LEGAL

The plot: James Spader moves his "Practice" character to an upscale Boston law firm filled with brilliant and emotional civil litigators.

Executive producers: David E. Kelley, Bill D'Elia, Jeff Rake, Scott Kaufer

What works: Spader. He's top-notch and the reason this show exists.

What doesn't: Could be in danger of getting too bogged down by "Ally McBeal"-style quirkiness — and the title could be better.

Bottom line: With no episode available for preview, the jury's out. But keep the focus on Spader (and lose the unfortunate title) and it should at least hold on to the "Practice" aud.

COMPLETE SAVAGES

The plot: Keith Carradine as a single father raising five teenage boys on his own.

Executive producers: Mike Scully, Julie Thacker-Scully, Mel Gibson, Bruce Davey

What works: Good-looking group of kids, and the Scullys are reliable, strong writers.

What doesn't: May be too formulaic, and perhaps needs more female presence.

Bottom line: Show seems to fit well into the "TGIF" formula and Gibson, if you haven't noticed, is on a roll.

DESPERATE HOUSEWIVES

The plot: Dark, sudsy comedic look at the life of housewives in the burbs, as seen through the eyes of one who just took her own life.

Executive producers: Marc Cherry, Michael Edelstein, Tom Spezialy

What works: Cast is strong, show is smart and the concept wholly original.

What doesn't: ABC may have to show extreme patience for this show to catch on. Let's hope they do.

Bottom line: Great, dishy fun, this could well be ABC's new watercooler show.

LIFE AS WE KNOW IT

The plot: Coming-of-age series about three teen boys and their relationships with families, friends and girls.

Executive producers: Gabe Sachs, Jeff Judah, Stu Bloomberg

What works: The spirit of "My So-Called Life" and "Freaks and Geeks" lives on in this decent teen drama.

What doesn't: The show starts out slow. Let's hope viewers give it a chance, as they'll be rewarded if they stick through it.

Bottom line: ABC hasn't been able to launch a drama on Thursday night in, well, forever. But here's incentive to stick with it: Ten years later, Alphabet execs still regret pulling the plug on "My So-Called Life."

LOST

The plot: Forty-eight survivors of a plane crash are stranded on a deserted Pacific island inhabited only by mysterious creatures.

Executive producers: J.J. Abrams, Damon Lindelof, Bryan Burk

What works: "Lost" is an exhilarating ride, the diverse cast is refreshing, the setting exotic and the production values top-notch.

What doesn't: It's still too soon to tell whether the show will sustain itself week after week, particularly with the supernatural plotline.

Bottom line: Abrams has outdone himself. If this doesn't work, then ABC just doesn't know how to promote what it has.

RODNEY

The plot: Standup comedian Rodney Carrington stars as a guy's guy living with his family in the American heartland.

Executive producers: Ric Swartzlander, David Himelfarb

What works: Carrington's a find, and his Middle America routine seems right in line with what appears to be working for ABC.

What doesn't: The show doesn't feel fresh or break any new ground.

Bottom line: Sandwiched after surprise hit "According to Jim," there's no reason "Rodney" can't hang around as a decent companion.

WIFE SWAP

The plot: Two wives switch keys and families for two weeks — with the swappee following the rules of her new household the first week, then instituting her own rules in week two.

Executive producers: Stephen Lambert, Jenny Crowther, Michael Davies

What works: The salacious title aside, "Wife Swap" is a surprisingly classy and intelligent look at the debate over one's place in a family.

What doesn't: But does classy and intelligent work in reality?

Bottom line: Nice companion piece for "The Bachelor," but Fox's "Trading Spouses" may already have stolen the show's thunder.

— *M.S.*

RETURNING SHOWS

8 SIMPLE RULES

Premiere: Sept. 24 (season 3)
Timeslot: 8 p.m. Friday (new)
Cast changes: None
Storyline: Mom works at school.

ACCORDING TO JIM

Premiere: Sept. 21 (season 4)
Timeslot: 9 p.m. Tuesday
Cast changes: None
Storyline: Jim and Cheryl are trying to conceive their fourth child.

ALIAS

Premiere: Midseason (season 4)
Timeslot: 9 p.m. Sunday
Cast changes: Mia Maestro joins as Sydney's half-sister, Nadia.
Storyline: Lauren is shot by Vaughn and Sydney discovers something disturbing about her father.

THE BACHELOR

Premiere: Sept. 22 (sixth edition)
Timeslot: 9 p.m. Wednesday

EXTREME MAKEOVER

Premiere: Sept. 23 (third edition)
Timeslot: 8 p.m. Thursday (new)

EXTREME MAKEOVER: HOME EDITION

Premiere: Sept. 26 (second edition)
Timeslot: 8 p.m. Sunday

GEORGE LOPEZ

Premiere: Sept. 21 (season 4)
Timeslot: 8:30 p.m. Tuesday (new)
Cast changes: Emiliano Diez becomes a regular.
Storyline: George continues to balance family life and work at the factory.

HOPE & FAITH

Premiere: Sept. 24 (season 2)
Timeslot: 9 p.m. Friday
Cast changes: Megan Fox replaces Nicole Paggi
Storyline: Faith continues causing commotion for Hope and her family.

LESS THAN PERFECT

Premiere: Sept. 24 (season 3)
Timeslot: 9:30 p.m. Friday (new)
Cast changes: Patrick Warburton becomes a regular.
Storyline: Claude keeps striving to succeed in her professional and personal lives.

MY WIFE AND KIDS

Premiere: Sept. 21 (season 5)
Timeslot: 8 p.m. Tuesday (new)
Cast changes: None
Storyline: Michael teaches his kids about life in his own comedic style.

NYPD BLUE

Premiere: Sept. 21 (season 12)
Timeslot: 10 p.m. Tuesday
Cast changes: Currie Graham and Bonnie Somerville join the cast.
Storyline: The 15th precinct gets a new commanding officer who immediately alienates the squad.

AUGUST 30, 2004 — VARIETY — TUNE IN: THE NEW SEASON — A13

Donald, 'Joey' keep Thursday tradition alive

_, MICHAEL SCHNEIDER

NBC is still worshipping at the altar of Donald Trump and Mark Burnett.

"The Lord giveth," says new NBC entertainment prexy Kevin Reilly, referring to the megahit "The Apprentice." "And in the godforsaken television business, by the Lord, I mean Mark Burnett, thanks to Donald Trump."

STRATEGY

This should have been a story about NBC's fate this fall in a world without "Friends" and "Frasier." But the huge success of "The Apprentice" — not to mention the resurgence of "Crossing Jordan," the midseason launch of a fourth "Law & Order" and the surprise summer hit "Last Comic Standing" — gave NBC a well-timed save.

Call it the luck of the Peacock. The net even avoided the "AfterMASH" syndrome with "Joey," the "Friends" spinoff that surprised many by not "sucking," the term popularized last year by NBC Universal TV chief Jeff Zucker.

"I think we've defied the odds with 'Joey,' frankly," Reilly says. "I think most people would have said, 'That show is going to be awful.' I think it's going to be special and it's only going to evolve from where it is. That was a big accomplishment."

"Joey" kicks off a Thursday night that likely will be tighter than ever in the ratings race with CBS.

Peacock, meanwhile, will try to revive its Tuesday night fortunes by returning "Next Comic Standing," followed by new animated series "Father of the Pride," one of the bigger gambles on the schedule.

NBC also will face off with the biggest threat to "Law & Order" in ages, as CBS' "CSI: NY" bows opposite the Dick Wolf staple Wednesdays at 10 p.m.

NBC's fall schedule includes just four sitcoms — a dramatic change from the days when the Peacock aired as many as 18. But the net promises the laughs aren't dead. ("I simply don't believe it," Reilly says.)

Peacock jumps out of the pack first, launching part of its schedule the week after the Olympics. By that point, Zucker believes viewers will be ready for series television.

"I think after that they'll be ready for their programs to come back," he says. "That's what we're excited about, to bring those programs back in originals right away."

NEW SHOWS

Father of the Pride

Joey

Medical Investigation

ATHER OF THE PRIDE

The plot: Big-bucks CGI-animated comedy follows the offstage antics of "Siegfried & Roy's" performing white lions.

Exec producers: Jonathan Groff, Jon Pollack, Peter Mehlman, Jeffrey Katzenberg

What works: Animation is sharp and boasts a feature-level quality. The animated versions of Siegfried and Roy steal the show.

What doesn't: Storylines seem a little too sitcom-conventional for such an unconventional show.

Bottom line: Properly promoted, show has a good shot, but animation is always a tough sell, especially for the big broadcast nets.

HAWAII

The plot: Modern-day "Hawaii Five-O" revolves around the cops of the Honolulu Police Dept. as they solve island crimes.

Exec producer: Jeff Eastin

What works: Eye-catching visuals and mindless plots make for a fun ride.

What doesn't: It could use more meat and a more authentic Hawaiian touch.

Bottom line: It's a tough time lot for NBC, and it's up against ABC's island actioner "Lost." But viewers may be looking for a Wednesday Hawaiian vacation.

JOEY

The plot: Matt LeBlanc's "Friends" character moves to Los Angeles, home to his sister (Drea de Matteo) and nephew (Paulo Costanzo), to pursue his acting career.

Exec producers: Scott Silveri, Shana Goldberg-Meehan, Kevin Bright

What works: One of the best sitcom spinoffs in recent memory, LeBlanc is strong and the show maintains the "Friends" comic sensibility.

What doesn't: The Hollywood-centric storylines may get tiresome. Will we frequently see Joey on auditions?

Bottom line: Bingo. NBC defied the odds and managed to keep the memory of "Friends" alive.

LAX

The plot: Heather Locklear, as the runway chief at Los Angeles Intl. Airport, locks horns with terminal boss and rival Blair Underwood.

Exec producers: Nick Thiel, Mark Gordon

What works: Timely drama doesn't take itself too seriously, does have fun with leads Locklear and Underwood.

What doesn't: Do we really want to spend an hour each week at the airport?

Bottom line: Perfect pairing with "Las Vegas," but will this flight be canceled before it lands?

MEDICAL INVESTIGATION

The plot: A National Institutes of Health medical team is called upon to stop outbreaks of mystery diseases.

Exec producers: Laurence Andries, Bob Cooper, Scott Vila, Marc Buckland

What works: Compelling, procedural drama led by strong perfs from Neal McDonough and Kelli Williams.

What doesn't: There's no worse title for a TV show this season.

Bottom line: Viewers, who continue to eat this brand of TV up, will likely schedule an appointment.

— M.S.

RETURNING SHOWS

AMERICAN DREAMS

Premiere: Sept. 26 (season 3)
Timeslot: 8 p.m. Sunday
Cast changes: Ben Taylor, Milo Ventimiglia and Daphne Zuniga join as recurring characters.
Storyline: The Pryor and Walker households continue dealing with the turbulence of the mid-1960s.

THE APPRENTICE

Premiere: Sept. 9 (second edition)
Timeslot: 9 p.m. Thursday
…t changes: Last year's winner, Bill …ic, settles in on the other side of …rdroom table.

CROSSING JORDAN

Premiere: Sept. 26 (season 4)
Timeslot: 10 p.m. Sunday
Cast changes: Ivan Sergei departs; Eugene Byrd joins as a recurring character.
Storyline: Jordan focuses more on solving crimes than dwelling on her past.

ER

Premiere: Sept. 23 (season 11)
Timeslot: 10 p.m. Thursday
Cast changes: Shane West joins the cast.
Storyline: Victims of road rage Pratt and Chen fight for their lives as their car careens off the road.

FEAR FACTOR

Premiere: Aug. 30 (fifth edition)
Timeslot: 8 p.m. Monday

LAS VEGAS

Premiere: Sept. 13 (season 2)
Timeslot: 9 p.m. Monday
Cast changes: None
Storyline: Gambling, girls and catching bad guys continue to take up the lives of Danny and Big Ed.

LAST COMIC STANDING

Premiere: Aug. 31 (third edition)
Timeslot: 8 p.m. Tuesday (new)

LAW & ORDER

Premiere: Sept. 22 (season 15)
Timeslot: 10 p.m. Wednesday
Cast changes: Jerry Orbach departs the force; Dennis Farina joins the NYPD.
Storyline: Stories ripped from the headlines.

LAW & ORDER: CI

Premiere: Sept. 26th (season 4)
Timeslot: 9 p.m. Sunday
Cast changes: None
Storyline: If at all possible, Goren tries to get even deeper into the psyche of the criminals he investigates.

LAW & ORDER: SVU

Premiere: Sept. 21 (season 6)
Timeslot: 10 p.m. Tuesday
Cast changes: None
Storyline: Benson and Stabler face some of the toughest cases of their careers involving stolen embryos, obscenity over the airwaves, cults, and the rights of rape victims.

SCRUBS

Premiere: Aug. 31 (season 4)
Timeslot: 9:30 p.m. Tuesday
Cast changes: Heather Graham will appear in an eight-episode story arc.
Storyline: J.D. and Elliot try to rebuild their friendship now that their romance is over.

THIRD WATCH

Premiere: Sept. 17 (season 6)
Timeslot: 9 p.m. Friday
Cast changes: Josh Stewart and Cara Buono join the cast.
Storyline: A main character is critically wounded.

THE WEST WING

Premiere: Oct. 6 (season 5)
Timeslot: 9 p.m. Wednesday
Cast changes: Alan Alda and Marley Shelton join the cast.
Storyline: Alda plays a Republican who seeks the presidency.

WILL & GRACE

Premiere: Sept. 16 (season 7)
Timeslot: 8:30 p.m. Thursday (new)
Cast changes: Bobby Cannavale returns for several episodes.
Storyline: Jack gets an executive job at a gay TV network.

Frog hopes exec shuffle shakes up ratings

By MICHAEL SCHNEIDER

WB, what happened?

Once the darling of critics, the Frog has stumbled in the past two seasons. With ratings down, several signature series retired and, most recently, the departure of honcho Jamie Kellner, followed by the biggest exec shuffle in WB history, it has been a rough patch for the web.

STRATEGY

Now, with chairman Garth Ancier and entertainment prexy David Janollari in place, the WB enters fall with a schedule that attempts to redefine (or at least clarify) its strategy.

As it approaches its 10th anniversary, the WB is looking to be more of a broadcaster, scheduling shows that wouldn't have been caught anywhere near the Frog in the past, namely, the Jeff Foxworthy sketch comedy "Blue Collar TV."

"We were getting a little too derivative in making shows that were cloning each other," Ancier says. "And when you're running a television network you can have ... a diversity of shows that appeal to different people. I think that's actually more healthy than having all shows that look alike on your schedule."

Net execs also have said they plan to spend more time promoting their older talent in addition to the WB's usual crop of fresh, young faces. Stars such as Foxworthy, Christine Lahti, Barbara Hershey and Gerald McRaney, who would have faded into the background in the past, now are much more visible on the web.

"We knew we did well with teenagers," says Ancier. "We knew we did well with 18- to 34-year-olds. We wanted to invite more people into the tent. ... I think to the degree that we have presented ourselves as just a teenage network, that's a very large mistake on our part."

WB saw promising returns this summer as new entries "Blue Collar TV" and "Summerland" posted solid numbers for the net. A third entry, gameshow "Studio 7," didn't fare as well, and won't air this fall after all.

Frog execs believe they've improved the net's flow this season, airing dramas on Mondays, Tuesdays and Wednesdays, a grab bag of reality and nontraditional comedy on Thursday, laffers on Friday and the combo of "Steve Harvey's Big Time," "Charmed" and new entry "Jack & Bobby" — which the WB will be pushing hardest — on Sunday.

NEW SHOWS

COMMANDO NANNY

The plot: Based on the life of reality producer Mark Burnett, a former commando for the British Special Forces who moved to the U.S. and became a nanny to make ends meet.

Executive producers: Mark Burnett, Rachel Sweet

What works: McRaney's a pro, and the plot seems to lend itself to countless stories.

What doesn't: Relies too much on cliche and not enough on its interesting, real-life premise.

Bottom line: Add more laughs, or viewers may go AWOL.

DREW CAREY'S GREEN SCREEN

The plot: Carey and his comedian buddies perform improv in front of a green screen; animators then add in other elements.

Executive producers: Drew Carey, Robert Morton, Ron Diamond

What works: Virtually the same crew that brought you "Whose Line Is It Anyway," Carey and pals are still masters of improv comedy.

What doesn't: The thrill of improv comes when audiences are forced to use their imagination. The animated bits take away some of those comedic elements.

Bottom line: A great idea on paper, but it isn't necessarily pulled off here.

JACK & BOBBY

The plot: Christine Lahti is a single mother raising two exceptional teenage boys, one of whom will eventually grow up to be president.

Executive producers: Greg Berlanti, Mickey Liddell, Thomas Schlamme

What works: Strong blend of Schlamme's "The West Wing" and Berlanti's "Everwood" sensibilities. Interesting idea for a show.

What doesn't: Producers reveal which brother ends up as president at the conclusion of episode one. How about a little mystery?

Bottom line: Hail to the chief: WB may have found its next successful drama.

THE MOUNTAIN

The plot: Oliver Hudson plays a free spirit who suddenly inherits control of a ski resort when his father dies — throwing him into conflict with the brother who should have been handed the reins.

Executive producers: McG, Stephanie Savage, Shaun Cassidy

What works: There's a void in this kind of campy, soapy, family-vs.-family drama, and "The Mountain" takes advantage of several familiar faces.

What doesn't: The show will be a tough sell opposite strong female-oriented competish ("The Bachelor," "Kevin Hill").

Bottom line: It'll be a hard climb for "The Mountain."

— M.S.

Commando Nanny

The Mountain

Jack & Bobby

RETURNING SHOWS

7th HEAVEN

Premiere: Sept. 13 (season 9)
Timeslot: 8 p.m. Monday
Cast changes: Barry Watson and David Gallagher return. Rachel Blanchard, Jeremy London, Scotty Leavenworth and Ashlee Simpson are no longer regulars.
Storyline: This season's theme is the Camden family being reunited.

CHARMED

Premiere: Sept. 12 (season 7)
Timeslot: 8 p.m. Sunday
Cast changes: Nick Lachey joins the cast for six episodes.
Storyline: Piper helps Leo deal with his grief of losing their unborn son.

EVERWOOD

Premiere: Sept. 13 (season 3)
Timeslot: 9 p.m. Monday
Cast changes: Scott Wolf and Anne Heche join the cast.
Storyline: Dr. Brown's no longer the new doc in town when a young doctor moves into Dr. Abbott's old office.

GILMORE GIRLS

Premiere: Sept. 21 (season 5)
Timeslot: 8 p.m. Tuesday
Cast changes: Jared Padalecki and David Sutcliffe return for several episodes.
Storyline: Lorelai and Luke's budding romance is complicated by the return of Rory's father, Christopher.

GROUNDED FOR LIFE

Premiere: Sept. 17
Timeslot: 9:30 p.m. Friday (new)
Cast changes: None.
Storyline: Claudia and Sean wind up preparing for the arrival of the newest Finnerty while getting ready to ship their first-born off to college.

ONE TREE HILL

Premiere: Sept. 21 (season 2)
Timeslot: 9 p.m. Tuesday
Cast changes: Barbara Alyn Woods is now a regular.
Storyline: Two new characters arrive to Tree Hill, which shakes up Brooke. Haley and Nathan deal with their marriage.

REBA

Premiere: Sept. 17 (season 4)
Timeslot: 9 p.m. Friday
Cast changes: None
Storyline: Brock and Barbra Jean's relationship hits the rocks and Van and Cheyenne face obstacles in Van's career.

SMALLVILLE

Premiere: Sept. 22 (season 4)
Timeslot: 8 p.m. Wednesday
Cast changes: Sam Jones is no longer a regular on the show. Jensen Ackles joins the cast.
Storyline: Lois Lane comes to town to investigate a murder.

STEVE HARVEY'S BIG TIME

Premiere: Sept. 12 (season 2)
Timeslot: 7 p.m. (expanded to one hour)
Cast changes: Jay Anthony Brown joins the show.
Storyline: A new sidekick joins the crew.

SUMMERLAND

Premiere: Midseason (Season 2)

WHAT I LIKE ABOUT YOU

Premiere: Sept. 17 (season 3)
Timeslot: 8 p.m. Friday
Cast changes: David De Lautour joins the cast. Michael McMillian is no longer a series regular.
Storyline: Holly returns from a summer in Paris with a new look, new attitude and new guy.

No longer an afterthought, net climbs 'Hill'

By JOSEF ADALIAN

After nearly a decade of trying, UPN finally may have found its groove.

While pre-season buzz and $4 will get you a venti latte at Starbucks, CBS' little sister has never headed into a fall launch with as much perceived momentum as it does this year. Thanks to reality smash "Top Model," a summer sensation called "Amish in the City" and a pair of critically admired new dramas, UPN seems ready at last to shed its image as the (Shasta) McNasty net.

STRATEGY

"Two years ago UPN's schedule suffered multiple personality disorder," admits UPN Entertainment prexy Dawn Ostroff. "There were different programs every night of the week that were geared toward different audiences."

Under Ostroff and her boss, Viacom co-topper Leslie Moonves, UPN has solidified its Monday comedy block and figured out a way to flow audience to Tuesday nights, which this fall will offer a mix of comedies and drama. Even more important, net has campaigned hard to bring top talent to UPN, from Tyra Banks ("Top Model") and Taye Diggs ("Kevin Hill") to Joel Silver ("Veronica Mars") and Missy Elliott.

"The quality of the programming has been upgraded considerably," Moonves says. "The schedule now has a clear sense of direction that makes a lot of sense."

Gutsiest move for UPN is the shifting of "Top Model" to Wednesdays, where the net hopes it'll provide a boffo lead-in to "Kevin Hill." Latter skein has some of the best advance buzz of any new show, and UPN execs hope "Model" will boost "Hill" in the same way "Survivor" helped make "CSI" a smash.

Monday comedy block should be even stronger, with the net consolidating three of its best laffers on one night and bringing in newcomer "Second Time Around." Even Friday —traditionally an afterthought for UPN — could get an upgrade now that "Star Trek: Enterprise" has moved to the night where "The X-Files" once thrived.

Moonves is so high on UPN, he's even considering a sixth night of programming. Even more amazingly, "We could very well turn a profit this year," he says.

NEW SHOWS

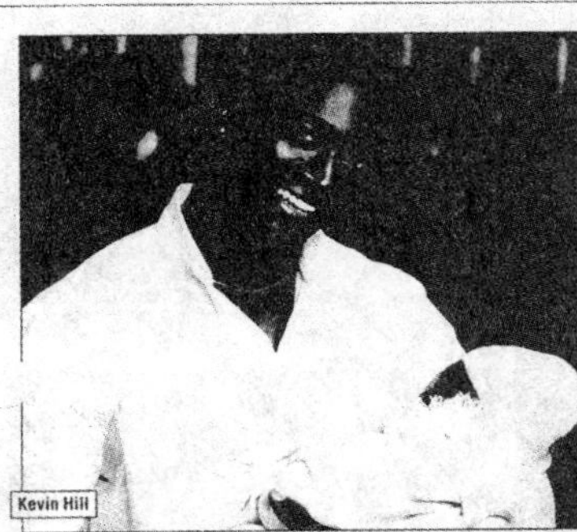
Kevin Hill

Second Time Around

KEVIN HILL

The plot: Taye Diggs is a super-smooth lawyer whose straight-out-of-Maxim bachelorhood ends abruptly when he's forced to take care of his late cousin's 6-month-old baby.

Exec producers: Bruce Davey, Alex Taub, Nancy Cotton

What works: Diggs. He oozes charm in every scene, and the ladies will eat him up.

What doesn't: We know this isn't "Law & Order," but the court cases could be a little less prefab.

Bottom line: Creator Jorge Reyes has fashioned a critical fave with mass appeal. It's hard to see how this won't be UPN's biggest drama hit since "Star Trek: Voyager."

VERONICA MARS

The plot: A teen girl gumshoe (Kristen Bell) solves the mysteries of a small town while figuring out the cosmic puzzle called adolescence. Think "Buffy" without the superpowers.

Exec producers: Joel Silver, Rob Thomas

What works: Good-looking cast, girl power vibe.

What doesn't: Does everyone on TV have to fight crime and injustice? Can't they, like, just be normal people?

Bottom line: Timeslot's not too tough, and the show's got some critical buzz. Could be the sleeper of the season.

SECOND TIME AROUND

The plot: The first marriage didn't work out but now Ryan (Nicole Parker) and Jackson (Boris Kodjoe) are giving holy matrimony another shot.

Exec producers: Ralph R. Farquhar, Claude Brooks

What works: Parker and Kodjoe are immensely watchable, and Farquhar ("Moesha," "The Parkers") is UPN's comedy king.

What doesn't: It's an awfully thin premise to stretch out over 100 episodes.

Bottom line: It's the net's only new comedy and it has a primo slot following "Girlfriends. If it doesn't work, producers have no one to blame but themselves. —*J.A.*

RETURNING SHOWS

ALL OF US

Premiere: Sept. 21 (season 2)
Timeslot: 8 p.m. Tuesday (new)
Cast changes: None
Storyline: As the wedding approaches, Tia wonders just how much Neesee she'll be able to handle for the rest of her life.

AMERICA'S NEXT TOP MODEL

Premiere: Sept. 22 (third edition)
Timeslot: 8 p.m. Wednesday (new)

EVE

Premiere: Sept. 21 (season 2)
Timeslot: 8:30 p.m. Tuesday (new)
Cast changes: None
Storyline: Shelly finds herself walking away from love when J.T. says he thinks she's not the marrying type.

GIRLFRIENDS

Premiere: Sept. 20 (season 5)
Timeslot: 9 p.m. Monday
Cast changes: None
Storyline: After quitting her job at a law firm, Joan searches for a new career.

HALF & HALF

Premiere: Sept. 20 (season 3)
Timeslot: 8:30 p.m. Monday (new)
Cast changes: None
Storyline: Mona and Spencer adjust to discovering they're more than just friends following last season's passionate kiss.

ONE ON ONE

Premiere: Sept. 20 (season 4)
Timeslot: 8 p.m. Monday (new)
Cast changes: None
Storyline: Even with the "Flex Files" in syndication, Flex still has to deal with 17-year-old Breanna's teenage independence.

STAR TREK: ENTERPRISE

Premiere: Oct. 8 (season 4)
Timeslot: 8 p.m. Friday (new)
Cast changes: None
Storyline: The Enterprise ventures further into uncharted territory while advancing last season's twisting timeline plot.

— Capsules by Paula Hendrickson

Eve

TIMESLOT BATTLES

Capsules by Rick Kissell

SUNDAY

'JACK & BOBBY' (WB) vs. 'DESPERATE HOUSEWIVES' (ABC), 9 p.m.

Desperate Housewives

What's at stake: A pair of intriguing new dramas butt heads in an hour that also includes NBC's tough "Law & Order: Criminal Intent" (but at least they don't have HBO's "The Sopranos" to worry about). Neither net has had great success in this timeslot, so both shows may get the time needed to build an audience.

ABC perspective: The Alphabet's drama woes in recent years have been well chronicled, but no skein appears to have a better chance at reversing that trend than this sexy soap about a group of female friends who live in the same suburban cul de sac. While the family-friendly "Extreme Makeover: Home Edition" wouldn't seem the ideal lead-in, it's ABC's hottest show among young adults.

WB perspective: This drama, the tale of a pair of teenage brothers in the Heartland — one of whom eventually will become president — is one of the most ambitious efforts from the Frog in recent years and could connect with a broader aud than typically watches the net. First, though, it must overcome a title that just doesn't work (it's not about the Kennedys!) and a challenging sked situation: fantasy hour "Charmed" is far from the ideal lead-in.

Bottom line: There might be some overlap between these two dramas, so the WB's early preem date for "Jack & Bobby" could give it the extra boost it needs to attract viewers early. "Desperate Housewives" looks to be one of the best bets of the fall season, and could be the show to put ABC on the road to a ratings recovery.

MONDAY

'CSI: MIAMI' (CBS) vs. 'LAX' (NBC), 10 p.m.

What's at stake: A pair of dramas go head-to-head opposite ABC's always tough "NFL Monday Night Football." Pigskin action will win out in most male demos, leaving the established CBS crime skein and the new NBC hour — a behind-the-scenes look at the comings and goings at the Los Angeles airport — battling for the remaining men and the large, available female audience.

CBS perspective: No reason to change a good thing, and "CSI: Miami" was one of only a few sophomore series last year to improve its ratings in its second season, ranking No. 11 among all series in adults 18-49. Its strong appeal among a variety of key demos — old and young, male and female — makes it tough to beat, especially when "Monday Night Football" ends its run in winter.

NBC perspective: Net did pretty well in the hour last season with reality dating show "Average Joe" but would prefer to have a scripted success here. "LAX," starring Heather Locklear and Blair Underwood, could draw young femmes but appears to be neither smart enough nor trashy enough to attract a loyal following.

LAX

Bottom line: Even with its star power, "LAX" seems too lightweight up against "CSI: Miami," although it looks to be a good fit with lead-in "Las Vegas." If auds begin to tire of the forensics fever that has struck primetime in recent years, "LAX" might have a shot.

TUESDAY

'SCRUBS' (NBC) vs. 'RODNEY' (ABC), 9:30 p.m.

What's at stake: NBC's hospital comedy takes on one of the fall's most promising new laffers in ABC's "Rodney," starring Rodney Carrington as a standup comedian juggling his career and family life. It's hard to imagine that two comedies could have less crossover audience than this pair, suggesting that both could survive quite nicely.

NBC perspective: "Scrubs," popular with young adults but never a broad hit, has bounced back and forth between the net's

Rodney

Tuesday and Thursday sked but looks better in this Tuesday slot, where there's less pressure and a lower rating can still be considered a success. Coming out of untested but seemingly compatible new laffer "Father of the Pride," this fourth-year comedy should challenge for the 18-49 lead and possibly prevail in 18-34.

ABC perspective: In a return to its more blue-collar Tuesday comedy roots, "Rodney" seems like a good fit with "According to Jim" and will benefit from heavy promotion during "Monday Night Football." Net has not had a really strong show in this 9:30 slot in nearly 10 years, but this reps perhaps its best shot since then. Look for it to play well across the 18-54 demos in Middle America, among both men and women.

Bottom line: By playing to different audiences and meshing well with their lead-ins, both "Scrubs" and "Rodney" should become strong performers in a timeslot without a lot of tough competish otherwise.

WEDNESDAY

'LAW & ORDER' (NBC) vs. 'CSI: NY' (CBS), 10 p.m.

What's at stake: NBC's longtime dominance of Wednesday's 10 p.m. slot is in jeopardy when the latest edition of forensics phenom "CSI" (starring Gary Sinise and Melina Kanakaredes) takes on the original "Law & Order." Did we really need another New York-based crimeshow, though? Viewers will provide that answer.

NBC perspective: With "West Wing" on the downslide, NBC has declined on Wednesdays, putting additional pressure on "Law & Order," which ranked 17th among all programs in adults 18-49. The loss of veteran actor Jerry Orbach probably couldn't have come at a worse time for the show, which has replaced the audience fave with Dennis Farina.

CBS perspective: From "Central Park West" and "Courthouse" to "Wolf Lake" and "Presidio Med," it's been one drama disaster after another for the Eye net in this hour, so there's tremendous upside potential for timeslot growth with "CSI: NY." It doesn't have a great lead-in (new laffer "Center of the Universe") and CBS is playing down expectations for it, but "CSI: NY" is capable of winning this battle.

Bottom line: New York is "Law & Order's" domain, so give a slight edge to the incumbent. There is room for both to do well in the same hour, although their ratings will suffer as fans of the popular franchises are forced to pick between them for the first time.

CSI: NY

THURSDAY

'THE OC' (Fox) vs. 'JOEY' (NBC), 8 p.m.

What's at stake: NBC looks to keep the "Friends" flame lit awhile longer with Matt LeBlanc starrer spinoff "Joey," which takes on Fox's transplanted teen sudser "The OC." Both skeins will have to contend with CBS' surprisingly durable "Survivor" franchise, which is back for a ninth edition.

NBC perspective: Its Thursday foundation has cracked some in recent years, but the likable "Joey" could help the net remain on top for the night in the key young-adult demos if it delivers roughly 70% of what "Friends" had been generating in the timeslot. Like its progenitor, "Joey" should be a broad performer for NBC, winning its slot in adults 18-49 and faring best among women 18-49, especially the younger half of the demo.

The OC

Fox perspective: The net, which has been a speck on the rear-view mirror of NBC and CBS on Thursdays in recent years, is making a bold move by shifting "The OC" to lead off the night. Show fared well on Wednesdays in its first season but really didn't put up great numbers until it was positioned behind "American Idol" halfway through the season. Now off on its own and asked to compete against "Joey" and "Survivor," "The OC" should win its hour in teens but will be hard-pressed to come in better than third in most key ratings categories.

Bottom line: Fox will improve its standing with "The OC," but the net's patience may be tested if numbers drop too much and the show loses its buzz. "Joey" isn't expected to be another "Friends" for NBC, but the net is counting on enough of the longtime laffer's viewers to stick around for a show whose pilot, at least, has hit potential.

pilots produced, 30 were picked up for fall. Additionally, another 37 were picked up for midseason, or for limited summer runs. At this point, 67 producers begin celebrating and simultaneously panicking over the enormous amount of preproduction work that has to be done between this moment and August. The other 58 producers simply begin drinking and praying the other shows die a quick, painful death.

JUNE 2004

Former President Ronald Reagan succumbs to Alzheimer's. A day of national mourning is declared as the country bows its head and, in a form of hypnosis, is forced to watch the "Mr. Gorbachev, tear down that wall!" speech over and over until we nod in unison like bobble-head dolls, agreeing that he was a great president. President Bush lauds the former president as his role model, as his handlers decide he needs a similar career-making phrase that will establish him in the pantheon of great American presidents. They consider "War—what is it good for? A lot," and "Islam—suck it!" until the president finally settles on "Mr. Gorbachev—tear down that wall!" "Fahrenheit 9/11" opens in U.S. Karl Rove comes down with a case of bleeding hemorrhoids. Scott Peterson goes on trial for murder, essentially the pilot of the only true American reality show—the infamous murder trial. I guess infamy is the new fame.

As I read the trades, tracking the new fall schedule, I also begin watching some of the pilots that were shot for this previous season. Writer's Christmas. My assistant gets them from Paramount on a weekly lending library basis. We screen them during lunch. 67 shows. Holy shit. One is worse than the next. Typical network garbage. Same dumb situations. Same stale jokes you see coming a mile away. (Shouldn't you have to take some kind of test to get creative license?) But I watch two with slightly more interest than the others.

When a writer's show is passed on, it's like being dumped or having a beloved pet die. And the grieving process, following the 5 Kubler-Ross steps, begins with denial, which doesn't last long. It is what is it. Lingering too long here is the road to madness. Followed by anger, usually directed at those who passed on it, and coming out along the lines of "they should get cancer and die," which was how my grandmother used to refer to anyone who cut us off in traffic. You skip over "bargaining." There's nothing to bargain for. Then depression. That lasts forever. It's part of what got you into this business in the first place. Then acceptance. OK, that has a better chance of occurring if, when you screen the pilots that were picked up by that network, you have to agree: "Shit, that was better than what I had," much in the same way that you found out the girl who dumped you is dating someone taller, younger, richer and better looking. You go, "OK, I get it." They should still both drive into a bridge abutment and die in a fiery inferno, but I get it. Still, if that's the case (with the shows, not the girl), you move on, still hoping they fail. But if you look at the shows that made it instead of yours and it's a shitfest—it eats you alive.

I check out the two big CBS comedy pilots for this year. The two shows they decided were this year's comedy flagship, winnowed down from hundreds of pitches: Jason Alexander in *Listen Up*, a family show based loosely on the life of sportswriter Tony Kornheiser; and John Goodman in *Center of the Universe*, about a guy and his wacky family. Now, forget for the moment that, while each of these actors was brilliant in *Seinfeld* and *Roseanne*, respectively, each had since failed with their subsequent "comeback" shows, Jason Alexander's *Bob Patterson* on ABC and John Goodman's *Normal, Ohio*, on Fox, in which he played the world's largest and worst-dressed gay guy. The track record for spin-offs is abysmal. The TV landscape is littered with the corpses of series with actors coming off hit shows, either as spin-offs of that character, or in a completely new arena. Not only do most get cancelled, most of them are pretty bad in and of themselves. Remember Michael Richards' wacky post-*Seinfeld* detective? This is the result of network-think; based on the show business equation: success=opportunity, meaning that if an actor was part of a successful show, then the audience must want to see that actor again. Not necessarily true. What they want to see, in theory, is that character. *Frasier* debuted at a time when the country had a *Cheers* hard-on. Most other spin-offs, as well as the shows actors jump into following a hit, tend to fail.

As for the pilots I watched, only four stand out as unique: *Desperate Housewives* on ABC. (Fast forward—a huge hit, and one that was based on a spec script that was passed on by NBC.) *Lost* on ABC (a hit), *Complete Savages* (produced by Mel Gibson—cancelled) and the John Stamos pilot, midseason for ABC. (Fast forward: it eventually made it to a second season, then died.) Ironically, an article from last year declared ABC in the toilet.

PERSPECTIVE

Every so often, while you're in the middle of chewing out your liver over some bit of show business injustice, something happens to give you some perspective. In this case, it was the gruesome murder and decapitation of 91-year-old formerly blacklisted, now retired screenwriter Robert Lees, whose credits included *Abbott and Costello Meet Frankenstein*.

P'acklisted Screenwriter Murdered

L NGELES, June 15, 2004

A homeless man suspected of beheading a 91-year-old screenwriter and stabbing to death the man's neighbor was arrested outside a Hollywood studio minutes after his photograph was broadcast on television.

One of those killed was 91-year-old Robert Lees, a major screenwriter in the 1940s and early 1950s before being blacklisted during the Communist scare of the '50s, reports **CBS News Correspondent Steve Futterman**. He wrote several films featuring Abbott and Costello, and later, under an assumed name, for the television series "Rawhide" and "Alfred Hitchcock Presents," among others.

The other victim was a 67-year-old retired doctor who was booking a flight when he was killed. The Southwest Airlines ticket agent heard the commotion and called police.

Arriving officers spotted Hal Engelson's body through a window, and forced their way inside. In the rear of the home they found Lees' severed head, Police Chief William Bratton said.

Kevin Lee Graff, 27, was arrested Monday after guards at Paramount Studios recognized him from a televised news conference and called police, Bratton said.

The man had been turned away at the studio gates, where he had asked guards for the telephone number of a female employee, and "something didn't feel right" about him, guard Isaac Macias said.

Graff had been talking to himself and making obscene gestures at passing cars. That prompted guards to keep their surveillance camera trained on him, security Sgt. Craig Phillips said.

M ents later, Phillips saw the news conference and recognized Graff.

"I turned to the camera on my monitor. I said, 'That's him! That's him!'" Phillips said.

Police did not find a weapon on Graff.

The motive for the killings was under investigation and it was unclear whether Graff knew the victims.

"It's too early in the investigation to understand why those two particular houses, those two particular people were chosen, if they were chosen at all," Bratton said.

The studio is about 2 miles from the home where police on Sunday found the body of Engelson.

The killer took Engelson's car, a Mercedes-Benz sedan, which later was found several miles away.

Lees also wrote under the name J.E. Selby, according to the Writers Guild of America.

Helen Klein, a neighbor, said she often drove around the neighborhood in his car, which had a "War is Not the Answer" bumper sticker.

"He is the guy you want for the neighbor next door," said Jeff Mesino, another neighbor. "He would say, 'Take the tools from my garage whenever you want.'"

Lees spoke in April 2002 at an event held by the Academy of Motion Picture Arts and Sciences to cap several months of exhibits about the blacklist, academy spokesman John Pavlik said.

"I think he was one of the funniest writers in Hollywood in his time," Dave Wagner, an author and authority on the blacklist period, t Futterman.

Lees had been a member of the Communist Party.

"He was finally called up by the House Un-American Activities Committee in 1952, took the Fifth Amendment, and he was out," said Wagner.

His wife, Jean Abel, died of cancer in 1982. His longtime girlfriend, Helen Colton, found his body in his home when she went to pick him up for an event at the academy headquarters in Beverly Hills.

Colton, 86, saw Lees' body on the floor of his bedroom, covered by blankets, and called police.

" as unreal, but I couldn't believe it," she said. "I was befuddled for a moment. It was like a movie, not real life."

So, there it is: one second you're a working writer in Hollywood, you're making money, sitting in your office, taking studio notes like "Abbott's too mean," or "Costello's a loser and he's coming off gay; can we give him a love interest." Or "Frankenstein's so stern, could we get him to smile in this one, or maybe the boys can do 'Who's on First' with him in the middle. It might be a funny bit. Think about it."

Still, you're successful. You even survive the blacklist writing under a pseudonym. You make it into your 90s, a body of work behind you, you have a girlfriend, you're well liked in the neighborhood, and you're still living a vital life. Then some maniac breaks into your home and cuts your head off. You've got to wonder as your head is rolling toward the dishwasher whether you would have made such a big deal out of the daily show business agonies if you knew how it was all going to end. It makes me wonder if I should just relax already and not infuse it all with such importance. Maybe take a few weeks off, go to Hawaii, enjoy the money and time while it's there. But I don't. Because I'm an idiot. Particularly in light of the fact that the street this guy was living on was only two blocks from the house I rented for a year, which has no meaning whatsoever, but somehow gives you credibility when you relate the story to someone. Like, it could've been you. Which is how most people here relate an event. "I dated a woman who lived two blocks from O.J." "I used to eat in the restaurant where Robert Blake ate before allegedly shooting his wife." (And getting off.) In Hollywood, events are often meaningful as they relate to "me."

June 15

David Isaacs, Ken, Dave and I work up our pitch and go into Paramount. Divorced woman, big job, high-maintenance kids meets single guy starting a new business. Set in New York. Log line: A combination family show and romantic comedy about "two people who fall in love at the worst time of their lives." We pitch it. Goes well. Other than that they don't see Julia Louis-Dreyfus in the lead, which is mind-boggling. Putting aside whether we could actually get her, in theory, she's so perfect it's frightening. Either way, they agree to take it out and, toward that end, deals have to be made with my colleagues as they are no longer directly affiliated with Paramount. That's after a 17-year run at the studio for Ken and David, working on *Cheers*, *Wings*, *Frasier*, and *Becker*, as well as producing several of their own shows, and over a dozen years for Dave Hackel, mostly on *Wings* and *Becker*.

JULY 2004

Two regular cast members of CSI don't show up to work, reportedly in an attempt to garner more than the $100,000 an episode they were being paid for their services on the show. CBS' Les Moonves' response: "Here's my offer—nothing." Then he fires them. They cave. He rehires them. It takes balls to negotiate. It takes giant balls to re-negotiate. Or giant leverage.

July 12

Rose Catherine has given me the go-ahead to pitch Showtime a one-hour show. We set up a time to rehearse the pitch next week. The meeting is set. Then cancelled. Twice. Then set a third time. I show up, sit in her office, at which point she's immediately called into a meeting she'd forgotten about with Paul Reiser, who just signed a deal with Paramount. So they ditch me. The "meeting" version of "I've got a bigger name on the other line." Meanwhile, the deal with Ken, David, and Dave is still pending. We can't go in to pitch before it's done and none of us understand what's holding it up.

July 15

Sometimes shows are generated from a writer's inspiration. An idea he or she is dying to do. Other times, it's a deal that's thrown in your lap. This was the case with the Daryl "Chill" Mitchell project. My agent sets up a meeting with Perry Simon, former NBC executive and former head of Viacom Television, but now that Viacom television no longer exists, he has a development deal with Paramount. He says he has an idea he wants to discuss; I have no idea what it's about. So we meet in his office and he says he's got a tape to show me. The tape is of Daryl Mitchell, an actor whose career I've followed from the first moment I saw him on *The John Larroquette Show*. The second he came on screen, you knew this guy was funny. So was the show, until NBC improved it to death by taking a dark, funny show about the night manager in a bus station, a recovering alcoholic, and, through a series of improvements, like changing night to day, fixed it out of existence. But Chill was always funny, as he was later on *Veronica's Closet*. Then, three years ago he had a motorcycle accident that left him paralyzed. In fact, when I'd heard about it, other then the "there but for the grace of God" moment, as I also have a motorcycle, I tried to get him on *Becker*, but was too late. *Ed* on NBC grabbed him up and he was on that show for two years. But now he's looking to get back in with his own show.

Perry and I have lunch and discuss his idea, which was to make him a small claims court judge, a pulpit from which to rant. My initial reaction is that the premise seems a little "sitcom-y," but I can tell he's passionate about it and that if I raise any objections, he'll just hire someone else to write it, so I shut up and go with it. He says he's meeting other writers and will get back to me. He has a deal to go to NBC with it. NBC ends up passing on the idea as they have a character in one of their other pilots—a black guy in a wheelchair—who, while only in one scene, tested high, so now he's recurring in the show and they're afraid of having two black guys in wheelchairs on one network. I guess there's no overlap in having hundreds of white people in their 30's looking for love and success in the big city, but somehow the two wheelchair-black-guys phenomenon strikes them as redundant. So, if we do this, we'll be going to CBS first. Déjà vu. Fuck.

AUGUST 2004

The 2004 Olympics are held in Athens, Greece. The force of air generated by a simultaneous worldwide yawn by 6 billion people causes hurricanes to strike Florida. George Bush accepts Republican nomination. (He wins.) I try to watch the Republican convention but have to turn it off. Between Dick Cheney, Zell Miller, and George Bush, if I wanted to watch two ogres and an amusing jackass, I'd rent "Shrek 2."

August 2

My friend with the family show idea calls me again. He's got something else. Hardly a family show. Essentially it's *Sex and the City* but with hookers. Escorts. I check with Rose Catherine to see if they'd be open to this idea.

August 10

I pitch my one-hour idea to Showtime. Not a great audience. Almost comatose, in contrast to their living-dead counterparts at CBS. For a moment, I consider that maybe it's me but decide it's not. It's them. I walk out feeling like I just ate a bad lunch.

August 13

Showtime passes. No explanation. Just pass. And on my birthday, the bastards. In my bitterness, I begin to wonder about the product on their network. While HBO is setting the gold standard for programming, with *The Sopranos*, *Deadwood*, *Sex and the City*, *Six Feet Under*, *Costas Now*, *Real Time with Bill Maher*, *Real Sports with Bryant Gumbel*, and *Curb Your Enthusiasm*—(and since *Entourage and Extras)*, Showtime has failed to ignite the public with anything. In fact, between *The L Word* and *Queer as Folk* they've almost pulled off the impossible—that of making lesbians unsexy and gay guys unfunny.

I suggest taking it to F/X, which has broken ground with *Nip/Tuck* and *The Shield*. Maybe they're up for a more risky comedy. The response from Paramount: forget it. Don't bother going to F/X. They're not looking for this type of show so it'll be an impossible sale. One month later, I check out *Variety* online with my morning coffee and nearly do a spit take reading an article that F/X just picked up a comedy pilot with the exact same premise. So much for "You'll never sell it at F/X." (Fast Forward: the show: "It's Always Sunny in Philadelphia," just got picked up for a back order. Another interesting companion show—*Starved*—did not.)

August 15

Still haven't heard anything on the Chill Mitchell project. Rose Catherine insists I'm "still part of the deal" but have to get in the room with Chill to see if we click.

August 26

A three-hour lunch with Chill, his manager, Perry and his associate. We talk about the show, life, politics, whatever. We all laugh, so I assume I passed the audition. I've got several shows working at this point but agree to stay with this if it goes and not to follow the path of the "creator/deserter"— a writer who creates a show, gets it on the air and then, for whatever reason, doesn't want to be part of the day-to-day production, but still draws a weekly fee from creating it and eventual syndication royalties if it makes it all the way. Sweet.

On the Escorts show, I'm passed from the comedy department to the drama development person. I give her the general idea over the phone, which she likes, and we set a meeting to go in and pitch her in detail. Still waiting for them to finish the deal with Ken, David and Dave on the Julia Louis-Dreyfus (hereafter referred to as "JLD" as her name is a bitch to type over and over). She still has no idea this show exists but that's OK. We're not saying we have her attached. Just that it would, in theory, based on the lead character, be perfect for her. Paramount still disagrees. My partners and I agree this is insanity. They're just wrong. Flat out wrong. This is not a matter of taste or opinion. This is factually incorrect. Still, it's all moot until we get in to pitch. The agents check it out and insist the deal will close any day now. Our goal was to get into the networks in August to beat the fall rush, as this idea seems like one that could easily be pitched by someone else and the last thing you want to hear is "Great idea. Too bad we just bought one like it yesterday." The one time in TV where ideas are not shit is when someone beats you in with something so similar it cancels yours out. But now they say the deal will be done by September. In all, two months to make a deal in which no money is changing hands.

SEPTEMBER 2004

Dan Rather embroiled in fact-checking gaffe regarding phony letter regarding George Bush's military service. American death toll in Iraq reaches 1000. In the sixties, the nightly news would report the "body count" both Americans and Vietnamese, with the same statistical dispassion reserved for sports scores. God, how we love our stats in this country.

999 soldiers dead and we're not ready to report it. The thermometer hasn't hit that high mark yet. Shit, if only one more would get killed we'd have that milestone number to lead off the news. Oh, wait. One more dead? Great. Now we've got our 1000. Still, somehow "death toll" doesn't seem inclusive enough, since every dead soldier had other soldiers they served with, not to mention family, friends, neighbors, and relatives, all of whom are grieving. We need a new phrase or idea to encompass this. Maybe "pain index." Or "misery quotient." Or "suffering barometer." Then we could throw it on the back of the nightly weather report, right behind the "pollen count."

THE 2004-2005 NETWORK TV SEASON

September officially begins the fall season representing the pride of each network's development efforts and the consensus of the respective experts involved that this is the best and brightest they have to offer and each show is in its proper time slot. Before the month is over Fox's *Method & Red* is cancelled. The WB moves *Drew Carey's Green Screen Show*, *The Mountain*, and *Blue Collar TV* to other time slots. *Tru Calling*, also on Fox, has production stopped, its order cut, and its future uncertain. Also, Fox's much-heralded boxing reality show *The Next Great Champ* starring Oscar De La Hoya is cancelled due to extreme apathy, causing those involved with Sylvester Stallone's *The Contender* on NBC to shit a brick. CBS pushes *The Amazing Race* to November.

On the upside, *Jack & Bobby* on WB and *Joey* on NBC are given full season orders. *Joey*'s not getting "*Friends*-level" numbers, but they'll only cancel the sole *Friends* spin-off in its first season under threat of death. (Fast forward: they cancel it after its second season.)

schedule 2004 SEPTEMBER

Day	Network	8-8:30	8:30-9	9-9:30	9:30-10	10-11
MONDAY	ABC	The Benefactor / ABC Monday Night Movie (after football ends in January)		Monday Night Football		Grey's Anatomy (after football ends in January)
	CBS	Still Standing	Listen Up	Everybody Loves Raymond	Two and a Half Men	CSI: Miami
	NBC	Fear Factor		Las Vegas		LAX
	FOX	North Shore / Athens		The Swan 2 / 24		
	WB	7th Heaven		Everwood		
	UPN	One on One	Half & Half	Girlfriends	Second Time Around	
TUESDAY	ABC	My Wife & Kids	George Lopez	According to Jim	Rodney	NYPD Blue / Blind Justice
	CBS	Navy NCIS		Clubhouse		Judging Amy
	NBC	Last Comic Standing / The Contender		Father of the Pride	Scrubs	Law & Order: Special Victims Unit
	FOX	The Billionaire: Branson's Quest for the Best / American Idol		House		
	WB	Gilmore Girls		One Tree Hill		
	UPN	All of Us	Eve	Veronica Mars		
WEDNESDAY	ABC	Lost		The Bachelor		Wife Swap
	CBS	60 Minutes		The King of Queens	Center of the Universe	CSI: NY
	NBC	Hawaii		The West Wing / Revelations		Law & Order
	FOX	That '70s Show	Quintuplets / Related by Family	The Bernie Mac Show / American Idol	Method & Red 9/30 off air / The Bernie Mac Show	
	WB	Smallville		Blue Collar TV 9/1 [illegible]	Drew Carey's Green Screen Show 9/1 [illegible]	
	UPN	America's Next Top Model / The Road to Stardom With Missy Elliott		Kevin Hill		
THURSDAY	ABC	Extreme Makeover		Life as We Know It		Primetime Live
	CBS	Survivor: Vanuatu		CSI: Crime Scene Investigation		Without a Trace
	NBC	Joey 9/30 full season	Will & Grace	The Apprentice 2		ER
	FOX	The O.C.		Tru Calling 9/14 pushed indefinitely		
	WB	The Mountain moves to Wed. @9		Studio 7		
	UPN	WWE SmackDown!				
FRIDAY	ABC	8 Simple Rules	Complete Savages	Hope & Faith	Less Than Perfect	20/20
	CBS	Joan of Arcadia		JAG		Dr. Vegas
	NBC	Dateline NBC		Third Watch		Medical Investigation
	FOX	Specials / The Inside		The Next Great Champ 9/22 encores cancelled / Jonny Zero		
	WB	What I Like About You	Commando Nanny	Reba	Grounded for Life	
	UPN	America's Next Top Model (repeat)		Star Trek: Enterprise		
SATURDAY	ABC	The Wonderful World of Disney				
	CBS	The Amazing Race 9/16 pushed to tues. in Nov.		Crime Time Saturday		48 Hours Mysteries
	NBC	NBC Saturday Night Movie				
	FOX	Cops	Cops	America's Most Wanted		

Day	Network	7-7:30	7:30-8	8-8:30	8:30-9	9-10	10-11
SUNDAY	ABC	America's Funniest Home Videos		Extreme Makeover: Home Edition		Desperate Housewives / Alias	Boston Legal
	CBS	60 Minutes		Cold Case		CBS Sunday Movie	
	NBC	Dateline NBC		American Dreams		Law & Order: Criminal Intent	Crossing Jordan
	FOX	King of the Hill / Kelsey Grammer Presents: The Sketch Show	Malcolm in the Middle / King of the Hill	The Simpsons	Arrested Development / Malcolm in the Middle	The Partner / Arrested Development, American Dad	
	WB	Steve Harvey's Big Time		Charmed		Jack & Bobby full season [illegible]	

KEY: NEW SHOW; NEW TIME; Fox Nov.-Jan.; Fox Jan.-June

September 3

Pitched the "escort" idea to Stacy Adams at Paramount. Went well. She likes it. Has to run it by her boss, but she thinks we could go to F/X. Meanwhile, I hear a rumor that Garry Hart is out as President of Paramount TV, and will be replaced by David Stapf, who was our current programming exec at CBS on *Becker*. This shouldn't derail any of the three projects I have working. It shouldn't. Then again, it could.

September 9

Rumors confirmed. Les commemorates the new pitching season by officially throwing out the first executive. Garry Hart is out. David Stapf is in. Garry goes indy prod and sets up camp on the lot. (Next time I see him, instead of a tie, he's wearing an enormous smile.) The other execs haven't officially heard their fate, but know it would not be unwise to get hold of some packing boxes. Usually they keep the old guard around until the new people get their footing and the old guard starts to think that maybe the new regime will keep them around. Then they fire them.

In another desperation move, I take my revised pilot, which isn't going to fly as an hour show, and turn it into a play. It's basically a two-act structure anyway. Toward that end, I call a guy I know who's done theater, and send it to him to see if it strikes him as play-worthy.

On other fronts, I'm getting ready to pitch the WB and ABC next week on the Daryl Mitchell show. This feels more sitcom-y than anything I want to do, but if that's what the networks are putting on then I have to protect myself and at least play the game in the event that everything else I'm trying bombs out.

Meanwhile, the first of the "Let's analyze the fall season" articles starts appearing in the papers.

Daily Variety
9-10-04

FRESH FALL FARE FLAT

Most firstrun skeins sluggish; Eye reality hot

By RICK KISSELL

Maybe it's still too early for auds to get pumped up for fresh fall fare but most of the firstrun programs on the broadcast nets are drawing modest ratings.

While CBS continues to shine with its summer reality tandem of "The Amazing Race" and "Big Brother," and NBC is off to a solid start with laffer "Father of the Pride," other new and returning skeins are doing just OK — at best.

Peacock vets "Fear Factor" and "Scrubs" have been below par with the first two weeks of their early fall segs, and Fox wasn't at full throttle with the relaunch of its returning Wednesday comedy lineup this week, although its "That '70s Show"-led block won the night among young adults.

The second regular seg for NBC's "Hawaii" dipped 27%.

Also on Wednesday — still more than a week before the official start of the fall season — the second regular seg for NBC cop drama "Hawaii" tumbled by 27% from its mediocre preem and already looks to be in trouble.

"Hawaii" (2.4/8 in adults 18-49, 8.44 million viewers overall) tied ABC's repeats of "My Wife and Kids" for a distant second-place finish behind Fox in 18-49 and lagged CBS' "60 Minutes" (2.0/6 in 18-49, 9.89m) in total viewers.

And it figures to only get tougher for "Hawaii," as competing dramas "Smallville" on the WB and "Lost" on ABC invade the time period Sept. 22.

For Fox, "That '70s Show" (3.9/13 in 18-49, 7.85m) dominated the 8 o'clock half-hour in key demos and was the night's top show in 18-49, but even its numbers were on the low side. *Turn to page 19*

Continued from page 2

Also winning in 18-49 for Fox were "Quintuplets" at 8:30 (3.1/9 in 18-49, 6.20m), which retained a tame 79% of its lead-in, and "Bernie Mac" at 9 (3.2/9, 6.58m). "Quintuplets" was the night's top draw among teens (4.0/16).

At 9:30, "Method & Red" at 9:30 (2.2/6 in 18-49, 5.01m) fell off quite a bit, placing third in 18-49.

National ratings for Tuesday of this week, meanwhile, showed that CBS' "Amazing Race 5" (5.1/13 in 18-49, 10.85m) and "Big Brother 5" (4.4/11, 9.76m) both hit season highs in 18-49 as they near their Sept. 21 finale.

■

Thanks to "Father of the Pride" and a Sunday NASCAR race, NBC prevailed in key demos for the Aug. 30-Sept. 5 frame, according to final Nielsen nationals, which weren't issued until Thursday due to Hurricane Frances-related processing delays at the ratings company's Florida offices.

The Peacock averaged a 2.8 rating/9 share in adults 18-49, comfortably ahead of its bunched rivals, with CBS second (2.3/7) and Fox and ABC tied for third (2.2/7). Net also won in adults 25-54 (3.2/9) and total viewers (7.48 million), edging past CBS (7.16m) in the latter.

Numbers were muted some for the Big Three due to low-rated coverage of the Republican National Convention on three nights and overall lower viewing levels before Labor Day weekend.

Leading the way for NBC was the premiere of "Father of the Pride" (5.4/15 in 18-49, 12.39m), which became the highest-rated entertainment program on any net since the May sweep (*Daily Variety*, Sept. 2).

Also, a Nextel Cup NASCAR race dominated primetime on Sunday in key demos (3.1/11 in 18-49, 8.21m).

Elsewhere, Fox did well Wednesday with a special two-hour preview seg of reality series "Renovate My Family" (4.0/12 in 18-49, 8.26m) but stumbled Monday with the preview of another unscripted show, "Complex: Malibu" (1.7/5, 3.46m).

CBS was paced by "Big Brother" and "Amazing Race" on Tuesday, edging past NBC's premieres to take the night in 18-49.

And…the reviews, from which writers whose shows weren't picked up look for revenge. Venal prick that I am, I found mine. Critics are brilliant when they see the obvious; i.e., they agree with you.

Variety – 9-17-04

TELEVISION:
BRIAN LOWRY

Listen Up

(Series, CBS, Mon. Sept. 20, 8:30 p.m.)

Filmed in L.A. by Regency Television in association with CBS Prods. Executive producers, Jeff Martin, Lindy DeKoven; co-executive producers, David Litt, Daphne Pollon; producers, Jason Alexander, Suzy Greenberg; co-producer, Linda Figueiredo; director, Andy Ackerman; writer, Martin; camera, Nick McLean; editor, Darryl Bates; music, Brian Kirk; production designer, John Shaffner; casting, Leslie Litt. **30 MIN.**

Tony Kleinman .... Jason Alexander
Bernie Widmar ...... Malcolm-Jamal Warner
Dana Kleinman .... Wendy Makkena
Megan Kleinman .... Daniella Monet
Mickey Kleinman .... Will Rothbaar

Whatever modicum of good will "Listen Up" engenders in the course of a mostly undistinguished half-hour dissipates near the end, when star Jason Alexander — best known for "Seinfeld," but also an accomplished song-and-dance man — inexplicably bursts into a musical number. With that, the show labels itself another vanity piece, a bit better than Alexander's last at-bat for ABC, "Bob Patterson," but still a swing and a miss. Although the show should do a reasonably good job sustaining its lead-in, that owes more to inertia than material that demands to be seen, much less heard.

Jason Alexander and Malcolm-Jamal Warner are dueling sportscasters in the CBS sitcom "Listen Up," from Regency Television.

FALL TV PREVIEW

Using Washington Post sports columnist Tony Kornheiser as its inspiration, the series teams Alexander with "Cosby" kid Malcolm-Jamal Warner as the opinionated hosts of a sports talk program — as if the yammering idiots on Kornheiser's "Pardon the Interruption" and ESPN companion "Around the Horn" begged for company.

Like most such sitcoms, however, the job is just half the life of Tony Kleinman (Alexander), who begins writing a general column for the lifestyle section and, in no time flat, alienates his 14-year-old daughter Megan (Daniella Monet) by embarrassing her in print.

In the pox-on-both-their-houses department, Tony is an obvious dunce for being so clueless as to his daughter's feelings, but the kid — while outwardly adorable — proves such a whiny brat it's hard not to hope he writes another column, if only to roll it up and smack her with it. Clearly, this newfangled parenting approach isn't yielding dividends, because the level of father-daughter discourse is all sniping, no talk.

The addition of Wendy Makkena (a role recast after last spring) helps bring a little zest to the domestic side, and Warner exhibits decent chemistry with Alexander as his squabbling co-host. Still, there are few laughs, with the one modestly funny visual moment coming when Tony — banned from attending his daughter's soccer game — tries to hide behind a rock and ends up looking like a pervert.

There are doubtless additional lessons here about second-banana syndrome pertaining to the "Seinfeld" co-stars. In Alexander's case, he's a bigger-than-TV comedic presence, much like Nathan Lane, whom he followed onstage in "The Producers." Neither is easily contained by the sitcom format. And while "Seinfeld" provided Alexander an ideal role, its unique tone can't easily be replicated, as Michael Richards and Julia Louis-Dreyfus can attest.

Thematically, "Listen Up" seems perfectly suited to its time-slot, a family comedy about a sports journalist nestled next to "Everybody Loves Raymond." Yet the halo from the established show just exposes how meek a prospect this rookie is.

CBS has fared surprisingly well even with mundane comedies in the first hour of its Monday lineup, but the stakes have been raised with "Raymond" preparing to sign off. In that context, it's hard to fathom "Listen Up" helping CBS fill the void left by one of TV's top-rated sitcoms.

VARIETY.com Reed Business Information

Welcome IAN GURVITZ (

Advertise | Contact Us | Help | Link

FILM | TV | WORLD | BUSINESS | MUSIC | INTERNET | HOME ENT | LEGIT | LEGAL | TORONTO FILM

NEWS | COLUMNS | REVIEWS | CHARTS | EVENTS | SPECIAL REPORTS

Home > Reviews - Center of the Universe

Last Updated Sep. 28, :

V TELEVISION HAVE Variety headlines delivered daily by email

SEAR
All
advan

Recently Reviewed

Posted: Sun., Sep. 26, 2004, 6:00am PT

EMAIL REVIEW
PRINT REVIEW
EMAIL AUTHOR

Center of the Universe

(Series -- CBS, Wed. Oct. 6, 9:30 p.m.)

Taped in L.A. by Tannenbaum Prods. in association with Warner Bros. Television and CBS Prods. Executive producers, Andy Ackerman, Eric Tannenbaum, Kim Tannenbaum, Mitchel Katlin, Nat Bernstein, Alan Kirschenbaum; producer, Bari Halle Cannon; director, Ackerman; writers, Bernstein, Katlin.

John Barnett - John Goodman
Kate Barnett - Jean Smart
Tommy Barnett - Diedrich Bader
Lily Barnett - Melinda McGraw
Miles Barnett - Spencer Breslin
Art Barnett - Ed Asner
Marge Barnett - Olympia Dukakis

"Th

By BRIAN LOWRY

Critics invariably have a least-favorite new series each fall, and CBS has generously obliged with "Center of the Universe," a colossal waste of a talented cast in a show with little point or purpose. John Goodman has the title role as the set-upon guy who holds a crazy family together, but crass writing and overly broad gags result in a series that makes "Yes, Dear" look like "Masterpiece Theater." Blessed with a hammocked berth between "King Of Queens" and "CSI: New York," sheer inertia is this sitcom's best chance of not becoming a chalk outline.

John Barnett (Goodman) and his wife Kate (Jean Smart) love each other, but oy, the relatives. Their kid ("The Cat in the Hat's" Spencer Breslin) is a nerd who favors sport coats, John's brother (Diedrich Bader) is a slacker, his sister (Melinda McGraw) has man trouble, and his Viagra-popping dad (Ed Asner) is aggravating his equally nutty mom (Olympia Dukakis).

TV Reviews From the Same Period

Revenge of the Middle-Aged Woman *9/23/04 9:19pm*

Hustle *9/23/04 2:31pm*

Clubhouse *9/23/04 2:28pm*

Dr. Vegas *9/22/04 1:44pm*

CSI: NY *9/21/04 4:42pm*

56th Annual Emmy Awards *9/19/04 8:29pm*

BOX
Weeken
Sep. 24

1 The F
2 Sky C World
3 Mr. 3(
4 Resid Apoca
5 First [
6 Cellul
7 Shaur
8 Wimb
9 Witho
10 Hero

Despite all that to keep them busy, in the premiere, John and Kate decide to renew their wedding vows, an event of course threatened by members of the wacky brood each imploding for one reason or another. This forces John to make like the COTU and reestablish order in his little world.

Beyond the fact that nearly everyone here has been in a much better comedy, there's something decidedly retro about the program, with producing team Mitchel Katlin and Nat Bernstein aspiring to a level of zaniness that never materializes. Although everyone appears to be giving their all, the tone is thus uniformly lifeless -- perhaps because the entire show feels as if it were pieced together from parts of old sitcoms.

Credit Goodman's work ethic between this and his voice stint on "Father of the Pride." After a seminal comedy like "Roseanne," though, it's too bad he hasn't been more selective in subsequent sitcom choices, as anyone who remembers "Normal, Ohio" can attest.

The Larry Elder Show *9/19/04 5:19pm*

Complete Savages *9/19/04 6:00am*

The Mountain *9/19/04 6:00am*

Veronica Mars *9/19/04 6:00am*

Lost *9/19/04 6:00am*

Rodney *9/19/04 6:00am*

Current Reviews...

The same can largely be said of CBS' comedy development, with "Two And A Half Men" representing a recent anomaly by actually being funny. Granted, the network clearly has no intention of reinventing the wheel, but sister Viacom networks Nick at Nite and TV Land already serve up more laudable reruns nightly for those hungering for this kind of warmed-over dish.

Camera, Steven V. Silver; editor, Bill Lowe; music, Rick Marotta; casting, Nikki Valko, Ken Miller. 30 MIN.

'Center of the Universe'

John Goodman and Jean Smart celebrate 20 years of blissful togetherness.

The new CBS comedy "Center of the Universe" stumbles onto the primetime air trapped seemingly in a creative vacuum between amusement and poignancy, struggling to locate both but settling instead for tepid interaction and innuendo. This isn't necessarily a shock, considering CBS' delay in getting the show onto the schedule — often an indicator of trepidation. But it's surprising given this show's impressive pedigree, headed by Emmy-winning producer-director Andy Ackerman ("Cheers," "Seinfeld," "Frasier") and an impressive cast of TV veterans who include John Goodman, Jean Smart, Ed Asner and Olympia Dukakis.

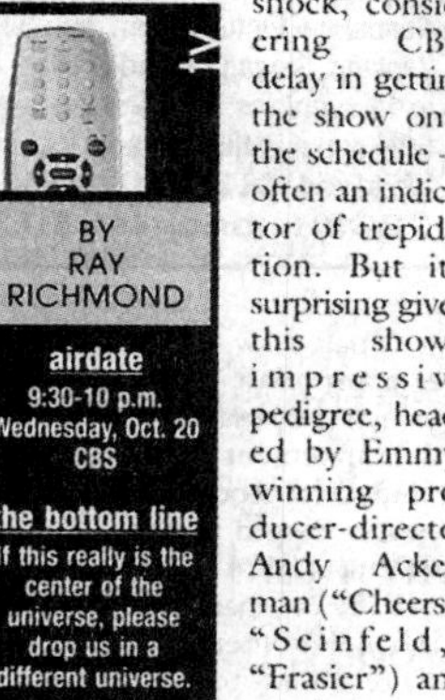

tv
BY RAY RICHMOND
airdate
9:30-10 p.m. Wednesday, Oct. 20 CBS
the bottom line
If this really is the center of the universe, please drop us in a different universe.

In other words, there is an awful lot of talent being wasted in "Center of the Universe," which packs no comedic punch whatsoever. Airing opposite the fading but still formidable "The West Wing" on NBC, "The Bachelor" on ABC and "The Bernie Mac Show" on Fox, its life could well be a short one.

As things unfold in the pilot, we meet John and Kate Barnett (Goodman and Smart), a happily married couple with the requisite eccentric family. They are about to renew their wedding vows after 20 blissful years together. But uniting their immediate kin under one roof for the renuptials proves a chore given everyone's cloying dopeyness. There's his meddling mother, Marge (Dukakis), and his feisty daddy, Art (Asner), who likes to pop herbal sexual supplements like they're candy.

We also meet John's gleefully oblivious brother, Tommy (Diedrich Bader), who has inexplicably been hired to work at John's security company. And John's sister, Lily (Melinda McGraw), is another handful: a therapist with more emotional issues than all of her patients combined. Barely introduced in the opener is the couple's 12-year-old son, Miles (Spencer Breslin), who seems to travel to the beat of his own bizarre drummer because, hey, it's a family tradition. It looks like things aren't going to work out for the big event because of a distinct lack of cooperation. But the day is finally saved. Or whatever.

Scribes Nat Bernstein and Mitchel Katlin (who also co-created the show and are among

See **"CENTER"** *on page 10*

CENTER OF THE UNIVERSE
CBS
Warner Bros. Television Production Inc. in association with CBS Prods.

Credits: Executive producers: Andy Ackerman, Eric Tannenbaum, Kim Tannenbaum, Mitchel Katlin, Nat Bernstein; Producer: Bari Halle Cannon; Director: Andy Ackerman; Writers: Nat Bernstein, Mitchel Katlin; Director of photography: Steven V. Silver; Art director: Scott Heineman; Costume designer: Mary T. Quigley; Editor: Bill Lowe; Music: Rick Marotta; Sound mixer: Bruce Arledge Jr.; Casting: Nikki Valko, Ken Miller. **Cast:** John Barnett: John Goodman; Kate Barnett: Jean Smart; Tommy Barnett: Diedrich Bader; Lily Barnett: Melinda McGraw; Miles Barnett: Spencer Breslin; Art Barbett: Edward Asner; Marge Barnett: Olympia Dukakis; Minister: Holmes Osborne.

'Center'

Continued from page 6—

the exec producers) craft a premiere teleplay that is utterly lifeless and certainly laughless. It isn't that it's offensive or implausible; it's merely inert, with the cast reduced to going through the motions. How CBS could have purchased this show based on the pilot material is a bit baffling, unless the network chieftains figured that with these big names involved it would ultimately improve.

That may yet happen for "Center of the Universe," but there is no evidence of it during the first installment.

Good luck in Week 2. This show is going to need it. ■

Hollywood Reporter
10-20-04

September 14

Pitched the Chill Mitchell show to David Janollari at WB. Nice guy. He actually laughs, which is always encouraging. (Fast forward: He's not in that job anymore, as the WB, as mentioned, no longer exists.) The pitch goes well, but it's probably not for them. No angst-ridden teenagers living in small towns looking for love while shooting each other soulful looks. Next stop on the pitch tour—CBS. We crowd into a small conference room. Perry has a five-minute presentation DVD on Chill he wants to show. Despite a ten-foot-tall stack of equipment in the cabinet, no one knows how to work it. So much for technology.

Now it's my turn. I look across the table at the same sphinx-like executives I pitched to exactly a year ago who bought and then passed on my project. What flashes through my mind is a sepia-tone photograph a friend and colleague, Russ Woody, used to bring into the writers room at *Becker* for show and tell, along with the erotic birthday card he once got from his mother. (In case you're wondering what kind of people end up doing this work.) This picture was of his old relatives in Texas, circa 1930s dust bowl. Looked like a Grapes of Wrath casting call. Stern, weather-beaten farmers in overalls and wives in gingham dresses, posing against the side of a barn holding pitchforks and shotguns, looking like they'd just as easily shoot the first possum or Jew that wandered on to the property. A colder, more life-beaten, downtrodden, stomped-on, god-forsaken group of individuals I have never seen. Yet, I would rather be pitching to those people right now than facing the CBS development execs again.

So I just start talking. I pitch my heart out. And they…just…sit there. Jokes greeted with polite smiles. People shifting uncomfortably in their chairs like they were muffling farts. I walk out thinking that pitching to these people is like having sex with your first cousin. There's supposed to be some pleasure associated with the act, but somehow it just feels unclean. I'm exhausted. I walk to my car getting mentally ready to pitch to Fox tomorrow morning, but first I need to go home, stand under a hot shower and try to scrub off the shame.

September 17

I get to Fox several hours early, which is a stupid habit I can't break. I hit the commissary, have some coffee, go over my notes, walk around the lot, trash the gift shop, and just waste time. We'll be pitching to Gail Berman, head of the network, whom I've never met, but I figure no matter what happens, it'll be good to make the connection. (Fast forward: she's hired at Paramount in movie development, just around the time I leave.) I still have an hour to kill, when my cell phone rings. It's Perry. The Fox meeting is cancelled. Like a trip wire, my mind goes right into "Assholes, why do they always wait for the last minute, etc…" but before I can get too far, he continues, saying it's cancelled because CBS wants to buy the show.

OK. So, that's good. After nine months of pitching all over town, I finally make a sale. My momentary elation is just that…momentary, as he quickly gets to the "but." "But," he says, they don't like the A story (the main story) I pitched, which was about Chill's character reconnecting with the girl who dumped him after his motorcycle accident. Too dark. Too depressing. They want something lighter. More "up." Oh, fuck me. I just got off this ride. Same people. Same situation. Somehow they know how to get right to the heart of a story, find what is most appealing, interesting, and human about it, then rip it out. Like a pig rooting for truffles. It's part of the answer to the question of why network television is so mediocre. There are business people in charge who use a "take no chances" approach to the process. The only people who can fight them on this are those with enough clout to shut them up, and that usually means having one bona fide hit under your belt so that you can argue them down, or better yet, pitch directly to their bosses so you don't have to bother with what the underlings think. But getting that first hit means you have to successfully navigate these waters in the first place.

So, now we have to figure out a new A Story, re-outline, get the outline approved and go to script. That process will take months, as before, with even more people involved, and more notes along the way. It's going to be excruciating, but my attitude this time will be to give them what they want. Make them happy, whatever it takes, and grab whatever satisfaction I can from being able to pay my bills and keep whatever stock I might have in the business alive, while hoping to find something to love about the project as time goes on.

Now, bitching aside, the underlying fear in all this is that your level of success may truly be a reflection of your talents reaching their own level. If you're at all prone to introspection or self-doubt, you have to come to terms with the possibility that you may only be as good as you are and not as good as you think you are, and that creating something that climbs out of the pack may be beyond your reach and talent. Not everyone can do everything, and if you work steadily and survive, you're already ahead of most people. If you make millions, you're way ahead of most. But, still, the drive to do something that makes a mark, gets attention, and is called "good" by someone who's not a direct family member never goes away. I guess it's good to have goals as they can spur you on to keep thinking while honestly examining your own abilities along the way and either accepting them for what they are or figuring out how to get beyond them. With that in mind, I call Stacy Adams on the drive back, who said we could go to Showtime with the Escorts project. I also hear that the deal on the JLD show that has been stalled for months will soon be finalized.

September 20

I've come up with another A story for Daryl Mitchell and will go back in to Paramount to pitch, hoping we can get approval so we can go to outline. Meanwhile, we're still waiting on the JLD deal to get finished. As well, the deal to pitch the Escorts show to Showtime is still pending. Given the odds of success, it feels good to have a few things working.

September 22

And so it begins. Having worked up a brand-new A story with my producing partners, we went in to pitch the brand-new studio development people on the changes. Absent is Rose Catherine, who was eventually let go, replaced by another former CBS exec. After the obligatory small talk, I launch into my pitch, breaking down the new story, throwing in jokes to give them the flavor of it, and ending with a scene and joke we liked from the first pitch. Then there's a beat. Then came the words you hate to hear after a pitch: "Here are my concerns."

And their concerns went right down network main street. The character is too reactive. It's too down. We need to capture Daryl's cheerful spirit and energy and the warmth he exudes when you meet him. The way he just reaches out to people and makes them feel at ease. All fine qualities for a person to have in real life, but not for a character. Characters are interesting because of their flaws, faults, needs, and desires, not in spite of them.

Once again I think back to successful shows. The characters are damaged. That's what makes them interesting. The one half-hour show on network TV (other than *Scrubs*) that most writers respect and that shows any creative spark is *Arrested Development* on Fox, sort of a "dysfunctional family" show, which is a phrase often used in pitches to describe a family that fights a lot but, as must be the case with most network fare, really loves each other. These people don't do that. They simply dysfunction and try to screw each other at every turn. That's why it's funny. Most of these characters are not redeemed. Whether Fox keeps the show on despite the iffy numbers remains to be seen. So far, they've stood by it. Winning several Emmys certainly helped justify that decision. But eventually, if it doesn't get ratings, it will dissolve into that cult favorite netherworld inhabited by *Freaks and Geeks*. Still, it works creatively because the characters are all damaged.

The new Paramount execs suggest that instead of focusing on Chill's character's problems, we have him get involved in the problems of those around him, straightening out their lives and giving them hope with his cheerful spirit, warmth and energy. We need to root for him. I'm thinking: he's a nice, funny, guy who's in a wheelchair. Unless he strangles puppies in his spare time, it's not going to be too tough to get the audience on his side. Outside I nod and smile. Inside, I'm freaking out, 'cause basically what I'm hearing is *Touched By A Wheelchair*. "Even though he's in a wheelchair he doesn't let that get him down and he's just the most positive, happy, plucky wheelchair judge you've ever seen, putting aside whatever secret pain he might be in to take care of the wounded birds around him," like the soldier who, riddled with bullets, still crawls into the middle of a firefight to pull out his wounded comrade. Fuck me, but this is so tragically unfunny.

Frankly, if you walked into Beverly Hills right now and swung a dead cat, you'd hit at least a dozen writers and if you asked them on the spot whether they could create a half-hour comedy based around a flawless character, the answer would be a resounding "Are you out of your fucking mind?" If the character has no drive, no desire for anything, no problems to solve on his or her own, then he's perfect, and perfect people are dull and humorless. This is Writing 101. Characters need flaws. That's where the humor comes from. And I'm writing a show for an actor who is funny and is going to read this script with one thought in mind: "Where am I funny?" Answer right now: Nowhere. You're not. But you help many, many people. This is a recipe for disaster. And I can't argue.

If this were a writers' room, and we were breaking a story, the people there would know how wrong this was and you could make your case intelligently by saying that's really fucking idiotic. It's sappy. You're cutting his comedic balls off by making him so pure. We'll never be able to hang jokes on a character who has no attitude; he's like a fucking motivational speaker. But these are studio people and if they don't like something—that's it. It's dead. And they speak for the people at the network because they know what's going to fly over there because they've just come from working there. Plus I'm trying to do several other projects with Paramount, so arguing with the new folks will just add a sour overtone to everything else and will work against me for the remainder of my deal. But, again, I signed on for this, it's the only project I've sold so far, and this is Daryl's shot to get back on the air so I agree to keep thinking. The experience is like one of those vomit burps ("verps," I think Tim Allen called them), where the food shoots back up into your throat just enough to leave a vile, rancid taste in your mouth. Then you have to choke it back down and continue digesting.

Perry calms me down and we agree to work out yet a third A story and re-pitch it. So, now it's almost back to square one, recreating this pilot again so that it's happy, and peppy and no one gets down and everyone's left smiling and wanting to see more. Then and only then does it have a chance to move on in the process toward being shot. And once they're all happy, they say "See, we were right, this works." Well, it works because it's the only idea that was allowed to live. All other ideas were confiscated like a six-pack smuggled under some face-painted idiot's coat on the way into a football stadium. Sometimes you need to give them the kind of show they want if you're ever going to have a chance of getting on. The ultimate fear is that once it's been stripped of any depth, intelligence, or emotion, you've basically produced yet another network sitcom, and when it comes time to be reviewed it gets lambasted by the critics for being yet another typical piece of network garbage, and the person whose name is all over that review as the "overpaid hack sitcom writer responsible for this shit" is yours.

OCTOBER 2004

Boston Red Sox break the 86-year-old "Curse of the Bambino" and win the World Series. Yankee fans are gracious, saying: "Hey, even the sun shines out of a dog's ass one day." Ann Coulter (the illegitimate daughter of Foghorn Leghorn and Sharon Stone) publishes a book: How to Talk to a Liberal. The title goes on longer but is not worth repeating, much like any of the venomous bullshit this woman spews. Essentially, she's just old swine in new bottles. For more information on this subject, read Al Franken's Lies and the Lying Liars Who Tell Them: A Fair and Balanced Look at the Right. Thank God for Al Franken—the Van Helsing of the left.

The fall season goes on, once again proving William Goldman's adage about show business: "Nobody knows anything." Fox moves *North Shore* to Thursday. NBC moves *LAX* to Wednesday. CBS moves *Clubhouse* to Saturday. NBC cancels *Hawaii*, while pushing *The Contender* to midseason, as FOX moves schedule — 2004 OCTOBER

Day	Network	8-8:30		9-9:30		10-11
MONDAY	ABC	The Benefactor / ABC Monday Night Movie (after football ends in January)		Monday Night Football		Grey's Anatomy (after football ends in January)
	CBS	Still Standing	Listen Up	Everybody Loves Raymond	Two and a Half Men	CSI: Miami
	NBC	Fear Factor		Las Vegas		LAX 10/15 moving to Wed. @8
	FOX	North Shore moves to thurs @9 / Athens		The Swan 2 / 24		
	WB	7th Heaven		Everwood		
	UPN	One on One	Half & Half	Girlfriends	Second Time Around	
TUESDAY	ABC	My Wife & Kids	George Lopez	According to Jim	Rodney	NYPD Blue / Blind Justice
	CBS	Navy NCIS		Clubhouse moves to Sat.		Judging Amy
	NBC	Last Comic Standing 10/11 Pulled off air / The Contender 10/6 Pushed to Midseason		Father of the Pride	Scrubs	Law & Order: Special Victims Unit
	FOX	The Billionaire: Branson's Quest for the Best / American Idol		Next Great Champ 10/6 moved to cable		
	WB	Gilmore Girls		One Tree Hill		
	UPN	All of Us	Eve	Veronica Mars		
WEDNESDAY	ABC	Lost 10/20 Full season		The Bachelor		Wife Swap
	CBS	60 Minutes		The King of Queens	Center of the Universe	CSI: NY
	NBC	Hawaii 10/15 on hiatus/cancelled		The West Wing / Revelations		Law & Order
	FOX	That '70s Show	Quintuplets / Related by Family	The Bernie Mac Show / American Idol	Method & Red / The Bernie Mac Show	
	WB	Smallville		Blue Collar TV	Drew Carey's Green Screen Show	
	UPN	America's Next Top Model / The Road to Stardom With Missy Elliott		Kevin Hill		
THURSDAY	ABC	Extreme Makeover		Life as We Know It		Primetime Live
	CBS	Survivor: Vanuatu		CSI: Crime Scene Investigation		Without a Trace
	NBC	Joey	Will & Grace	The Apprentice 2		ER
	FOX	The O.C.		Tru Calling		
	WB	The Mountain 10/20 moves to Sun. @9		Studio 7		
	UPN	WWE SmackDown!				
FRIDAY	ABC	8 Simple Rules	Complete Savages	Hope & Faith	Less Than Perfect	20/20
	CBS	Joan of Arcadia		JAG		Dr. Vegas
	NBC	Dateline NBC		Third Watch		Medical Investigation 10/20 Full season
	FOX	Specials / The Inside		The Next Great Champ / Jonny Zero		
	WB	What I Like About You	Commando Nanny 10/21 pulled fr production	Reba	Grounded for Life 10/26 not picked up	
	UPN	America's Next Top Model (repeat)		Star Trek: Enterprise		
SATURDAY	ABC	The Wonderful World of Disney				
	CBS	The Amazing Race		Crime Time Saturday		48 Hours Mysteries
	NBC	NBC Saturday Night Movie				
	FOX	Cops	Cops	America's Most Wanted		

Day	Network	7-7:30		8-8:30		9-10	
SUNDAY	ABC	America's Funniest Home Videos		Extreme Makeover: Home Edition		10/20 Full season Desperate Housewives / Alias	Boston Legal
	CBS	60 Minutes		Cold Case		CBS Sunday Movie	
	NBC	Dateline NBC		American Dreams		Law & Order: Criminal Intent	Crossing Jordan
	FOX	King of the Hill / Kelsey Grammer Presents: The Sketch Show	Malcolm in the Middle / King of the Hill	The Simpsons	Arrested Development / Malcolm in the Middle	The Partner / Arrested Development	American Dad
	WB	Steve Harvey's Big Time		Charmed		Jack & Bobby moves to 10/20 Wed @9	

KEY: NEW SHOW · NEW TIME · Fox Nov.-Jan. · Fox Jan.-June

14 www.hollywoodreporter.com

The Next Great Champ to cable. WB moves *The Mountain* to Sunday, and pulls *Commando Nanny* from production, which is lenient as it was singularly the most insipid, lame, amateurish pilot

I watched. Apparently, being based on the life of Mark Burnett (*Survivor*) wasn't enough to guarantee its success. My personal analysis is that Gerald MacRaney's throat cancer was the direct result of having this awful dialogue come out of his mouth. The WB also cancels *Grounded for Life* after a respectable run and moves *Jack & Bobby* to Wednesday. On the upside, ABC gives *Lost* and *Desperate Housewives* full season orders.

October 1

We've worked up our new A story for the Chill Mitchell pilot, agreed among ourselves that it will work for the studio, and now it's back into the maw of Paramount to get it approved so that it can go to the development mavens at CBS for their approval, just so that we can get to the outline stage. Once again I'm mired in pre-anger mode. I keep running over in my head that I've written/produced over 300 episodes of television. I've been in more rewrites, broken more stories, fixed more broken scenes than all of the people whose approval I need combined. Yet I'm still subject to the whims and tastes of people who have never done any of these jobs.

I also can't stop thinking about how, on the one hand, network television is getting dumber by the second, with more bugeaters and bachelorettes coming every day. Yet at the same time, some hour shows are leaking through that have actual style, and substance. *Lost* on ABC is one. Every so often, something makes it through the system, whether nurtured by an intelligent executive or pushed through by a producer with enough clout to tell everyone to fuck off. And the dumber network gets, the smarter cable gets. I guess the people in this country who finished college need someplace to relax, too.

Meanwhile, the JLD deal seems that it will close soon. That's five months after it was approved. Once again, we'll have to start one step back and re-pitch it to the new folks, which is set up for next week. But the "Escorts" deal, also approved by the development people, is still mired in business affairs. I've been calling agents on all sides of this, trying to get a simple deal made so we can, once again, go out and pitch.

As a sidebar, a fourth show I'd gotten involved with and tried to get through the system here was shot down, as there was no interest from CBS or UPN and, for the moment, that is mostly what this company is interested in. A side effect from the fact that Paramount is virtually an in-house production company for those two networks, coupled with the fear that if they pass on a show that goes on to become a hit on another network, they will look foolish. Even though it could also be a Paramount-produced show, which would strengthen them as a studio, but obviously the focus is on the upside of the former, and not the latter. So, as someone who has been put in the position of salesman, my territory has just been limited.

We finally pitch the third Chill Mitchell story to Paramount. This time, Daryl's practically curing cancer. But, I need story approval so I can write. And I get it, with a few cursory notes but assurance that it should fly at CBS. I walk out relieved, much in the same way one is relieved when they stop beating your head against the wall.

October 4

Monday. Another day in development. *Last Comic Standing* was cancelled. Maybe now all those unfunny people will finally stop following their dreams of stardom and go back to law school, or get married and have babies. Like the world needs a place for bad comics with no imagination or insights but three minutes of material that kills in some backwater Holiday Inn on Komedy Klub Night to strut their stuff on national TV.

Finally, the deal for the JLD show is done. After six months. Meetings have been set next week to pitch at CBS and UPN. One Thursday, one Friday. I don't like Friday pitches. They feel like the obligatory meetings that get scheduled when people have one foot out the door for the weekend, not the ones they want to take seriously during the week.

Meanwhile, I'm waiting for CBS to call back and see if they like, and more importantly approve, the story we sent over, so that I can begin to write the script. I'm also trying to get in touch with the executives at Paramount to see if we can take the Escorts show into Showtime, but no one's returning my calls.

PHONE CALLS

In the daily working of show business, phone calls are a barometer of your importance, in that you are as important as the people who will return your calls. This is one of the goals in Hollywood: to rise to a position of power wherein your calls get taken immediately, at which point you can turn around and begin not returning others' calls. It is a supreme position of power not to return calls. It is also a supreme position of power to have your calls returned. The early evening cell phone call often becomes the "I'll call this asshole back" version of the message you leave at the end of business when you know the person won't be there but you want the credit for having returned the call. But if your call gets returned eventually, you've got some power. The call gets returned that week. More power. In a day or two. Even more power. That day. Even more power than that. In a few moments. You're someone. And ultimate power is when they take the call that moment. In the office. If someone takes your call immediately, it means you're more powerful than they are. Or they need something specific from you today. Or possibly it's a friend. Most people here talk "up," rationing their time and enthusiasm for those who can do them some good. Someone never calls you back; assume that, in their eyes, you're shit.

Not to say I haven't not returned calls. I've done it. Out of necessity: when staffing a show, agents call by the minute. You're bombarded with hundreds of spec scripts and resumes. And most of these people have credits. You can't possibly return every call. Or read every script. Or meet every writer. You do the best you can. Besides, you can't hurt an agent's feelings. They just keep calling, which can create the illusion that you have actual power. Instead of momentary power. Your show gets on the air. Stays on the air. You approach actual power. You can savor the feeling. But you should also save your money. In reality, you're not the pretty girl at the prom. You're just the girl at the prom who puts out. But don't delude yourself into thinking you're actually attractive. Your show gets picked up, gets ratings, stays on the air, makes it to syndication, and you cash in, you have power, at least to the extent that you've got "fuck you" money, don't need anyone, and can do another show from a position of strength because now they want you but you don't need them. But, if your show gets cancelled, the phone stops ringing. Immediately.

On the advice of a friend, I send a copy of the play I'd written to a guy I'd met who works at the Mark Taper Forum. My fear is it's not developed enough as a play to meet his expectations, but I send it anyway as maybe he'll see enough in there to put it through whatever development process they might have. It's a world with which I'm unfamiliar. Sometimes scripts are like carrier pigeons. You let them loose and see if one returns with good news.

More often than not, they're like canaries sent into coal mines to check for gas.

On a side note, Christopher Reeve died this weekend. My first thought, other than for his family, was of Chill Mitchell and how this must make him feel. He knew the guy. He's obviously in a similar position. I wonder if it weakened his resolve. On the one hand, it's all the more reason to want to create a show that reflects the emotions someone in that position must experience. On the other hand, it's also a reason to say fuck it. Just give them the show they want, and get it on the air.

THE FALL SEASON

When you go through the development process and crap out, you develop a sporting interest in the shows that did make it on the air, particularly at the network where you were in play. Actually, it's more of a psychological sporting interest in that you hope every new show dies a miserable death. This season, the two big shows that CBS put on have limped out of the starting gate. The Jason Alexander show—*Listen Up*—is doing fairly, though certainly no breakout hit. (Fast forward: cancelled.) And the John Goodman show's premiere has been postponed, but that hasn't stopped the critics from stomping all over it. Chances are it will break its leg jumping out of the gate and will be taken aside and shot soon enough. (It was.) So all their combined wisdom and expertise in programming their own network has given rise to two more shows about fat guys and their families. Of course, midseason shows are already in production, the producers of those shows praying the others get cancelled so that they can get their shot. Six years ago, that was the case with *Becker*, which went on the air and ran 5 1/2 years, and was treated, for the most part, with all the regard a pimp has for an aging hooker. She still brings in some money, but she's not the prettiest girl in the stable.

By now, you might have the impression that I'm bitter. But why should I be? I'm working; I'm making a ton of money. (Maybe it's the adage: A miserable Jew is a happy Jew.) OK, here's a reason. I just saw a network promo (a commercial for an upcoming show the network runs to either create or continue interest in a show) for the Jason Alexander show *Listen Up*. It's a scene in which he's talking to Steve Young, former SF 49er quarterback, who we used on *Wings* 10 years ago and it was barely stunt casting then. The promo joke from Jason's character: "You've got a Super Bowl ring. All I've got is ring around the collar." Holy fuck. Even one of my cats farted when that came out of the TV. I mean, it's 2004, and a show that is part of the network's fall lineup, a show they're promoting as a breakout comedy hit, does a joke referencing a thirty-year-old nitwit commercial that has all but evaporated from public consciousness.

But to break it down further, you need to understand the sequence of events that had to take place in order for this joke to appear in a network promo. First, some writer on the show had to either write that in a script or pitch it in the room and not receive the proper response for pitching a joke about 'ring around the collar," which is death by stoning. Yet, the writer survived, *and* the person running the room deemed the joke funny enough to be in the script. Then, it had to survive the table reading, and a week's worth of script rewrites, run-throughs and show night, where the audience actually had to laugh at it. Then it had to go through the editing process, and not get cut out for time, or for being the dumbshit joke it is. Then, having made it all the way into the final cut of the show, the network promo department had to deem it funnier than every other joke in the show that week and pull it out all on its own for the promo, as the small snippet of humor that will represent the show and entice viewers to tune it in.

The second I saw this, I thought of the Amsterdam red light district with the hookers hanging in the windows, beckoning customers. That joke was the equivalent of sticking a fat chick with acne, hairy legs and a screaming brat in each arm in one of those windows. Yet this was the joke that CBS declared funny. In a show CBS declared funny. Starring an actor who was brilliant enough to push children and an old lady out of the way to get out of an apartment fire in *Seinfeld* and made you laugh yourself sick. God help me, I may not survive this much longer.

October 3

Vomited up an outline on the Chill Mitchell project to send to CBS for story approval, but first have to give it to Perry Simon for notes.

October 5

The deal finally having been completed for the JLD show, we now have to pitch it to the new Paramount administration. So we do. They show their enthusiasm by saying, "Let us talk about it."

October 11

Paramount is fine with the JLD idea, or they're resigned to the fact that we've been working on it so long, it wouldn't kill them to let us go out and pitch it, so they set up meetings beginning next week.

October 12

After getting the new Chill Mitchell A story through Perry and then Paramount, it finally goes to CBS, and a conference call is set up for today at five o'clock, which means I have to sweat out the entire day once again immersed in pre-anger over what I expect will be a slew of notes I despise, rendering something I'm already lukewarm about into a story I fully detest. At which point they say, "Go write." And "Have fun with it."

Of course, by the time the call rolls around the notes are cursory, just a few requests for clarification. We hang up. I drain the backwash from the beer I've been sucking on, take a deep breath, and mentally prepare to begin writing the next day. The fact that they've requested a draft in three weeks doesn't even allow for the usual two or three days of writing procrastination built into starting any project. I have to start immediately.

October 13

I begin vomiting. Meanwhile, I've been trading calls with Maria Crenna to get an answer on the Escorts project. Trading calls means I call them during regular business hours and they call back after 6 when they know I won't be in the office but want credit for returning the call, which puts it back in my court. I try her again. Not available. I try the drama development person. Same thing.

October 14

After almost two weeks of phone tag I finally get through to Maria, who tells me they're passing on the show. "The whole (escorts) thing is an area we just don't want to get into." Several months work down the drain. So that's that. I'm back down to two projects. Writing one. Pitching the other next week.

October 21

Pitching the JLD project today to CBS. What's that line from Henry V: "Once more into the breach"? This project has been in the works since the beginning of the year. The pitch is solid, we've put so much work into it, and it feels about 15 months pregnant. I feel like they're assholes if they don't buy it, especially with their two big shows this year premiering like two big farts in the wind. Reviews awful. Shows awful. Ratings not great for Jason Alexander, and the John Goodman show hasn't even premiered yet. It got pushed several times, including last night because of the 7th game of the Boston/New York ALCS, in which Boston just bitch-slapped the Yankees, but that's another story.

In the CBS waiting room I bump into Larry Miller, one of the funniest comics I know, and his wife, Eileen, a writer. They just finished a pitch. Larry and I worked together on a pilot for him about 8 years ago and spent a lot of time laughing, even though I was dead on my feet from sleep deprivation as my then two-year-old daughter refused to sleep. In the end, he pulled out of the project to act in a pilot by a friend. I was happy for him in that I like and respect Larry, plus I was too exhausted to continue. In the end, that pilot went to series. I was offered a job but turned it down as I had two years security on *Wings*. It premiered after *Frasier*. And died. But the writer of that show went on to create *Becker*, offered me a job and I took it, happily. Everything comes around.

We go in to pitch to CBS. Same room. Same corpses. I walk outside looking for a small animal to kick or a stop sign to beat my head against.

Meanwhile, a guy I play softball with, a talent manager and producer, calls. He and his partner have an idea they want me to get involved with about a guy in his fifties playing a John Derek-type guy with a young wife, and several ex-wives. The actor they have in mind—Ted Danson. And CBS says they'd be happy to work with him again, even after canceling him just last year. Not a bad idea, as TV ideas go. But Ted's the only one who could pull it off, as no network is likely to greenlight a show with an over-50 lead. Still, I agree to get involved, or at least follow the process as far as it goes.

As well, my Chill Mitchell first draft is done, so at least I have a document to play with over the next few weeks before I have to turn it in and start the notes process again.

It occurs to me while I'm writing this that I never heard from the guy at the Taper, who I sent the play to. I'm assuming the silence means he didn't like it and is just trying to find the words to communicate that, or he will just let it go without responding, or possibly hasn't read it yet. I usually assume that someone reads a script immediately upon receiving it. I usually do, though I've had lapses on occasion. Still I suppose I have to let this fantasy go and hope that all this work over the last year will boil down to one, maybe two pilots written for CBS. Two chips on the roulette table.

October 23

Pitched our JLD show to UPN where it was well-received, but we're 99% sure it's a pass. It's just not for their target audience. I go home and relax, waiting for some word from CBS, which comes in the form of an early afternoon bit of disappointment in a call from my partner saying he heard from his agent that they were passing. Got a confirmation call a few hours later from Paramount saying they just "didn't respond," which is the usual catchall phrase accompanying a pass, so we discuss our next moves—setting up meetings at NBC and ABC, though we first have to wait for UPN to pass officially. Nothing like a Friday afternoon hope-dashing buzz-kill to set the weekend off to a pleasant start.

October 26

Talk to Kevin, who's miraculously still at Paramount. He says we didn't get the official pass yet because the UPN exec got food poisoning and is not at work. In the meantime, I mention to him that the pilot I wrote a year ago for CBS is technically the property of Paramount, or will be officially in December, and there's no reason it couldn't get submitted to NBC or ABC. Call it creative salesmanship or hopeless desperation. Either way, he sees no reason not to check it out. Otherwise, it just sits on the shelf collecting dust.

Bumped into Warren Littlefield, the head of NBC when I did the Tony Danza show, and who's now on a production deal at Paramount. He was walking around the lot after lunch. We talk for a moment, mostly about Paramount business affairs department (the lawyers who make all the deals) bitching about how backed up they are and how they're slowing down any producer with a project because you can't get in to pitch without having all the appropriate deals in place, but by the time they're done the season will be over. As he hears it, they've already got around 50 drama projects in development here. And from what I've heard, nearly that many comedies. Makes you feel special with your one precious little script.

October 27

Pitch meeting set up with ABC for JLD…for November 8. Also, banging away on revisions for the Chill Mitchell pilot, which I will turn in next week and begin the note process, which will still have to go through the layers of Paramount before it even gets to CBS. But hopefully, their notes will "CBS-proof" it, as they tend to know where the minefields are.

NOVEMBER 2004

Yasser Arafat dies. Palestinians in mourning. Bush wins re-election. Democrats in mourning. On both counts, world holding its collective breath.

The fall TV season continues. NBC cancels *LAX*. I guess the audience just couldn't get behind the notion that Heather Locklear was in charge of running a major urban airport. Sexism? You be the judge. UPN cancels *Second Time Around*. (This was too

schedule — 2004 NOVEMBER

Day	Network	8-8:30	8:30-9	9-9:30	9:30-10	10-11
MONDAY	ABC	The Benefactor / ABC Monday Night Movie (after football ends in January)		Monday Night Football		Grey's Anatomy (after football ends in January)
	CBS	Still Standing	Listen Up 11/12 full season	Everybody Loves Raymond	Two and a Half Men	CSI: Miami
	NBC	Fear Factor		Las Vegas		LAX 11/22 cancelled
	FOX	North Shore / Athens		The Swan 2 / 24		
	WB	7th Heaven		Everwood		
	UPN	One on One	Half & Half	Girlfriends	Second Time Around 11/10 not picked up	
TUESDAY	ABC	My Wife & Kids	George Lopez	According to Jim	Rodney 11/16 full season	NYPD Blue / Blind Justice
	CBS	Navy NCIS		Clubhouse 11/9 benched for sweeps		Judging Amy
	NBC	Last Comic Standing / The Contender		Father of the Pride 11/2 benched for sweeps	Scrubs moves to tues @9	Law & Order: Special Victims Unit
	FOX	The Billionaire: Branson's Quest for the Best / American Idol		House		
	WB	Gilmore Girls		One Tree Hill		
	UPN	All of Us	Eve	Veronica Mars 11/9 full season		
WEDNESDAY	ABC	Lost		The Bachelor		Wife Swap 11/1 full season
	CBS	60 Minutes		The King of Queens	Center of the Universe	CSI: NY 11/5 full season
	NBC	Hawaii		The West Wing / Revelations		Law & Order
	FOX	That '70s Show	Quintuplets / Related by Family	The Bernie Mac Show / American Idol	Method & Red / The Bernie Mac Show	
	WB	Smallville		Blue Collar TV	Drew Carey's Green Screen Show cancelled 11/16	
	UPN	America's Next Top Model / The Road to Stardom With Missy Elliott		Kevin Hill 11/9 full season		
THURSDAY	ABC	Extreme Makeover		Life as We Know It		Primetime Live
	CBS	Survivor: Vanuatu		CSI: Crime Scene Investigation		Without a Trace
	NBC	Joey	Will & Grace	The Apprentice 2		ER
	FOX	The O.C.		Tru Calling		
	WB	The Mountain		Studio 7		
	UPN	WWE SmackDown!				
FRIDAY	ABC	8 Simple Rules	Complete Savages 11/16 full season	Hope & Faith	Less Than Perfect	20/20
	CBS	Joan of Arcadia		JAG		Dr. Vegas 11/3 benched for sweeps
	NBC	Dateline NBC		Third Watch		Medical Investigation
	FOX	Specials / The Inside		The Next Great Champ / Jonny Zero		
	WB	What I Like About You	Commando Nanny	Reba	Grounded for Life	
	UPN	America's Next Top Model (repeat)		Star Trek: Enterprise		
SATURDAY	ABC	The Wonderful World of Disney				
	CBS	The Amazing Race		Crime Time Saturday		48 Hours Mysteries
	NBC	NBC Saturday Night Movie				
	FOX	Cops	Cops	America's Most Wanted		

Day	Network	7-7:30	7:30-8	8-8:30	8:30-9	9-10		10-11
SUND.	ABC	America's Funniest Home Videos		Extreme Makeover: Home Edition		Desperate Housewives / Alias [illegible]		Boston Legal
	CBS	60 Minutes		Cold Case		CBS Sunday Movie		
	NBC	Dateline NBC		American Dreams		Law & Order: Criminal Intent		Crossing Jordan
	FOX	King of the Hill / Kelsey Grammer Presents: The Sketch Show	Malcolm in the Middle / King of the Hill	The Simpsons	Arrested Development / Malcolm in the Middle	The Partner / Arrested Development	American Dad	
	WB	Steve Harvey's Big Time		Charmed		Jack & Bobby		

KEY
- NEW SHOW
- NEW TIME
- Fox Nov.-Jan.
- Fox Jan.-June

bad. I liked this pilot. It was smarter and had more class than their other shows. Apparently, that was its death knell.) CBS cancels *Clubhouse*, possibly as revenge for the Yankees blowing a 3-0 lead in the ALCS. WB cancels *Drew Carey's Green Screen*. CBS benches *Dr. Vegas*, Rob Lowe's post-*West Wing* vehicle. This is a lesson to any actor who gets on a hit show. *Never Quit!* Ride the fucker into the sunset. Bank the cash and parlay whatever fame and clout you have into getting a movie part during your four-month hiatus. But never assume the success is permanent. Never assume the public loves *you*. What they love is the character you're playing. I once was in a casting session on *Becker* and counted five actors waiting outside in the hall to read, all of whom were once in the cast of a hit network show.

Meanwhile, CBS awards *Listen Up* a full season order though only two additional episodes for *Center of the Universe*, the traditional network pre-cancellation show of lukewarm support. Full season pickups go to *Rodney* on ABC, along with *Wife Swap*, *CSI: NY* on CBS, *Kevin Hill* on UPN, and *Complete Savages* on ABC, which also moves *Alias* to Wednesday. In an unrelated move, NBC moves *Scrubs* to Tuesday, where it's still funny.

November 2

Father of the Pride taken off the schedule at NBC for sweeps. No way they'll renew it, as it costs around $2 million per episode, along with the huge lead-time it takes to produce an animated show, on top of the fact that it's getting shitty ratings. NBC is in trouble. We're going in tomorrow with our pitch, hoping to make a sale. Meanwhile, CBS announces they bought two divorce-related shows. Maybe they liked them first, or best. Who knows? Can't hate them yet for passing, I still have a project with them.

November 3

Pitched JLD to NBC. Drove through the same gate and had coffee in the same commissary where, seven years earlier, I sat with my notes getting ready to pitch the Tony Danza pilot. I remember having hope then, too. We pitch to Cheryl Dolins who, Ken Levine pointed out, was a P.A. for them on *Cheers*. Everyone grows up. Pitch went well. She's smart. Gets it. And actually laughs, which is a new and refreshing experience. They seemed to respond. We all left on a high.

November 4

The high is short-lived. NBC passes. Liked us and the idea but orders from on high, they don't want to do anything with kids. Or at least that's the story we're told. On to ABC.

November 5

Waiting for an answer on sending my old pilot to NBC, which can't happen until everyone here has read it and signed off on sending it over. Finished first draft of the Daryl Mitchell pilot and sending it to Perry. It's almost a year since I was writing the other pilot for CBS, and now I'm about to go through the same process, only with an actor aboard.

November 8

Same day I hear we got passed on by ABC, I get a call from Garry Hart, former President of the studio, who's now on an Indy Prod[45] deal, to see if I have any interest in doing a pilot for Lewis Black. We meet in his office, and he gives me a copy of the pilot they did for Lewis last year. I watch it. It's awful. Clunky, old school. Typical sitcom. Plus, Lewis, while brilliant as a standup,

---

[45] Indy Prod. A network or studio executive who's let go but is given an "independent production" deal at the studio or network where they were employed.

isn't an experienced actor and this played to that weakness, instead of to his strengths as a comic. It's common knowledge that if you're doing a show starring a comic who has his or her own voice but may not necessarily be a skilled actor, you protect that person by surrounding them with actual actors. They did this on *Roseanne*. *Raymond*. *Seinfeld*. They didn't do it here. Garry and I discuss what to do and come up with an idea.

November 9

Another typical development day. Jamming on finishing the studio notes for the Daryl Mitchell project, which I was having a hard time embracing but am playing the game. Got a call from Kevin Plunkett. The old CBS pilot I did last year that we sent to NBC. Pass. "Have one like it in development"—a phrase you often hear, whether it's bullshit or not. Another bit of hope killed. That's the interesting thing about working here. On almost a daily basis, the business generates just enough hope to set you up for the next disappointment.

Met with Perry quickly on one scene I couldn't crack, and then went over to Garry Hart's office to pitch an idea to Lewis Black over a speakerphone, while he was in Ohio preparing for a gig. I hate pitching over the phone, but there isn't much of an option here. If he likes it, we approach Paramount with the goal of going to either ABC or Showtime. I prefer the latter. CBS wouldn't buy this in a million years. Too strident for their delicate sensibilities. And he's too old for UPN. I'm hoping that, since I'm in partnership with the former head of the studio, he'll know how to cut through the bullshit and get things done, maybe even going over the heads of some of the underlings. We'll see. The phone connection is shitty but Lewis seems to like it.

Then ran out for a meeting with Keith Addis, Ted Danson's manager, to pitch the other idea for the John Derek-type guy. It goes well, but Keith said, as I assumed, that Ted's not going to commit to anything without a script and so far, no one's paying for a script. That would involve pitching to Paramount, and it's getting late in the season. Left Keith's office in the dark, made a few wrong turns and fought bumper to bumper traffic all the way home. During the past several weeks, we've pitched JLD to CBS, UPN, NBC, and ABC. Pass, pass, pass and pass. Six months of working out a pitch, stories, casting, deal making…for nothing. (Fast forward: CBS produces a pilot with another writer starring JLD as a divorced mom. It premiers in March, 2006 to good reviews and ratings.)

MIDSEASON ASSESSMENTS

This is around the time of year that articles start appearing in *Variety* and the *Reporter*, assessing the fall season, while trying to identify any trends. Here's one such article from the 11/12 issue of *Variety*, the headline of which gives heart to TV writers who are mostly praying for the "reality" genre to die, which will lead to more scripted shows and therefore more jobs. The first article isn't quite the "reality" epitaph but does make the point that those shows are subject to the same audience whims as scripted shows, and that oversaturation will cause the audience to gag, perhaps signaling a course correction on the parts of the networks.

REALITY LOSES BITE

Variety 11-12-04

By JOSEF ADALIAN

It's been a brutal week for reality shows, but don't count out the unscripted genre just yet.

In the past six days alone, the nets have launched three reality shows, and all three have struck out with viewers. Fox scored back-to-back flops with "My Big Fat Obnoxious Boss" and "The Rebel Billionaire," while it turned out the joke was on NBC with the underperforming "$25 Million Hoax."

news ANALYSIS

Earlier in the season, ABC's "The Benefactor" was such a loser, the net quickly found a way to get it off the air two weeks sooner than planned. A slew of controversy surrounding Fox's "The Next Great Champ" couldn't get viewers to care about boxing. And when the Peacock got greedy with the success of "Last Comic Standing" by rushing a new season of the show on the air barely two weeks after the end of the previous season, the audience thought the net was joking — and stayed away in droves.

Turn to page 42

Continued from page 1

All this failure in such a short amount of time — coupled with the runaway success of ABC's "Desperate Housewives" and "Lost" — will no doubt have some alarmists declaring reality is dead.

A closer look at the genre's track record this fall reveals that viewers are still in love with unscripted shows. They're just punishing networks for launching skeins that are too familiar or rushed together too quickly.

"With quantity comes failure," admitted Mike Darnell, Fox's exec VP of alternative programming. "You can't do this much quantity without doing shows that are similar to other shows. It becomes a combination of mediocre shows or shows that are so similar to other shows, they don't stick out."

Cablers hurt, too

Broadcasters aren't the only ones suffering negative side effects from their addiction to reality. Cablers are also finding it harder to get auds interested in unscripted projects.

Bravo, which struck gold with "Queer Eye," has lost its gaydar with "Top Model" clone "Manhunt." Spike TV's "Apprentice"-like "I Hate My Job" has viewers saying, "I Don't Really Like This Show." And TBS' "He's a Lady" might as well be called "He's a Dud."

In the case of Fox, the net seems to have incorrectly bet that a heavy dose of reality would keep the net's pulse racing in September and after baseball. Just as ABC flooded the market with reality shows in the first quarter of 2003, Fox is devoting nearly two-thirds of its primetime sked this month to unscripted fare.

Alphabet's plan flopped, resulting in a sea of failure. Fox is doing a bit better, but not much.

The good news: Viewers still seem ready to embrace originality when it comes to reality.

ABC's "Wife Swap" is the unsung hero of the season, this week beating the mighty "Law & Order" Wednesday at 10. Fox has also seen encouraging numbers for kiddie makeover show "Nanny 911," while its "Wife Swap" clone "Trading Spouses" is quietly posting solid results.

NBC also has reason to cheer "The Biggest Loser," which — while not a Nielsen heavyweight — has suppressed the net's performance in the 8-9:30 p.m. Tuesday slot.

All four shows have one thing in common: They're new concepts that haven't yet saturated the marketplace.

Nets also have to be relieved that existing reality franchises are still doing fine.

"Survivor" still thrives on Thursdays, while ABC's "Extreme Makeover: Home Edition" has exploded in its second season. "The Apprentice" is down from last season, but still mighty, while UPN's "America's Next Top Model" has found its (long) legs after a shaky start.

Still, Darnell and others concede there may simply be too many reality skeins on the air.

"The volume was bound to implode on itself, and now we're seeing the result," said one industry veteran.

Alt rocked

While nets have traditionally used reality skeins to plug holes in their midseason skeds or keep the lights on during the summer, this year saw a fall launch packed with more reality skeins than ever before. Greedy for a quick ratings fix, webheads have once again forgotten that reality is supposed to be *alternative* programming — not the bread-and-butter of a sked.

"Unfortunately for alternative, when it becomes the staple that it is now, you're just going to have failure," Darnell said. "And you're going to have almost as much failure as in any other area."

Indeed, despite all the hoopla over ABC's hourlong hits, it's been an awful year for new scripted dramas.

CBS has already killed two of its three new hours, pulling the plug on "Dr. Vegas" and "Clubhouse." NBC has also dumped "Hawaii," while "LAX" seems headed for a final descent any day now. The WB's "Jack & Bobby" and "The Mountain" barely have a pulse.

Laffers suffer

And comedy? It's still pretty dead. NBC airs just 90 minutes of comedy each week vs. 3½ hours of reality.

But while scripted vets are used to a world in which 80% of new shows bite the dust in their first year, the high mortality rate is something new for reality producers and execs. Ditto the overwhelming workload demanded when nets order up so much fare so quickly.

Producers on many skeins are working 20-hour days battling to get shows done in record time. Producers of "Biggest Loser" had to switch gears at the last second and turn hourlong episodes into 90-minute segs with hardly any notice.

Some wonder if all the rushing doesn't lead to inferior shows — though "Loser" and "Nanny 911" are doing fine. It certainly taxes the strength of reality execs, whose relatively small staffs now find themselves juggling one or two dozen projects at a time.

Darnell, the symbolic face of TV's turn-of-the-century reality wave, insists he and his staff can keep up. He also remains convinced reality has joined sitcoms and dramas as a permanent third staple of network TV.

The exec believes Fox and other nets are "still finding our way in this genre," learning new lessons about what viewers do and don't want. He predicts more original reality ideas come January — and he has no doubt the next "American Idol" or "Survivor" is out there.

"If it's good and it's unique and it's loud, it'll work," he said.

The second is an interesting take on the current state of "sitcoms." The third, a midseason report from thefutoncritic.com on which shows were given additional script orders. As you'll see, this doesn't necessarily protect them against cancellation. In fact, the awarding of additional scripts is the traditional "let's wait and see" from the network. Anything short of an instant back nine order will start making producers nervous.

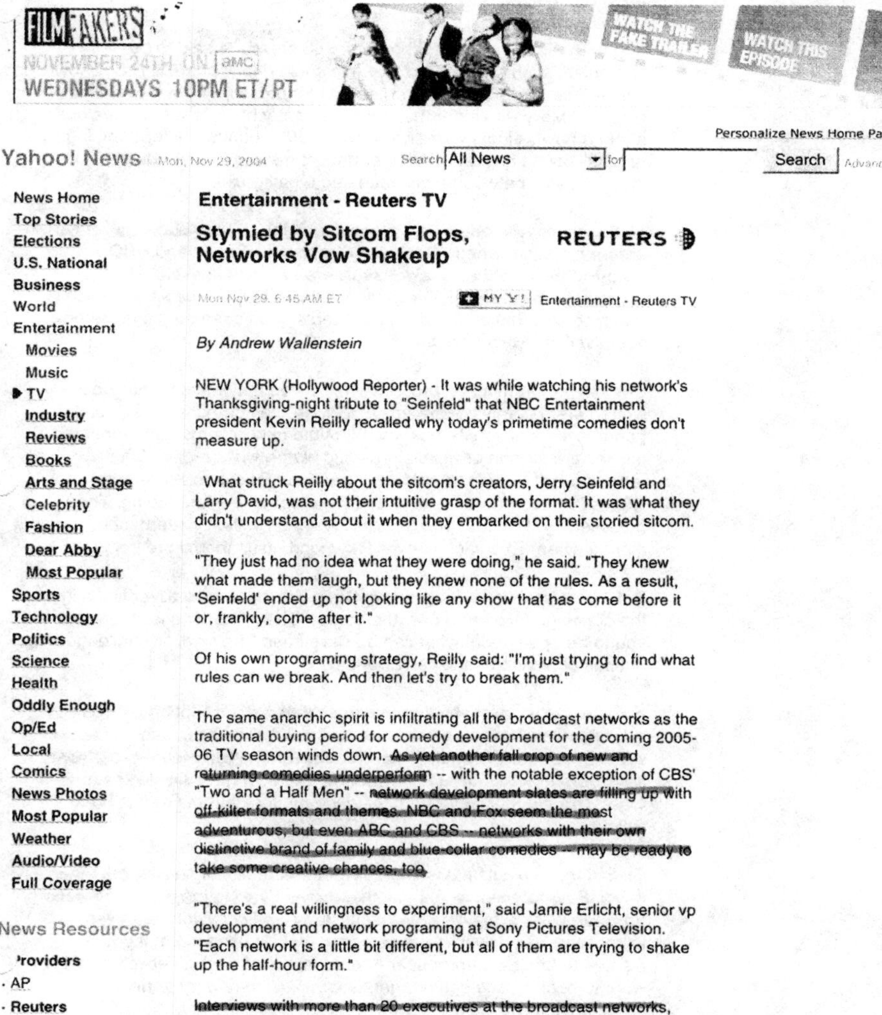

Personalize News Home Page

Yahoo! News Mon, Nov 29, 2004 Search All News for Search Advanced

News Home
Top Stories
Elections
U.S. National
Business
World
Entertainment
Movies
Music
TV
Industry
Reviews
Books
Arts and Stage
Celebrity
Fashion
Dear Abby
Most Popular
Sports
Technology
Politics
Science
Health
Oddly Enough
Op/Ed
Local
Comics
News Photos
Most Popular
Weather
Audio/Video
Full Coverage

News Resources

Providers
· AP
· Reuters
· E! Online

Entertainment - Reuters TV

Stymied by Sitcom Flops, Networks Vow Shakeup

REUTERS

Mon Nov 29, 6:45 AM ET MY Y! Entertainment - Reuters TV

By Andrew Wallenstein

NEW YORK (Hollywood Reporter) - It was while watching his network's Thanksgiving-night tribute to "Seinfeld" that NBC Entertainment president Kevin Reilly recalled why today's primetime comedies don't measure up.

What struck Reilly about the sitcom's creators, Jerry Seinfeld and Larry David, was not their intuitive grasp of the format. It was what they didn't understand about it when they embarked on their storied sitcom.

"They just had no idea what they were doing," he said. "They knew what made them laugh, but they knew none of the rules. As a result, 'Seinfeld' ended up not looking like any show that has come before it or, frankly, come after it."

Of his own programing strategy, Reilly said: "I'm just trying to find what rules can we break. And then let's try to break them."

The same anarchic spirit is infiltrating all the broadcast networks as the traditional buying period for comedy development for the coming 2005-06 TV season winds down. As yet another fall crop of new and returning comedies underperform -- with the notable exception of CBS' "Two and a Half Men" -- network development slates are filling up with off-kilter formats and themes. NBC and Fox seem the most adventurous, but even ABC and CBS -- networks with their own distinctive brand of family and blue-collar comedies -- may be ready to take some creative chances, too.

"There's a real willingness to experiment," said Jamie Erlicht, senior vp development and network programing at Sony Pictures Television. "Each network is a little bit different, but all of them are trying to shake up the half-hour form."

Interviews with more than 20 executives at the broadcast networks, studios and talent agencies affirm that desperation is encouraging more experimentation than ever. But tempering that sentiment is a deeply ingrained skepticism shared by many over whether networks will walk the talk next fall.

"I would be surprised if we didn't end up with more of the same," one studio chief lamented.

Traditional family-oriented sitcoms are still quite well represented on development slates. But there are plenty of others that stray from the living-room couch or coffee shop, where many sitcoms are centered; NBC is considering one set in a retirement community and another in a trailer park. And the usual cavalcade of stand-up comics are seeing some of their spots taken by more marketable pop stars such as the rock band Barenaked Ladies (news - web sites) (Fox) and Melissa Etheridge (news) (ABC).

And then there's a few real howlers: Fox brass are said to be particularly high on a project that one could dub "That '70s B.C. Show": It imagines Jesus as a slacker teen under pressure from his parents -- God and Mary -- to enter the family carpentry business. NBC has one about a newly single woman who loses 300 pounds -- after dumping her 300-pound husband. Another project making the rounds depicts the friendship between a divorcee and a gay ghost.

All this quirkiness bears the influence of cable, where such innovative programing as Comedy Central's "Chappelle's Show" and HBO's "Curb Your Enthusiasm" has spawned renewed interest in sketch and improvisational formats. Given the gradual parity the cable audience is reaching with that of broadcast, concepts once deemed too niche now seem viable, executives say.

Comedy programing on broadcast television may have had its obituary written prematurely before, as CBS' "Men" has demonstrated, but the genre is certainly on its sickbed. All of the new sitcoms that premiered this fall are sinking or at least treading water, while many of the returning half-hours that have managed to make a splash -- from NBC's "Scrubs" to Fox's "Arrested Development" -- are fading. The holes left by "Friends" and "Frasier" last year will only seem more glaring when "Everybody Loves Raymond" joins them in retirement.

But Fox executive vp programing Craig Erwich spots a silver lining in the dark cloud hovering over the genre. "The good thing is, it forces you to be open about what can be developed," he said. "It challenges notions of what can and can't work."

Industry veterans are finding that the old genre descriptions of comedy -- family, workplace, urban, rural -- are slowly being replaced by a new set of buzzwords, including "form-breakers" and "promote-ability." One holdover, however, still reigns stronger than ever: "distinctive point of view." "It's the most important thing, no matter what the form," Sony's Erlicht said.

To find those points of view, broadcasters are casting a wider net than usual. Several agents said that their greater inclination is to hear ideas from film writers, playwrights, novelists and ad copywriters -- even lower-rung industry folks are getting a shot. "It used to be, if you wanted to bring a co-producer or producer for a pitch, (networks) didn't want to hear it," one senior agent said. "Now they want to hear just about anything."

More open minds at the networks also are a reflection of a lesson learned -- re-learned, really -- from the ABC hit "Desperate Housewives." Absent the breakout new series that typically drives droves of copycats in development, the most influential comedy on the air is actually a drama (one ABC has submitted as a comedy for the Golden Globes to capitalize on the category's weak competition).

That "Housewives" creator/executive producer Marc Cherry -- a veteran comedy writer who struck out with his last few projects, including the short-lived 2001 CBS comedy "Some of My Best Friends" -- succeeded with a serialized soap opera amid a sea of procedural dramas from top-shelf producers is now cited as inspiration for countering conventional wisdom when there's little left to lose.

Cherry's breakthrough has served the comedy world a timely reminder: The best scripts are almost always conceived by a fresh voice. That held true for the breakout comedies of recent years, including "Malcolm in the Middle" (Linwood Boomer) "Will & Grace" (David Kohan and Max Mutchnick) and, of course, "Seinfeld" (David and Seinfeld).

Still, the traditional sitcom is in no danger of extinction; even HBO has signaled its intent to invade this territory. Lee Dinstman, executive vp at Agency for the Performing Arts, says their syndication value is too rich to ignore.

That's abundantly clear at CBS, where "Men" is shaping up to be the next syndication bonanza, with ratings rivaling lead-in "Raymond." The network played it safe this season by installing more family comedies that imitate "Raymond's" bumbling-dad conceit, including "Listen Up" and "Center of the Universe," both of which were recently picked up for additional episodes.

However, sources say CBS might shake up its comedy offerings next season. Development executives there are expected to focus on workplace comedies and female-driven fare -- Jenna Elfman (news), Holly Robinson Peete, Aisha Tyler and Susie Essman are among the actresses being considered for their own vehicles. All those close-knit families currently on CBS' schedule might also soon rub up against a little turbulence; the network has at least six projects in development that deal with divorce.

ABC might also get antsy: Despite riding high with "Housewives" and "Lost," the network's Tuesday and Friday comedy blocks will likely need fresh blood next season. Family fare may step aside for potential form-breakers like a vehicle for "Saturday Night Live" alum Chris Kattan with touches of "Curb"-like improvisation and broad physical comedy as well as an Elton John (news)-produced chronicle of an aging rock star.

Nevertheless, pessimism runs high that all these unorthodox projects will be around in September. "Development season represents what the networks want to be," one literary agent said. "Their schedule in the fall is what they are."

Reuters/Hollywood Reporter

the futon critic - the web's best primetime television resource Page 1 of 1

ıe >> newswire >> wednesday, november 17, 2004 sections: jump to a section

newswire
most recent headlines

- **Development Update: November 11-12**
- **CBS to Stick With 'Listen Up,' 'Center of the Universe'**
- **Development Update: November 8-10**
- **UPN Halts 'Second,' Moves Forward With 'Cuts'**
- **The WB Pulls Down Its 'Green Screen' for Sweeps**
- **Development Update: November 3-5**
- **'C.S.I.: N.Y.' Investigates Full Season Order**
- **Development Update: October 28 - November 2**
- **Eight Fall Newcomers Earn Script Orders**
- **Development Update: October 26-27**

more from the newswire >>

Monday, November 1, 2004 - 11:09 AM
Eight Fall Newcomers Earn Script Orders
By Brian Ford Sullivan

LOS ANGELES (thefutoncritic.com) -- Eight new fall series - ABC's "Rodney" and "Complete Savages," CBS' "dr. vegas" and "Clubhouse," UPN's "Second Time Around," "Veronica Mars" and "Kevin Hill" as well as the WB's "The Mountain" - all inched closer to full season orders over the weekend as their respective networks gave additional script orders to each.

Leading the pack was the Alphabet's "Rodney," which received a commitment for nine additional scripts, followed by "Savages" (six), "Kevin Hill" (four), "Veronica Mars" (four), "The Mountain" (four), "Second Time Around" (three), "dr. vegas" (two) and "Clubhouse" (two).

Said orders cover the gamut from solid success stories (UPN's "Kevin Hill," which is up over 40% from UPN's Wednesday, 9:00/8:00c hour last season) to middling performances (ABC's "Rodney," which is on par with "Less Than Perfect's" numbers in the Tuesday, 9:30/8:30c half hour last season) to downright failures (CBS' "Clubhouse" which is down 23% from "The Guardian," the show it replaced from last season).

Nevertheless, whether any of the group will get the production green light for additional episodes beyond their initial 13-episode order will be decided in the next several weeks.

Meanwhile in other freshman series news, FOX and producer Rocket Science Laboratories also confirmed over the weekend they won't be moving forward with the reality entry "The Partner." The series was originally targeted for the Sunday, 9:00/8:00c hour this fall but was instead replaced by "My Big Fat Obnoxious Boss." "With the numerous boardroom-type unscripted programs on the various network's schedules, we have decided to focus our mutual efforts on other unscripted material," the pair said in a joint statement to the press.

archives
find previous months here

- **most recent news stories**
- **most recent press releases**

showatch
for more on these projects

visit the showatch section!

more from the showatch >>

November 10

Racing to finish the revisions on the Chill Mitchell pilot so it can get into Paramount before the weekend. Call from Garry Hart, who spoke to Lewis Black's agent who heard the pitch went well, but alluded to a possible holding deal[46] in the works at another studio, which would shut us out, so Garry's calling Paramount to see if we can get in to pitch quickly, like Monday, and if they like it, maybe make a deal with Lewis to preempt that. Problem is, this is not a CBS show, so that won't encourage them to make a deal. We

[46] Holding deal. Networks or studios make deals with actors, paying a certain amount of money to tie up their exclusive services for a specific amount of time.

will suggest taking it to Showtime, which may or may not excite them. They also own Comedy Central, where Lewis is known for his segments on *The Daily Show*, but to do a half-hour comedy for that network I'm assured would be cost-prohibitive, that is, assuming they're even interested in getting into that business. Ideas on one hand—financial realities, corporate affiliations and competing networks on the other. Ideas do not live for their own sake. Ideas live in context of who's on what deal where, what bit of talent will make it more attractive, what studio you're at and does the network they're trying to program for want this specific project.

November 12

Gave my first draft of the Chill Mitchell script to Perry, and wait for the response. I ask him to call me over the weekend, and by mid-Saturday I'm already neurotic, having heard nothing, until I pick up a phone message from Perry. Loved it. Have notes, but great job. That's all you want to hear. OK, now I can relax. For the rest of the weekend.

November 15

I go to get Perry's notes. Upon walking in I notice his script has about 35 dog-eared pages, and instantly flash on a meeting years ago in Warren Littlefield's office at NBC on the Tony Danza pilot. I walked in to see at least a dozen executives and rack focused on each of their scripts with multiple dog-eared pages, each symbolizing some problem or concern. Then I re-focus on their unsmiling expressions. Warren begins the meeting with "Just so you know...this is us happy." "Shit, I'd hate to see them unhappy," I thought at the time. I didn't have to wait long. I relate this to Perry and he laughs, insisting his marked pages are for things he liked as well. I sigh in relief. It's just not something I'm used to. In short, his notes aren't bad. Some insights. Caught me on a couple weak jokes I tried to sneak by with. He has some suggestions and I have a few days to do a rewrite and turn it back in.

November 16

Doing my rewrite. Notes, whether they enhance a project or eviscerate it, are annoying, second only to the experience of actually having to sit down and execute them. I have my process. Take a day to let them sink in. Take the next day or two to incorporate them onto the page in pen, deleting runs that took weeks to perfect, replacing them with the new stuff, then weaving it all back together so it works again. Some things actually improve, some good jokes are killed, and other things are just punched sideways. Still as I look at it today, it is better in some respects. The script goes back in to Paramount.

November 17

Have heard nothing from Paramount, other than Perry and the exec were trading calls. Since I read disaster into everything, I'll read it into this. I know they've got a shitload of projects in development, so this is not their top priority. Still, I'd like to know what's going on so I know how much rewriting I'll have to do.

November 18

After sweating this out for days, I finally get a call from Perry, who finally heard from Paramount. A quickie response from a cell phone saying, essentially, they want to schedule a notes conference call for the next day and address some things about Chill's character.

November 19

Have the conference call. Not a disaster, but the feedback is along party lines. He's too mean. Too harsh. Jesus, I've already made him a saint, do I have to make the wheelchair roll on water? Evidently so. Everyone should love this guy and want to talk to him, confide their problems, and confess their sins. He specifically noted a few scenes in which he felt he was too mean. Just when you think the studio/network executive cliché isn't true, one of them speaks up and personifies it. Get out the meanness detector. Stripmine the nasty jokes out. Make sure everyone's lovable. Then wrap it in bunting and send it in. Shit. They just don't get it. The edges are where the jokes come from. If they had seen him in *Larroquette*, *Veronica's Closet*, *Ed*...they would know that. Now, they are slowly and surgically slicing out any instance of it. He's losing humanity and humor, and approaching divinity. But, my attitude has to be strategic. I need to do their notes or it will never get to CBS at all, let alone with the studio's blessing. I need to deliver what they want, at least on paper, to ever be able to get to a stage where I can slowly add back the jokes that he needs to have if he's going to have any character at all. The fact that they don't get this is tragic.

November 22

Turned in another revision to Perry on the Chill Mitchell pilot, based on Paramount's notes, and he assured me he'd read it right away and get back to me with either final thoughts or a "go ahead" to send it in. So once again, I'm sitting in my darkened office, waiting for a phone to ring. I re-read the notes I'd made over the last year, mostly from my previous CBS pilot experience and, once again, I find myself in that most dangerous of places—

with hope. Perhaps this time I'm better positioned. It's a softer script, with an actor attached with whom they want to work, a producing partner who was a former network executive and who knows how to work the system.

As a sidebar, my brother and agent call to set a meeting to "strategize" about the future. Meaning: with six months left on my deal, if I totally crap out this pilot season, they need to start sniffing around for other opportunities. A job on an existing show that might have a development component wrapped in. Or not. Maybe just a job. But the tone of these sessions, and we've had them in the past, is almost funereal. Meaning, you're not there, yet. You still need to struggle for this next job. Finally Perry calls and OK's the script to go in to Paramount, which it does, on the anniversary of the Kennedy assassination, so I will just sit in my office, work on other projects and wait for the network to blow the back of my head off. Call from Garry Hart's office—Paramount can't meet with us until after Thanksgiving. The result of them being busy. Still, I take it personally.

November 26

The yet-again revised Chill Mitchell script has gone into CBS and it occurs to me as I'm driving home on Laurel Canyon that they probably won't read it until after Thanksgiving. I've been told that Paramount won't meet with us on the Lewis Black project until after the holiday so, at this point in time, after pushing and driving myself all year, I'm finally at a position where I can stop. I go home and get a message from the guy to whom I sent the play back in October. Hadn't heard from him so I assumed he didn't like it. Then I hear the message, saying he read it immediately and liked it and was going to get back to me when he was suddenly rushed to the emergency room and spent two weeks in the ICU with what turned out to be West Nile Virus. He apologizes for not getting back and says "Let's talk after the holidays." This was a first. I've had people not like something I'd written; I've never had a script actually put someone in the hospital with a near-fatal disease.

November 29

Monday morning after Thanksgiving. A script went to Chill Mitchell over the holiday and I haven't heard from him, so my antennae are back up. Silence=Death. My agent has it, as does my brother. Haven't heard from either of them. Sent an email to Perry about this silence and he says not to read anything into it, but I can smell evil brewing. Got a call from Kevin Plunkett. They'll hear the Lewis Black pitch on Wednesday. Also spoke with Garry Hart about having lunch earlier to go over it. Maybe we'll luck out and sneak in under the wire with a last-minute thing.

November 30

Meet with Marc and Jay to discuss my flailing career. Their response to the Chill Mitchell pilot: "Not your best work." Meaning they hated it, because only when people hate something do they feel forced to voice a negative response. Otherwise, it's lukewarm praise, couched in stock phrases and left-handed compliments. It's frustrating because I wrote it to order, took out anything too rough and, in doing so, sanitized the humor out of it. My agent urges me to spec a pilot as a writing sample for future work. After almost 20 years, I need new material. It's daunting. The price of not creating a hit show. Still, at the end of the day, if this doesn't get picked up, all eyes fall on me as the one who couldn't deliver the script, even though I'm playing along every step of the way. If I shot my mouth off and told them how I thought it would be funny, I might get to write it, but they'd never pick it up. Interesting dilemma.

Now that it's pre-Oscar time, the studios begin sending out videos, DVDs and scripts of their contending movies. It's a boon for Guild members, who suddenly find themselves with free movies showing up on their doorsteps. Now that I'm in the Directors' Guild, I may even get a better class of freebie. Although the first delivery came yesterday and wasn't DVDs but screenplays. *Sideways* and two others. I immediately read *Sideways* and was left with that most conflicted of writer feelings: this is so fucking good I wish I'd written it.

DECEMBER 2004

Earthquake in Indian Ocean causes tsunami that devastates south Asia, killing over 150,000 people. I feel like such a shallow asshole for putting so much importance on my career that I donate $100 online to the Red Cross. Well fuck you, it's a hundred bucks they didn't have before me. Rumor of some musicians getting together to do a We Are the World-type song for the tsunami victims. Seems hard to pull off as not many words rhyme with "tsunami," other than "mommy" or "pastrami" and I'm not sure how they'd work them in.

Not many end of the year changes on the network schedules, except for a few shows moving timeslots.

schedule 2004 DECEMBER

Day	Network	8-8:30	8:30-9	9-9:30	9:30-10	10-11
MON.	ABC	The Benefactor / ABC Monday Night Movie *(after football ends in January)*		Monday Night Football		Grey's Anatomy *(after football ends in January)*
	CBS	Still Standing	Listen Up	Everybody Loves Raymond	Two and a Half Men	CSI: Miami
	NBC	Fear Factor		Las Vegas		LAX
	FOX	North Shore / Athens		The Swan 2 / 24		
	WB	7th Heaven		Everwood		
	UPN	One on One	Half & Half	Girlfriends	Second Time Around	
TUESDAY	ABC	My Wife & Kids	George Lopez	According to Jim	Rodney	NYPD Blue / Blind Justice
	CBS	Navy NCIS		Clubhouse		Judging Amy
	NBC	Last Comic Standing / The Contender		Father of the Pride	Scrubs	Law & Order: Special Victims Unit
	FOX	The Billionaire: Branson's Quest for the Best / American Idol		House		
	WB	Gilmore Girls		One Tree Hill		
	UPN	All of Us	Eve	Veronica Mars		
WEDNESDAY	ABC	Lost		The Bachelor		Wife Swap
	CBS	60 Minutes		The King of Queens	Center of the Universe	CSI: NY
	NBC	Hawaii		The West Wing / Revelations		Law & Order
	FOX	That '70s Show	Quintuplets / Related by Family	The Bernie Mac Show / American Idol	Method & Red / The Bernie Mac Show	
	WB	Smallville		Blue Collar TV	Drew Carey's Green Screen Show	
	UPN	America's Next Top Model / The Road to Stardom With Missy Elliott		Kevin Hill		
THURSDAY	ABC	Extreme Makeover 12/8 moves to thurs @ 9 in Jan.		Life as We Know It 12/8 moves to thurs @ 8 in Jan.		Primetime Live
	CBS	Survivor: Vanuatu		CSI: Crime Scene Investigation		Without a Trace
	NBC	Joey	Will & Grace	The Apprentice 2		ER
	FOX	The O.C.		Tru Calling		
	WB	The Mountain		Studio 7		
	UPN	WWE SmackDown!				
FRIDAY	ABC	8 Simple Rules	Complete Savages	Hope & Faith	Less Than Perfect	20/20
	CBS	Joan of Arcadia		JAG		Dr. Vegas
	NBC	Dateline NBC		Third Watch		Medical Investigation
	FOX	Specials / The Inside		The Next Great Champ / Jonny Zero		
	WB	What I Like About You	Commando Nanny	Reba	Grounded for Life	
	UPN	America's Next Top Model *(repeat)*		Star Trek: Enterprise		
SATURDAY	ABC	The Wonderful World of Disney				
	CBS	The Amazing Race		Crime Time Saturday		48 Hours Mysteries
	NBC	NBC Saturday Night Movie				
	FOX	Cops	Cops	America's Most Wanted		

Day	Network	7-7:30	7:30-8	8-8:30	8:30-9	9-10	10-11
SUND.	ABC	America's Funniest Home Videos		Extreme Makeover: Home Edition		Desperate Housewives / Alias	Boston Legal
	CBS	60 Minutes		Cold Case		CBS Sunday Movie	
	NBC	Dateline NBC		American Dreams		Law & Order: Criminal Intent	Crossing Jordan
	FOX	King of the Hill / Kelsey Grammer Presents: The Sketch Show	Malcolm in the Middle / King of the Hill	The Simpsons	Arrested Development / Malcolm in the Middle	The Partner / Arrested Development / American Dad	
	WB	Steve Harvey's Big Time		Charmed		Jack & Bobby	

KEY
- NEW SHOW
- NEW TIME
- Fox Nov.-Jan.
- Fox Jan.-June

December 1

Having lunch with Garry Hart to discuss the Lewis Black pitch. Later a notes conference call with CBS on Chill Mitchell. Pitching Paramount on another show after that. A busy show business afternoon. Get notes from CBS via conference call. Lasts all of 10 minutes. A few things on a few pages, which ordinarily would be a good thing, but their palpable lack of enthusiasm leads me to believe this is once again just an obligatory call and they have no intention of putting it on. But the most telling note of all was that Daryl was too "passive" throughout. Translation: unfunny and with no attitude. Why? Because throughout the entire process I was systematically noted to remove anything that had the slightest amount of attitude, for fear of making him too unlikable. They make him vanilla then complain he's too white when they're the ones who comedically whitewashed him.

Now I have to go back in and strengthen his attitude and give him more jokes and do what I wanted to do in the first place, albeit with a story that is uninteresting. Only now the project has a stink on it, so now I have to change something I'm not happy with into something I might be happy with but they may not be. Or may be. When you get no accurate information, you're shooting in the dark. Then again, it all may be bullshit if they have no intention of putting it on. At this point, they might as well just change the network voice mail: "You have reached CBS; if you know your party's extension, please dial it now. If not, please press 2 for a directory of employees. If you're calling for your network notes: start the story sooner, make it more joyful, and the characters less mean. Oh, and lose the masturbation joke at the end of the first act."

The pitch for Lewis Black, however, goes great. Would be a show I'd love to do.

Therefore, it will not happen.

December 2

Show business gets interesting: while I'm struggling with the Chill Mitchell pilot, knowing I've got to make it funnier, better, more solid, I get a call from Garry Hart who tells me, as we knew might be a possibility, that Sony is offering Lewis Black a holding deal. So...if he makes that deal with a rival studio, we can't go in with him to pitch. So the plan is to try to get to the networks, pitch the idea and if we sell it, then Paramount could make a preemptive deal with him, but they'll never pony up blind money before that. The other possibility is going in, in partnership with Sony, but that's not likely, nor desirable from a creative standpoint—too many cooks—but it is desirable when compared to everyone winding up with nothing.

Still December 2

4:30 pm. Already dark. The cheesiest of Christmas music is blaring out of speakers outside my office, where they've set up for the annual lighting of the Paramount Christmas tree, where the executives descend from the mountain and address the below-the-line folks[47] telling them how important they are and blathering on about the Paramount family. There's eggnog and sandwiches and I think if I hear one more Christmas carol right now I'll yack. Meanwhile, I have a meeting with Perry Simon in ten minutes to figure out how to handle these notes. There's something about failure and lack of momentum with a project. After a while, you can just smell it. And I can smell it. Still I'm going to kill myself on this rewrite. I know this moment. I've lived it. And I'm living it again. I can see myself walking out of here for Christmas, after a year's work, with no projects and a completely uncertain future, with six months on a deal to get something going.

[47] Below the line. The people on any production who do the hardest work and are paid the least. The reference is to a production budget which delineates "above the line" inflated salaries for actors, writers, producers, directors, and below the line, the crew people who actually do the heavy lifting.

December 3

Meetings set for next week on Lewis Black project. Monday with the studio to go over the pitch, and Thursday with ABC, where I've already been this year and struck out. Meanwhile, on the other project: I am in rewrite hell. Lost between conflicting sets of notes on a story that I didn't originally pitch but was the only one I could get approved.

December 8

Will finish the Chill Mitchell rewrite tomorrow. Think I cracked a couple of scenes I was killing myself over and I think it's better, but I still don't think it will go. Going tomorrow to pitch ABC on Lewis Black idea. Again, I don't think they'll pick it up. Not their style, but I have to keep trying.

December 12

Have turned in yet another draft to Paramount and, once again, am waiting for notes. ABC responded to the Lewis Black pitch with an equivocal pass. They don't want to do a show in a bar, where it was set, but I guess they liked elements of it so there are further discussions to have. Pitching it to NBC tomorrow.

December 13

Spend the afternoon with Garry Hart. Started with a quick phone call with Stephanie Leifer at ABC (no longer in that job) who said she liked elements of what we pitched, but added that we need to come in with a concept that's more daring, new, and different in order to attract them. Garry and I take a walk around the lot playing the most dreaded of development games: "what if." "What if he were a cop, fireman, doctor, lawyer, Indian chief…" If you find yourself playing these games around this time of year—well, if you're on a development deal with an office, assistant and salary, it's not that horrible. If you're alone in a studio apartment in the Valley with dishes piled in the sink, catshit stinking in the box, dust balls rolling past your feet, several days' beard growth and a computer with nothing on the screen but a blinking cursor—then shoot yourself.

THE MYTH OF THE BLINKING CURSOR

The myth about writing is that all you have to do is get a computer, install some scriptwriting software, get a beverage, turn on the computer, type "FADE IN" then sit back and wait for an idea. For some idiotic reason it's even portrayed this way in movies, from writers who should know better. This is not the way it happens. By the time you sit down to write, whether it's a book, TV script or movie, you've got an outline and notes scribbled in margins, along with, depending on your habits, various other notes on voice recorders, matchbooks, random slips of paper, or scribbled in ink up and down your arm, all the result of having lived with the idea long enough, and thought about it long enough, to know what you're writing about. Sitting down to write is not a random act. It's the intentional result of thinking over time about an idea that begins to take shape and form itself into a story. It might start from a character, a scene, a moment you're working from, or working toward. In any case, there is pre-thinking involved. And passion. And a desire to get it down on paper. But no one sits down to write having no clue what they're writing about. If you find yourself sitting at the computer staring at the blinking cursor, looking for an idea, the idea you might want to look for is that of finding a new profession.

Where was I? Oh, yeah. Those "what if" conversations. Nothing ever comes of them. Until something does. We actually trip over an idea that begins to come alive, which you know because you can pitch on it, imagine characters, stories—you can see the world. It was definitely something we could go back to ABC with. But we decide to pitch the old idea to NBC tomorrow. Play it safe, as it's already worked out.

December 14

I'm sitting in the NBC commissary having a Coke and rubbing ice on my swollen lip that I injured by rolling my own car window into my face in a *Three Stooges*-like moment in my garage at 5:30 in the morning. Great. Now I have to go up and pitch with an attention-diverting physical deformity and temporary speech impediment. But what's really weighing on my mind is the notion that I think this new idea is better, and that we can position it with NBC that it just came to us and it's so hot and if you don't buy it we'll go to another network. It feels like something we can sell. So when Garry comes in I make my pitch. He agrees. As does Kevin. We go upstairs with a game plan.

Garry introduces it. I pitch: "The first words of the script tell the story—INT. KUWAIT HILTON." And I pitch a show about reporters covering the Iraq war from Kuwait. Perfect for Lewis. Daring for TV. Shades of *Salvador*. *Year of Living Dangerously*. But most similar to *MASH*. We seem to pique the interest of the 5 people in the room and leave. Downstairs we feel some excitement. This could work. In a moment of creative salesmanship, Garry immediately calls Stephanie Leifer at ABC and asks for 5 minutes right away. She says OK. We race over, a few minutes away, and run upstairs and pitch it again. She's intrigued. Will get back to us. We go down again, feeling like we may have something, along with an interesting story to tell of how it happened.

December 15

Morning comes. No response from anyone. No pass. No sale. Just nothing. So much for enthusiasm. Meanwhile, the revised Chill Mitchell script went back to CBS, though I'm not feeling very hopeful. But I've felt this way with them before. Maybe they'll come back with more notes. Maybe with a polite "Thank you, but no." All I can do is wait for the phone to ring. Besides, the town is in pre-holiday shut-down mode, and most people are probably heading out already. It's the time of year for those in good positions to enjoy their families and the fruits of their labors and for those still sweating it out to either get loaded, go away, or hang by the phone praying that some executive read their script and loved it so much they had to call the agent who immediately called the client to perk up their holidays and remove some of the painful waiting. These are the fantasies you go through. They rarely happen. Better to leave town or start drinking.

December 22

Left the office for the holiday, nothing more to do. Driving up Laurel Canyon, I remember it's almost been a year since I wondered what it would be like driving up Laurel Canyon in a year, stuck in traffic, with nothing to show for a year's work. Now I know. Merry motherfucking Christmas. The car in front of me stops short, long enough for me to notice the bumper sticker reading: ISRAEL. GOD'S GIFT TO THE JEWS. SOURCE: THE *BIBLE*. Ironically, it's on a Mercedes station wagon. Wonder what God felt about the Jews when he gave them the gift of the Holocaust and if that would fit on a bumper sticker.

JANUARY, 2005

George Bush inaugurated. War continues as Iraqi elections come off as promised with high voter turnout reported. Facing overwhelming evidence that this is what the Iraqi people want, the insurgents get together and go "Well, fuck it, they voted, that's it, let's go home." Oh, wait, they don't do that. Instead, they set off more bombs.

Meanwhile, here's how the TV season looks, based on the shows that were on in the fall. And just for some broader perspective, here's a list 59 shows dating back to July, 2003, that the networks banked on being popular that all ended up getting cancelled.

schedule

ON AIR STATUS

Day	Network	8-8:30	8:30-9	9-9:30	9:30-10	10-11
MON.	ABC	The Benefactor / ABC Monday Night Movie (after football ends in January)		Monday Night Football		Grey's Anatomy (after football ends in January)
	CBS	Still Standing	Listen Up	Everybody Loves Raymond	Two and a Half Men	CSI: Miami
	NBC	Fear Factor		Las Vegas		LAX
	FOX	North Shore / Athens		The Swan 2 / 24		
	WB	7th Heaven		Everwood		
	UPN	One on One	Half & Half	Girlfriends	Second Time Around	
TUESDAY	ABC	My Wife & Kids	George Lopez	According to Jim	Rodney	NYPD Blue / Blind Justice
	CBS	Navy NCIS		Clubhouse		Judging Amy
	NBC	Last Comic Standing / The Contender		Father of the Pride	Scrubs	Law & Order: Special Victims Unit
	FOX	The Billionaire: Branson's Quest for the Best / American Idol		Next Great Champ		
	WB	Gilmore Girls		One Tree Hill		
	UPN	All of Us	Eve	Veronica Mars		
WEDNESDAY	ABC	Lost		The Bachelor		Wife Swap
	CBS	60 Minutes		The King of Queens	Center of the Universe	CSI: NY
	NBC	Hawaii		The West Wing / Revelations		Law & Order
	FOX	That '70s Show	Quintuplets / Related by Family	The Bernie Mac Show / American Idol	Method & Red / The Bernie Mac Show	
	WB	Smallville		Blue Collar TV	Drew Carey's Green Screen Show	
	UPN	America's Next Top Model / The Road to Stardom With Missy Elliott		Kevin Hill		
THURSDAY	ABC	Extreme Makeover		Life as We Know It		Primetime Live
	CBS	Survivor: Vanuatu		CSI: Crime Scene Investigation		Without a Trace
	NBC	Joey	Will & Grace	The Apprentice 2		ER
	FOX	The O.C.		Tru Calling		
	WB	The Mountain		Studio 7		
	UPN	WWE SmackDown!				
FRIDAY	ABC	8 Simple Rules	Complete Savages	Hope & Faith	Less Than Perfect	20/20
	CBS	Joan of Arcadia		JAG		Dr. Vegas
	NBC	Dateline NBC		Third Watch		Medical Investigation
	FOX	Specials / The Inside		Jonny Zero		
	WB	What I Like About You	Commando Nanny	Reba	Grounded for Life	
	UPN	America's Next Top Model (repeat)		Star Trek: Enterprise		
SATURDAY	ABC	The Wonderful World of Disney				
	CBS	The Amazing Race		Crime Time Saturday		48 Hours Mysteries
	NBC	NBC Saturday Night Movie				
	FOX	Cops	Cops	America's Most Wanted		

Day	Network	7-7:30	7:30-8	8-8:30	8:30-9	9-10	10-11
SUND.	ABC	America's Funniest Home Videos		Extreme Makeover: Home Edition		Desperate Housewives / Alias	Boston Legal
	CBS	60 Minutes		Cold Case		CBS Sunday Movie	
	NBC	Dateline NBC		American Dreams		Law & Order: Criminal Intent	Crossing Jordan
	FOX	King of the Hill / Kelsey Grammer Presents: The Sketch Show	Malcolm in the Middle / King of the Hill	The Simpsons	Arrested Development / Malcolm in the Middle	The Partner / Arrested Development	American Dad
	WB	Steve Harvey's Big Time		Charmed		Jack & Bobby	

KEY
- NEW SHOW
- NEW TIME
- Fox Nov.-Jan.
- Fox Jan.-June

MOVED TO CABLE | FATE T.B.D. | CANCELLED

Ca ed TV Shows -- The TV Graveyard Page

You are here: About > Entertainment > Primetime TV > Cancelled TV Shows > Cancelled TV Shows -- The TV Graveyard

Primetime TV

Canceled Shows: The TV Graveyard

We loved them the networks didn't.

AS OF 1/24

Home

Essentials

- TV Shows A-Z
- TV Listings
- TV Show Pictures
- TV Spoilers
- TV Shows on DVD

Primetime TV Offers

- TV Show DVDs
- Fox TV DVD
- Smallville Season One DVD
- ER Season One DVDs
- Alias Television
- What are offers?

Articles & Resources

- TV Shows
- TV Show DVDs
- TV Listings
- TV News, Gossip & Reviews
- Cancelled TV Shows
- TV Episode Guides
- TV Spoilers
- TV Actors & Actresses
- TV Award Shows
- TV Show Pictures
- TV Characters
- TV Theme Songs
- TV Quotes
- TV Multimedia

Buyer's Guide

Before You Buy

Top Picks

- Raid Rory and Lorelai Gilmore's Closet
- Gifts for "O.C." Fans
- Raid Sydney Bristow's Closet
- ɔduct Reviews

Articles

TV Blog Season Premiere Dates TV Shows A-Z List

You may be able to find some of these cancelled shows on DVD. Check out list for the best prices here.

Show	Network	Date
Center of the Universe	CBS	Saturday, January 22
life as we know it	ABC	Monday, Janaury 24
The Mountain	FOX	Tuesday, Jan. 11, 2005
LAX	NBC	Monday, November 22, 2004
Grounded For Life	WB	Tuesday, Nov. 9, 2004
Dr. Vegas	CBS	Monday, Nov. 8, 2004
Clubhouse	CBS	Monday, Nov. 8, 2004
Commando Nanny	WB	Wednesday, Oct. 20, 2004
Hawaii	NBC	Tuesday, Oct. 19, 2004
The Complex: Malibu	FOX	Monday, Oct. 18, 2004
The Benefactor	ABC	Monday, Oct. 18, 2004
Who Wants to Marry My Dad?	NBC	Tuesday, Oct. 12, 2004
Method and Red	FOX	Tuesday, Sep. 28, 2004
Still Life	FOX	Tuesday, Aug. 10, 2004
The Jury	FOX	Friday, Jul. 2, 2004
Life of Fire	ABC	6/18/04
10-8	ABC	6/18/04
My Life Is A Sitcom 2	ABC Family	6/3/04

Hack	CBS	5/19/04
The District	CBS	5/19/04
The Guardian	CBS	5/19/04
Becker	CBS	5/19/04
The Jamie Kennedy Experiment	WB	5/17/04
It's All Relative	ABC	5/17/04
Life With Bonnie	ABC	5/17/04
I'm with Her	ABC	5/17/04
Married to the Kelly's	ABC	5/17/04
All About the Andersons	WB	5/17/04
Good Morning Miami	NBC	5/17/04
Miss Match	NBC	5/17/04
Whoopi	NBC	5/17/04
The Tracy Morgan Show	NBC	5/17/04
Happy Family	NBC	5/17/04
ED	NBC	5/17/04
The Parkers	UPN	5/10/04
Angel	WB	5/4/04
The Practice	ABC	4/20/04
Cracking Up	FOX	3/6/04
The Stones	CBS	3/6/04
Century City	CBS	3/5/04
Wonderfalls	FOX	3/5/04
Kingdom Hospital	ABC	3/5/04
Frasier	NBC	3/23/04
The Handler	CBS	3/16/04
Jake 2.0	UPN	3/16/04
Love Again	FOX	3/9/04
Karen Sisco	ABC	1/23/04
Friends	NBC	1/26/04
A Minute with Stan Hooper	FOX	1/15/04
Lyon's Den	NBC	1/7/04
Wanda At Large	FOX	12/8/03

Tarzan	WB	11/7/03
L.A. Dragnet	ABC	11/5/03
Skin	FOX	11/4/03
Boomtown	NBC	11/4/03
Coupling	NBC	11/1/03
Luis	FOX	10/28/03
The Brotherhood of Poland, N.H.	CBS	10/28/03
Cedric the Entertainer Presents	FOX	10/21/03
The Mullets	UPN	10/21/03

January 3

Happy New Year. I return to my office with fear and loathing. I've successfully managed to spend the holidays in denial over the one project I've got in the works, but now that I'm back I have to face the likelihood that it's not going to go. Just to begin confirming that fact, I call Perry Simon, who assures me he hasn't heard anything and will follow up with CBS. Still I sense a lack of genuine enthusiasm in his voice, so I know it's a pass. I talk to Garry Hart about our Lewis Black project that has now transcended Lewis Black into a show about journalists covering the Iraq war that, having been passed on at ABC and NBC, we now want to take to Showtime. Interesting that when ABC passed, they said it was "too current." I'm thinking that's the exact reason they should put it on, which speaks volumes as to what is wrong with network television. Without waxing on about the golden age of TV, there was a time when they put a show on the network because it had something to do with what was going on in the country, or in the world. Now it's a justification for passing on it.

I talk to Garry Hart. Despite my earlier thoughts of doing this as a multi-camera show, I tell him that I think it should be single camera. As unique as it might be to do it multi-camera, the arena is too real, and doing it in front of an audience would make it more joke-dependent and trivialize it. Meanwhile, I've been in touch via email with a freelance journalist in Baghdad who has agreed to help as a consultant. I still need to speak with him so that we can go in with some knowledge about that world. This is not one you can just make up.

January 4

Another interesting show business morning. Starts with a call from the manager I'd talked to about a project potentially involving Ted Danson. They called CBS, who said they'd be interested in hearing the pitch if Paramount liked it. They call Paramount, and although Maria Crenna supposedly heard it years ago, she doesn't remember, so they'd be open to hearing it again. The meeting is set for Thursday.

Meanwhile, I try to call the journalist I'd been emailing in Baghdad. After repeated attempts through cell and satellite phones, we make contact. Forgetting for the moment that I'm sitting in my comfy office in Hollywood and talking to a guy in a war zone, and putting aside the relative triviality of my little enterprise next to his, we have a pleasant 45-minute conversation in which he tells me what it's like hanging out with other journalists in the Al Hamra hotel in Baghdad and covering a war, but for some idiotic reason I can't find a legal pad to make notes on, so I start frantically grabbing whatever paper I can find and scribbling on it. Backs of script pages. Lunch menus. Anything. I just need to get it down.

After we hang up, I call Garry Hart, excited—which usually spells doom for any project, but I decide to go with it. The occasional good feeling, being a rarity, should be enjoyed in that moment, either for its own sake, or as a device to gain strength to handle the shit yet to come. He calls Paramount so they can hear the pitch and give us their blessing to go on to Showtime. Then he calls back, saying Les (Moonves) has insisted in a staff meeting that all pitches go to CBS first. Not that they'd put this show on. Despite the fact that they are the network of *MASH* and *All in the Family*, they wouldn't have the balls to do that again. There's no fat guy and bitchy wife in it. So, I wait for that meeting to get set. From one project, to two, to three...what next?

January 5

In true showbiz schizophrenia I'm pitching two shows to Paramount this week. One: the John Derek-type guy with multiple ex-wives in his life. The other: a single-camera cable show about reporters in Iraq covering the war. Toward that end, I've been downloading articles on the war off the web as fast as I can. Pieces from other reporters. Web log entries from Iraqis communicating what it's like from their side. I buy a few books on Amazon written by reporters who covered the war. Still I feel like a total fake, pitching a show like this. The subject is so serious, and I'm so ignorant. Still, I worked on *Wings* without having flown a plane and *Becker* without being a doctor, and most people who worked on *MASH* never went to war. I know I'm going to be blowing some smoke in these meetings, but with the research I'm doing, at least I'll know more than the people I'll be pitching to, so maybe I can pull it off.

In the larger show business world, two new shows premiered. One: *Medium*, a midseason show starring Patricia Arquette as a crime-solving psychic. It did well, and may be the one bright spot at NBC. The other premiere was a show called *Committed*, one of the pilots I watched months ago and hated with a white-hot passion. A cutesy, nauseatingly fake madcap romantic comedy with a bunch of wacky characters acting wackily. The premiere numbers were fair, and if there's a God who is truly on the side of righteousness, it will be cancelled soon, and with extreme prejudice. Though it does seem to fit the current NBC model of wacky white people making lots of sex jokes while looking for love and success in the big city so, who knows, it could be a huge hit. (It wasn't. It was cancelled.)

In the actual world, the tsunami "death toll" approaches 150,000 and, once again, *ET* gets to the heart of the matter by interviewing Leo DeCaprio, who noted that he made a movie in the region and felt particularly touched by the disaster. I think it's fair to say most every human being in the world was particularly touched, whether or not they'd been on location there, so why do I need to hear Leo's account? Not that this is his fault. He's an incredible actor and seems like an intelligent guy and, like any compassionate person, if someone sticks a mike and camera in your face and asks what you thought of the disaster, it's only normal to communicate sorrow and sympathy for the victims. That's not the problem. The problem is, why am I seeing this on TV?

ENTERTAINMENT NEWS: PIMPS IN THE CELEBRITY WHOREHOUSE

First off, let's get the hypocrisy part of this out of the way. If you're a producer on a show and you hear *ET* is coming to interview one of the stars, your reaction is; "Great, free publicity for us!" and you move the production schedule around to accommodate them. But as a viewer, sitting home watching one of these shows, listening to the opening theme, seeing the host or hostess strut out onto the set and smiling with an almost deranged glee over whatever super-hot breaking celebrity news they have to impart, I want to blow my brains out. From a creative standpoint, whoever invented the concept of entertainment news should be shot. War is news. Entertainment is often what you seek out to forget about the news. Or occasionally to shed some light on it or make fun of it. Though from a business standpoint, whoever invented these shows should be given their weight in gold, as they pull off one of the most brilliant feats of alchemy in broadcasting: that of presenting advertising and promotion as content.

Entertainment Tonight and *The Insider* are owned by Paramount, *Access Hollywood* by NBC, and E! Channel is partly owned by ABC; as such, these shows often serve to hype whatever product their parent companies have in the pipeline. Even the morning and evening talk shows serve their corporate masters: *Survivor* castoffs appear on the CBS morning show, and the winner on *Letterman*. Winners and losers on *The Apprentice* or *Amazing Race* become newsworthy by appearing on *The Today Show*. In business, it's called "corporate synergy." In reality, it's fake news. And not Jon Stewart's brilliant fake news, which is often more real than real news. This is bullshit news. Pure public relations. Promotion in the guise of programming.

Actually, the first network to do this was MTV. Although the network launched the music video industry, it carried a sidebar benefit in that every video was, essentially, a commercial for an artist's upcoming release. But at least the videos were entertaining in their own right and added a new dimension to music. The entertainment news shows report—and yes, they actually use the word "report"—celebrity marriages, break-ups, arrests, weekend grosses (or the inflated ones released by the studio), along with providing the latest "news" from reality shows and celebrity trials, as if any of this shit matters. Though they occasionally will stick in a minor chord music cue when reporting a celebrity death.

Not that these shows are the only ones guilty of this. The other pimps in the celebrity whorehouse are magazines, from the cheesy supermarket gossip rags right up to *People*, *Us*, and *Entertainment Weekly*. Then there are the Barbara Walters softball interviews with recent Oscar winners and on Bravo, the king of the celebrity asskissers—James Lipton, the host of *Inside the Actor's Studio*, or, as we called it in the writers room, "Inside the Actor's Anus." This guy's unbelievable. With sycophantic glee and a "Tell us about the wonderfulness that is you," interview style, he can snake his tongue up an actor's ass from six feet away and tickle their eyeballs from the inside. Don't get me wrong: I love actors. Especially the people I've worked with over the years. I'm amazed by what they do. It inspires respect, admiration and, at times, even awe. And even when they morph into celebrities many stay human. Which is not easy when you become "a star" and find yourself living in that fishbowl. I watched Ted Danson handle fame with about as much class as anyone could. So believe me when I say I truly like and respect most actors. It's the hero worship I don't get. These people are not curing cancer, they're just pretending to be a guy who cures cancer.

Even *Rolling Stone* does its own hip version of the celebrity interview, usually in the form of some young journalist's first-person account of interviewing a waifish young actress—coming upon her sitting on a bench in Washington Square Park where she's almost unrecognizable in her jeans, frumpy shirt, and funky little hat, where's she's drinking espresso, chain-smoking Marlboro Lights and reading Hemingway, almost as if she was oblivious to the fact that the journalist her publicist arranged to interview her might be stopping by, so they take a walk around the Village and smoke a joint while discussing her latest movie, along with how she's deep down a very spiritual 19-year-old and really wants to do theater for a few years before going back to college to finish her Anthropology degree, then maybe work for the U.N. saving children, that is before having children of her own, though not before traveling around Europe for a year or two, but right now she's set to do a half-dozen upcoming features, all with actors and directors she feels lucky and privileged to be working with, but after that she'd really like to take a break and fall in love, if only she could meet the right guy and by that she means not some Hollywood actor but a real person, which leaves the reporter with the illusion that he might just get to sleep with a movie star—which he doesn't.

It's not that I don't get the public interest in celebrity. We're all voyeurs. If we weren't, the paparazzi stalking famous couples eating dinner or shopping for baby clothes would be somewhere shooting bar mitzvahs. What they shoot sells because people buy the magazines they're published in. Maybe it's just the looser definition of the term "celebrity." There was a time when this at least had a tangential relationship to talent, but now 15 minutes of fame has morphed into 15 minutes of infamy as we're force-fed the latest news of every celebrity murder, drunk driver, bar brawler, wife beater or child molester. This hit home a few months ago as I was driving down Robertson Boulevard in Beverly Hills and noticed a swarm (or is it a gaggle? It can't possibly be a pride) of paparazzi with their white telephoto lenses chasing some young girl and her two friends across the street, angling for a shot. Only when she finally stopped running and turned to allow them the privilege of a photograph did I realize who it was: Kelly Osborne. Basically the daughter of a star who had her few minutes while their family show was on, then did a shower-worthy version of a Madonna song and played make-pretend rock star for about an hour. But someone's making a buck by taking shots of her because somewhere, some magazine will buy them—but only because someone, somewhere must still want to see them. America is a great country, but frankly, sometimes it's just such a very silly place.

Still January 5

Déjà vu. Almost a year after my cell phone rang with my brother and agent on the line telling me CBS was passing on the one project I had, I get the same call from the same people in the same "the governor turned down your appeal" tone to tell me they're passing on the Chill Mitchell script. No reason given; it doesn't really matter. A pass is a pass. Six months' work—over. I toss the script in the files and get ready for two upcoming pitches in the next two days, though the timing is odd as this is not the time of year to start pitching and, at least with one project, if it gets the Paramount OK the next step is…God help me…back to CBS.

January 10

Fox cancels *The Mountain*.

January 11

I take a walk around the lot, which is usually the only way I can find out any information. I see a crew guy from *Becker* who tells me that *The Bad Girl's Guide*, the Jenny McCarthy show for UPN, has started production on Stage 19, where we did *Wings*. I know the woman running it, which might have theoretically led to some consulting work except for the fact that I inadvertently insulted a friend of mine who represents Jenny by saying, in effect, it's not exactly the kind of show I'd like to work on, though I may have said it less politely and in a roomful of people. Oh, well… I also bump into another acquaintance who tells me a semi-famous comedienne/actress walked off the *Girlfriends* set yesterday 'cause her trailer wasn't big enough. Just another day in show business.

January 17

Reading everything I can to become as informed as possible for pitching the reporter show to Showtime. The more I read, the more excited I get. Could be an amazing show. Of course, there are three shows in various stages of development at this moment about the war. Steven Bochco is doing one for F/X. But it's about soldiers and the families on the home front. There's another at HBO. And a comedy at Fox, but it's a multi-camera show about people setting up a Voice of America-type TV station in Baghdad. Similar, not the same. Undaunted, I press on.

January 18

Fox cancels *Tru Calling*.

January 20

We pitch the war correspondents show to Showtime. Same people. Same narcoleptic response. It's usually a bad sign when the person you're pitching to can't stop yawning and his associate drops her pen and stops taking notes. Out on the street, I bitch to Garry Hart that these people just don't get it. That's why they're sucking ass next to HBO. This could be a hot show for them. Timely, promotable. Actually having something to do with the world. But I can smell a pass.

January 21

Variety reports the cancellation of the John Goodman show—*Center of the Universe*. For some insanely petty reason I feel vindicated.

January 26

ABC pulls the plug on *Complete Savages*. Single dad. Five

sons. Sloppy house. Still, it had its own style, and Keith Carradine was funny in the lead. This is one I thought might make it.

January 27

Showtime passes on the reporter show. "Have something like it in development," "Don't want to do a comedy around the war," just about every response other than "We hate you, don't come back." I go right into anger mode. Fine, good luck with Kirstie Alley and *Fat Actress*. I'm sure it's less interesting to do a show about the lives of reporters living in a war zone than one featuring a 300-pound Scientologist going down on a bowl of spaghetti. Watch, it'll be a huge hit. Still, I had to get that out.

So for the moment, I'm done. Crapped out after a year and a half's work, two pilot scripts, a dozen network pitches backed up by countless meetings, phone calls, note sessions.... That's it. A moment I could feel in my gut was going to happen over a year ago, and now it's here. I was hoping to be in production on a pilot at this point, not just for its own sake but because it would make a more interesting next chapter to this book, but instead I'll track the rest of the season and spec out the war reporter pilot as a writing sample, per my agent's suggestion. Maybe I'll start writing another spec pilot I've been playing with for years, or even take a week's vacation somewhere to cool out and mentally prepare to pack up my office and move out.

I also have to think about interviewing for a job on someone else's show or, for the first time in 13 years, face the possibility of flat-out unemployment. The last time I was in this spot, I was offered a job in New York on a show with Malcolm-Jamal Warner that I turned down and soon after landed a job as a consultant on *Wings* with a mere 6-show guarantee, their way of protecting themselves in case I sucked. I ended up staying for 5 years, until the end of the series. I wonder if something like that will happen this time.

Either way, it means going out into the great unknown with very little control over my fate. Ebay's starting to look real good.

FEBRUARY 2005

Jury selection on the Michael Jackson trial begins. Both prosecution and defense question prospective jurors during voire dire, trying to weed out those who look smart enough to nail book deals before they do.

This is the time of year that every writer with a project in play gets final notes and soon learns their fate. Pilot orders are beginning to filter in. In an interesting sidebar, *Variety* reports the advent of a Sundance-like festival entitled The New York Television Festival, being held in September for aspiring television writer/producers that will showcase 30-40 rough homemade pilots. This will be interesting, as it could open doors for people who could never get into a network to show what they can do. Representatives of every network, studio, and agency will certainly flock to the event, looking for "new talent." I'm sure the talent is out there. The talent is already here. The question is what the networks will do with it. If the goal somehow changes to putting on the best product it can find, opening up creativity on all fronts, this may be the shot in the arm the industry needs. My feeling is it won't matter what they see. Given their meat grinder approach to development, once they've smoothed all the edges and gotten everyone to love each other, they can still turn the most original, brilliant idea into hamburger.

February 3

One of the better pilots I saw this season—the John Stamos show—has just been given a premiere date in March on ABC. An article in Zap2it.com describes the show, now entitled *Jake in*

Progress, as "a midseason comedy, though with its lack of laugh track and single-camera shooting style, it might not exactly fit with the other more traditional sitcoms on the network's schedule." They're right. It might not. But this does open up an opportunity to mention another of these annoying notions that entertainment journalists trot out every now and then–

THE LAUGH TRACK

Let's put this to rest once and for all. There is no such thing as a "laugh track" anymore. This is a device left over from when shows were shot on film without an audience and, once mixed, the laughs were put in, on the assumption that the audience at home might not realize something was funny unless shown by example where to laugh. In time, shows began shooting in front of a live audience so that the laughter you heard at home was actual laughter from that audience. Watch a *Cheers* re-run, you'll hear one of the cast in voice-over saying: "*Cheers* was filmed before a live studio audience." Their way of telling you that the laughs were real. As they have been on every other multi-camera show since.

The only place the "laugh track" rears its ugly head anymore is in a single camera show where all the laughs are inserted in post-production, though it is usually at the insistence of the network and over the dead body of the writer/executive producer. Even executives are backing off, finally realizing how cheesy it sounds. Yet journalists still trot out the phrase "laugh track," which carries with it the snide implication that no actual human could laugh at this shit. The laugh track has not been a part of multi-camera production for years. When a show is shot in front of an audience, those laughs are real. However, sometimes a scene will be pre-shot before the audience comes in, or shot again in pickups after they leave. If, in editing, portions of the audience takes and pickup takes are used in the scene, you need to equalize the laughs. Toward that end, there is a guy who shows up at every mix with a laugh machine to make sure all the laughs are balanced. Occasionally, the laughs on a joke will be heightened to keep pace with the rest of the scene, or they will be added because the audience just didn't get it. As well, on occasion, you'll get an audience that was so giddy, or so worked up by the warm-up guy, that they laughed themselves sick at everything—jokes, setups, straight lines. It's like they showed up on Nitrous. In that case, those laughs are removed and replaced with human ones or none at all. But the "laugh track"—the machine that inserts laughter into a show where it never existed, does not exist. This is something entertainment journalists should know, but most don't bother to find out because it's more fun to use the pejorative "laugh track" as a way of slamming the entire genre of half-hour shows than to find out the truth.

February 6

Super Bowl Sunday and not a tit nor ass in sight. You barely knew the respective sides had cheerleaders. Thanks, Janet Jackson, you fucked it up for the rest of us. War still on. Doesn't stop Fox (why in God's name would it) from turning the 40-minute pregame show into a flag-waving war pageant, complete with military choirs singing America the Beautiful while jets fly overhead. Watching this spectacle, an emotion began to well up inside, just as it has in past years, and as the flags waved and the veterans put their hands over their hearts and the deaf folks signed the words to this tribute to this great land of ours, the only words I could think of were probably the same words in the heart of most every other American football fan: JUST PLAY THE FUCKING GAME!!!

February 7

Network pilot orders are trickling in. This morning's *Variety* mentions a few, each interesting in its own right. NBC/Universal is producing a show for NBC, (in-house[48]) starring Aidan Quinn as a minister who deals with the stresses of his dysfunctional family by popping Vicodin and talking to a live Jesus. (Fast forward: Several stations around the country refuse to air the

Variety 2-7-05

8 ▪ VARIETY.COM DAILY VARIETY

LEMONS & MERMAIDS

Nets play pilot card; Quinn toplines 'Daniel'

By MICHAEL SCHNEIDER

Pilots added to the mix Friday include a Fox sitcom set at a used-car dealership; an NBC laffer based on the life of poker champ Annie Duke; and a high-concept WB entry about a mermaid in Miami.

Meanwhile, Aidan Quinn has been cast as the lead in the Peacock's "Book of Daniel," while KaDee Strickland ("The Stepford Wives") will star in the ABC legal drama "Laws of Chance."

Beyond the pilot realm, Fox's "Arrested Development" has scored Ben Stiller to guest star in an episode later this spring as Tony Wonder, a rival magician to Gob Bluth (Will Arnett). Stiller shot his part on Friday.

Stiller is no stranger to Fox, where his "Ben Stiller Show" earned an Emmy — after it was canceled — in 1992.

Meanwhile, in his first major episodic TV role, Quinn would play Episcopal minister Daniel Webster in "Book of Daniel." The NBC U TV Studios project, from Jack Kenny and Flody Suarez (with James Frawley directing), revolves around

Quinn

Strickland

Quinn's character, who deals with the stresses of his dysfunctional family by popping Vicodin — and talking to images of God.

Quinn will next be seen in the made-for-HBO film "Empire Falls."

Strickland, meanwhile, will play the lead character Chance in "Laws of Chance," which is based on real-life Houston assistant district attorney Kelly Siegler. Gary Glasberg, Gina Matthews and Grant Scharbo produce for 20th Century Fox and Roundtable Ink.

As for the pilot pickups, Robb and Mark Cullen ("Lucky") will exec produce the ensemble laffer "New Car Smell" for 20th Century Fox TV.

"All In," meanwhile, revolves around the character based on Duke — a single mom who's a whiz around the poker table, but who could use some of those same smarts in raising her kids.

Jack Burditt ("I'm With Her") will exec produce, along with Lisa Kudrow and Dan Bucatinsky. Warner Bros. TV is producing the cast-contingent pilot for NBC.

Then there's the untitled drama/fantasy project at the WB about a mermaid who attempts to live on dry land in Miami.

Brad Kern ("Charmed") will exec produce for Spelling TV, along with Aaron Spelling and E. Duke Vincent.

(Josef Adalian contributed to this report.)

[48] In-house. A show produced by the network's own production company.

show due to the live Jesus.) Still the subject matter is not entirely new, bearing a resemblance to *Joan of Arcadia*, or even a Norman Lear show from 1991 called *Sunday Dinner*, starring Robert Loggia and (now famous again) Teri Hatcher as his young wife who used to talk to God in private asides. Unfortunately, the latter show got a little too precious, as she referred to the good Lord as "Larry." CBS cancelled it. God Almighty isn't fond of nicknames, which occurred to me as I watched a news report on the upcoming Robert Blake trial, and flashed back to him on *The Tonight Show with Johnny Carson* sitting on the couch like the funky rebel he was, nonchalantly waving a prop cigarette and referring somewhat cheekily to "the big guy" and "the man upstairs." (Wonder how the big guy felt about him allegedly busting a cap in his wife's head? Not a value judgment, just a passing observation.) In any event, characters talking to God isn't new on TV. Somebody steal someone's idea? No. Will it work? Maybe. It's all execution.

Similarly, Fox announced a half-hour (20th Century Fox for Fox network—again, an in-house production) called *New Car Smell*, set at a used car dealership—an idea that hasn't been around since…last year, when NBC produced *Beverly Hills SUV*, about a high-end car dealership. The pilot never got picked up.

Also at NBC, a show based on the life of a woman poker champ—a single mom who's a whiz at the poker table but can't seem to bring those same talents to bear raising her kids. Jesus. This notion has too many incarnations to quote chapter and verse but every year it rears its head in one form or another. Shelley Long did a show post-*Cheers* called *Good Advice*, about a marital therapist whose own marriage falls apart in the pilot. The advice columnist whose life is shit is a premise that has been done ad nauseum. Two years ago Alicia Silverstone was on NBC as a matchmaker who just couldn't find the right guy. Why does this concept keep living?

Because it's easily understandable to development executives as the obvious contradiction is a source for humor—you see, the person's an expert in one area of life, but a failure in that same aspect of their own life. Hundreds of these shows have come and gone over the years. I can't think of one that was ever a hit. Oh yeah, *Frasier*. That made it.

Then the WB weighed in with an untitled drama/fantasy about a mermaid who attempts to live on dry land in Miami. OK, let's break this down. It's 2005. There's still a war in Iraq. The present administration is sending messages to Iran and Syria to watch their asses 'cause we're not above bombing the shit out of you, too, 'cause as everyone knows, inside the heart of every oil-rich Muslim is a freedom-loving American Christian waiting to get out. Evidently, as long as the neocons are in power, the motto for the 21st Century is "Armageddon: Bring It On." And while some networks are preparing shows that seem to deal with the war, the WB opts to keep us entertained in that Bob Hope USO-show denial sort of way by pretending none of this exists and instead diverting our attention with the ongoing story of a mermaid in Miami. Parenthetically, the USO show is a concept I never quite got. Sure, laughter's cathartic. Takes your mind off the danger. But what's the concept behind visiting GIs in a war zone and parading beautiful women on stage in front of them as if to say this is the kind of American girl you may never get home to fuck again 'cause you're going to die. Do they really need reminders of that? Isn't this the sort of tactic you'd use to torture a captive instead of entertain a troop? But who knows? The mermaid thing could work. Seems dumb as shit on the surface, then again, in 1984 Tom Hanks and Ron Howard did *Splash*, and it worked. It's all execution. I also wonder if this show, as it's set in Miami, will feature a person of Latin heritage, which is my awkward segue into another topic: diversity.

DIVERSITY

NBC will host industry forum for minorities

By Susan King
Times Staff Writer

Seniors, the disabled, blacks, Latinos and other minorities are being encouraged to attend NBC's first industrywide diversity expo Saturday in Studio City.

Marc Hirschfeld, executive vice president of casting for NBC Entertainment, said that this is the first event in which broadcast networks are pooling their resources and staff together to offer workshops that focus on skills and identify potential talent.

"I wanted it to be an opportunity especially for actors, writers and directors of color to take advantage of all opportunities," Hirschfeld said.

"That really meant inviting the other networks to participate."

Diversity Outreach Expo 2005, an all-day forum, will offer a variety of workshops and panels on résumé writing, acting, screenwriting and directing. Speakers include Kevin Reilly, president of NBC entertainment; Arthur Forney, director-producer of "Law & Order"; actor Orson Bean; and Ron Taylor, Fox's vice president of diversity development.

Information and advice will be provided for seniors and people with disabilities working in entertainment, as well as racial and ethnic minorities from Southern California.

"We wanted to embrace diversity in the broadest sense of the word and give opportunities to portions of the entertainment community that were being overlooked and neglected," Hirschfeld said.

Though he worried that few people would attend, NBC has already received 1,500 RSVPs.

Among the workshops and panels being offered: "Creating an Eye-Catching Resume," "Second Stage: A Panel for Senior Actors in the Biz," "Directing Your Way Into Hollywood" and "How to Interview Like a Star." Representatives from more than 25 organizations and entertainment companies will be available to talk about resources.

The forum will be at the Sportsmen's Lodge Event Center, 12833 Ventura Blvd. The doors open at 9 a.m.

The expo is no longer taking RSVPs, but those interested in attending can still show up.

This article from the *L.A. Times* references "NBC's Diversity Outreach Expo 2005." Diversity is network-speak for putting ethnic people on TV, both in front of and behind the cameras. The article quotes people saying all the right things. "Opportunity." "Embracing ethnic diversity." Over the years I have been to a half-dozen CBS-sponsored events—five at the Directors' Guild and one at the Writers' Guild. Each gathering featured the same people, same speeches, same noble thoughts and, in the case of the DGA, the same disgusting hors d'oeuvres. Like cat puke on a cracker. Unbelievable.

The DGA building on Sunset Boulevard is imposing. The theatre, where members can see recently released movies in the company of other directors and not suffer the public, is legendary for its comfort and state-of-the-art acoustics and design. The pictures on the wall in the function room where they have the event are of the most famous directors in Hollywood history. This is a prestigious organization. Yet, every year the same thought occurrs to me: why can't these people put out anything more appetizing than snot on a Saltine? Maybe I'll mention that when I send in my next dues statement. Where was I? Oh yeah, diversity.

Every year I read a version of this article about someone at one of the networks stating their desire to make television reflect our rainbow-like society. In fact, each network and many studios have hired vice presidents of diversity, whose function, it seems, is to hold seminars such as this in which people come together to say the right things. The question is, Do they *do* the right thing? When I was working on *Becker*, I would read this article every year. The reporter would examine shows on TV at the moment and show an ethnic breakdown of the casts. Oddly enough, except for maybe one article, we were never mentioned, even though, as a show set in the Bronx, two of the five main characters were African-American. And no one ever called us to ask about it. If they had, I could have told them that I had been in on casting hundreds of guest star parts over the years, and the casting process—with the few exceptions of casting someone's mother or brother, in which case race would play a factor—was completely color-blind. It wasn't about ethnicity. It was about talent. And the doors were totally open, because we made every effort to have the show reflect the neighborhood in which it was set. To do otherwise would have been idiotic. Yet despite the networks' annual diversity seminars, the only way to judge their track record is to check out what they put on the air.

Look at shows that have been recent hits. *Seinfeld*, *Will and Grace*, *Just Shoot Me*—all set in New York. All pretty white. *Cheers*, set in Boston, white. *Raymond*, *King of Queens*. White and fairly white. In fact, other than Damon and George Lopez on ABC, I can't think of another show on a major network that predominantly features a diverse cast. Of course there's UPN, which has been home to "the black shows"—*Girlfriends*, *The Parkers*, *One on One*, *Moesha*, *Sister Sister*. This is the audience they're going after. It is also the audience that the major networks don't seem to chase.

Does network TV mirror the ethnic makeup of the country? According to the 2000 census, America is 75.1% white, 12.3% African—American, 3.6% Asian. According to SAG[49], the ethnic breakdown of characters on TV in 2003 was: 73.5% white, 15.3% African America, and 2.5% Asian. Pretty close. Still, there doesn't seem to be much diversity in the casts of half-hour shows. Hour dramas are a different story. Look at *ER*, or *Law and Order*. Each set in a city, each features a diverse cast.

In terms of the networks' desire to diversify, you can check out the actors they currently have under holding deals. Of the roughly 76 deals at the various networks, 9 are with African—American actors, 6 are with Hispanic actors, and 2 fall into that quaint census category of "other." But this doesn't make the networks discriminatory. They're not. They have been and will always be about one thing: money. If Halle Berry or Denzel Washington decided tomorrow they'd do a network show, they'd be on the air in a second because they would deliver a huge audience. And that audience is not just based on color. There are plenty of white kids out there are buying hip hop CDs. Is TV beginning to feature more non-white actors? Yes. Is it because the industry is making a concerted effort to put more shows on starring people of different

[49] SAG. The Screen Actors Guild.

backgrounds? Partially. Are there black executives at the networks? Some. Should there be more? Probably. Is there racism in Hollywood? No, not overtly, though it does exist in its more insidious form in people who can't escape their cultural upbringing. As generations die off, race will probably become less of an issue among children and we'll all get together as one, waiting to hate the next person who moves on the block. (Human nature being what it is.)

Ultimately, Hollywood is not prejudiced based on race or ethnic background. Dave Chapelle signed a two-season deal with Comedy Central, supposedly worth $35-50 million. *Everybody Loves Raymond* could have just as easily been *Everybody Loves Raheem*. Or *The Cosby Show*. If it had a loveable star and got great ratings, it'd be on CBS Monday night for years. Hollywood is prejudiced against only one thing: failure. Success is welcomed with open arms, no matter what color package it arrives in.

February 8

NBC announces several schedule moves. Even before premiering, they're moving *The Contender* to Sundays and *American Dreams* to Wednesday for the rest of the season. They have to be scared shitless over the fact that the Fox boxing series *The Next Great Champ* bombed. They also announce the premiere of *The Office*, an American version of a clever British comedy. I saw the pilot last June. It was true to the original, but the original was really dry. I don't know if America gets "dry." (Fast forward: it's a hit, due in part to the lead, Steve Carrell, becoming a movie star in *The 40-Year-Old Virgin*. If you're producing a show, you can't pray for better luck than that.) Also on the way: *Law & Order: Trial by Jury*, part of NBC's plan to force-feed the audiences *Law & Orders* until they gag. Though they'd better do something as they've dropped to fourth place among viewers 18-49, after winning that audience demo four years in a row and eight out of the last nine. If they don't come up with a hit soon, NBC may soon appear as a victim on *CSI*.

February 11

Arthur Miller dies. Though he made it to 89, wrote *Death of a Salesman* and fucked Marilyn Monroe. All in all, you have to look back from your deathbed and think, not a bad run.

A crawl on CNN related a pronouncement by Les Moonves, head of CBS and Paramount TV, regarding Dan Rather's upcoming retirement and proclaiming the end of the "voice of God"-style of news anchor while alluding to the possibility of putting in a team to anchor the evening news. The meaning: one of the anchors is going to be an attractive woman. Stay tuned for the "Six o' Clock News Show." On a similar note, articles in the trades recently referred to rumors about *Nightline's* imminent demise, as CNN announced the upcoming premiere of an evening show called *Showbiz Tonight*. I'm relieved CNN's finally going to cover show business, just in case I miss anything not covered by *ET*, *Access Hollywood*, *Extra*, *The Insider*, *People*, *US*, *Entertainment Weekly*, *The Globe*, *The Enquirer*, or any of the other ten million celebrity news magazines or channels.

An article from Zap2it.com reports that, even though *Arrested Development's* season was cut short, ending its season before May sweeps and having its episode order reduced from 22 to 18, Fox Entertainment president Gail Berman insisted that the show was not being cancelled. (It was.)

February 15

Michael Jackson collapses on his way to court, sending him to the hospital with "flu- like" symptoms, delaying his trial for a week while his lawyers debate the wisdom of calling Kobe Bryant as a character witness in a molestation trial. The defense listed other possible celebrity witnesses including Elizabeth Taylor, Deepak Chopra and illusionist David Blaine, who they're hoping will somehow make these charges disappear. If I were the judge I'd suggest a compromise: MJ pleads guilty and the judge sentences him to ten years in juvenile hall. The state gets spared an expensive trial; MJ's behind bars but still gets to have pajama parties with young boys. It's win-win, except for the networks and world press who would lose a juicy story to cover, but maybe the audience would win one for a change and not have to endure the "breaking news" reports ten times a day.

Meanwhile, more pilot pickups are announced; recent ones include a show about a married father of two teenage sons who announces he's gay; two brothers—one straight, one gay—who end up running the family business; a woman whose mother meets the man who was her anonymous sperm donor; and a crook who wins the lottery and tries to make amends in his life. Now these are hardly the only shows picked up, but they are indicative of two interesting trends in TV. One: the gay-themed show, shades of *Will and Grace* and the failed John Goodman show—*Normal, Ohio*—where many of the jokes are based on that one premise; and two: the premise pilot, where the situation revolves around a big change coming in the first episode, which goes back to much of what is wrong with TV. When seen in a logline[50], it's very clear what the pilots are about: the discovery or introduction of a new situation, along with the main character and those closest to him or her finding a way to deal with it. These types of shows are attractive to development people because they have an easily understandable built-in conflict in the pilot, in the introduction of

[50] Logline. A one-line description of a pilot.

the new situation. And it's easy to write to that situation because the jokes hang on who knows what, who's hiding what, and how that information finally comes out.

INT. DINING ROOM—NIGHT
The family is having dinner.

SISTER

I don't know what's wrong with me. All
I want to do is meet a nice guy and settle down.

SECRETLY GAY DAD

I hear ya!

And the audience howls. The studio and network execs smile. The producers preen.

The problem becomes, how do these shows function in series? Usually not well, for the simple reason that the pilot tends to be about the premise and not the characters, and once the premise runs dry, unless the characters and their interrelationships are solid, the series gets old real fast. You can usually pull off maybe a half-dozen episodes as variations on the original theme before it starts feeling stale. Again, look at the most successful shows in the last two decades. Possibly only *Frasier* had a premise-y beginning—about *Frasier* relocating and living with his dad, but who cared; someone from *Cheers* was still on TV. And it was a solid show. Otherwise…*Taxi*, *Cheers*, *Raymond*, *Friends*, *Seinfeld*…Not one relied on some huge gimmick to anchor the series. We just came into a situation and met a group of characters. This is another fact executives just don't seem to get.

February 16

Just when I think I'm out… I have lunch with Garry Hart and assume it's just to bitch, until he surprises me, saying he called

HBO to see if they would hear the Baghdad reporter show pitch, and they said they would, so the meeting is set for the 18th. Shit, now I have hope again.

February 17

An article from *AP*, appearing on AOL news, details *Arrested Development's* struggle to stay on the air, describing it as "ferociously clever and daringly breaking the *laugh-track*, multi-camera sitcom mold." Some entertainment reporters just don't know shit.

February 18

I'm ready to go to HBO for what will most likely be the last pitch on this deal. I've got the material down cold but, as proof of God's sense of humor, I've also got a huge, honking zit on the tip of my nose. I'm going in to try to sell a show about journalists in a war zone—admittedly a serious subject. In terms of my background, it could be construed as out of my league, as most of my experience is in multi-camera half-hour. This is one time I have to do everything I can to be taken seriously, which is going to be near impossible, given the fact that I'm sporting a red clown nose that no concealer on Earth will hide. I mean the fucking thing is practically glowing like neon, and no amount of self-deprecating jokes I could make in the room could ever deflect attention from it. I might as well go in with a red bicycle horn and honk it as I go. Months of hard work and research, and I could get subverted by a zit. I work out on my home treadmill that morning, praying for some divine intervention. The phone rings. The woman at HBO we're supposed to pitch to is out sick. Meeting rescheduled for next week. Thank you, Jesus.

February 21

In an article in *Television Week* about the lack of breakout comedy hits from this season, several network executives are interviewed, saying there might be more of a willingness to take a chance in this upcoming season. Shelley McCrory, senior VP of comedy development for NBC/Universal, is quoted, saying "Comedies are supposed to make people laugh" and "We reminded ourselves that characters who are likeable are not necessarily the pathway to funny." THANK YOU!!! But this observation shouldn't be buried in 2-point type in a magazine article; it should be carved in stone on the entrance to the network.

February 24

HBO pitch set for 11. Then rescheduled for 4. But it's on, with promises not to cancel. Thankfully, the zit is gone and I look human again. Still, while taking my almost eleven-year-old daughter Hana to school this morning, she asks what I'm doing today. I tell her I'm going to HBO to pitch a show about journalists covering the war. She tells me it's not a good idea. No one's going to watch it. It's really going to suck. *Et tu, Hana?*

I get to HBO early, going over my notes. The waiting room is impressive, the décor somewhat reminiscent of the Moloka bar in *A Clockwork Orange*. I run into a writer I know and her partner, also waiting to pitch. He eyes me with that same suspicious, competitive "I hope you tank" look all writers exchange in a network lobby. Then we go in. The pitch goes well. They're intelligent, receptive people, who actually laugh in the right spots. In the end, they say they'll get back to us when they're ready, as HBO is on its own timetable. Whether it's a pass or not, it doesn't take away from the satisfaction of pitching something I care about to a network who, if they put it on, won't try to sanitize it.

MARCH 2005

Michael Jackson trial in full swing. Over a thousand reporters from news organizations all over the world are camped outside, covering the event, although none I imagine has found an angle as insightful as E! Entertainment Television who, in partnership with British Sky Broadcasting, has hired a Michael Jackson impersonator to star in the network's "Michael Jackson Trial" — a daily half-hour series based on the singer's courtroom ordeal. According to the article in the New York Times, the show will use transcripts to re-enact the actions in the court, which is closed to cameras. According to Jackson impersonator Edward Moss, "It's the role of a lifetime." In a related story, attorney Johnnie Cochran passed away. I guess you've got to give the man credit for balls and style and some good works—well, aside from the obvious; but, as with everyone else, it comes down to basic mortality: "If you can't respire…you must expire." Meanwhile, in actual reality, AP reports that the number of U.S. troops killed in Iraq has topped 1,500, adding that at least 1,030 of those deaths resulted from hostile action, as opposed to the remaining 470 who perished from injuries received in a pillow fight.

March 2

The Hollywood Reporter lists the comedy pilot pickups for this season along with an assessment of each network's strengths and weaknesses. Citing a dearth of comedy hits, the networks are sinking more money into new pilots. Seems that reality might finally be on the decline, and the article refers to some networks taking more chances, though the writer notes that, when push comes to shove, they might just retreat to the comfort of more traditional approaches.

Reporter
3-2-05

Nets hungry for comedy

Sitcom pilot orders jump for '05-'06

By Andrew Wallenstein

Pilots
2005-06
Comedy
Chart begins on page 26.

Starved for new comedy hits, the broadcast networks are feasting on half-hour pilot orders for the 2005-06 season.

"This year, there is a dramatic rise in the number of comedy pilots being produced," Warner Bros. Television president Peter Roth said. "This speaks to the belief that there is a hunger for comedy by the American public. The comedy quotient, which may have been satisfied recently by reality series, can be brought back in scripted form."

But given the dwindling amount of new comedies that made it to air last season — not to mention the erosion of many of the genre's veterans — skepticism is considerable that casting a wider net will result in a bumper crop making it to air.

Last fall, the six networks ordered a total of 36 half-hours, down from 50 in the 2003-04 season. Not a single new 2004-05 sit-

See **COMEDY** *on page 26*

Comedy

Continued from page 1—

com has managed to break out of the pack, while the number of new half-hours that have reached hit status since 2000 — CBS' "Two and a Half Men" most recently — can be counted on one hand.

NBC Universal Television Studio co-president Angela Bromstad doesn't believe that any one theme or strategy governs comedy selection this year. "I don't think it's anything other than let's pick the best written, funniest original voices out there," she said.

NBC leads the pack with at least 19 pilots ordered, but most of them are contingent on casting. Few expect them to actually produce more than 14. The WB Network is said to have as many as 15 pilots in production but is keeping a tight lid on many of them.

The abundance of comedy pilots is said to make casting a nightmare.

"It's been a really competitive casting season," Regency Television president Robin Schwartz said. "The more comedies there are, the more it stretches the talent pool."

With the genre in such dire straits, there has been plenty of talk about shaking up the conventions of comedy, from tapping fresh writing voices to unorthodox concepts including projects incorporating improvisational or unscripted elements.

Single-camera projects abound, and sources said ABC and Fox are looking to have single-camera directors take on multicamera projects in order to infuse them with a fresh visual sensibility.

But with the most critically acclaimed comedy series in recent years, Fox's "Arrested Development," still facing ratings woes, many believe the networks won't stray that far from the tried and true. Executives likely will take their cues on how risky to get from the performances of several format-bending midseason comedies rolling out this month, including NBC's "The Office" and ABC's "Jake in Progress."

"The thing most interesting in development this year is you can't quite get a beat on what any one network is looking for," UTA agent Matt Rice said. "They're all looking at a variety of things, and that's a good thing."

After getting less than stellar results from "Listen Up" and "Center of the Universe," CBS likely will move away from adding another traditional family comedy from a male perspective. Female voices could get a shot on the network with potential projects including a vehicle for "Curb Your Enthusiasm" star Susie Essman, from 20th Century Fox Television/Paramount/Watson Pond Prods.; an adaptation of a BBC comedy titled "According to Bex," about a single woman's love life, from Touchstone TV, and "Washington Street," which stars Cynthia Watros as a single mom who mixes with the tenants in her apartment building, from Warner Bros./Paramount.

Perhaps the most coveted time slot for a new comedy is CBS' Monday 9:30 p.m. slot, with "Men" expected to move to 9 p.m. after "Everybody Loves Raymond" concludes its run this season. Among the projects believed to have a shot at landing the post-"Men" slot are "Three," from "Friends" producers Andrew Reich and Ted Cohen, about a married couple and their divorced male friend; an untitled comedy about a family of doctors from "Frasier" alumnus Joe Keenan and Christopher Lloyd, and "Old Christine," about a woman trying to rebound after a divorce, from Kari Lizer ("Will & Grace").

NBC looks likely to try at least one off-kilter concept in the fall judging from the many oddball premises it is developing. Among the stranger possibilities include "Early Bird," about a twentysomething who lives in a retirement community, from NBC Uni TV/3 Arts Entertainment, and "My Name Is Earl," which stars Jason Lee as a thief who wins the lottery, from 20th Century Fox TV. A real sleeper in the mix is a scripted/reality blend from "Da Ali G Show" executive producer Dan Mazer from NBC Uni TV/DreamWorks.

With its Tuesday and Friday comedy blocks struggling, ABC will likely look to make multiple half-hour pickups. The network is considering more traditional series with such stars as Freddie Prinze Jr. and Kevin Sorbo attached. There are a number of dating series in contention that could work as a companion for "Progress" should it return next year.

ABC also seems to be interested in doing something set in the real estate world, ordering "Hot Properties" from Warner Bros. in addition to the similarly themed drama "Westside." NBC also has a real estate comedy planned titled "Hot Property" from 20th Century Fox TV/Brad Grey TV.

Fox seems intent on developing an ensemble workplace comedy, with possibilities including "New Car Smell," from producers Robb and Mark Cullen; "Kitchen Confidential," from "Sex and the City" producer Darren Star; and an untitled police precinct comedy from "The Simpsons" writing veterans Bill Oakley and Josh Weinstein.

UPN is looking to add comedies that will skew to the young female audience base it is continuing to build with such series as "Kevin Hill" and "Veronica Mars." The WB is lining up talent including Anne Heche and Camryn Manheim; and reality/scripted hybrid "Nobody's Watching" already is getting buzz.

Despite the best efforts of the executives developing comedies, some said it is inevitable that 2005-06 will see a repeat of this season, where the strongest comedy happens to be an hourlong show — ABC's "Desperate Housewives." Many of the projects in development on the hourlong side ape "Housewives'" comedic elements, industry insiders said. ■

But an article in the same issue points to a trend even more disturbing than another *Who's My Daddy*, as it details two Washington lawmakers' attempts to subject cable TV to the same indecency regulations as the over-the-air networks. The article cites

Pay TV targeted by pols

Senators call for same indecency regs b'casters face

By Brooks Boliek

WASHINGTON — A pair of powerful lawmakers want to put pay TV services under the same indecency regulations as over-the-air broadcasters, contending that viewers can't tell the difference between the services.

Sen. Ted Stevens, R-Alaska, chairman of the Senate Commerce Committee, and Rep. Joe Barton, R-Texas, chairman of the House Commerce Committee, said Tuesday that it isn't fair for broadcasters to come under different rules than cable and satellite TV services, especially because the raciest programs appear on cable and satellite television.

"The problem is most viewers don't differentiate between over-the-air and cable," Stevens said during the National Association of Broadcasters' annual state leadership conference. "Cable is a greater violator in the indecency arena."

Stevens brushed aside constitutional questions about whether the government has the right to regulate indecent speech on pay TV services.

"I think that's wrong," he said. "I think we have the same power to deal with cable as over-the-air

Indecency

Continued from page 1—

because of the combination of the two."

As defined by the FCC and the courts, material is indecent if it "in context, depicts or describes sexual or excretory activities or organs in a patently offensive manner as measured by contemporary community standards for the broadcast medium."

Although obscene speech receives no First Amendment protection, indecent speech does. The government, however, has the ability to restrict it as a legitimate way to protect children. Indecent speech can be aired between 10 p.m.-6 a.m.

Because most people receive their TV via cable or satellite, the government has the power to regulate indecent content, he said.

Stevens doesn't want the regulations to stop with the most popular tiers, either, telling reporters that HBO and other premium channels should come under the same regulations.

His opinion was seconded by Barton.

"If we can work out the constitutional questions, I'd be supportive of that. I think they ought to ... to the extent it's possible, (play by) the same rules," Barton told reporters. "It's not fair to subject over-the-air broadcasters to one set of rules and not subject cable and satellite to no rules. So I'm supportive of what the senator says."

Both men chair the key congressional committees that oversee the broadcast and cable industries.

National Cable and Telecommunications Assn. spokesman Brian Deets said the lawmakers' remarks raise serious free-speech questions. The U.S. Supreme Court has said that the government can regulate the cable business but only in an economic context. Representatives for HBO and Showtime declined comment on the matter.

"We believe any regulation of cable content raises serious First Amendment objections and will oppose efforts to impose regulation on cable programming," Deets said. "As the U.S. Supreme Court has found, the subscription nature of cable service, and the ability of cable customers to block unwanted programming through the use of tools offered by local cable systems, strongly differentiate cable from broadcasting, which is distributed free and unfiltered over the air."

Stevens also said he strongly supports keeping language in indecency legislation that would increase the fines performers face for indecent broadcasts from $11,000 per incident to $500,000 and removes the FCC rule that gives performers a warning after the first incident. That language was included in legislation that won House approval last month that would raise the fines from $32,500 per incident to $500,000.

Last year, the performers clause was removed from the Senate legislation but was insisted on by the House. Although the bill failed to win approval in the last Congress, it is expected to win this year.

"They (performers) know they can get away with it, and the risk is on the networks," Stevens said. ■

Reporter 3-2-05

the FCC definition of indecent material as that which "in context, depicts or describes sexual or excretory activities or organs in a patently offensive manner as measured by contemporary community standards..." No more shit, sex, and body parts. (And I was just starting to make notes about a new show to pitch to cable about a crime-fighting duo, entitled *Assfucker and Diarrhea Man*.)

This is a dangerous precedent. You outlaw shit, sex and body parts, most of American comedy goes away, and cable TV goes away as the last refuge for viewers who need to be treated as educated adults and entertained accordingly. Once again the current administration, led by the President, the Fredo Corleone of the American far right, is taking steps to sanitize all aspects of the media so that by the time they're done, there'll be nothing left to watch other than football, *The 700 Club*, and *Fox News*.

I usually don't donate money to big charities or PACS. I like to give personally, handing out spare change to bums outside 7-11s. Think globally, act locally. Yet if someone were enterprising enough to start the Cocksucker Fund, as a way of fighting this kind of censorship in cable TV, they could put me down for 100 bucks.

March 3

Fox cancels *North Shore* while ordering a second season of *House*, an interesting new one-hour medical show about a misanthropic doctor played by Hugh Laurie. Actually one of the bright spots on their schedule, or any network schedule this year. (Cut to six months later: I'm hooked on this show. Hugh Laurie is great.)

March 4

The Hollywood Reporter runs an article about Julia Louis-Dreyfus starring in a CBS comedy about a divorced woman. Just not the one we pitched. *Fat Actress* premieres this weekend on

Showtime. A review in the *Reporter* is complimentary, citing two choice moments in the show that involve "Alley having cramps in a bathroom stall and running out of toilet paper and…mooning the press from behind double-glass doors at the back of an ambulance." That's a lot of ass stuff and bodily fluids, I wonder if the FCC is aware of this. I know two members of Congress who'll be setting their TiVo's. And after five months' of hard time, Martha Stewart emerged from prison ready to resume her life, and begin the Mark Burnett/Donald Trump-produced reality show, for which, a month earlier, hundreds of hopefuls stood out in the New York rain and sleet in a line that was five deep and stretched for blocks, proving that the one natural resource this country will never run out of is talentless egomaniacs who'll pay any price, bear any burden, meet any hardship, and oppose any foe just to get their faces on the TV.

March 7

Fat Actress premieres on Showtime. The roll-out is huge: full-page ads in the trades, billboards, and bus posters. She is literally and figuratively ubiquitous. Then I watch the show and agree with Tom Shales. It's painful. Heard a radio promo for NBC's/Sylvester Stallone's *The Contender*, using that melodramatic, "Once in a lifetime a show comes along…" voice-over style, making it sound like Jesus was coming back as the ring announcer, and going on to describe the human drama that will unfold beginning tonight. Then at the end of the promo came the informational tag, citing the date and time, ending with "Premiering right after *Fear Factor—Twins*!" OK, so a "*Rocky*-like, rags-to-riches, hopes and dreams, poor guy getting beaten to a pulp in the ring to carve out a better life for his family" show makes its network debut right after a show featuring twins eating bug larvae. Step right up to the midway and see The Human Sword Swallower right next to the Bearded Lady!

March 8

HBO passes on the journalist show. Shit! Fuck! Dammit! OK, I'm over it. Move on. Moments later a friend from back east who works in P.R. emails me, saying he's got a great idea for a TV show and would I be interested in it. I momentarily wince, then he emails me the idea…and it's not bad. I later run it by Garry Hart, who just smiles, saying he's heard this pitch a million times.

March 9

The Contender premiere ratings are OK but not a knockout. (See what I did there? I used a boxing term to write about a boxing show. If this TV writing thing bottoms out, maybe I can get a job as an entertainment journalist.) Anyway, the results were similar for the premiere of *Fat Actress*. If only Stallone would fight Kirstie Alley for 15 rounds—that I'd tune in to see. Meanwhile, Fox puts out a casting call for squabbling couples for a reality special entitled *Marriage 911*, a show coming from the producers of *Nanny 911*, saying if the show does well in the ratings it could become a series. Fox also announces the cancellation of *Jonny Zero*, a show featuring former bouncer Franky G. Or it might have been *Franky G*, featuring former bouncer Jonny Zero. I can't remember. Either way, it got its ass kicked by *Reba* on the WB.

March 14

NBC announces they're restructuring their development departments, creating two separate comedy and drama divisions—one for in-house productions and another for outside projects. According to Kevin Reilly, NBC Entertainment President, "In any given project, an army of execs are involved—that's not particularly healthy for creativity." No shit.

March 16

Walking around the lot at lunch, I bump into a line producer I know who's doing a pilot. I ask how it's going and she just rolls her eyes. The reason: executives interfering at every turn, micromanaging everything—right down to where to hold the table reading and even what direction the actors will face. Her comment: "Why don't these people just back off and let the people who know how to do the jobs simply do them?" I just nod and continue my walk.

APRIL 2005

Pope John Paul II dies. I sit in my office, contemplating my professional mortality and look around, wondering how many boxes it's going to take to pack up all my stuff. In honor of the Pope's passing, I resist the urge to begin stealing office supplies.

MAY 2005

Deep Throat reveals himself as former FBI agent Mark Felt. Nobody much cares anymore. Personally, I would've cast Al Haig. Iraq war still on.

Here are the networks' fall schedules for the 2005-2006 season, as well as midseason pickups. For fun, you can compare them with last year's and see what's left. Or check out the 31 new shows on the schedule. But do it quickly. Before the year is out, 11 will already be cancelled. On that subject, you can reminisce about out the 138 series that either finished their runs or were cancelled within the last 2 years.

2005-2006 Prime Time Network Schedule

MONDAY

Network	8:00PM	8:30PM	9:00PM	9:30PM	10:00PM	10:30PM
abc	Wife Swap RDF Media / Diplomatic		Monday Night Football ABC Sports			
	King of Queens (9/19) Sony / CBS	How I Met Your Mother (9/19) 20th	Two & a Half Men (9/19 WB / Tannenbaum / Lorre	Out of Practice (9/19) Paramount	CSI: Miami (9/19) CBS / Alliance / Bruckheimer	
NBC	Surface (9/19) NBC Universal		Las Vegas (9/19) NBC Universal / DreamWorks		Medium (9/19) Paramount / Gramnet / Picturemaker	
	Arrest. Development (9/19) 20th / Imagine	Kitchen Confidential (9/19) 20th / NewLine / D. Star	Prison Break (8/29) 20th / Adelstein Parouse			
upn	On on One (9/19) Paramount / Greenblatt-Janolari	All of Us (9/19) Warner Bros / Overbrook	Girlfriends (9/19) Paramount / Gramnet	Half & Half (9/19) CBS / SisterLee		
WB	7th Heaven (9/19) Spelling		Just Legal (9/19) Warner Bros / Bruckheimer			

TUESDAY

Network	8:00PM	8:30PM	9:00PM	9:30PM	10:00PM	10:30PM
abc	According to Jim (9/2 Touchstone / Brad Grey	Rodney (10/4) Touchstone	Commander in Chief (9/27) Touchstone / Battle Plan		Boston Legal (9/27) 20th / David E. Kelley	
	NCIS (9/20) Paramount		Amazing Race (9/27) CBS / Touchstone / Bruckheimer		Close to Home (10/4) Warner Bros / Bruckheimer	
NBC	The Biggest Loser (9/13) NBC Unviersal		My Name is Earl (9/20) 20th	The Office (9/20) NBC Universal / Reveille	Law & Order: SVU (9/20) NBC Universal / Wolf Films	
FOX	Bones 20th		House NBC Universal			
upn	Amer. Next Top Model Encore (9/27) 10 x 10 Entertainment		Sex, Love and Secrets (9/27) Paramount / Axelrod-Edwards			
WB	Gilmore Girls Warner Bros		Supernatural Warner Bros / Wonderland			

WEDNESDAY

Network	8:00PM	8:30PM	9:00PM	9:30PM	10:00PM	10:30PM
abc	George Lopez (9/28) Warner Bros	Freddie (10/5) Warner Bros / Mohawk	Lost (9/21) Touchstone / Bad Robot		Invasion (9/21) Warner Bros	
	Still Standing (9/21) CBS / 20th	Yes, Dear (9/21) CBS / 20th	Criminal Mind (9/28) Preview 9/22 Touchstone / Paramount		CSI: New York (9/28) CBS / Alliance / Bruckheimer	
NBC	The Apprentice: Martha Stewart (9/21) Mark Burnett		E-Ring (9/21) Warner Bros / Bruckheimer		Law & Order (9/21) NBC Universal / Wolf Films	
FOX	*That '70s Show* (11/2) Carsey-Werner	Stacked (11/2) 20th	Head Cases (9/14) 20th			
upn	America's Next Top Model (9/21) 10 x 10 Entertainment		Veronica Mars (9/28) Warner Bros / Silver Pictures			
WB	One Tree Hill (10/5) Warner Bros / Tollin-Robbins		Related (10/5) Warner Bros / Class IV			

Network	8:00PM	8:30PM	9:00PM	9:30PM	10:00PM	10:30PM
abc	Alias (9/29) Touchstone / Bad Robot		The Night Stalker (9/29) Touchstone		Primetime Live ABC News	
	Survivor: Guatamala Survivor Ent. Group		CSI (9/22) CBS / Alliance / Bruckheimer		Without a Trace (9/29) Warner Bros / CBS / Bruckheimer	
	Joey (9/22) Warner Bro	Will & Grace (9/29) NBC Unviersal	The Apprentice (9/22) Mark Burnett		E.R. (9/22) Warner Bros	

2005-2006 Prime Time Network Schedule

THURSDAY

Network	7:00PM	7:30PM	8:00PM	8:30PM	9:00PM	10:00PM
FOX	The O.C. — Warner Bros / Wonderland		Reunion — Warner Bros / Class IV			
UPN	Everybody Hates Chris (9/22) — Paramount	Love, Inc. (9/22) — Paramount / Lapidus	Eve (9/22) — WB / Greenblatt-Janollari	Cuts (9/22) — Paramount / Greenblatt-Janollari		
WB	**Smallville (9/29)** — Warner Bros / Tollin-Robbins		**Everwood (9/29)** — Warner Bros			

FRIDAY

Network	7:00PM	7:30PM	8:00PM	8:30PM	9:00PM	10:00PM
ABC	**Supernanny (9/23)** — Ricochet Ltd.		Hope & Faith (9/30) — Touchstone / Industry Ent.	Hot Properties (10/7) — Warner Bros	20/20 — ABC News	
CBS	Ghost Whisperer (9/23) — Touchstone / Paramount		Threshold (9/16) — Paramount		Numb3rs (9/23) — Paramount / Scott Free	
NBC	**Dateline** — NBC News		Three Wishes (9/23) — NBC Universal		Inconceivable (9/23) — Touchstone / Tollin-Robbins	
FOX	**Bernie Mac (9/23)** — 20th / Regency	**Malcolm in the Middle** (9/30) — 20th / Regency	Killer Instinct (9/23) — Regency			
UPN	**WWE Smackdown!** — WWE Entertainment					
WB	What I Like About You — WB / T-R	Twins — Warner Bros	Reba — 20th	Living with Fran — Regency		

SATURDAY

Network	7:00PM	7:30PM	8:00PM	8:30PM	9:00PM	10:00PM
ABC	ABC Saturday Movie					
CBS	Crimetime Saturday		Crimetime Saturday		48 Hours Mystery — ABC News	
NBC	**NBC Saturday Movie**					
FOX	Cops — 20th / Barbour-Langley		America's Most Wanted — 20th			

SUNDAY

Network	7:00PM	7:30PM	8:00PM	8:30PM	9:00PM	10:00PM
ABC	**America's Funniest Home Videos (10/2)** — Vid di Bona		Extreme Makeover: Home Edition (9/25) — Endemol		Desperate Housewives (9/25) — Touchstone	Grey's Anatomy (9/25) — Touchstone
CBS	60 Minutes (9/25) — CBS News		Cold Case (9/25) — Warner Bros / CBS / Bruckheimer		CBS Sunday Movie (9/25)	
NBC	Dateline — NBC News		**The West Wing (9/25)** — Warner Bros		Law & Order: CI (9/25) — NBC Universal / Wolf Films	Crossing Jordan (9/25) — Warner Bros / Tailwind
FOX	Animated Encores	**King of the Hill** — 20th	The Simpsons — 20th	The War at Home — Warner Bros / ACME	Family Guy — 20th	American Dad 9:30pm — 20th
WB	**Reba - Beginnings**		Charmed (9/25)		**Blue Collar TV (9/25)** — Warner Bros / Riverdale	

Bold = New Time Period / Shaded = New Program

Rev. 9-19-05 R\L\Primesch\05-06.xls

2005-06: Mid[illegible]son Pickups

Network	Program	Producer	Talent	Commitment
ABC	Crumbs	Touchstone	Fred Savage, Jane Curtain	
ABC	Emily's Reasons Why Not	Sony / Pariah		Jan - Mon 9pm
ABC	In Justice	Touchstone		
ABC	Jake in Progress	Touchstone / Brad Grey	John Stamos	Jan - Mon 9:30pm
ABC	Less Than Perfect	Touchstone		
ABC	Sons & Daughters	NBC Universal / Broadway Video		
ABC	The Bachelor	Next Ent / Telepictures		Jan Launch - Mon 8pm
ABC	The Evidence	Warner Bros / John Wells		
ABC	The Miracle Workers	DreamWorks / Renegade 83	Reality	
ABC	What About Brian	Touchstone / Bad Robot		Jan - Mon 10pm
CBS	Everything I Know About Men	Touchstone / Paramount	Jenna Elfman	
CBS	Old Christine	Warner Bros	Julia Louis-Dreyfus	Pilot + 12
CBS	The Unit	20th	Dennis Haysbert	
Fox	Free Birds	Fox 21		
Fox	Nanny 911	20th / Granada		
Fox	The Loop	20th	Bret Harrison	
Fox	Trading Spouses	20th		
NBC	Fear Factor	Endemol		
NBC	Four Kings	Warner Bros / KoMut	Seth Green	
NBC	Scrubs	Touchstone		
NBC	Thick and Thin	NBC Universal / Broadway Video	Jessica Capshaw, Chris Parnell	
UPN	South Beach	Paramount / Nuyoriacan / Flame TV	Vanessa L. Williams	
WB	Bedford Diaries	HBO / Warner Bros		
WB	Misconceptions	20th TV / Imagine		
WB	Modern Man	Warner Bros / Bruckheimer		
WB	Pepper Dennis	20th TV		

Cancelled series 2005-2006

the futon critic
the web's best television resource

home >>
calendar >>
· this month's highlights >
· what's new tonight? >
· when does (insert show) come back? >
charts >>
devwatch >>
· abc pilots >
· cbs pilots >
· fox pilots >
· nbc pilots >
· the cw pilots >
dvd >>
listings >>
moviewatch >>
newswire >>
pr >>
rant >>
ratings >>
search >>
showatch >>

SHOWATCH
(find out what's renewed, what's canceled and what's coming soon)

genre: all
network: all
status: canceled/ending (2005-2006 season)
studio: all
title:
Submit

- **AIRLINE (A_AND_E)**
- **ALIAS (ABC)**
- **APPRENTICE, THE: MARTHA STEWART (NBC)**
- **BOOK OF DANIEL, THE (NBC)**
- **CHARMED (WB)**
- **CURRENT AFFAIR, A (SYNDICATION)**
- **EMILY'S REASONS WHY NOT (ABC)**
- **GROWING UP GOTTI (A_AND_E)**
- **HEAD CASES (FOX)**
- **HOT PROPERTIES (ABC)**
- **INCONCEIVABLE (NBC)**
- **JUST LEGAL (WB)**
- **KILLER INSTINCT (FOX)**
- **KITCHEN CONFIDENTIAL (FOX)**
- **MADE IN THE U.S.A. (USA)**
- **MALCOLM IN THE MIDDLE (FOX)**
- **NIGHT STALKER, THE (ABC)**
- **REUNION (FOX)**
- **ROLLERGIRLS (A_AND_E)**
- **SEVENTH HEAVEN (WB)**
- **SEX, LOVE AND SECRETS (UPN)**
- **STRONG MEDICINE (LIFETIME)**
- **THAT '70S SHOW (FOX)**
- **THRESHOLD (CBS)**
- **TOO LATE WITH ADAM CAROLLA (COMEDY_CENTRAL)**
- **WANTED (TNT)**
- **WEEKENDS AT THE D.L. (COMEDY_CENTRAL)**
- **WEST WING, THE (NBC)**
- **WILL & GRACE (NBC)**
- **YES, DEAR (CBS)**

contact us at: **letters@thefutoncritic.com**

From the beginning of my Paramount deal there's been some confusion over the end date. For some reason I always had in my head that it was at the end of June. With that in mind, and keeping one eye on staffing season, I play around with a few other projects and try to lay the groundwork for an exit strategy. Then, through a total fluke, I find out my deal is up at the end of May. Shit. My assistant and I start scavenging packing boxes from around the lot while I meet on some of the few shows looking for staff. Some shows I like. Some shows I despise. In either case, if offered, it's a job. No jobs are offered, so that's that.

Over a period of a few days, I pack up and make repeated trips in (former head of Paramount TV) Kerry McCluggage's golf cart, which he left behind when his Indy Prod deal ended. I take down the two Hirschfeld drawings of the *Wings* and *Becker* casts that were Christmas presents that have hung on my wall for the last year and a half and load them up to take home and hang in my office there. After all the projects, meetings, lunches, phone calls, note sessions, story sessions, outlines, rewrites, and hours at the computer to crank out two pilot scripts, it all ends in nothing. I drop my key in the office, make the Anatevka drive to my car with the last of my stuff, and drive off the lot, 13 years after I first drove on. Now, I am officially a writer off a deal, a Hollywood *ronin*, "between projects," or, as it's known in the real world—unemployed. Well, except for the residuals coming in from *Becker* and *Wings*. Thank God for residuals.

JUNE-AUGUST 2005

War's still on. Robert Novak says "shit" on CNN and gets bounced off the air. Peter Jennings passes away. Michael Jackson acquitted of molestation charges. Canada and Spain legalize gay marriage. Jackson immediately makes plans to begin construction on Neverland du

Nord in Montreal and Euro Neverland in Madrid. Two Supreme Court vacancies open up, hurricanes devastate the south, the world gets hit with more terrorist bombings, earthquakes, 5 plane crashes, and the Koreans clone a dog. (Note: I did not stoop to any kind of cheap joke about enriching their food supply.)

Undaunted, I bring my stuff home and immediately spring into action by selling my Porsche. It's been collecting dust in the garage, and my daughter doesn't fit in the back anymore, so after placing several newspaper ads and a listing on Ebay, taking numerous phone calls, a few test drives, and doing some last-minute repairs, I get a buyer and watch some guy drive it away with the same smile I had on my face 13 years ago when I bought it. Still, no regrets. This will be the first move in Operation Downsize.

After 13 straight years of production, I'm now on my own, working out of my home/office, though I tell myself that I've been here before and fought/written my way back in, and can do it again. As I ponder that, I also start walking around the house looking for shit to sell, while my agent and brother tell me not to panic, as they're going to start setting studio and producer development meetings all over town so I can reconnect with people I haven't talked to in years, or meet the new people in those jobs. I figure "Yeah, yeah," lots of meetings. I start pacing off the square footage of the house, getting ready for when I have to put it on the market.

Then…they start setting meetings. Like fucking crazy. I drive to two, three offices a day. From one end of town to the other. Studios, independent production companies, directors and actors with pilot deals and pet projects, or pod producers, some with network deals. Most are "general, look-see, what do you want to do" kind of meetings, though some involve specific projects. They all begin with an offer of bottled water. I take it. Then we talk. What are you working on? What are you passionate about? We want your passion. I tell them I'm passionate about this Iraq script, which I've written on spec. Their jaws drop as they say they'll never be able to sell it. But they've got ideas they're high on they run by me. Like the one about the black couple who moves into an all-white neighborhood, with ensuing hijinks. I check the date on my cell phone, just to confirm that this is, in fact, 2005 and not 1975. It is. I hear other ideas. Some I pursue until I lose interest or the other parties hook up with another writer.

Meanwhile, I take a trip to Vegas to help my friend Wayne, who sold a reality show to CBS with Jon Lovitz. I find myself in an un-air-conditioned trailer in the parking lot of a mini-mall on a hot Vegas Sunday night, lying on my back below camera holding cue cards for Jon, thinking "This is not the show business I signed up for."

I continue going to meetings and, just for amusement, leave a water bottle on the floor of the passenger side of my car from every one, just as a way of marking time, as well as setting up a future income stream. At the end of the meetings, I count 50 bottles. I make a note: at 2 1/2 cents refund per bottle, if they could set up 100,000 meetings a month, I might be able to cover my nut and never have to write a word.

Eventually, all these meetings lead to three projects. One is brought to me by a producer I know about divorced men and their kids, a subject with which both of us have become intimately familiar. I like the area, and he and the other producers like my take on it, so we agree to go pitch. It's single camera, half-hour.

The second is a fairly traditional multi-camera show about cops that the development guys at Dreamworks have. Again, they like my ideas and I like working with them. They're smart and aggressive. We agree to go pitch.

The third begins with a blind pilot deal[51] with Touchstone, through Brillstein-Grey. It ends up being sort of a quirky family show that goes through several permutations along the way, but we also get our ideas together and plan to hit the networks. I also explore godfathering a pilot starring a female comic. She wants to write it but is not an experienced writer. We have several meetings but eventually it just evaporates, leaving me with three projects. In the course of the next weeks, I pitch at ABC, NBC, CBS, FOX, HBO, and the WB. Some places more than once.

SEPTEMBER 2005

Saddam Hussein goes on trial. C'mon, does this one really need a trial? Then again, it would be good TV. New Orleans is devastated by Hurricane Katrina. The federal government immediately springs into action by finding other people to blame for not immediately springing into action. If only the hurricane hit Fallujah, then they'd have been ready. Meanwhile, as I'm now back in pilot mode, I attend an agency's comedy showcase on the lookout for "new talent."

THE COMEDY SHOWCASE

Another pilot season ritual is the "comedy showcase," where an agency puts together a half-dozen fresh young comics and gives them 20 minutes each at a local club in front of an industry crowd as a way of sparking interest among writers, producers, and studio or network people. It falls somewhere between a bachelor auction and the hookers at the Bunny Ranch lining up for prospective customers. In the past, while in production, I would toss these fliers right in the garbage. It's just not something you have time for.

---

[51] Blind pilot deal. A writer is paid to write a pilot, the subject of which will be mutually agreed upon later.

But given my present circumstances and growing bottle collection, I figure the time to be a snob is over, so when my agency emailed me about their showcase and said they'd put my name on the list, I said I'd go.

Besides, I used to love going to comedy clubs, dating back to the late 70s in New York. Catch a Rising Star, The Comic Strip, The Improv, and Caroline's. There was always somebody great either on the bill or dropping in at midnight for a surprise set. This was the early "observational comic" era. I remember seeing Sam Kinison for the first time at Caroline's and was in awe. (Years later we would work together on a show I created that, like many, started out with hope, and ended in disaster. Still I admired the guy. Even his memorial service was hysterical.) I saw the comic once known as Jay Leno at Dangerfield's, where he did 2 1/2 hours of material, some of it based on events that happened that day. I remember laughing my ass off at Gilbert Gottfried, Bill Maher and Richard Belzer, or seeing Jerry Seinfeld and Larry Miller at the Comic Strip and Robin Williams both at The Copacabana, as well as at Catch a Rising Star, where he dropped in for a set around midnight. That was when standup still had some danger attached to it, and before TV began eating comics for sitcom breakfast.

Over the years, the observational comic invasion hit LA, and the local clubs—The Improv, Comedy Store, Laugh Factory, The Ice House in Pasadena, and The Comedy/Magic Club in Hermosa Beach—became the launching pads (or Petri dishes) for half-hour TV. It seemed every standup got his or her shot with a pilot that either never made it to air, got on and got cancelled or, like *Seinfeld*, *Raymond*, or *Roseanne*, went all the way. The downside of this phenomenon, however, was a blandness invasion of comedians from every American town, and of every ethnicity and sexual orientation, doing some version of the same set, based on their particular situation. Still, I thought, there's always the possibility that some unique voice is going to crawl out of the pack. So, with that optimism, I drove down Laurel Canyon to the Laugh Factory on Sunset, found the officious door person with the clipboard, and was immediately hit with "you're not on the list," which is right up there with people fucking up your studio drive-on pass on the list of Hollywood indignities. I ask them to check again, spelling my name slowly and carefully. Then they find it. Turns out I was on the list.

The velvet rope was lifted and I was allowed inside, where I got a glass of watery Cabernet, and immediately ran into twenty people I knew, all on the same mission. Still, I was curious; eager to be amused, surprised, or shocked.

As the house lights went down, people immediately cradled their Blackberries and cell phones below the table and the MC introduced the comics, who took the stage one by one and began working their hearts out. And they did work it. And everyone was funny, energetic, likeable, and got laughs from an industry crowd that is notorious for being too hip to laugh. The one problem: it was boring as shit. Whether from comics being coached to do their time-tested, safest 'A' material for a crowd that had the power to put them on TV, or because this is all they had, it all came out pretty generic, to the point that, regardless of age, sex, physical appearance, ethnicity, or sexual orientation, they almost had the same act, something you could almost construct from Madlibs. It could stem from someone's cultural background, sexual orientation, particular physical characteristics, like being fat, or short, or attractive, or not so attractive but, just for fun, let's pick ethnic. And it might go something…like this:

"JOHNNY ETHNIC"

M.C.: "All right…let's bring up our next comic, hailing from AMERICAN CITY, put your hands together for JOHNNY ETHNIC. Mild applause, JOHNNY ETHNIC bounds on stage with tons of energy and a big smile as he confidently rips the mike from the stand and begins to work the crowd.

JOHNNY ETHNIC: "All right! Awesome! Woo! All right! It's really great to be here! Actually, I'm married, so it's great to be anywhere! So, how you all doin'? (Mild applause. War whoops from the drunks, particularly the bachelorette party at the front corner table.) All right. I'm JOHNNY ETHNIC. I don't know if you can tell from my UNIQUE PHYSICAL CHARACTERISTIC, but I'm ETHNICITY. I come from a large ETHNICITY family. The funny thing about growing up in ETHNICITY families is that, in white families, if you INFRACTION at school, when you got home, your dad would go CALM REACTION IN WHITE-SOUNDING PARENTAL VOICE. But in my house, it was ANGRY-VOICED PARENTAL DISAPPROVAL IN FUNNY ETHNIC ACCENT. (Cut to audience reaction. Bachelorette table cracks up, orders 8th round of drinks, as the bride-to-be braces herself, gets up from the table and wobbles down the aisle to go throw up in the can.) Thank you. I just moved out to LA from HOMETOWN. Anybody here from HOMETOWN? (Some applause.) Yeah, so you know what I'm talking about. It's tough living in LA. I mean, in HOMETOWN if you wanted to ACTIVITY, all you had to do was VERB. But in LA, if you try to ACTIVITY, all you get is FUNNY-SOUNDING REACTION IN EITHER VALLEY GIRL OR STONER

VOICE, USING THE WORDS "DUDE" AND "AWESOME." (Cut to couple in audience. She turns to him, whispers: "That's so true.") Thank you. So…I just had a baby. (AWW'S AND APPLAUSE.) Well, I didn't, my wife did. Though I did have something to do with it…at least that's her story and she's sticking to it. Though I did wonder when the kid came out looking all DIFFERENT ETHNICITY, I'm like, "Bitch, did you fuck a OCCUPATION PERFOMED BY PERSON OF OTHER ETHNICITY?! "But the one amazing thing about your wife having a baby is that her breasts are suddenly the size of LARGE FRUIT. And I'm like, all right! But, the one thing they don't tell you is that you never get your hands on them! The kid's there like 24/7. And I'm like, dude, you'll get your turn in 16 years, give daddy a chance. (Mild laughs and applause from parents in audience. One husband turns to wife and nods. Embarrassed, she playfully hits him on the shoulder.) Comic turns to guy in couple. Yeah, this dude knows what I'm talking about. He's shaking his head. And (re: wife) she's all…don't even go there! Thank you! Goodnight, I'm JOHNNY ETHNIC!"

And on and on.... Sure, this is often the road to a pilot but, Christ, if this is all you've got, why bother with comedy as a career? If you can't be brilliant, why shoot for redundant and mildly amusing? Once upon a time, starting with Lenny Bruce, through people like Dick Gregory, Mort Sahl, Richard Pryor, George Carlin, Sam Kinison, Bill Hicks, Bill Maher, Dennis Miller, or Chris Rock, standup used to be dangerous. Or insightful. Or angry. Or intelligent. Even provocative or occasionally subversive. (Not that's it's entirely gone—just check out Sarah Silverman's act.) Still, for the most part now, it's McComedy.

At the end of the night I get up to leave and notice Chris Rock hanging out in back. I overhear him talking to someone about going on later. Shit, if I didn't have to leave I'd go back outside and stand on line like a civilian to see him, as his HBO specials rival early Richard Pryor. One of the shows that looks like a breakout hit this season is *Everybody Hates Chris* on UPN.

Depressed, I drive home and watch *Martha Stewart's Apprentice*, which I TiVo'd. Holy shit. I know it was a drag for her to go to prison, but why do the rest of us have to suffer? Whether you think she deserved to go to the can or that she was railroaded for being a successful businesswoman and engaging in an activity that used to be referred to as "the old boys' network," or "business as usual," that doesn't mean she gets to parlay that infamy into a bad show. She's virtually The Donald with a wig…a blond wig…. a better wig. OK, he's a stiff. As an actor, I wouldn't cast him to play Donald Trump. But he works on his own show, and he was actually funny on *SNL*, playing a parody of Donald Trump.

But this show just reeks of phoniness, starting with the bullshit opening montage of her walking through her office, stopping to chat with underlings and giving on-the-fly instructions. Then the contestants. Or whatever the fuck they're called. Like a Chinese menu of backbiting wannabe media monsters. The cute chick. The tough chick. The Brooklyn street guy. The upper-crust bow-tied prig. This is such manufactured garbage. And her version of Trump's "You're fired" catchphrase—a modest, polite "You just don't fit in," which is probably something she heard on her first day in jail by some lifer holding a broomstick. Then to top off the fake sincerity, they add Martha writing a thank-you note to the vanquished contestant. What they should have done is the Bond villain version, so at least when someone's let go, they could walk halfway across a bridge as we cut to Martha tapping a pedal that makes a section of the bridge drop and the contestant fall into a pool of piranhas. Now that's entertainment. This show is a bad thing. I hope it gets cancelled quickly. Early ratings and reviews say it will. (It did.)

September 22

Fox cancels *Head Cases* after just two airings, leaving four unaired episodes on the shelf. But for me, a good show business day. This book, which up to now I've been writing on spec, the manuscript lying in the corner of my office like some stuffed, dead cat, suddenly comes alive. My brother sends it to a publisher and in a matter of days, we have a deal to put it out. I'm shocked at the prospect of actually having this published. Then I wonder, "Oh, shit, what did I write? And about whom?" I immediately re-read it and think about mitigating one or two statements. Or putting them in a more generous context. Or hiring a lawyer.

Then it's off to pitch the divorced guys and kids show. First at ABC, where it's politely received, but I'm sure it's a pass. I could just see that light in their eyes flicker out mid-pitch. Then to NBC. Back one more time, sitting in the commissary, waiting for a meeting, going over my notes. Deja fucking vu all over again. Then I make my way upstairs, wait for a while, then get summoned inside, where I knew two of the four women there. I'm in a roomful of women ready to pitch a show about divorced guys, some of whom have attitudes bordering on misogynistic. This feels utterly pointless.

Then the strangest thing happens. They respond. With actual laughter and nods of understanding. And they ask smart, insightful questions. I don't know if they'll ultimately buy it, but it was a good meeting. Probably helps that they're coming off great premiere numbers for *My Name is Earl*, which gives NBC credibility and also adds to the possibility that they'll feel that different types of shows can work on their network.

On the way out I scan the assistant's walls, seeing memos and writing staff and director lists for various shows. I notice the name of one of the directors we hired on *Becker* off one of those diversity nights is on the list for *Earl*. I've seen him since and his career is taking off. Nice guy. And talented. I'm happy for him. Also noticed spec pilot scripts lying around from writers whose names I recognize. Everyone's cranking out material, trying to stay alive and keep their homes. One of the biggest hits on TV right now started as a spec script written by a writer who was in the process of unloading his house. In a few years, he'll be able to buy his entire block.

September 23

On my way to ABC again, to pitch yet another idea, I get a message on my cell phone, which, if you've been reading carefully, doesn't ring at my house. Only Verizon dead zone for miles. It's from one of the producers of the divorced guys show we pitched yesterday at NBC. And which, she says, they bought. Holy fuck. A roomful of women and they buy a show about guys. Total shock. And appreciation. I applaud their taste. We still have a meeting set up to pitch it at Fox, which we decide to keep, as a deal's not done until it's done and, if by some fluke, another network wants it, you could find yourself reaping the benefit of a bidding war. Either way, it's a good show business week and certainly takes the pressure off the rest of these meetings with one sale in the bank.

I get to ABC early to have lunch in the commissary, and bump into the editor, and occasional director, from *Becker*, who's there for a meeting. We haven't seen each other in over a year so we catch up. He's been working on different shows, most recently the Lisa Kudrow HBO show *The Comeback* which is not, unfortunately for him, coming back. Too bad. It started growing on me. But he says the experience was a good one. As opposed to a series and network pilot he did where in both cases notes were shoved down the producers' throats. The series is gone. The pilot never made it to air. He went on, unprompted by me, saying how it feels that no one wants to make good TV. They just want the same old shit. Made me feel like I wasn't alone in this.

Meanwhile, as I'm waiting for this book deal to be finalized, I'm wondering if I've shot myself in the foot, or the head, actually, because of some of the less than warm and fuzzy things I've written. But part of this book has been an attempt to describe the emotions of working as a writer in Hollywood and the angst you go through at the mercy of others. So in that regard, it was all true the day I wrote it so I'm standing by it. With some minor revisions. I may be pissed off. I'm not suicidal.

September 27

Pitch the divorced guys show to Fox. (Fast forward: to several execs who are no longer in those jobs.) Again, it went well. Easier pitching when you know you've already got a sale and that somebody else wants it.

September 28

Another cell phone message. Shit, I love Verizon, but I seriously wish they would stick a cell, transmitter, or tower in my neighborhood. Again, it's from one of the producers on the divorced guys pilot. Now Fox wants it, too. I smell a bidding war. Meanwhile, I go to Touchstone to pitch the family show, though to my mind, a more unusual and subversive one, centering around a young kid who, in Emperor's New Clothes fashion, questions the existence of God, which throws his family, school, and community into a tailspin. It's an idea that's always fascinated me. Unfortunately, it doesn't fascinate anyone else in the room, and the executives involved think it will never fly at the network as the subject matter will scare them and, even more importantly, the current marching orders are "no shows centered on kids." So, I let it go and we begin to re-develop the idea.

OCTOBER 2005

7.6 earthquake hits Pakistan. Does $8.95 in damage. ("THANK YOU! I'M JOHNNY KARACHI! LOOK FOR MY UPCOMING SHOW THIS FALL ON CBS!") Bird flu mentioned as possible worst worldwide epidemic since 1918 flu that killed millions. OK, fine, but it's not here yet, Meanwhile, there's another Yankees/Boston AL EAST pennant race. Time to rehearse the curse. Yankees lost the first game. They're tied. Two games to play Saturday and Sunday. I have to do revisions on one pilot pitch and add to this book but, for the moment, fuck show business, earthquakes, and bird flu, it's the Yankees and Boston again. This is reality.

October 3

Walking back into CBS to pitch the redeveloped kid show, which has now become more of a family show, but I've got a huge lump in my chest. Not because I know they'll never buy it, but because I know this book, in which I've been less than kind to some of these people, is on the way. Again, not personal, strictly business; still I feel guilty. And I have to come here twice in the next week. Like having a root canal followed by a colonoscopy. Inside the building I start bumping into executives right and left. The UPN entourage is there for some big meeting, including one woman I've known since high school. I go up to the third-floor waiting room and run into more CBS execs, including one of our contacts from *Becker*. They offer water. I take it. Evian. Small bottle. Warm. But it's free. And worth 2 1/2 cents down the line. In another six months they may be lobbing these bottles at my head.

I check in with the receptionist and make myself comfortable on the couches along with the six other people on their way in to pitch. I overhear a rumor about a big Hollywood marriage in which the husband was supposedly gay. Gotta love the rumor mill.

Then I wait. I'm not looking forward to this. Then the receptionist calls over and tells me that the meeting is, in fact, not today, but was changed to next Monday. A fact that doesn't seem to have been communicated to me.

With relief and embarrassment I skulk out of the building, knowing I have to return tomorrow to pitch yet another project, but still I get a reprieve today. I drive back up Laurel Canyon. Again it's backed up. Fucking people just won't learn how much I hate to be in traffic. By the time I get home I've got messages and emails informing me that the times and dates of every other meeting I've got have been switched and my head is spinning trying to keep track of it all. But this is development…without an office or assistant. I wish my cats could type and answer a phone instead of eating my plants and puking on the rugs. Fucking useless.

October 6

WB cancels *Just Legal* after 3 weeks on the air. Four shot episodes sit on the shelf.

October 7

F/X announces the 13-show, second season pickup of *It's Always Sunny In Philadelphia*, the show about guys who hang out in a bar that was somewhat similar to the one I'd written for CBS that got passed on. I like this show. And it was originally done as a spec pilot, which most people consider a pointless and insane move. Until it works. Then it's genius. F/X also pulls the plug on *Starved*, its companion show.

October 10

NBC cancels *Inconceivable*, a single camera show about a fertility clinic, while cutting back the order on *Thick and Thin*, a midseason show, to just six episodes.

I pitch the redeveloped family show at Fox and, despite the similarity to *Malcolm*, I could sense during the meeting (due to the distinct absence of laughter) that I was losing them. My fault. I'm pitching this too dramatically but, honestly, I can't even remember what it's about anymore. I remember it started as a show about a kid who begins challenging the adult world around him by announcing in school that he doesn't believe in God and all hell breaks loose. It's now morphed into some kind of weird family show, with the focus taken off the kid, and even though I'm pitching it I'm not sure I even understand what I'm pitching or could write it if it sold. And I could sense they knew that. The feedback I got the next day was exactly that. But they are open to discussing it more. The studio development guy at Brillstein-Grey is working his ass off to help me sell this and I'm afraid I'm not giving him much help.

Pissed off at myself for doing a mediocre job, I race home to catch the rest of the Yankee game, which was, ironically, on Fox, where I just was and could have ducked into someone's office and locked the door. Still I make it into my garage, try to get out of my car and tangle the cell phone earpiece around the steering wheel. I try to untangle it but forget which direction was tangled and which was untangled, so the more I wrap it around the wheel, the tighter it gets, and the more I choke myself. I finally get it loose. There's a metaphor in here somewhere for what our cell phones and hectic lives are doing to us, but I'm in no mood to ponder it, as the Yankees are on. They end up losing. No more playoffs. OK, now I'm depressed.

So I switch channels, finally remembering to TiVo *My Name is Earl*, NBC's breakout show. Before it comes on, I have to wade through 15 minutes of *The Biggest Loser*, a fat people weight loss reality show. The in-show sponsors: a fitness center and diet drink. Product placement. Gotta love it. And this segues into the real commercials. First one up: a popular brand of American cheese. Jesus. Talk about a perpetual motion machine. Eat the processed cheese, make more fat people to be future contestants. Our version of the Koreans cloning a dog. (Shit, I wasn't going to do that.)

October 11

Show business keeps getting interesting. The one show I've sold (divorced dads and kids at NBC), for which I'm waiting for all the deal-making to finish so I can begin to write, has hit a snag. One set of producers is not content with their deal and tell me that the project could go away. Personally, I don't care about the money, in the sense that, in success, there's money for everyone, but my brother and agent say they will handle it. So I go into panic mode, as I do when something is out of my hands.

Then I race back across town to pitch the redeveloped family show to ABC. I get off the elevator and see my friends, Ken and David, who just got done pitching. We immediately laugh because we just saw each other at Touchstone the day before. Everyone's on the same train. We commiserate for a while until they find out that ABC's not buying their show because they have one like it in development. I feel bad. These are true friends I want to succeed.

I go in to pitch, having lightened up the story from the other day. I'm sick of the sound of my own voice and don't want to do this, but I do it anyway—and it's working. Getting laughs. They seem to get the show. I wish I did. I have no idea what I'm talking about. I doubt they'll buy it but still, the pitch was enjoyable.

October 12

I pitch the redeveloped family show to the WB. I get some laughs, but it smells like a pass. The *LA Times* runs an article that the new Geena Davis show, ABC's *Commander in Chief*, is the only new series to crack the top ten, for the second week in a row. I haven't seen it. I'm not sure I plan to. I'm sorry. I just can't accept Geena Davis as the president. Everyone knows Martin Sheen is the president. Or may be on his way out, I haven't been watching *West Wing* lately. But since part of enjoying fiction involves the suspension of disbelief, I figure if the American public can suspend disbelief long enough to accept George Bush as president, maybe it's not such a huge mental leap to get to Geena Davis. Or maybe it's just wish fulfillment.

October 13

Yom Kippur. Show business atones for its sins, laboring under the delusion that one day ought to take care of it. I pay dues to my religious heritage by taking my daughter bowling. My rationale is that the bowling alley's attached to Jerry's Delicatessen, which technically makes it Jew-adjacent.

October 14

Pitch the redeveloped family show to NBC, where I've already sold one show (although that's got deal problems). I pitched a second one with no response, but that probably means a pass and now I'm going in to the same audience for a third time. It goes well but I don't smell a sale. Meanwhile, there's a phone conference call scheduled with Fox to allay some of their concerns about the kids show and hopefully get it picked up. They feel it's too satiric, not fun enough. Can't say I blame them, it's not even amusing me anymore.

October 15

The unhappy producer calls me on my cell while I'm out of town at a wedding with my girlfriend. (Luckily the phone doesn't ring during the ceremony. Not that I turned it off. It's pilot season. I'm too neurotic not to be reachable.) Anyway, he informs me that our deal is in serious jeopardy and that I could get bounced off the project. The insecure part of me panics, though I know this is a scare tactic and not the way to handle this problem. Negotiations are for agents and managers. That's what they do. You don't call someone up directly. It's just not done. So I tell him I'm not going to negotiate and if it means I'm off the project, then I'm off. Then I hang up. And wet myself.

October 17

The NBC thing is still up in the air, though my agents and brother tell me it will sort itself out. It's now four o'clock and it hasn't yet. Meanwhile, I'm waiting on a conference call with Fox to answer some of their concerns about the redeveloped family show. The more I change it, the closer it gets to something I'm told they'll buy and the further away from what I initially wanted or now even understand. I'm so lost, to the point that I don't know what I'm saying and feel like I'm totally blowing smoke. Between the studio and network comments I'm slowly hearing the same phrases. Where's the fun? How do we know they all care about each other? It's almost insidious the way it happens piece by piece. Death by 1000 cuts.

Meanwhile today's *LA Times* runs an article about Aaron Sorkin, the creator of *West Wing*, who just sold a spec script to NBC called *Studio* 7 (the title later changed to *Studio 60 on the Sunset Strip*), a satiric look at the TV business. In the pilot, the executive producer of an *SNL*-type show has an on-camera meltdown, saying: "This show used to be cutting-edge political and social satire, but it's gotten lobotomized by a… broadcast network hell-bent on doing nothing that might challenge their audience." Later in the article, a reference is made to *Sports Night*, another show created by Sorkin, and a moment when ABC insisted on using a laugh track on a single-camera, non-audience show. His comment was that the experience made him feel like he'd "put on an Armani tuxedo, tied my tie, snapped on my cuff links, and the last thing I do before I leave the house is spray Cheez Whiz all over myself." Yes.

Later that day I have the conference call with Fox, trying to explain how the redeveloped family show will be funny. And fun. I'm running off at the mouth, but flailing. I'm not even convincing myself. The fact that it's pouring outside adds to the gloomy feeling of this call, and the fact that my ceiling's leaking in three places reminds me that I've been somewhat remiss in fixing the leaks. Along with the warped kitchen floor, it makes me think I should be doing a better job if I want to sell this and get paid so I can repair my house. We hang up. I'm pretty sure I blew it.

That night I get a call from a friend who's a former *Becker* writer and fellow guitar player (some of us from *Becker* along with other friends have gotten together for the last two years and jammed in a studio twice a month). He sends me an email describing a meeting he had with the same producer I wrote the Chill Mitchell pilot for last year. The subject of the meeting: writing a pilot for Chill Mitchell. I fucked up, bring on the next guy.

October 18

The NBC show deal resolves itself. The producers are happy again. We talk on the phone and make nice. I hope the process goes back to being civilized and professional. That's all I want. To me, the money is almost irrelevant. If you get a show on the air and keep it on for ten years, you've made a fortune and bought yourself even more opportunity. So what's the difference how many gross points you have when down the line you'll still be hiring lawyers to sue the studio for a fair accounting of revenues that have come in, when they suddenly say "We're not in profit yet." That's why I don't negotiate.

October 19

Conference call with the two sets of producers and NBC Studios to discuss some general ideas for the outline on the divorced dads with kids show. Cheryl Dolins, the exec who bought the pitch, leads the call and, other than adding a few thoughts I'd already heard and that I had easy fixes for, said: "I liked what you pitched, go do that, don't hold back on anything." And that was it. I hung up the phone and almost cried. There was no pain here. No attempt to change or eviscerate the story. No one had to be nicer, warmer, sweeter. Just do what you pitched. I may be setting myself up for a major fall, but so far, this is amazing. This is the way it should be.

Though it's interesting that because they are succeeding wildly with *My Name is Earl* and even *The Office* is doing better, they have to be feeling that doing unique shows based on a writer's vision may be the way to go. She even mentions this show as a companion piece to *Earl*, which I'm sure is being mentioned to every single writer writing a half-hour for NBC. Next season there will be no better time slot on their network. Something to shoot for. That said, I'm going to jump on this immediately, by beginning the short period of writing procrastination by doing some errands and getting ready for another pre-pitch conference call at 4 on another project, with another set of producers. If I sell that, I'm going to really be in deep shit.

October 20

Commander in Chief gets a back nine order from ABC. Obviously, her poll numbers are better than those of the actual commander in chief. Reading development reports about several shows about divorce, now that I have to start my outline for the NBC show, hoping it's not the subject du jour. Also going to CBS tonight to pitch the Dreamworks cop show, a show they'll never buy in ten million years. A pointless exercise. I may request a 6-pack of water. Tomorrow I go back to Fox to pitch the same show, but altering the concept to fit with the younger, more blue-collar demographic they're after. Again, it could get morphed into something I don't know if I can write. Part of me wants to hit them up while I'm there with the original idea for the redeveloped family show, which was about the kid who says he doesn't believe in God and causes a furor. Curious to see what their reaction would be.

I fight my way through traffic to get to a 5:45 meeting at CBS at a time when most sensible people are heading home, just to pitch them a show I know they'll never buy. But at least when I get there the guard is pleasant and the smile from the stunning third-floor receptionist takes the sting out of suffering through *Survivor* on the waiting room TV.

I look around the waiting room at the other writers waiting to go in. Same guys in jeans and sneakers, clutching the same ten pages of folded-up pitch notes. And the same self-important female executive along with them, with the Blackberry and the Bluetooth earpiece like the one who was at Fox about five meetings ago in the waiting room, clacking on the phone, and every other word out of her mouth was "awesome." Her new car was "awesome." Her babysitter was "awesome." The wine she had at dinner last night was "awesome," at a restaurant that was "totally awesome." Shit, get a fucking imagination. Or a thesaurus.

October 21

After going over my notes all day I get on the Fox lot an hour early, driving down into the bowels of the parking structure. I walk around the lot, and stop in at the studio store to buy my daughter the new *Family Guy* movie DVD she's been haranguing me for. I know I'm going to get it for her eventually, so I might as well buy it here for less. Then I hit the commissary to go over my notes. My partners from Dreamworks show up, and we review last-minute game plans and adjustments. They inform me we're pitching to Peter Liguori, who's the head of TV. Liguori came from F/X—home of *The Shield*, *Nip/Tuck* and *Over There*, the Steven Bochco Iraq show. Shit, I thought I was in the lounge, now I'm playing the main room.

We go in, everyone's introduced: some people I know, some I don't. A few pleasantries and then I start talking, going through my pitch, though I've got so many scribbled notes I'm afraid of "going up"[52]. But I don't. And I hear laughter. I'm thinking: What's that sound? But I sense it's going well. I get to the end, he asks a few good questions which, miraculously, I have answers for, we all shake hands and split.

I'm not off the lot 10 minutes when the Dreamworks guys call me on my cell and tell me we've sold it. Damn. My first thought is: now I've got to write it. Two pilots at once. This could get interesting. Or ugly. The last time I tried this, 17 years ago, I had an anxiety attack and took the ambulance trip to the UCLA emergency room with nitroglycerine under my tongue. But I was inexperienced, and freaked out over what seemed like an overwhelming amount of work with a very short deadline. Plus I was working on a show at the time. I hope it doesn't happen again, but so far, the people I'm working with, all the way up the line, seem bright and their notes are insightful, so it seems like we're moving in the same direction. Time will tell. I will try to frame my thoughts this weekend and start jamming on Monday.

---

[52] Going up. An actors' term for totally forgetting one's lines while onstage.

October 24

I start the first of two outlines that are virtually due simultaneously, though maybe I can buy a few days between drafts. I make some progress, then take a lunch break, just in time to turn on the TV and see that insurgents have set off three bombs in Baghdad, targeting two hotels where journalists and workers live. I am more than a little intrigued, as I wonder if one of them was the Al Hamra, where that journalist I spoke with was living. I watch the news, trying to see if they mention the hotel. They don't. You'd think it would be one of the more important aspects of the story. I go online and try to search it out. First stop, CNN's website, where they have a report, which I click on, but first have to wade through a 50-second commercial for some antacid. So much for the immediacy of online news.

October 25

2000 dead in Iraq. Gotta love those milestones. I hope somebody's working on the memorial.

NOVEMBER 2005

President nominates Harriet Miers for Supreme Court to fill Sandra Day O'Connor's seat. Her qualifications: having run the Texas state lottery. She has less experience as a judge than Judge Judy. Since when is "inexperience" something you put on a resume? I mean, shit. If you were going to hire a dogcatcher, wouldn't the first question you ask be: have you ever caught a dog? Then the nomination is withdrawn. Most disappointed is Rachel Dratch at SNL, as she bears an uncanny resemblance to the nominee and it would have provided material for years to come. Judge Alito nominated.

F/X cancels or doesn't pick up any more episodes of *Over There*. Never quite caught on. NBC gives limited six-show back order to Amy Grant feel-good show *Three Wishes*. Evidently, one of the rules on *Three Wishes* is that you're not allowed to wish for a full season back nine. Interesting...*My Name is Earl*, the show about a white-trash career criminal trying to set his life straight and a show that could be the comedy flagship for NBC for years to come, beats out the one about handing real people their lifelong dreams. Funny beats feel-good any day. *Martha Stewart's Apprentice* continues to struggle and will never get a pick-up. So there is some justice in the world—to be spared an extra half-hour of watching these preening, backbiting goons masquerading as corporate hopefuls. Still you just know, looking at the faces of these poseurs that one day, one of them is going to end up as a network comedy VP.

November 2

I fight bumper-to-bumper traffic to get to an outline notes meeting with my producing partners on the NBC divorced guys show that I initially hoped would be a slam dunk but then suddenly smelled big changes. And I was right. Though in this case, the changes were for the better. First draft needed work. But they were toward the goal of enhancing what we were going after, not eviscerating it. I'll take those notes anytime. Not that it's any less irritating to get them, but you can't discount them. Then I get a call about a water main break at my house while the driveway is being repaired, so I rush back home in traffic just long enough to write a check to repair it. Not even noon and I'm out 350 bucks.

So now I'm juggling two outlines, finishing one, sending it off to the first set of producers for notes, and scribbling on the second. It'll be a writing horserace for the next two months to get two scripts written, through the notes pipeline of producers, studio execs, and finally network execs before they get it for the December and holiday reads. Then it's time to relax and sweat again. Amazing how the results immediately alter your future. Could go two for two, both shows into production. One for two…or the oh-fer. Then it's back to nothing.

A couple years ago I saw two producers I knew who had shot two pilots for two different networks and were walking around the Paramount lot on a Friday afternoon having a conversation that I didn't have to overhear to know the subject: how are we going to produce two shows at once? We split up, each run one, compare notes in the morning, etc.... By Monday morning neither of their shows had been picked up, either for the fall schedule, or midseason, and they were back to zero.

November 4

I go to Beverly Hills for a haircut before meeting two of my producing partners on the divorced dads and kids show, so that we can sit down together and beat out a revised outline. Although I would prefer to do it alone, when there are a lot of notes, this is the safest way to proceed, as when you're done, everyone is in sync. Can't afford to do my version and not be in agreement. It's a waste of effort and, more importantly, valuable time.

Walking around, I bump into one writer I know who did an episode for a mutual friend's show, but even though he wanted to hire her on staff, the execs at the network vetoed it, saying she wasn't right. There was a time you could hire the people you felt were best qualified. So we bitch about that.

Then I run into another guy I know who tells me the story of an actress from a hit show who's got another pilot, only the original production was postponed three months when it was decided the script wasn't right. So they fired the original writer and brought on another one to completely rewrite it. And now, finally, it's been shot. Another victim of the process. We bitch about that.

Then I go into Starbucks and make small talk with the barrista while waiting for my cappuccino. He asks how my day's going. I give a perfunctory "OK," and ask how he's doing. He pauses, which I thought was unusual, as I just assumed it was Starbucks' corporate policy that these people put out a high-on-life kind of attitude. But he's not. Says he's just so-so as the reserve unit he's in just got called up to go to Iraq and he leaves tomorrow. I tell him good luck and I hope it ends soon. Another one of those perspective moments.

November 5

Working outside at The Grove (an outdoor mall near CBS) on a Saturday, trying to jam through a quick first-pass rewrite on the revised divorced dads and kids outline. I'm trying to put it back together and get it back to the producers in a couple days so I can jump on the cops show outline and get that to the people I promised it to by the end of the week. Still, too much work is better than no work anytime. Though in an effort to avoid it for a moment, I glance over at someone's paper and read that Tom Cruise has hired a veteran publicist to replace his Scientologist sister. He needs someone. After the Oprah/Brooke Shields/Matt Lauer fiascos, his image as a first-class lunatic is being carved in stone. And perhaps it should be.

One of the unfortunate offshoots of the celebrity whorehouse is that as opposed to being content to be looked up to as life role models or fashion icons, some of them use their names and reputations to tout whatever nonsense they've glommed onto and refer to as their "religion" and source of their inner "spirituality." In L.A., one is usually deemed "spiritual" simply by eating brown rice, doing Yoga, and driving a hybrid car to a charity benefit. And celebrity spirituality has become the lunatic cherry on top of the idiot sundae in the discussion of religion in this country. Not that actors don't have the right to explore the nature of their being. They're human. (Well, most of them). But can't it be done by keeping their mouths shut and their beliefs close to their hearts instead of pontificating or bullying non-believers, as if their ability to play the hero in a movie or put on a costume and sing and dance on stage was somehow an indication that their interpretations of life's mysteries had some extra validity? Truly religious people don't do that. They simply and humbly live ethical, charitable lives, doing good works where they can. The only ones who shoot their mouths off in an attempt to convert the rest of the world are the ones who belong to cults.

CULTS

Recent newspaper articles about the Tom Cruise/Katie Holmes affair have used words like "faith" and "religion" to describe Scientology. This is how sloppy the discussion of religion in this country has become, so maybe we can take a few minutes to clarify things. Scientology, despite the "church" tax-exempt status, is not a religion. Scientology is to religion as fast food is to food and the Third Reich was to representative democracy. Scientology is a business masquerading as a religion but is in reality a cult.

When properly understood, religions are grounded in a mystical or spiritual experience and an attempt to communicate the value of that experience and how it can enrich human life, not on the lunatic ravings of a failed science fiction writer and megalomaniac. Religions don't charge by the course, or put ads in local papers offering "breaking into the industry" seminars. Religions don't attack those who criticize it. Religions, when truly practiced and understood, teach compassion and acceptance.

Scientology is a cult, like Est or any of the other lunatic fringe organizations that have sprouted up over the years and that have served as a refuge for life's disenfranchised. It is essentially a con game designed to prey upon the weaker element of society, *and* its adherents are divided into two types of people: 1) the sadly gullible segments of the population who need some new belief system to make sense of life; and 2) the thieves who bilk the first kind of person out of their life's savings. Yes, people get lost and look for answers. Especially when they feel their own traditions have failed them. But the answer is that there is no easy answer. Religion is not a panacea, but cults sell themselves by offering attractive, oversimplistic solutions to life's mysteries. But those who run Scientology and other cults like it indoctrinate the weak-minded into the club by giving them a brand new reality: new mythology; new rules of behavior, new language with special secret words, and a new set of friends who believe the same nonsense so that gatherings of the faithful turn into a communal circle jerk and collective mind fuck. This is and always has been the difference between religions and cults.

Those who start or join cults call them religions because it lends an air of respectability, gets people comfortable with a word and concept they already know, and gets them tax-exempt status so they can make their money without giving the government their cut. Check out how much real estate the church of Scientology owns just on Hollywood Boulevard. Now, of course, these people will deny, deny, deny all day long. They will make the argument of how much property the Catholic church owns. But priests don't stand outside the church waving fliers like 42nd street hustlers, trying to rope people in off their streets for "free personality tests" using what is essentially a lie-detector to gauge people's personalities;

or, to be more precise, discover their weaknesses and fears so they can be preyed upon.

I remember seeing the Grand High Kommisar or whatever he calls himself on *60 Minutes* years ago. Whoever was interviewing him asked about the fact that they had aggressively tried to discredit one of their critics, going after him with harassing phone calls, even private investigators. The guy responded: "When we're attacked, we have a right to defend ourselves." Sure you do. If you're in your home and some lunatic breaks in. But this is not what religions do. I could stand outside the Vatican tomorrow screaming "The Pope's an asshole," and "Catholicism's bullshit!" and although some faithful passersby might beat the crap out of me, I wouldn't get an unexpected visit from the Spanish Inquisition. ("No one expects the Spanish Inquisition!")

That's the point. Religions and the people who practice them do not need to go after their critics. They are secure enough in their beliefs to shrug off criticism as merely an opinion, and therefore nothing that's going to shake anyone's faith. But those who run cults know that their institution is based on a lie, and any criticism has the power to shed light on the nonsense they refer to as their beliefs and could bring the whole house down. That is why they are so vehement in silencing their critics. Those who write articles about the subject should not use terms like "religion" and "faith" to refer to Scientology. Words like "cult" and "con game" are more accurate, as the people who run these games are thieves and liars. Talking serpents, if you will.

If I wanted to learn more about religion and the nature of human life, I might first look into The Bible (either Testament), the Buddhist Sutras, Hindu Upanisads, The Koran, or the writings of any mystic, monk, philosopher, poet, or scholar over the last several thousand years of recorded history before taking the word of the guy who danced in his underwear in *Risky Business*. (Cut to March, 2006. South Park's hilarious episode on Scientology—"Trapped in the Closet"—is pulled off the air and Isaac Hayes, who plays "Chef," and is an avowed Scientologist, quits the show, citing the episode's bigotry against his religious beliefs. The creators of the show fight back, citing the fact that he had no problem with the show when it lampooned anyone else's faith. Some news reports cite a possible reason for pulling the show is fellow Scientologist Tom Cruise's threatened refusal to promote *Mission Impossible 3*, which is an upcoming Paramount movie, which is owned by Viacom, which also owns Comedy Central, which airs *South Park.)*

ZEN-TASTIC!

And while we're on the subject of religion, a recent *LA Times* article carried the headline: "Phil Jackson and L.A. Together A-Zen." The article about the possible return of Phil Jackson to coach the Lakers was all well and good. But this bastardization of one of the most profound and elegant traditions in Buddhism borders on the criminal and has to stop. And I mean now. No, really, I'm not fucking around on this. This cheeky, pseudo-clever working in of the word zen into everything from "Zen-sational" new tofu recipes to infinte "zen in the art of" manuals cheapens a 2500-year-old tradition that is quite possibly the most aesthetically, spiritually, and intellectually refined of all schools of religious thought. So, all you clever magazine writers and cookbook editors, please knock this shit off. I know you think this kind of Buddhist name-dropping makes you look clever, but it doesn't.

Zen Buddhism is a tradition that dates back to the Buddha's enlightenment under the Bodhi tree in India in 500 B.C., and, as practiced all over the world, has kept alive and intact a spiritual discipline and search for enlightenment, along with a refined sense of art, aesthetics, humor, and wisdom. Don't cheapen it with "Zen and the Art of Dating" *Cosmo* headlines.

November 9

Turned in second draft of divorced guys outline. Got quick notes. Again, I hate notes, but these are good ones. Things I missed. Sometimes the process works.

November 10

Arrested Development has its order cut back and is shelved for sweeps. This is its death knell, though you can't fault Fox for not staying with it. This is what a network should do. They also dump *Kitchen Confidential* for sweeps. So that's gone.

November 14

WGA (Writers' Guild of America) calls for more information regarding product placement in television and movies. AOL announces it will begin airing reruns of WB shows (same company) on demand. The delivery systems of television shows keep expanding. Maybe one day they'll just stick a chip in our heads.

Making it official, Fox cancels *Arrested Development* and *Kitchen Confidential.* I guess the WB was along for the hunt and got a taste for blood, as it cancelled *Seventh Heaven* after ten seasons in what was, according to sources, a "cost-cutting measure." It simply became economically unfeasible to produce more shows. Strange things going on at the WB. Massive layoffs. Shows' orders suddenly cut back. According to a source, it all stems from a controversy over the falling stock price. Small consolation if you're on one of those shows. (Cut to May, 2006, *Seventh Heaven* is resurrected on The CW.)

Meanwhile, after several drafts, I've gotten the divorced dads and kids outline past my producing partners, and now it's with the NBC Universal Television (NUTS) development people for their reaction before it goes into NBC. This worries me a little, as this group was not in on the initial pitch, and people who were not part of the process tend to want to flex their creative muscles at this stage and put their imprimatur on the material. So I've asked one of my producing partners, who is tighter with these people than I am, to monitor the situation, as I know she will. Meanwhile I'm sure I'll get notes on the cops show outline from the guys at Dreamworks, to whom I sent the first draft on Friday. Would have preferred to hear from them over the weekend so that only makes me more agitated, but I'll try to be patient and wait it out until the phone rings.

Mid-morning. The phone has not rung and, once again, I am officially neurotic. I swear, this never changes. No matter how many outlines and scripts I've handed in, any silence past the point where you should have gotten a reaction brings nothing but dread. "We have problems." "Even though I know we approved the story, seeing it on paper, it doesn't quite work. We need to rethink…" I've got two pilots to write in less than two months and, as before, need story approval to do so. Every day I'm not writing is wasted time and puts more pressure on the days remaining. It never stops.

Mid-afternoon. Still no calls from anyone. I hate the fucking waiting game. Though the afternoon's headlines brought with it news of *Martha Stewart's Apprentice*'s cancellation. No more to say about it.

Late afternoon. I can't stand the silence. I'm so fucking neurotic. I call Dreamworks. Turns out they're very happy with the outline, just running between meetings and had no time to call. All I needed to know. I can stop worrying…for now.

Early evening. I'm still at my computer when I get a call from the producer and friend who brought the divorced guys project to me. He asks if I know anything about the fight our respective agencies are having regarding packaging fees.[53] I tell him I don't know anything about it, and that I just want to do the work. Shit, I don't need this aggravation. Hard enough to get the creative side of this right without the business side intruding into the process and making bad blood among people who have to work together. My agent calls me later in the evening to calm me down...again, assuring me that agents often have disagreements about packaging fees and they'll sort it out. What is so exasperating about these moments is that I'm reduced to the level of a child, having to have my fears assuaged that even though mommy and daddy are fighting they still love each other very much, so just go to sleep and don't worry.

November 15

E-Ring gets a back order. *Night Stalker* gets cancelled. Get a call from my partners on divorced guys and kids pilot. NUTS liked the outline, everything fine, except one nagging comment: it seemed to be "angry." Uh-oh. We discuss this for a while and how to handle it; perhaps fleshing out some of the female characters—but after I hung up, something kept nagging at me. Then I figured it out. First of all, it wasn't angry. It was written from the point of view of guys in a situation that most guys who are in this situation will tell you, is a difficult situation. Lots of pressures and conflicting emotions. I tried to write it from an honest place, which was exactly what I'd pitched and was told to stick with. But more importantly: Why is "it seems angry" a criticism? Must all of half-hour television be purged of any negative emotions? Or real

---

[53] Packaging fees. The fees agents take out of a show's budget when one of their clients has created it or they've put several elements in the project, such as talent and other producers.

emotions? The reason people watch TV or go to movies is for the emotions. Whether it's fear, laughter, love, sex…or anger. People go to their living rooms, or to a darkened movie theater in order to feel. But, again, those in charge don't understand this point. Or I keep forgetting that what they mean is that it's supposed to be funny. And "funny" most often translates as "happy," or at least "not sad." Right. Tell that to Charlie Chaplin.[54]

Notes call from Dreamworks guys on the cops show outline. Loved it. Have a few thoughts. Nothing major. That's all you want to hear. Ever. From anyone. Nice to work with people who get it.

November 16

Call from the producer on the divorced guys project. I anticipate more headaches, but it's all fine. Just regarding a *Variety* article on the projects he's got going on, this one included. He gives me the name of a reporter to talk with—they actually want to speak with the writer. I recognize his name and call back. We have a pleasant ten-minute conversation and I hang up, wondering what I might've said that could be misquoted and turned into another nightmare. Probably nothing, but that's just where my head goes. Outlines getting passed up the approval ladder one at a time. Both will hit the networks within a week, at which point there'll be notes calls and then a go-ahead, hopefully, to write. At that point, I'll have to write two scripts within about 3 weeks. Luckily the outlines were very detailed, so I'll have a good head start.

November 17

Variety article comes out detailing the project. Thank God I didn't say anything stupid. And they spell my name right, which is all anyone really cares about.

---

[54] Charlie Chaplin. A dead silent film comedian.

November 18

Still waiting for story approval on both outlines. Meanwhile, in the real world, the Al Hamra hotel, which I'd written about in that Baghdad pilot, was bombed yesterday. No one hurt, but plenty of damage. I check to see if the journalist I'd been corresponding with was there. He wasn't, but wrote about the incident on his blog.

Locally, Robert Blake's civil trial ended in the jury holding him responsible for his wife's death and awarding her family $30 million. And dat's the name of dat tune.

Notes meeting set for Monday at 3 for NBC divorced dads and kids show. Of course, no other information is forthcoming, so once again, I have to sweat it out. Then the meeting time's changed to 5. Then another call comes in regarding a notes call on the cops project. Two sets of notes in one day. I smell the aggravation from across the weekend, but I tell myself to calm down and not see disaster around every turn. That calm lasts about two hours, when I get a call from one of my producing partners on the divorced dads show, who got a call from the network with their "headlines," meaning their "concerns." They like the show, the characters are clear and well-drawn, but...and here it comes...they're feeling a little sad when they read it. Where's the joy in the show? Where's the fun? They're afraid it's coming off too down. I swear to ever-loving Christ I am not making this up, here we fucking go again. I churn this over in my guts all weekend.

November 21

Of course after getting all worked up, when the NBC conference call finally happens, it's almost perfunctory. I get the go-ahead to write, while agreeing to address the "sadness" and "fun" issues, which I will cover by having some character get kicked in the balls. Just do it, and work backwards to the reason. The kick in the nuts: comedy insurance.

The call on the cops show, while a bit more substantive, involved some well-taken points that we said we would address. We agree to talk again after Thanksgiving. Starting Monday I'll have to write two pilots in about three weeks. Time to go to the mattresses.

November 22

I get a call from a guy I used to know, pitching me an idea for a show roughly based on a unique situation in his life. It was one of those "My life would make an interesting TV show" kind of moments. He was calling to say that he'd run it by a company that had a TV deal and they were "interested." "Interested" is one of those key words used in Hollywood to describe a situation in which you tell someone an idea, and if they don't either berate, insult, or shoot you, but instead say "Hmm, let me think about it," they are suddenly classified as "interested." So now the person pitching the idea can have lunch with friends and say "I pitched an idea to X company, and they're interested." I know. I've used it myself on several occasions.

Now the fact is, it wasn't a bad idea, on its face. In fact, it wasn't dissimilar from a show that had been on one of the networks recently and was quickly cancelled. Not because of the idea, but because it was poorly executed. Actually, it wasn't executed as much as assassinated. But the similarity would have made it a tough sell, as anyone hearing the pitch would surely cite that cancelled show as a reason not to buy it. Still I felt it was too premise-heavy.

Of course looking back at the early sitcoms, most of them were based on big, contrived premises. *Gilligan's Island*, *My Mother the Car*, *Mr. Ed*, *The Beverly Hillbillies*, *Green Acres*, *I Dream of*

Jeannie, *Bewitched*.... Now I grew up watching those shows. Part of me has an affection for these shows, but, to be honest, they were mostly, well...stupid. Perhaps it was because TV was in its nascent stages of development, and advertisers had more clout. No one was looking to offend anyone, just entertain the public and sell Chevys. But, after all this time, you hope the goal would be to reach a little higher. A two-year-old ties his shoelaces for the first time, you get excited and whip out the video camera. A 40-year-old does it, you just sigh and look at them as retarded. I have that same feeling when I see shows or hear pitches based on the "big fat silly premise." "Sitcom" or "situation comedy" is a misnomer. At best, and shouldn't that be what you aim for, it's "character comedy." And the source of any idea should rest with those characters, not on some contrivance.

Ted Koppel's final show on *Nightline*—the "Tuesdays with Morrie" segment. A fitting end on many levels—to go out on a show about dying with dignity. One can only hope that the new show and hosts will retain the level of intelligence shown by the former. Time will tell whether it will get show-bizzed up along the way.

November 23

CBS announces midseason shows. *The New Adventures of Old Christine*, the JLD divorce project that someone else did, will go on and I'll watch it with some interest.

November 28

ABC announces the cancellation of *Alias* after 5 seasons and critical raves but falling ratings on Thursday night. I track the first three episodes of the post-Ted Koppel *Nightline*, to see if the tone of the show would change. First night's story subject: marching bands. Second night: a Thanksgiving profile with a segment on a place that specializes in "turduken" (Google it yourself, I'm not explaining it), and another segment on cranberry sauce, featuring many high-profile chefs holding forth on the merits of canned vs. fresh. Third night: profile of some modern-day ghostbusters in Seattle. And for a moment, I was worried that the quality would slip. Fourth show, they finally get back to Iraq, following the ambassador around the country in a 10-minute segment. This was followed up by a piece on a deaf high school football team. Baby steps.

I start writing the divorced guys script, as I've got network story approval and have a few days before getting network notes on the Fox cops project.

November 29

The President goes on TV to announce to the nation that the war in Iraq is going well and he details his plan to end it, which involves turning it over to the Iraqi army. Wasn't this called Vietnamization about 30 years ago? I continue to vomit, both my script and from the speech. *Nightline* shows signs of life with a 10-minute segment following soldiers on patrol in Iraq and how they're involving the Iraqi police. It's followed by another segment of people who pray outside the Supreme Court 24/7, hoping for divine intervention with the court. Meanwhile I'm waiting on a conference call with Fox to get their notes and praying for divine intervention that they're not bad.

The call is scheduled for 11. Then postponed 'til 3. Then postponed 'til tomorrow at 5.

November 30

I scribble my way to the end of a very clunky first draft of the divorced guys and kids pilot just in time to take the Fox notes call. Between Fox, Dreamworks, NUTS, and me there are about 10 people on the line. Essentially, they're happy with a lot of what's there...BUT...and this is not a bad "but," their note is "take it further." Fox it up. Take chances. Push the characters more, make them more unique both from a creative standpoint and a marketing standpoint. Make this something that the powers that be at Fox will look at and feel "This is something we haven't seen." "This is new." "This is unique." Now whether in the end that is in fact what they will put on the air is occasionally another story, but it's a far cry from the "pull it back, they're too mean, we have to know they love each other" days at CBS.

I take the notes with enthusiasm and start thinking of ways to push it more. The one show they cite as an example is *The War at Home*, the new family show with Michael Rappaport that I initially didn't love but, after watching it with my daughter, am starting to like. It's sort of a modern *Married with Children*. Dreamworks wants another outline. I say there's no time. It'll take the better part of two weeks to climb back through the approval process. We agree to discuss ideas for changes, but the fact that they think they need another outline tells me they and the network want more substantial revisons and that worries me.

DECEMBER 2005

Measles outbreak in Romania. Paramount announces plan to buy Dreamworks, signaling an outbreak of firings.

December 1

CBS cancels *Threshold*, whatever that was, while cutting the order of *Still Standing* back to 18 episodes, after previously cutting *Yes, Dear*'s back to 13. Could this signal the beginning of the end of the Dumb Fat Guy/Bitchy Wife paradigm? We can only watch…and wait. Dreamworks calls to schedule a call at 11 tomorrow to discuss story revisions on the cops show.

December 5

Jamming on revising the draft of the divorced dads show while I go back to Dreamworks with ideas for story revisions on the cops show. They like some and send me back to think harder on others. Another phone call with Fox scheduled for next Thursday. Gives me the better part of a week to work on one script, revise the story on another, and hopefully get approval one week into December—which probably gives me about two weeks at most to bang out a first draft and go through the approval chain again.

Nightline airs a series of segments from a correspondent in Baghdad. Still, the most dramatic change from the Ted Koppel format is that of breaking the show into three distinct segments, more like *60 Minutes*. Not that this can't work, obviously, but the original intent of *Nightline* was to focus on one story in more depth. That was what made it unique.

CBS making a play to get Katie Couric from NBC to anchor the 6 o'clock evening news as Dan Rather's permanent replacement. Given her popularity on the *Today Show*, I guess it seems like a good move. CBS news has been trailing the big 3 in the ratings and this would certainly add new blood. Also, it would certainly give CBS the cutest evening news anchor among the 3, except for the fact that it looks like Elizabeth Vargas will be part of a co-anchor team taking over the ABC evening news, so I'd have to swing my cutest anchor vote over to her. I guess we'll have to wait to see who gets the Cutest Evening News Anchor Emmy to see if I'm right.

Meanwhile CBS announces they're going to develop a show around Al Sharpton tentatively titled *Al in the Family*. Other shows in the pipeline include an afternoon talk show exploring social and psychological issues in marriage and divorce called *I'm O.J. You're O.J.* and another prime time half-hour entitled *Iraq?—You Rock!* starring Saddam Hussein.

December 6

Trying to blast through two first drafts at once, just to have documents to work from, when I go online. There, staring me in the face on the AOL home screen, is a report that a movie producer I've known for years, Gregg Hoffman, passed away at 43. Like many people out here, Gregg struggled for years to get that one ellusive hit, and finally got it, in spades, with the movie *Saw* and more recently *Saw II.* And made millions. Then died. Out of nowhere. Just like that. I call my friend Wayne to ask what happened. He's in shock. He just had lunch with him two days ago. In reality, unlike most Hollywood movies, the hero doesn't always triumph in the third act. Sometimes he dies in the second act, leaving people in the theater scratching their heads, going "What the fuck." For some reason, life occasionally refuses to follow dramatic structure.

December 8

Conference call with Fox to address their notes at five, though I've already started writing as I don't have time to wait. It's at the end of a day that began at a memorial service at Mt. Sinai for Gregg. Several hundred people there. Utterly senseless, and tragic; a nice guy who just died too young.

As I sat there, I remembered the last time I was at this place (or next door at Forest Lawn) for Sam Kinison's memorial. That was the other pilot I did. Sam and Tim Matheson. It embarrasses me to this day that one of the last things he did involved him being shrunk down through the magic of blue screen[55] to 18 inches high. Sam was definitely not less than life-size. But at least in the original pilot presentation, the gimmick worked. And frankly, if you were going to cast someone to personify a guy's inner lust come to life, that's the guy. And he was funny. For 5 out of 7 shows. For the other two he was MIA. On those days, the game was "where's Sam?" For some reason, I still have the 15-year-old interoffice memos detailing his no-show days. His people made excuses and ran interference because that is what they'd been doing for years, but one day when he did show up hours late and completely wasted, I sat in his dressing room with another producer as Sam moaned and groaned and slurred his words while insisting he was ready to work. It was sad. I admired the guy. I despise the phrase "comic genius," but if you're going to use it to refer to someone, it could apply to Sam. He was hilarious. And dangerous. And I knew he only took this TV job for the cash. And it was not his fault that the show went down. Then, a month or two later after cancellation, I woke up to CNN around midnight (yeah, I tend to leave the TV on all night) to hear the report of his fatal car accident while en route to a gig in Laughlin. Hundreds attended the memorial. Along with the obligatory media trucks.

I get back from the funeral with several hours to get ready for a conference call. I am in no mood for this. Not after watching a young kid shovel dirt into his father's grave and looking at the sadness in his eyes. I can't shake that image and also can't help internalizing it. Like most people. What if that were my funeral? And my daughter? Shouldn't I really concentrate on living life to the fullest, appreciating every moment, instead of agonizing over a television show? The easy answer is: yes. The real answer is: I'm not capable of doing that.

---

[55] Blue screen (or green screen). A process in which an actor is set against a blue or green background, which drops out on film so they can be placed in front of any background in post-production.

However, the experience also made me remember that I haven't called my lawyer in over a year to go over all those "final arrangements." I just have no time, and, frankly, who's ever in the mood to deal with that shit? Though it does occur to me that this book could function as some sort of public record and a way to avoid getting Schiavo'd, so I might as well do it here and now. OK…

EXTREME MEASURES. If for some reason I am in some kind of coma or vegetative state and extreme measures have to be taken as the only way to keep me alive—TAKE 'EM! TAKE 'EM ALL! I DON'T CARE IF THERE'S NOTHING LEFT OF ME BUT A TOENAIL OR A BALL OF SNOT WADDED UP UNDER A BEDPAN, IF THE SNOT HAS A PULSE, GATHER MY FAMILY, PUT THE YANKEE GAME ON TV, HOOK UP A MORPHINE DRIP AND KEEP ME GOING!! I'm not kidding. Who knows what's reversible these days? Or in ten years. If you need to harvest a single lung or kidney along the way, be my guest (as long as it doesn't kill me), but as long as the word "reversible" can still modify the word "coma," then drag in the machines!

DEATH. If it turns out that I am, in fact, mortal like everyone else, which is a notion I still reject or, quite possibly, remain in denial over. (Frankly, I resent mortality. You put all this effort into a life, and then one day out of nowhere it's like, OK, you're done. Fuck that. It's insulting.) But if I do, in fact, die—and I mean after they're absolutely sure, after employing every single test known to medicine—then all right. Have a funeral. But keep it simple. Don't let some anonymous day player rabbi emote a perfunctory account of my life based on quick conversations with family and friends. It always sounds like such horseshit. "And who can forget how much he loved golf, and Oreos, and his favorite TV show…" Let some people speak. But don't drag it out. I hate when they drag those things out. Everyone's a saint in death. No reason to torture the living over it for two hours. (Although if anyone checks their watch or Blackberry during the service, toss their fucking ass out.)

FINAL ARRANGEMENTS: NO BURIAL. NO CASKET. NOTHING IN THE GROUND. Even in death, I wish to remain above ground. Just wrap me in a white shroud and set up a funeral pyre like they do in India. If it's not legal in L.A, find out where it is legal and do it there, even if there's some travel involved. I always liked traveling, I just never seem to find the time. Or a boat trip might be nice. Take me out beyond the three-mile limit and do it at sea. Just figure it out. At the moment, it's not my problem. Drag out a wooden raft, put me on top, shoot some flaming arrows onto it like they did in *The Vikings* and barbeque my ass into oblivion. And if anyone feels like roasting a marshmallow or grilling a burger, go ahead. I won't complain.

OK, so at least that's taken care of. Oddly enough, today is the 25th anniversary of John Lennon's murder. Takes great people to make history. And insignificant, twisted, mentally deranged assholes who can get their hands on a gun to change it. I was in New York at the time, but didn't go to the west side to light a candle and join my generation in singing "Imagine" outside the Dakota, holding hands with strangers and to swaying back and forth in tearful, rhythmic devotion. I just don't have that Kumbaya spirit. I'd rather process it in private.

So now that I've bummed myself out properly, I have to get my notes together for the Fox cops show conference call, which has been moved from 2:30 to 5:30 and then back to 5:00. The call finally happens and because I've been beating myself over it, it goes well. Even though it's like pitching all over again. I'm selling like a madman. But they're happy and I've got the go-ahead to write, which I've already been doing.

December 9

I blast my way to the end of a draft of the cops show. It's clumsy, clunky, and 10 pages too long, but it's something to work with. Now I can put it aside and jump back on the other one.

December 10

Richard Pryor dies. Madlib comics take notice: that's brilliant, angry, funny, dangerous standup. Aim for that, or go work in a bank.

December 12

Writing both pilots at once. First drafts have to get out this week. Meanwhile, the trades are already announcing early pilot pickups. Lights a fire under everyone else. Article in today's *LA Times* by Paul Brownstein about *Nightline*. Again, critics are brilliant when you agree with them, and he articulated exactly what I've been feeling about the revamped show. While it's still hitting important issues, the depth and analysis that Ted Koppel gave an individual subject seems to have disappeared, replaced by each story getting a somewhat lighter touch. More of a news magazine than a forum for news analysis. The hotter graphics, theme music, and promos for Jimmy Kimmel all make it feel just a little too slick. Not that *60 Minutes* suffered with the 3-story format, but an important forum for an in-depth look at a single event has disappeared from the news landscape.

December 14

Sitting around unshowered and unshaven, writing like a madman on two first drafts simultaneously, trying to get them both done and out, getting calls from producers politely asking when they'll see a first draft.

In actual show business news, the trades announce that *Arrested Development* may get sold to Showtime or ABC. It's a rare occurrence that a cancelled show makes an appearance on another network. *Taxi* did it at the end of their run. As have several others shows, but it's not the norm.

In the actual world, it's reported that the Iraq war will cost half a trillion dollars. *The Fog of War* is playing on HBO, and I watch Robert McNamara during Vietnam use much of the same language and tough talk about "winning this thing" and "not cutting and running." Though looking back with the wisdom of hindsight, he says: "If we can't persuade nations with comparable values on the merits of our course, we'd better re-examine our reasoning." Hindsight's a beautiful thing.

December 16

Turned in the first draft of the divorced guys show and already I'm worried. The network notes on the outline were that it was too angry and too sad, and I have a feeling it's not light enough. As well, there are at least seven women on the way up the approval chain, and I have to account for that. Meanwhile I kept working on this right up to the moment it went in, trying to make it as good as possible, then I take a break and go to the mall to do some Christmas shopping. I see a guy with a shaved head, except for a tiny Mohawk down the middle, wearing a tight-fitting T shirt with the logo: "Got Pussy?" I think maybe I'm working too hard.

December 17

Still no response on the draft, even though it's the weekend. People just don't get the courtesy part of this. You turn in material, you want a quick response. Don't just leave someone hanging, they only assume the worst. As I do. As I am. Meanwhile, in the actual world, it's the meeting of the oxymorons as journalist Robert Novak joins Fox News.

December 19

Monday morning. The calls trickle in. First from one producer on the divorced guys script: "Nice job, good first draft, have notes to make it funnier, let's meet..." Basically, faint praise heralding lots of notes and heavy rewrites. I spend the day getting the cops script ready to go to Dreamworks and wait for a call from the other producers, which finally comes in the late afternoon and echoes the other one. Lots of "ums," and "uhs" and rising intonation "Good jobs," and "Now we have the bones of a story that works, time to add some flavor..." I've heard this note before. I've given this note before. It's the "We have some work to do to punch this up" note. And they're probably right. And their notes will probably be decent and I'll agree with most of them and execute them. It still doesn't make the process any less annoying. Once again, I'll be writing and rewriting two projects right through the holidays, which doesn't put me in that season of good cheer frame of mind. Then again, I'm not sure what does.

December 20

Waiting for my notes meeting on the divorced dads script, anticipating a hefty rewrite. I get a call from one of the guys at Dreamworks who read the cops show script and was very pleased. A good call to get, as maybe I'll only have a monster rewrite on one project, as opposed to two. Then the meeting starts and, as I sensed, there were a lot of notes. Many of them good ones, well-taken points, others just punching it sideways, but I have to agree, the script needs work. As a veteran writer once told a newcomer regarding a first draft: "Just run it through the typewriter one more time." Similarly, this needs another cycle. We debate a few points and I leave. Per my routine, I give it a day to settle, rinse any bile from my system, and get back to work.

Still, there is something that can happen along the way in this process. At some point there's an emotional shift in your attitude, and you find yourself not writing so much as just tailoring a suit to fit someone else. Maybe it's just me, but when the opinions start to roll in, you just say: "Sure, whatever you want." And I'm self-aware enough to know that it might just be a defense mechanism to deal with the emotions of not receiving the praise you're after, but either way, I know it's there. I also know as the rewriting continues I can start to get back into it and re-create it, but I'm writing with a crowd in my head. The potential danger is that you stop hearing your characters talking and start hearing the other opinions. Hopefully, you hear both.

December 21

Received Dreamworks' cops show notes over the phone. Overall, they're happy. The notes—not bad, all things considered, but the basic note is they still want me to go further. "Pretend you're writing this for HBO." Now, I'm thinking, OK... So far in the pilot I've got an armed robbery, a naked blow-up doll, a woman cop decking a berserk suspect, physically threatening another cop, and a guy getting blown in a parked car while two cops on stakeout observe. I'm not sure how much further to take this, but I'll be happy to give it a shot.

December 26

After a Christmas Day break I jump back on both rewrites, going from one to the other like the cowboy in the runaway stagecoach scene leaping between horses. I digest all the notes and spit them back out. Finish one draft today. Switch to the other tomorrow. Both scripts have to go back to the respective parties this week, to get them to the studio—in both cases NUTS—before the end of the year. From there it's more notes, then they go into the respective networks—Fox and NBC—in the early part of January as part of the annual pickup/rejection festival. The one upside of all this is that I will be able to, once again, go into the end of the year with at least some hope of getting at least one show picked up.

December 28

Both scripts going back to producers tomorrow for what will, I'm sure, result in more last-minute notes. I take a break long enough to visit my accountant for the year-end wrap up. All in all, and by most standards, it was a lucrative year, but I know that a year from now, short of some good luck, the house is going on the market. Which might not be so bad as, on the way out, my neighbor stopped to inform me that there have been three home-invasion robberies in our neighborhood in the last several days. I take note of that and stop by the hardware store to pick up a Walking Tall-size piece of lumber, and a "Beware of Dog" sign. I don't actually have a dog; just four neurotic, chickenshit cats. But at least the sign is a moderate deterrent, as it leaves room for doubt in the mind of a thief. And you don't have to walk the sign in the middle of the night. I've got enough on my hands panning for catshit twice a day.

In the last few days there was an article about Congress debating making cable systems a la carte so people could choose which stations to get. Their goal is to keep Cinemax away from the kids, but it gave rise to an interesting sidebar, in that Pat Robertson is against it as well, afraid that too many people will opt not to receive the *700 Club*. He's probably right. Given the choice between watching soft-core porn or a pompous, pious asshole laboring under the delusion that he speaks for God, I think I know which way most people would go. Well, I know which way I'd go.

December 31

New Year's Eve. It's raining, which is often my cue to stare out a window and reflect on my past and the future—which, at the moment, is tied to my two little pilot scripts. I check Futoncritic.com to see what the development landscape is at the moment. As of today, including my two little scripts, there are 352 projects in development among 34 different networks, falling under the headings of alternative, animated, comedy, drama, game shows, improv/sketch, newsmagazine, sports, talk show, and unspecified.

By my rough count, there are 138 comedies and 148 dramas. Of those, there are 37 cop/PI shows, 4 medical shows and 8 lawyer shows, with other subjects ranging from cult deprogrammers, to the goings on at an ultra-hip New York hotel, to terrorists who plan on taking over Miami's South Beach, to thieves planning on robbing Beverly Hills jewelry stores during Oscar week, along with comedies about an actress who's a recovering alcoholic, a group of con artists posing as a typical suburban family, a 10-hour limited series about people who work at an LA news station years in the future, a rock super-group hiring a female shrink to help them work through their dysfunction, several *X-Files-*, *Alias-*, or *24*-style shows, a reality show centered around the son of Jim and Tammy Faye Bakker, a makeover show starring Mr. T and one called *America's Cutest Puppy*. As well, there's the usual assortment of comics with shows based around their acts, people moving back home or in with relatives after life-changing experiences, and 20-somethings or 30-somethings looking for love in various big cities. How unique or insipid these turn out to be—who knows? Ideas—

mostly shit. It's execution. The difference between *Lost* and *Gilligan's Island*.

Two shows I think will be the hits of the fall season: *Studio 60 Live from the Sunset Strip*...the Aaron Sorkin show for NBC. The script was great, as is the cast, and NBC will promote the shit out of it. The other will be *The Class* for CBS, a spec script co-written by one of the creators of *Friends*, which was the subject of a fierce bidding war, ending up at CBS with a 13-episode commitment, amid rumors of a huge purchase price for the script itself.

Recent promos have also heralded the triumphant return of Fox ratings monster *American Idol*, along with *Dancing with the Stars*, and a new show called *Skating with Celebrities*. I think I see where this is going. If my two pilots crap out, I'm going to pitch *America's Top Crack Whore*, *Puking with the Stars*, and *Queer Eye/Extreme Takeover*, where a band of gay mercenaries invades a foreign country, assassinates its leaders, then redecorates.

I drive into Beverly Hills to get some pizza, which is my usual head-clearing ritual. Mulberry Street Pizza is one of the only places in L.A where you can simulate the New York pizza experience by having a slice and a Coke at the counter while reading the *Post*. For once Laurel Canyon is empty, as show business usually relocates to Hawaii or Aspen for Christmas, and those who don't usually don't drive in the rain. People here have no concept of how to drive in the rain. They almost have no concept of rain, itself, with an almost primitive "water fall from sky" take on the phenomenon.

As I head down the hill I think back over the last 2 1/2 years of development, and that, after all that work, I'm still in the same "waiting to hear" mode. Turning in scripts. Waiting for phone calls that ultimately say yes or no. Either get ready for casting, or toss them on the pile and move on. Could get two pilots picked up, one, or none and go from frantic writing to hitting a brick wall and having to start fresh with something else, probably making good on the blind Touchstone pilot, while trying to beg my way on staff this May on a new or existing show. Two chips on the roulette table…and the wheel's spinning.

JANUARY-MARCH, 2006

World is still fucked. No need to do chapter and verse. Just read a paper. Or watch Nightline.

After several last-minute notes and rewrites on both scripts, they finally went into the respective networks on Friday, January 13th. Friday the 13th. Not that I'm superstitious but, c'mon, the deck is stacked enough as it is. Now it's back to waiting for the phone to ring. Though I'm not sure it's helping my cause at NBC that the executive who bought the project has been let go and I've heard that the new regime instantly shitcanned 80% of the pilots commissioned by the previous group, not even bothering to give notes. This happened with a friend's pilot. I do end up getting network notes over a conference call, mostly along the same line: "too sad, too serious, lighten it up, have more fun." Still, the fact that I got notes at least gives me a modicum of hope, or buys me a few extra days of delusion.

I execute the notes, turn the draft back in, and continue to wait, knowing that the same game is being played all over town. People jamming on last-minute rewrites, then hanging by phones, or trying not to. But I've been through this before and know the drill so I should be taking all of this in stride. I'm not. In fact, I'm quietly freaking out. One phone call is going to determine my immediate future. It will signal hundreds of thousands of dollars in pickup bonuses, pilot producing fees, and a possible slot on a fall schedule, carrying with it even more money…or none of the above. I can almost hear the intonation in my agent's sympathetic, though no less direct voice as he says: "Both networks are passing." Like two in the bonnet from a mob hit man. But without even the pre-hit fake-out of dinner, drinks, and hookers. I realize I'm being pessimistic, but the odds almost necessitate that pessimism is realism. To think otherwise is to set yourself up for a fall.

To pass the time, and take my mind off things, I pick up a book about Harry Cohn, founder of Columbia Pictures—a man who used to refer to writers as "schmucks with Underwoods," i.e.: typewriters. Filled with self-worth, I read a few pages, put the book down and turn on the TV.

Meanwhile, in the world of TV, Fox announces the end of *Malcolm in the Middle* and *That 70's Show*, after 7 years and 8 years respectively. ABC's attempt at establishing a comedy night in a post-Monday night football world—the Heather Graham show, *Emily's Reasons Why Not*, and the re-launch of the John Stamos show, *Jake in Progress*—took off and fell back to Earth like the Challenger. Horrible ratings, especially for the Heather Graham show, which was yanked after a single airing. And things don't look much better for the Stamos show. In fact, anytime the word "re-launch" is next to the title of your show, it's almost guaranteed that it's going to combust soon after takeoff.

American Idol came roaring back with enormous ratings, destroying everything in its path. It's like having the Super Bowl on your network, several times a week. HBO's starting to promote the new *Sopranos* episodes, premiering in March. Showtime putters along with a Golden Globe acting win for Mary Louise Parker for *Weeds*, as well as a pickup. Curious to see what's in the pipeline, other than the show about call girls I read about, somewhat like the show my friend and I wanted to pitch them a year ago but we were cut off mid-way by the development folks at Paramount, saying it was just not something they wanted to do.

It's TCA time in LA and the networks are trotting out to Pasadena for the winter press tour. NBC's moving shows all over the schedule, declaring they're stable after years of sucky ratings, while announcing *The West Wing* will be ending its run after 6 years due to sagging ratings, though the recent death of John Spencer is a sad sidebar. And *Will and Grace* will also say "ta-ta." The folks at *The Book of Daniel* learn their fate and it won't involve an afterlife. NBC's semi-controversial new show starring Aidan Quinn as an Episcopalian minister who's addicted to painkillers, deals with his dysfunctional family and occasionally talks to a Jesus only he sees is gone. Shot 8, aired 4. Over.

Also, on NBC, an announcement of Dick Wolf's newest show: *Conviction.* Check out this article in the *LA Times* business section just to get a real taste of what really drives network development and how show business is really done.

BARBARA NITKE *NBC Entertainment*

TV DRAMA: *Dick Wolf says "Conviction," his new NBC show, "reflects reality."*

'Law & Order' Creator Gets Fresh

A new series from Dick Wolf about young D.A.s stars a bunch of hotties, much to NBC's liking.

By MEG JAMES
Times Staff Writer

Dick Wolf, television's king of the procedural cop drama, built his empire on a string of grumpy old men. So when his newest series debuts in March, fans of the character actors who gave Wolf's "Law & Order" franchise gravitas — Jerry Orbach, Fred Thompson and Sam Waterston — will be in for a shock.

"Conviction," a sudsy look at the lives of seven New York assistant district attorneys, features a passel of beautiful people as its main characters, just one of whom is over 40. And that poor guy is killed off before the end of the pilot.

Asked last week whether "Conviction" is trading furrowed brows for fresh faces in a play for younger viewers, Wolf was characteristically frank.

"Unabashedly," said the 59-year-old hit maker. "That's who the advertisers want to reach. That's who the networks want to watch their shows. And it's not a mystery that people like watching people who are like themselves."

Wolf's wooing of the youth market, which he will officially unveil today in Pasadena at the semiannual gathering of the Television Critics Assn., couldn't come at a better time for NBC, the network he has made his home for more than two decades.

Last season, NBC plummeted from first place to fourth in prime time among 18- to 49-year-old viewers. Just as alarming to executives there was that their audience was rapidly turning gray. Two seasons ago, the median age of NBC's prime-time audience was just under 46 years old. This season, NBC's audience has "aged up" to 49 years.

"We're trying to turn a page right now," said Kevin Reilly, NBC's entertainment president. "We're trying to rebuild our schedule by introducing new shows that have distinct points of view. And the fact that Dick Wolf is on board with us says that he's turning a page too."

Wolf wasn't always "on board." Last year, NBC executives gave the quick hook to Wolf's fourth installment of his profitable franchise, "Law & Order: Trial by Jury." Wolf, whose shows have been the bedrock of NBC's prime-time schedule and made the company hundreds of millions of dollars, was furious.

Then, NBC delivered to Wolf what to him was the ultimate slap: It replaced his ripped-from-the-headlines show with "Inconceivable," a hormone-charged

[*See Wolf, Page C10*]

C10 SUNDAY, JANUARY 22, 2006 LOS ANGELES TIMES BUSINESS

Dick Wolf, to NBC's Liking, Aims Younger

[*Wolf, from Page C1*]
drama about a fertility clinic that survived on the air just two weeks.

NBC's reasons for canceling "Trial by Jury" were twofold, said executives involved in the decision. The network was trying to send a signal to advertisers and Hollywood's creative community that NBC was more than the "Law & Order" network. Plus, the median age of the audience for "Trial by Jury" was nearly 54.

But Wolf fumed that NBC seemed to have predetermined that the show would skew older when it placed it in the 10 p.m. Friday slot, when nearly half of the broadcast networks' audience is older than 50.

So when it came time to tear down the elaborate "Trial by Jury" sets, which had cost $2 million to build, Wolf refused.

And that, it turned out, would prove to be a masterful strategic move that eventually helped get "Conviction" greenlighted.

NBC isn't the only network sensitive about the age of its audience. Last May, CBS canceled its oldest-skewing shows: "60 Minutes 2," "JAG," "Judging Amy" and even "Joan of Arcadia." CBS was attempting to dial down the median age of its prime-time audience, which is 51.7. In comparison, ABC's audience comes in at 46.3 and Fox Broadcasting is the youngest of the Big Four networks at 41.8.

But NBC was in a particular pickle. "Our [median] age has climbed dramatically because we have older shows on our schedule," Reilly said. "Shows tend to get older audiences when they stay on the air longer."

For example, viewers who were in their mid-30s in 1990, when Wolf's first "Law & Order" launched, now are over 50. The median age of that Wednesday night show's audience is 52.1. "Law & Order: Criminal Intent," the Sunday installment, is even older: 53.2. Only the Tuesday night show, "Law & Order: Special Victims Unit," has a median within the desired demographic and just by a whisker: 49.

"Dramas have always skewed older," Wolf said. "You have to have a certain number of miles on the odometer to have the desire to sit down and watch something that requires some thinking."

So when Wolf agreed to stock the "Conviction" cast with nothing but hotties, he got a warm reception. Gone was the "Law & Order" signature in the title. Gone was the familiar percussive theme song. And most important, Wolf deviated sharply from his tried-and-true formula: building each episode around solving a single crime.

"Conviction" will have multiple story lines and delve deeply into the fears, foibles and sex lives of its young professionals.

MITCHELL HAASETH *NBC Entertainment*

THE YOUNG AND THE LEGAL: *"Conviction," a new NBC court drama, stars a passel of beautiful people as lawyers.*

And yes, it will be shot on those $2-million "Trial by Jury" sets that Wolf stubbornly refused to destroy.

"I knew I'd never get to build another set like that," Wolf said.

Reilly acknowledged that within NBC's Burbank office, "saving the sets" became "kind of this interesting inspiration. We had wanted to do a show about D.A.s — that concept was in the ether. And about the same time, Dick started talking about doing a show about young D.A.s."

Although NBC didn't greenlight "Conviction," which costs the company about $2.4 million an episode, just to save the sets, nobody minded that the recycling saved the network money and time.

"We were able to fast-track the show because we didn't have to spend time building sets," Reilly said. "We had the need and the opportunity to make it work."

Last week, NBC executives debated where in its lineup to place Wolf's new show. They don't have a lot of options.

NBC doesn't want to schedule it on Tuesdays opposite Fox's younger-skewing doctor drama, "House," or "American Idol," which returned last week to 35 million viewers, the show's biggest audience ever for a season premiere. Nor does NBC want to put "Conviction" in another suicide slot — Wednesdays at 9 p.m. — in which it would compete against ABC's juggernaut "Lost."

That leaves 10 p.m. Friday, the slot previously occupied by "Trial by Jury."

And that, say analysts and advertisers, won't go far in helping attract people under 35. The show's success "depends on where on the schedule NBC puts it," said Jason Maltby, president of national TV for ad-buying firm Mindshare. "And putting it on Friday night isn't going to help."

Shari Anne Brill, programming director for another ad-buying firm, Carat USA, agreed: "It's tough to launch a show at Friday at 10 when younger viewers aren't around."

While stopping short of revealing where in the lineup "Conviction" is likely to air, Reilly defended the Friday night slot, saying "Law & Order: SVU" and John Wells' "Third Watch" prospered in that hour.

Although Wolf grouses about the advertising industry's obsession with the 18-to-49 demographic, he has to admit that he's excited by the freshness of "Conviction." Instead of the police "procedural," his stock in trade, Wolf is calling the new show a "character-cedural."

He scoffs at any suggestion that he might be selling out to the youth-obsessed industry, noting that the average age of an actual New York assistant attorney is 28.

"The show reflects reality. If you walk into any courthouse around the country, you will see young people," he said. "What are people going to say, that I'm selling out to reality?"

And what a reality it is. In the first episode, a tousled assistant district attorney, played by 27-year-old Eric Balfour, accidentally leaves his badge in the bed of a character a colleague later describes as a "skinny chick with an octopus tattoo." Det. Lennie Briscoe, the iconic "Law & Order" character played by the late Orbach, never had problems like that.

Which is just the way Wolf wants it. On his trademark shows, he said, the main characters have always been portrayed as confident veterans whose personal angst rarely figures into the plot.

"You don't see Jesse Martin or one of Sam [Waterston's] assistants throwing up in the bathroom," he said. But with "Conviction," you will.

"It's great to see the legal system through the eyes of a newcomer," Wolf said. Come March, he'll find out whether TV viewers agree.

WB and UPN merged into a new entity called The CW. So six networks has now become five, the new entity being run by a collective of UPN and WB execs.

Home > WB, UPN merge

http://www.variety.com/index.asp?layout=print_story&articleid=VR1117936727&categoryid=14

To print this page, select "PRINT" from the File Menu of your browser.

Posted: Tue., Jan. 24, 2006, 9:12am PT

WB, UPN merge

Moonves plans Sept. start for new net

By MICHAEL LEARMONTH

And then there were five.

CBS Corp., Warner Bros. Entertainment and Tribune Co. announced Tuesday they're shutting down both the struggling WB and UPN and merging the two into a new entity called The CW.

Move will unite shows such as "Everybody Hates Chris," "Gilmore Girls," and "Veronica Mars" on one network, distributed by CBS and Tribune-owned stations.

The new fifth network, a 50-50 joint venture between CBS and Time Warner, will be distributed on CBS and Tribune-owned stations, reaching 95% of the country.

The net will be staffed by a combination of UPN and WB executives and an undisclosed number will be laid off as a result of the merger.

Dawn Ostroff, current president of UPN, will become President of Entertainment of the new entity and WB's John Matta, now COO of the WB, will become COO of The CW.

Move comes as the WB in particular has been struggling through tough times, with ratings down and profits non-existent. There's been much speculation in recent months that Time Warner might be poised to make a radical move to fix its WB problem, but the merger of UPN and the WB caught most industry observers by surprise.

"This new network makes sound business and creative sense at every level -- for our viewers, advertisers, affiliates and for the shareholders of our companies," said Barry Meyer, chairman and CEO of Warner Bros. Entertainment.

Fox stations currently affiliated with the UPN will be looking for new programming as of August when current affiliate agreements expire.

I try to stay busy and ignore the trades but in a weak moment I check *Variety* online to see what shows have already been picked up: one from Fox about a New York City psychiatrist who…wait for it…has difficulty finding happiness in her own personal life. One for CBS about moms juggling careers, relationships, and kids, including one about a recently divorced woman who works at a detective agency. NBC has one about a young couple dealing with the wife's large extended family, doesn't say whether anyone involved is ethnic, and another about a big-time real estate developer who loses everything and returns home to his small town. So it's urban professionals who have trouble with relationships, women juggling the familiar stuff, a young couple dealing with in-laws and a big city guy returning home to his small home town. If you've been following carefully, each of these falls neatly into the group of familiar pilot concepts. Doesn't mean they'll suck. Depends how they're written and produced. Still, when their backs are against the wall, it seems the networks buy the same old stuff. Oh, and there's also an NBC pilot that is described on Variety.com as "buzzworthy." It's about some ordinary people who discover they have superpowers.

I check out another *Variety* article about the season five ratings for *American Idol.* They're huge. 15% over last year. Beyond anyone's wildest imagination. A mere singing contest, a show that's been done in one form or another for years, from Ted Mack's amateur hour, through *Star Search*, is now commanding numbers that are off the charts. And the benefits stretch even further than simply inflated ad revenues. It's destroying the competition's shows in those time slots, even *Commander in Chief*, which looked hopeful for ABC. They'll have to move it. Plus it's a powerful launching pad for whatever new shows they have in the pipeline. Not that this guarantees success. The battlefield is littered with the corpses of shows that were launched after the Super Bowl. Still, delivering a mass audience to sample a new show couldn't hurt. This is huge.

And imitation being the sincerest form of imitation, NBC announces they're jumping into the world of singing competitions with an American version of the "Eurovision Song Contest," starting with an online competition to find singers from each state, with the winners advancing to the broadcast series. Voting will be in the hands of the viewers.

And on my two pilots, the wheel's still spinning….and then it stops…the ball drops…and lands on double zero. The first call comes from one of the producers on the NBC divorced dads show. It's a pass. Dead. Morte. Followed by the pro forma "but we're going to see if we can get it back and test the waters at other networks," which is the usual producer response to a pass. The same conversation is probably going on, in one form or another, at about 350 other venues around town. Human nature being what it is, there's occasionally some "garage sale"—type interest, as people are always curious about what someone else has thrown out, but it rarely leads anywhere. The fact that I've heard nothing but silence from Dreamworks tells me the other project is just as dead, just waiting for the official report from the coroner, which comes in the form of a phone call the next day. Pass. No reasons are given in either case, though the topline on the NBC divorced dads and kids show was that they wanted it lighter, while the cops show pilot for FOX they wanted darker. Like making fucking toast. I pile up the two stacks of notes, outlines, and drafts, dump them in a file box, and sit in my office wondering what I'll do next, while pondering the state of TV in general.

THE FUTURE OF TV
REALITIES, POSSIBILITIES, CONCLUSIONS, SPECULATIONS, AND MODEST PROPOSALS

HALF-HOUR COMEDY

The Iraq War is still going on with no end in sight with the administration staying the course with whatever the daily rationale is, while the rest of the world recovers from deadly hurricanes, tsunamis, earthquakes, terrorist bombings, and political scandals. And with all this going on, one of the hot new comedy shows in development at NBC is *Kung Fu Mom*, a show about two brothers who pay for their mother's retirement home by becoming bounty hunters and use kung fu as opposed to firearms to get the job done. OK, that's a cheap shot. It could be hilarious. But it does show that those in comedy development are happiest ignoring reality and producing light-hearted diversions. Put down the newspaper, turn off the news. Just stare at the shiny objects…

Despite the few shows that push the form creatively, by and large "sitcoms" remain stuck in almost 50's "Honey, I'm home" sensibilities. Comedically, socially, ethnically and intellectually. The question is, going back to one of those initial reactions people have about TV shows: Do they have to be that stupid? Answer: No. There is nothing inherent in the form that mandates stupidity or being a slave to traditional silliness. Whether it's called a "sitcom" or "character comedy," it's essentially a 20-minute, two- or three-act play, performed on a proscenium stage in front of four cameras and several hundred people, or shot single-camera film-style either on stage and/or on location. How that play is conceived, written, and produced is initially in the hands of writers, but ultimately in control of those who run the networks.

Not that anyone's rushing to bring back *Playhouse 90*, but it's still a sad fact that in order to cite examples of television comedies that pushed boundaries or either reflected or poked fun at the politics, society, or emotions of the times, one has to go back to the early seventies and shows like *All in the Family* and *MASH;* or the eighties and *Married with Children*—and the creators of those shows fought huge battles to keep their visions of those shows intact.

It's been said about baseball that it's "too much of a sport to be a business, and too much of a business to be a sport." The same could be said about TV. If you've been paying attention, you know that TV is ultimately a business, the purpose of which is to sell cereal. And, yes, it's also about entertainment. People turn on the box to forget about work and relax. Escapism is necessary, sometimes. But that doesn't preclude some slight nod to adult reality every now and then.

A writer I worked with on another show co-wrote a pilot about a terror cell in America, in which the terrorists were getting so Americanized that they slowly lost interest in their holy crusade. I heard it was hilarious. It was written about in the press as one of the greatest pilots that'll never get made. And of course, in this country, at this time, no network would have the balls to do it. Though I bet they'd do it in England. Or on HBO.

Will half-hour TV disappear as a genre? With some exceptions, it's looking very tired and old-fashioned at the moment—the same shows with the same premises, the same rhythms, the same stories, the same subject matter. But TV can only grow up if the networks allow it to. It's not that there are a lack of new ideas or approaches to the medium. But they all have to go through the same filtering system. Interestingly, the cable networks are finally developing multi-camera half-hours with, I assume, adult sensibilities, which is something I've wanted to do for years. With everyone who's grown up watching sitcoms, it's always felt like there would be a built-in audience for a more mature, intelligent show and it doesn't seem like the networks are eager to make that happen.

There was a running joke in the writers' room at *Becker*. When a joke was pitched that stunk, one of the writers would imitate Homer Simpson watching *Prarie Home Companion*, where he banged on the TV, yelling "Be More Funny!" The same critique could apply to network TV comedy as a whole, though it would go beyond that exhortation to "be more intelligent." Be more adult. Be more literate. Be more relevant. Have more balls.

Easily said. But how do you make something like that happen? One solution—and, admittedly, this will be seen as a modest proposal to those in charge—would be to hire some/more/any experienced writers and producers as development executives. I realize this notion will strike fear into the heart of any executive, as it would feel like giving the inmates the keys to the asylum. Still, the fact remains that TV will only be as good as those in charge of the process allow it to be. And those in charge of the process, with some exceptions, don't have the talent to create shows, nor the instincts or experience to know why things work or not. If they did, they'd probably be on the other side, pitching with the rest of us. Often when executives are hired, the article in the trades lauds their relationship with the creative community. Frankly, that relationship would be stronger if a writer or producer felt like they were dealing with someone who spoke their language and whose goal was to push a show to the height of its creative possibilities instead of forcing it back into the bland and familiar.

Ultimately, there would be nothing to lose. With all the money, research and strategic planning that goes into TV development, the networks still haven't hit on a quantifiable formula enabling them to mass-produce hit shows. If they had, there wouldn't be a writer in L.A. left alive. At heart, the process involves intangibles such as imagination and inspiration. So what would be the harm, even as a think tank-like experiment, in hiring a few writers charged with developing more interesting and intelligent shows, instead of simply paying annual lip service to it? Even if the failure rate were the same, the end product would be a better class of failures and, more importantly, a more interesting class of successes.

Again, I doubt this will ever happen. I once ran into a network president at a Lakers game and the conversation segued into the (then) budding reality craze. He said the best thing about reality TV—"no writers." I think he was joking, although the twinkle in his eyes when he said it made me nervous. But this is an indication of network-think. That writers are the enemy—children with silly ideas who must be watched over by the parental eyes of network executives because this is, after all, a business. But my contention is that putting business people in charge of a creative product is, in fact, bad business, as they are trying to mass produce a product that is, in essence, not mass-producible. Despite the fact that cookie-cutter shows and spinoffs occasionally succeed, the biggest hits in the history of television have been unique shows that arose from a writer's vision, or from a writer in collaboration with a comic, and his or her unique voice. These are singular phenomena. The way to get more of them is to allow writers the freedom to write and produce the shows they hear in their heads. The result would be a class of unique, more interesting and, I'm guessing, more intelligent shows. And more successes. Not less.

Now, at this point, you might ask: "Well, aren't you just trying to impose your personal tastes on the public?" I don't know. Maybe. And "Isn't it about giving the audience a choice and letting them decide what they want to watch?" Sure. That's one of the things we do well here. The whole freedom of choice, 31-Flavors thing. But, still, those in charge should at least have a taste/stupidity line they refuse to cross. As some comic once remarked: "There's a dial on my TV that says 'brightness' but that doesn't seem to work." In the long run, we ought to be dialing it up, as a dumbed-down audience is a dumbed-down electorate that can be more easily mislead, and the consequences of that should be apparent to anyone who picks up a newspaper.

But, in the same way writers usually trust their own, so do execs, and so the unholy alliance will probably continue. Not that quality doesn't arise out of it, but most often it arises in spite of it. Borrowing an analogy from another context, it's like that thing with the typewriters and the monkeys. Put enough of them in front of enough typewriters for enough time, and they'll eventually write *Hamlet*, though it will be completely accidental. Well, I guess there's enough time, and enough typewriters (or computers) and there's certainly no shortage of chimps.

ONE-HOUR DRAMA

The two biggest franchises at the moment are *Law and Order* and *CSI*, occupying six time slots between the CBS and NBC schedules, not including *Law and Orders* airing in syndication. Factor in *ER*, which has just been renewed through the 2007-2008 season, and other hits such as *House* and *Crossing Jordan*, and it's basically cops, lawyers and doctors. Maybe it's the fascination with occupations most people aren't smart enough or tough enough to be involved with. Or perhaps it's our fear of crime and disease and other of life's uncertainties that draws people to shows in which, most often, the criminal's caught and convicted and the patient is cured, though it is a tribute to the maturity level of *Law and Order*, *House*, and *ER* that that's not always the case. Only *24* and *The West Wing* seem to play with the form or delve into other arenas.

The biggest network hit at this time is *Desperate Housewives*, not much different in concept from *Peyton Place* or any of the nighttime *Dallas*-type soaps from the 70s, just very well-executed. But, in essence, an old-fashioned show. Cable remains light years ahead of the networks, with *The Sopranos*, *Deadwood*, *The Shield*, *Nip/Tuck*. If cable is the Renaissance, network TV is the Middle Ages, hamstrung by self-imposed boundaries. Again, the limits of this form are not inherent in it. They're imposed by executives, afraid of advertisers who would threaten not to buy time on a show they found objectionable, along with the special interest groups who set themselves up as societal watchdogs.

One has to wonder if it's profanity, nudity or ideas that people are afraid of. Commercial television in other countries features more mature subject matter, and neither those societies nor their governments seem in imminent danger of collapse. Maybe it's just who we are—a people who gobble up porn in private but flip out in public at an accidentally televised breast. It seems a shame that the shows on cable have been virtually exiled there because networks would never put them on. But it's not just a matter of being able to get naked and swear. It's about ideas and the depth of human emotions and experiences that ought to be reflected in the public airwaves. Perhaps network TV is just ceding those shows to cable and carving out the *Fear Factor* territory for itself. *NYPD Blue* created a stir years ago by showing a bare ass and letting an "asshole" leak through in dialogue. The question is: Why is this a big deal? Are we that immature a society that this should be an issue? Network TV will never mature if those in charge don't take some chances. But at long as it's about money and ratings, pushing a show to its creative limits is not the endgame.

REALITY

At present there are over 200 reality shows on about 35 networks. Obviously, reality is here to stay as the shows are popular and disposable. *Survivor's* been going for years, flogging the same premise with new characters and locations. Others like *Who's My Daddy?* come and go in a heartbeat. One of the biggest hits for NBC is a prime time game show: *Deal or No Deal*, starring a bald, soul-patched Howie Mandel, looking like Jafar from *Aladdin*. There was a time when hosting a game show was one of the layers of hell for a comic, just a rung or two above hosting kids' birthday parties. But a hit is a hit and this is a hit. At least for the moment, assuming they don't overexpose it like ABC did with *Who Wants to Be a Millionaire*. Maybe it won't matter, given the fact that it centers around money and contests and screaming contestants, and features an array of models, whose sole, Vanna-like job is to smile and open briefcases. Sex, money, and contests. This will be around for a while.

And I guess I must have missed something because it seems that *Last Comic Standing*, a show I thought was cancelled, is back on the air, only without Jay Mohr, but with two geeky, unfunny Simon Cowell wannabes, who apparently failed Sarcasm in college. And the dork parade of bad comics continues, each one praying for that *American Idol*-like "ticket to Hollwood" to compete in the finals or live in the house or whatever the fuck they do. One by one, they take the stage in all their mundane glory, and grab the mike for two minutes of shitty material. I watched a few episodes just for sport. Turns out TV commercials are stupid, and "men and women are different." Who knew?

It doesn't matter. The genre has planted itself on network TV and probably won't disappear, because as a form these shows reinforce our most popular fairy tales and myths of love, money, beauty, personal renewal, and instant gratification all rolled into one. People magically find true love, get rich, get turned into swans via liposuction and corrective surgery, or have the same thing done to their homes by beneficent goateed carpenter elves in the middle of the night. Of course these shows are seductive. They make us feel good because they cater—some might say pander—to the most unreflective, uncritical, naïve, childish and—OK, yes—romantic parts of all of us. However, from a business standpoint, these shows are brilliant. With TiVo giving viewers the ability to fast forward through the commercials, producers and networks have figured out how to remove the boundaries between content and advertising by selling corporate participation in the body of the show. Whether it's called "product placement" or "product integration" with all the corporate name-dropping and built-in sponsorship, *American Idol* and *The Apprentice* have become the virtual NASCARs of television.

Audiences can no longer run to the bathroom to avoid the commercials when the messages are woven into the fabric of the show. In fact, I'd heard that with shows already in syndication, there is a company that is in the business of digitally inserting products into scenes where they never existed. Retroactive product placement. Some might call this insidious. But, in the age of TiVo, this is genius. Or maybe evil genius.

NEWS

Ted Koppel's *Nightline* is gone, taking with it an important venue for in-depth analysis of a current news story. The new *Nightline* has substance, but frankly only time will tell if they air more stories centering around the news…or turduken. Or if it ultimately stays on at all, as there's more money in a late-night comedy/variety or talk show than one that is politically oriented, despite its inherent value as a source of intelligent perspective on the news.

The current anchor lineup on the big three networks: taking over for Tom Brokaw at NBC, intelligent and telegenic Brian Williams. Charlie Gibson steps in at ABC, as Bob Woodruff recovers from injuries received covering the war in Iraq, and Elizabeth Vargas goes on maternity leave; and in the most high-profile move, Katie Couric will soon make her debut in the chair once occupied by Walter Cronkite and Dan Rather at CBS. It will be interesting to see if any of these broadcasts get sexed up, as news succumbs to the ratings race, though one interesting aspect of these changes is that a hard journalism background was once the sole prerequisite for sitting in an evening news anchor chair. Now it seems that morning show likeability is considered to be a legitimate road to evening news show credibility.

The question is, is hard news going the way of the "voice of God" anchor, in favor of a dash of actual news, punctuated with stories featuring celebrity gossip, car chases, weekend movie grosses and infamous murder trials? We're served this steady diet of junk news until we gorge out on a particular topic, and then it's on to the next. And as news remains subject to ratings, being number one will continue to outweigh keeping the public informed. Between car chases, crime stories, and "I'm here at the courthouse" on-the-scene news reporting, not to mention the dramatic re-enactments of the trial, O.J. had no idea he was setting a paradigm. Frankly, if I were a Bond villain running a network, I'd just orchestrate one celebrity murder a year, and create a cottage industry to keep the ratings up and the ad dollars flowing.

Sadly, what's also missing from the prime time network landscape is news satire. Bill Maher ran from ABC to HBO (ultimately for the better) and Jon Stewart thrives on Comedy Central. Each is brilliant, but neither reaches the audience they could on a network. It's sad that to find a primetime network show that satirized the news you have to go back to the sixties and *That Was the Week That Was* or *Laugh-In;* or to *The Smothers Brothers* in the seventies, and they got bounced off the air for being too controversial. Of course, there's the Weekend Update segment of *SNL*, but that's on around midnight.

For a take on TV news from someone in a position to know, check out this guest column from Ted Koppel from the *NY Times*.

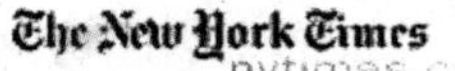

January 29, 2006
Guest Columnist

And Now, a Word for Our Demographic

By TED KOPPEL

Washington

NOT all reporters have an unfinished novel gathering dust but many, including this one, do. If that isn't enough of a cliché, this novel's hero is a television anchor (always plant your pen in familiar turf) who, in the course of a minor traffic accident, bites the tip off his tongue. The ensuing speech impediment is sufficient to end his on-air career and he finds himself, recently divorced, now unemployed, at home and watching altogether too much television.

After several weeks of isolation he discovers on his voice mail a message from an old friend, the opinion-page editor of his hometown newspaper. She is urging him to write a piece about television news, which, after some hesitation, he does — with a vengeance:

The earls and dukes and barons of television news have grown sleek and fat eating road kill. The victims, dispatched by political or special interest hit-and-run squads, are then hung up, displayed and consumed with unwholesome relish on television.

They wander the battlefields of other people's wars, these knights of the airwaves, disposing of the wounded from both armies, gorging themselves like the electronic vultures they are.

The popular illusion that television journalists are liberals does them too much honor. Like all mercenaries they fight for money, not ideology; but unlike true mercenaries, their loyalty is not for sale. It cannot be engaged because it does not exist. Their total lack of commitment to any cause has come to be defined as objectivity. Their daily preoccupation with the trivial and the banal has accumulated large audiences, which, in turn, has encouraged a descent into the search for items of even greater banality.

A wounded and bitter fellow, this fictional hero of mine, but his bilious arguments hardly seem all that dated. Now here I sit, having recently left ABC News after 42 years, and who should call but an editor friend of mine who, in a quirky convolution of real life's imitating unpublished fiction, has asked me to write this column examining the state of television news today.

Where to begin? Confession of the obvious seems like a reasonable starting point: I have become well known and well-off traveling the world on ABC's dime, charged only with ensuring that our viewers be well informed about important issues. For the better part of those 42 years, this arrangement worked to our mutual benefit and satisfaction. At the same time, I cannot help but see that the industry in which I have spent my entire adult life is in decline and in distress.

Once, 30 or 40 years ago, the target audience for network news was made up of everyone with a television, and the most common criticism lodged against us was that we were tempted to operate on a lowest-common-denominator basis.

This, however, was in the days before deregulation, when the Federal Communications Commission was still perceived to have teeth, and its mandate that broadcasters operate in "the public interest, convenience and necessity" was enough to give each licensee pause.

Network owners nurtured their news divisions, encouraged them to tackle serious issues, cultivated them as shields to be brandished before Congressional committees whenever questions were raised about the quality of entertainment programs and the vast sums earned by those programs. News divisions occasionally came under political pressures but rarely commercial ones. The expectation was that they would search out issues of importance, sift out the trivial and then tell the public what it needed to know.

With the advent of cable, satellite and broadband technology, today's marketplace has become so overcrowded that network news divisions are increasingly vulnerable to the dictatorship of the demographic. Now, every division of every network is expected to make a profit. And so we have entered the age of boutique journalism. The goal for the traditional broadcast networks now is to identify those segments of the audience considered most desirable by the advertising community and then to cater to them.

Most television news programs are therefore designed to satisfy the perceived appetites of our audiences. That may be not only acceptable but unavoidable in entertainment; in news, however, it is the journalists who should be telling their viewers what is important, not the other way around.

Indeed, in television news these days, the programs are being shaped to attract, most particularly, 18-to-34-year-old viewers. They, in turn, are presumed to be partly brain-dead — though not so insensible as to be unmoved by the blandishments of sponsors.

Exceptions, it should be noted, remain. Thus it is that the evening news broadcasts of ABC, CBS and NBC are liberally studded with advertisements that clearly cater to older Americans. But this is a holdover from another era: the last gathering of more than 30 million tribal elders, as they clench their dentures while struggling to control esophageal eruptions of stomach acid to watch "The News." That number still commands respect, but even the evening news programs, you will find (after the first block of headline material), are struggling to find a new format that will somehow appeal to younger viewers.

Washington news, for example, is covered with less and less enthusiasm and aggressiveness. The networks' foreign bureaus have, for some years now, been seen as too expensive to merit survival. Judged on the frequency with which their reports get airtime, they can no longer be deemed cost-effective. Most have either been closed or reduced in size to the point of irrelevance.

Simply stated, no audience is perceived to be clamoring for foreign news, the exceptions being wars in their early months that involve American troops, acts of terrorism and, for a couple of weeks or so, natural disasters of truly epic proportions.

You will still see foreign stories on the evening news broadcasts, but examine them carefully. They are either reported by one of a half-dozen or so remaining foreign correspondents who now cover the world for each network, or the anchor simply narrates a piece of videotape shot by some other news agency. For big events, an anchor might parachute in for a couple of days of high drama coverage. But the age of the foreign correspondent, who knew a country or region intimately, is long over.

No television news executive is likely to acknowledge indifference to major events overseas or in our nation's capital, but he may, on occasion, concede that the viewers don't care, and therein lies the essential malignancy.

The accusation that television news has a political agenda misses the point. Right now, the main agenda is to give people what they want. It is not partisanship but profitability that shapes what you see.

Most particularly on cable news, a calculated subjectivity has, indeed, displaced the old-fashioned goal of conveying the news dispassionately. But that, too, has less to do with partisan politics than simple capitalism. Thus, one cable network experiments with the subjectivity of tender engagement: "I care and therefore you should care." Another opts for chest-thumping certitude: "I know and therefore you should care."

Even Fox News's product has less to do with ideology and more to do with changing business models. Fox has succeeded financially because it tapped into a deep, rich vein of unfulfilled yearning among conservative American television viewers, but it created programming to satisfy the market, not the other way around. CNN, meanwhile, finds itself largely outmaneuvered, unwilling to accept the label of liberal alternative, experimenting instead with a form of journalism that stresses empathy over detachment.

Now, television news should not become a sort of intellectual broccoli to be jammed down our viewers' unwilling throats. We are obliged to make our offerings as palatable as possible. But there are too many important things happening in the world today to allow the diet to be determined to such a degree by the popular tastes of a relatively narrow and apparently uninterested demographic.

What is, ultimately, most confusing about the behavior of the big three networks is why they ever allowed themselves to be drawn onto a battlefield that so favors their cable competitors. At almost any time, the audience of a single network news program on just one broadcast network is greater than the combined audiences of CNN, Fox and MSNBC.

Reaching across the entire spectrum of American television viewers is precisely the broadcast networks' greatest strength. By focusing only on key demographics, by choosing to ignore their total viewership, they have surrendered their greatest advantage.

Oddly enough, there is a looming demographic reality that could help steer television news back toward its original purpose. There are tens of millions of baby boomers in their 40's and 50's and entering their 60's who have far more spending power than their 18-to-34-year-old counterparts. Television news may be debasing itself before the wrong demographic.

If the network news divisions cannot be convinced that their future depends on attracting all demographic groups, then perhaps, at least, they can be persuaded to aim for the largest single demographic with the most disposable income — one that may actually have an appetite for serious news. That would seem like a no-brainer. It's regrettable, perhaps, that only money and the inclination to spend it will ultimately determine the face of television news, but, as a distinguished colleague of mine used to say: "That's the way it is."

Ted Koppel, who retired as anchor and managing editor of the ABC program "Nightline" in November, is a contributing columnist for The Times and managing editor of The Discovery Network.

Frank Rich is on book leave.

POSSIBILITES

More international news. While each nightly news show features stories from around the world, they're most often told from an American perspective. Maybe the public would benefit from seeing segments of news reports from other countries, just to provide an idea of how we're viewed abroad, and add to our understanding of and perspective on a particular event. It might help us look more critically and objectively at our own cultural chauvinism and ultimate sense of rightness in the choices we make, promoting a more sophisticated understanding of world events and our place in them. I recently watched the documentary *The Control Room* about Al Jazeera. It might not be something the American public wants to watch, but it does add perspective. Then again, propaganda is easier to sell if it's left unchallenged. As of this writing Al Jazeera is expanding throughout the world, though still looking for a cable outlet in the U.S., something that is unlikely to happen.

CAMPAIGN FINANCE REFORM

Albeit another modest proposal, but one of the biggest sins on television has nothing to do with programming. It's political advertising. With all the talk of campaign finance reform, it seems no one has hit on the notion of banning political commercials from TV, as they serve no purpose other than to disseminate lies masquerading as facts. With a little creative misdirection, one side can throw marbles under an opponent's feet, screw with their poll numbers in key states at the right time, and force them to spend millions to respond in kind. The only result is a confused and misinformed electorate. Of course, banning these ads is an impossibility, as they represent too much of a cash cow to the networks and local stations, and too effective a political tool for campaign managers to ignore.

The Willie Horton, Max Cleland character assassination, and near-Orwellian "Swift Boat Veterans for Truth" ads served up nothing put propaganda and distortion. Effective? Yes. Honest? No. And not necessary. Somehow, we managed to elect individuals to national office even before radio. Televised debates give us a somewhat more honest look at the candidates, and the many political talk shows still leave room for the spinners to spin. If candidates were not forced to raise the millions needed to engage in this televised food fight, they would ultimately be less obligated to various special interests. This in itself would purify the political process, not just during an election, but after the winner takes office. As effective as they are, political commercials have no place in the democratic system, as they demean the very process we claim to respect.

TECHNOLOGY

Technology and the internet are expanding the options of how we watch TV. New delivery systems offer the capability of downloading shows to your cell phone, computer, Ipod, or TiVoing and burning them on DVD or portable video recorders. I am a gadget freak, so all of this is intriguing. But in the end, it's still about content. And ideas. The shows may be more portable, but what's the difference if it's the same old shit? As was once said about computers: GIGO: "Garbage in/garbage out." And, after almost 60 years of television, the basic experience hasn't really changed: despite technological advances that have made TV more colorful, controllable, changeable, flexible and portable, at heart, it's still people sitting down in their living rooms and turning on the box to be entertained, informed or, whenever possible, maybe a little of both.

THE 2006-2007 NETWORK TV SCHEDULE

Here is the schedule as announced by the networks at the Upfronts in May, along with a list of midseason shows and cancelled shows from last season. For fun and perspective, you can compare and contrast this schedule with ones from past years.

features/originals

TV Feature: 2006-2007 TV Broadcast Schedule

Entertainmentopia Editorial Policy

Entertainmentopia respects the personal opinions of our writers and fully embraces the first Amendment. Please be aware that editorials are not edited for content and are the author's personal feelings and in no way do they reflect the opinions of Entertainmentopia or Entertainmentopia Studios.

Since the start of the TV season we have seen more than a few shows miss their mark when debuting, and others, who debuted strong, are now looking at the cancellation axe. Here's Entertainmentopia's 2006-2007 TV Season update looking at the schedules for all networks, what shows are on the horizon, and what shows have been delegated to the trash heap. Also, if you are looking for a blast from the past, check out last year's TV Season Schedule.

Updated: May 25 @ 12:03PM MST

NOTE: NBC, ABC, CBS, FOX, & The CW UPDATED

Key

	Drama		**Movie**
	Comedy		**News Magazine**
	Reality/Unscripted		**Sports/Other**

Waiting in the Wings

All Times in Arizona Mountain Standard Time (MST)

These shows are either mid-season replacements or new shows waiting for a spot in the schedule to open up. Not all of these will make it to air, but a good majority should be given a shot. This will be updated periodically when new shows are announced or removed from the list.

Network	Show Title	Notes
NBC	Scrubs	Full Season Order; Return Date TBA
NBC	The Black Donnelly's	Debuts Jan '07 Thursdays @ 9PM
NBC	America's Got Talent	Debuts Jan '07 Sundays @ 7PM
NBC	The Apprentice	Debuts Jan '07 Sundays @ 8PM
NBC	Medium	Return Date TBA
NBC	Raines	Debuts Jan '07 Sundays @ 9PM
NBC	The Singles Table	Debut TBA
ABC	Supernanny	Debuts after The Bachelor ends
ABC	Set for the Rest of Your Life	Debuts after Dancing... ends
ABC	George Lopez	Midseason Wed. @ 7:00PM

ABC	According to Jim	Midseason Wed. @ 7:30PM
ABC	Day Break	Midseason/Replacement
ABC	Traveler	Midseason/Replacement
ABC	In Case of Emergency	Midseason/Replacement
ABC	Greg Behrendt's Wake-Up Call	Midseason/Replacement
ABC	Just for Laughs	Midseason/Replacement
CBS	The King of Queens	Midseason/13 Episode Order
CBS	3 LBS	Midseason
CBS	Waterfront	Midseason
CBS	Rules of Engagement	Midseason from Happy Madison
FOX	24	January 2007; Mondays @ 8PM
FOX	American Idol	January 2007; Tues@7PM/Wed@8PM
FOX	The Loop	January 2007; Wed @ 8:30PM
FOX	The Wedding Album	January 2007: Fri. @ 8PM
FOX	King of the Hill	January 2007; Sun @ 6:30PM
FOX	The Winner	Midseason from Seth MacFarlane
FOX	Duets	Midseason from Simon Cowell
FOX	On The Lot	Midseason
CW	Hidden Palms	Midseason

Cancelled Shows

Network	Show Title	Notes
NBC	Conviction	Dick Wolf's DA's get a life sentence
NBC	Joey	Friends spin-off put out of its misery
NBC	Four Kings	Ditto...
NBC	Surface	Going under for a long time
NBC	Teachers	Fired for shooting spitwads
NBC	Heist	Stealing is bad
NBC	The Book of Daniel	Never had a chance
NBC	E-Ring	What show was this again?
NBC	Three Wishes	The last one wasn't to be renewed
NBC	The Apprentice: Martha Stewart	One apprentice is enough
NBC	Inconceivable	This one is too easy...
ABC	Commander-in-Chief	Another lame duck President
ABC	Emily's Reasons Why Not	
ABC	Jack in Progress	Progressing into cancellation
ABC	Invasion	No longer invading the airwaves
ABC	Hot Properties	
ABC	Freddie	
ABC	Night Stalker	
ABC	Miracle Workers	

ABC	Less than Perfect	
ABC	In Justice	
ABC	Rodney	
ABC	Sons & Daughters	Improv doesn't seem to work
ABC	The Evidence	
ABC	Hope & Faith	We hope it's gone for good
CBS	Out of Practice	Out of work too
CBS	Courting Alex	Courting cancellation is more like it
CBS	Still Standing	Not for long...
CBS	Yes, Dear	...we are cancelled
CBS	Love Monkey	Catch reruns on VH1
CBS	Threshold	Most won't even remember it
FOX	The Bernie Mac Show	Stopped being funny years ago
FOX	Stacked	Was never funny
FOX	Arrested Development	I'm still in denial; Damn you FOX!
FOX	Kitchen Confidential	This show had promise too
FOX	Reunion	
FOX	Head Cases	
FOX	Free Ride	Boring and unfunny as they come
WB	Charmed	
WB	Living with Fran	
WB	Pepper Dennis	
WB	Modern Men	
WB	Survival of the Richest	
WB	What I Like About You	
WB	Twins	
WB	Blue Collar TV	
WB	Everwood	This should start some petitions
UPN	Eve	Thank god
UPN	Cuts	Ditto
UPN	Sex, Love, & Secrets	
UPN	One on One	
UPN	South Beach	
UPN	Half & Half	
UPN	Love, Inc.	Who greenlit this thing anyway?

Sources

Entertainmentopia has compiled this schedule via many sources including, but not limited to USA Today, Mediaweek, Reuters, AP, Variety, and the Hollywood Reporter. We hope you enjoy the new fall schedule and we will make any changes as they come in.

2006 Fall Broadcast Network Schedule

All Times in Arizona Mountain Standard Time (MST)

Monday

	7:00PM	7:30PM	8:00PM	8:30PM	9:00PM	9:30PM
NBC	Deal or No Deal		Heroes		Studio 60 on the Sunset Strip	
CBS	How I Met Your Mother	The Class	Two and a Half Men	New Adv. of Old Christine	CSI: Miami	
FOX	Prison Break		Vanished			
CW	7th Heaven		Runway			
ABC	Wife Swap		The Bachelor		What About Brian	

Tuesday

	7:00PM	7:30PM	8:00PM	8:30PM	9:00PM	9:30PM
NBC	Friday Night Lights		Law & Order: CI		Law & Order: SVU	
CBS	NCIS		The Unit		Smith	
FOX	Standoff		House			
CW	Gilmore Girls		Veronica Mars			
ABC	Dancing with the Stars		Let's Rob...	Help Me Help You	Boston Legal	

Wednesday

	7:00PM	7:30PM	8:00PM	8:30PM	9:00PM	9:30PM
NBC	20 Good Years	30 Rock	The Biggest Loser		Kidnapped	
CBS	Jericho		Criminal Minds		CSI: NY	
FOX	Bones		Justice			
CW	America's Next Top Model		One Tree Hill			
ABC	Dancing with the Stars		Lost		The Nine	

Thursday

	7:00PM	7:30PM	8:00PM	8:30PM	9:00PM	9:30PM
NBC	My Name is Earl	The Office	Deal or No Deal		ER (till Dec. 2006)	
CBS	Survivor		CSI		Shark	
FOX	'Til Death	Happy Hour	The O.C.			
CW	Smallville		Supernatural			
ABC	Big Day	Notes from the Underbelly	Grey's Anatomy		Six Degrees	

Friday

	7:00PM	7:30PM	8:00PM	8:30PM	9:00PM	9:30PM
NBC	Crossing Jordan		Las Vegas		Law & Order	
CBS	Ghost Whisperer		Close to Home		Numb3rs	
FOX	Nanny 911		Trading Spouses			
CW	Friday Night Smackdown!					
ABC	Betty the Ugly		Men in Trees		20/20	

Saturday

	7:00PM	7:30PM	8:00PM	8:30PM	9:00PM	9:30PM
NBC	Dateline		Drama Repeats		Drama Repeats	
CBS	Crimetime Saturday		Crimetime Saturday		48 Hours: Mystery	
FOX	Cops	Cops	America's Most Wanted			
CW						
ABC	ABC Saturday Night College Football					

Sunday

	6:00	6:30	7:00	7:30	8:00	8:30	9:00	9:30
NBC	Football Night in America		NBC Sunday Night Football					
CBS	60 Minutes		The Amazing Race		Cold Case		Without a Trace	
FOX	Comedy Rerun	Comedy Rerun	The Simpsons	American Dad	Family Guy	The War at Home		
CW	Everybody Hates Chris	All of Us	Girlfriends	The Game	America's Next Top Model (Encore)			
ABC	American's Funniest Home Videos		Extreme Makeover Home Edition		Desperate Housewives		Brothers & Sisters	

Return to Features Index – Entertainmentopia Home – Top

A LAST WORD ON THE FOUR PREDICTABLY ANNOYING RESPONSES I GET WHEN I TELL PEOPLE I WORK IN TELEVISION . . .

"We don't really watch TV."

Well, many people claim not to watch, though according to that same U.S. Census, adults 18 and over probably watch about 1,669 hours of TV a year. That's about 70 days. Again, not everyone's reading novels.

"Why is TV so dumb?"

There is a vicious cycle of simple/dumb shows succeeding, which means they get ratings so that the people at the networks assume that's what the audience wants, so they make more of the same kinds of shows, pre-dumbing it all the way through the process. At the same time, shows that take creative chances like *Arrested Development* end up getting cancelled, so it reinforces the thinking that America just wants its fun. This cycle will continue until more intelligent shows escape the system, meaning they get on the air and get good ratings so that they can stay on. Then, and only then, will the networks see the value in producing a more intelligent product and try to replicate it.

Then again, an article in *The Washington Post* related a story about forces on America's political right orchestrating a campaign that has led to policymakers in 19 states weighing proposals that question the science of evolution. Maybe they can look into gravity and photosynthesis while they're at it. Given that network TV is a reflection of the audience's taste and intelligence, maybe we're lucky that TV is as smart as it is.

"What's it like working in TV? I've got a great idea for a show."

And as to what it's like to work as a writer/producer in television, I imagine this has given you a taste. After almost twenty years in the business and 2 1/2 years of frustrating though extremely well-paid development, I've written four scripts for hire and 2 others on spec I would've killed to do but couldn't sell; pitched 16 different projects in about 35 meetings at 8 different networks; had maybe 130 development meetings, notes calls, lunches and story sessions resulting in notes I either despised or agreed with, but in either case had to sit down and execute, often involving tearing apart an outline or script and putting it back together, in draft after draft after draft.

At the end of it all, I'm still sitting here owing a studio a pilot I'll have to get to later in the year, but otherwise I've got nothing to show for all that work other than a few bucks in the bank, and the possibility of pitching or writing something else when pilot season rolls around again. Which I've started working on. On spec.

Oh, and I recently read an article in *TV Week* that HBO announced they were developing a comedy about reporters living at a hotel in Baghdad, while covering the war. Only they're doing it with some other writer, a year after they passed on the same exact concept I pitched them, with a script....

So…still think you've got a good idea for a TV show?

ACKNOWLEDGMENTS

To my assistant, Zuzana Cernik, for her invaluable research; to Michael Viner for publishing this book; to Julie McCarron for her graceful hand in editing it; and Sonia Fiore for her design and layout.